Practical Guide
to
Performance Appraisal

Richard I. Henderson

Reston Publishing Company, Inc.
Reston, Virginia
A Prentice-Hall Company

Dedication

To All Who Have Lived Through an Unbelievable Array of Performance Appraisal Processes and Ratings

Library of Congress Cataloging in Publication Data

Henderson, Richard I.,
  Practical guide to performance appraisal.

  Simultaneously published under title: Performance appraisal, second edition.
  Includes index.
  1. Employees, Rating of.   I. Title
  HF5549.5.R3H38   1984b   658.3'125   83–11230
  ISBN 0-8359-5576-1

Copyright 1984
Reston Publishing Company, Inc.
Reston, Virginia 22090
A Prentice-Hall Company

10   9   8   7   6   5   4   3   2   1

Printed in the United States of America

Contents

Preface

For as long as most of us can remember, we have heard these phrases: "You bad boy!" "Aren't you sweet?" "What a polite little girl." "He is so shy." From these behavior-shaping words of encouragement and discouragement, we move into and through school, simultaneously dreading and looking forward to a new kind of behavior-shaping technique—our report cards.

To some, a review of the report card provides a most enjoyable "high"; to others, it is downright depressing. For most of us, however, it elicits a broad range of emotions. From school we move into the world of work, where, for most of us, the grades or performance ratings we receive from our bosses and our organizations take on far greater importance than our report card grades in school.

As children, we could laugh off poor or unacceptable personal comments or school grades, but now, as jobholders and as supposedly mature adults, we cannot make light of our on-the-job performance ratings. Our current and future life styles are now on the line, and the ratings we receive have a huge impact on the way we live.

No longer can our grades be determined by a simple spelling test or an algebra examination. Now, many factors—some of which we have significant control over and some of which we have absolutely no control over—influence both our on-the-job behaviors and the results we achieve.

Since World War II, I personally have felt the extreme highs and lows that result from both excellent and terrible ratings. Over the past 20 years, as a student, researcher, teacher, writer, and consultant in the broad area of rewarding employees, I have come to realize that this frequently condemned tool of management that has so often and so correctly been called "a damned if you do, damned if you don't" operation, is, in reality, one of the most valuable and important tools available to management. Measurement is the name of the game, and in any productive society measurement *will* occur. This book describes the whys and hows of performance appraisal and what management and performance appraisal specialists can do to make the process successful.

This book was based on ideas and concepts I have gathered from thousands of sources including writers, consultants, practitioners, and both beneficiaries and victims of performance appraisal programs.

I would like to thank in particular Kathleen C. Robinson for her diligent review and comments; Michael Hornsby for his skill in relating real-world problems and opportunities to the theories and ideas presented in this text; and Charles F. Myers for his contribution of CAPA (Computer-Aided Performance Appraisal) and how to establish the procedures that will allow performance appraisal to use the communication processes of the electronic age.

Bikramjit S. Garcha and John B. Miner provided significant help in the area of measurement. Allan Dana and Kitty W. Clarke expanded my insights in the areas of interviewing and training. I also want to thank Rose Beohm for her tireless review of the entire manuscript.

Finally, I want to express my thanks for the excellent reviews and ideas presented by Jeffrey S. Kane. I often disagreed with the comments made by Jeff, but, in retrospect, I realize that Jeff's thoughts significantly influenced my actions, which in turn improved the book. The final book is my responsibility, however, and no other individual should be held accountable for missing concepts or concepts that some may believe to be poorly or even inaccurately portrayed.

This book, like the rest of my publishing efforts for the past 15 years, would not have seen the light of day without the patience of my live-in, poorly rewarded, often unfairly rated assistant—my wife and confidante, Jean.

To all who helped, I say a deep and heartfelt thank you, and may all of your ratings be distinguished, super, and magnificent.

Introduction

In the fall of 1981, a group of human resource professionals, who had a variety of personnel responsibilities for their respective organizations, and a small group of specialists involved in performance appraisal research met in Toronto. The purpose of the meeting was to discuss how to design and manage a performance appraisal plan that would meet the demands of the organizations for whom these professionals worked. From the start of the meeting, it was apparent that there were extremely divergent opinions, concerns, even fears as to the effectiveness of performance appraisal programs in general and their own systems in particular.

Toward the middle of the meeting, one of the more renowned specialists chastised the group, stating that they were making too many demands on their performance appraisal programs. He warned them that if they did not simplify their demands, they would "break the back" of their appraisal systems, thus crippling them and making them ineffective for any worthwhile organization use.

The general tenor of this meeting was no different from that of any other meeting where individuals responsible for performance appraisal gather. Despair and gloom, horror stories, and cries of "What can we do with this monster?" prevailed. After more than 30 years of personal interaction with performance appraisal programs, I have come to realize that performance appraisal is truly the orphan of human resource management. "Orphan Appie" is so mischievous and ill-mannered that no department or group wants to give it a home. Appie is always causing some kind of unwanted trouble and bringing those responsible much despair for its unacceptable behaviors.

It is possible that organizations are responsible for the poor behavior of Orphan Appie because they make unfair, inordinate demands on the poor soul. In fact, the pressures placed on this unwanted orphan can be described by the poem that follows (any similarity to Rudyard Kipling's "Tommie" is purely by design).

Orphan Appie

I went to Personnel, all happy and full of cheer,
But the administrator sez to me, sez he,
"We need no ratings here."
The clerks in the department laughed and giggled fit to die;
I went into the street again and to myself sez I:

———

Oh, it's Appie this, and Appie that, and Appie go away.
But it's "Thank you, Mr. Appraisal" when deciding on your pay.
When deciding on your pay, my boys, when deciding on your pay.
It's "Thank you, Mr. Appraisal," when deciding on your pay.

I went to see the President, as nice as I could be.
He gave me little room and said, "I can't pay your fee."
He sent me on to Planning, where they gave me little thought,
But when it comes to firing,
Lord, without me, they'll come to naught!

———

Oh, it's Appie this, and Appie that, and Appie step aside,
But it's "Thank you, Mr. Appraisal," when you wanta save your hide.
When you wanta save your hide, my boys,
When you wanta save your hide.
It's "Thank you, Mr. Appraisal," when you wanta save your hide.

Just what are the multiple demands organizations place on performance appraisal that may be causing unacceptable results? Among the more common are information inputs for

1. Compensation-related decisions.
2. Training purposes.
3. Employee development purposes.
4. Analyzing and validating selection criteria.
5. Making employee movement decisions (promotion, failure to promote, transfer, demotion, termination).
6. Organizational planning.

This book focuses on the actions an organization must take to design, build, and operate a performance appraisal program that is strong enough to withstand whatever load the organization expects it to carry. The book will specifically investigate the possibility of using performance appraisal for only one or two purposes, thus avoiding an appraisal usage overload that could result in the crippling of the entire program.

There is no doubt that organizations have made, are making, and will continue to make large demands on their performance appraisal systems. Instead of worrying about poor Orphan Appie's back, it is time now to provide some physical therapy (p-t) that will make Appie's back strong enough to carry whatever the load demands. There is always the possibility that the p-t program will result in some pain and torture (p^1-t^1), but it is only through this kind of hard work that Orphan Appie can be transformed from a child who causes all kinds of discomfort to a responsible member of the family of management.

Chapter 1

Human Barriers to Effective Appraisal of Performance

Many serious problem areas block accurate and timely measurement of employee performance. Any subject that arouses such a high level of interest and, at the same time, causes such discomfort must include significant topics that are difficult to understand and place in proper perspective. To gain an appreciation and an improved understanding of the many barriers that block successful appraisal of performance, it may be useful to first classify these barriers into two primary groups—technical and human.

The technical barriers are many and may appear to be more complex than the human barriers. In the long run, however, it may be far easier to come to grips with and develop solutions for the technical problems than it will be to overcome the human problems. It must also be recognized that there are continuous and critical interactions between the human-related problems and the technical problems involved in performance appraisal. The content of this book focuses primarily on the technical issues involved in the design and operation of a performance appraisal program. Through correct design and proper implementation of the technical components of the performance appraisal program, the human problems that block success can be minimized.

The technical problems that will be discussed in detail in later chapters of this book are:

1. Accurate and precise description of job content.
2. Identification and weighting of relevant performance dimensions and establishment of performance standards.
3. Allocation of sufficient resources and other support systems that influence successful accomplishment of assignments.

4. Non-job-related contributions that influence organizational productivity.

5. Measurement processes and rating instruments that relate to the multidimensionality of work and accurately reflect the kind of work and results expected of the ratee.

6. Use of raters who have the opportunity and ability to observe, recognize, and measure specific aspects of performance.

7. Timing of performance ratings.

8. Recognition of conflict among uses of rating data and information and design of programs to minimize use-oriented contamination of ratings.

9. Training of all involved personnel, leading to a more effective performance appraisal program.

10. Provision of information systems that can quickly store, retrieve, analyze, and disseminate relevant appraisal data to appropriate parties.

11. Establishment of monitoring and auditing programs that assist in quickly identifying and correcting program deficiencies.

12. Establishment of appeals programs that permit all ratees due-process protection.

In this chapter, the human barriers are identified, described, and analyzed from the perspective of ratees, raters, reviewers, administrators of performance appraisal processes, and users of appraisal data and information output.

Possibly the most critical barriers to accurate and valid measurement of employee performance lie deep within the genetic and learned makeup of all people. A wide variety of emotional, psychological, intellectual, and physical problems that, at first glance, may appear to be separate and irrelevant factors may combine in any number of different ways during the performance appraisal process to completely neutralize or lay waste to any program designed to measure employee performance. A review of some of the human problems that influence performance measurement and ratings assists in developing an appreciation of the extent and depth of these problems. Some of the issues are sufficiently universal to affect anyone involved in the appraisal process, while others influence the behavior of those involved only when they are performing the specific role of ratee, rater, reviewer, administrator, or user. An analysis will focus on the emotional, psychological, intellectual, and physical demands made on these five primary groups as they are directly involved in and significantly influenced by appraisal ratings.

Factors emanating from performance appraisal that influence ratees cover a wide and diverse number of human qualities. They range from the almost universal desire to be "number one," to the unacceptability of being rated "average," to the recognition that nobody is perfect, to the fear that excellent, even acceptable, levels of performance may lead to some kind of physical or emotional and psychological abuse from fellow workers, to the possibility that one black mark may result not only in current penalties but also in punishment that may occur in the future.

Almost all employees are extremely wary of performance ratings (with the possible exception of a small number of outstanding contributors who are extremely secure in their own capabilities and a similar small number of poor performers who either "don't give a damn" or feel that they can beat any appraisal process). This fear of performance ratings is reinforced by many actions and failures to act by immediate supervisors, administrators, and managers at all levels. Possibly the most common fear expressed by a ratee is that of rater subjectivity. What worries the ratee is that the rater will not measure his or her performance on the actual behaviors demonstrated and results achieved during the rating period, but will instead use a variety of subjective biases to rate performance. In other words, the actual rating may be based more on the sex, race, national origin, age, or religion of the ratee, or on performance in some past appraisal period, or even on physical or psychological makeup. In addition, some inconsequential behavior or result could unfairly color a more representative set of contributions. Employees also feel that those who perform certain kinds of work or have jobs in certain areas may receive unwarranted high or low appraisal ratings.

Non-Performance-Related Influences

These fears relating to unfair, highly subjective ratings receive significant reinforcement when ratees feel (often with considerable justification) that their supervisor or others rating performance do not (a) know the requirements of the ratee's job, (b) recognize the standards to measure job performance, (c) have the opportunity to observe many of the tasks performed or see the results achieved, and (d) communicate to the ratee what is expected of anyone performing that job.

As if all this isn't disturbing enough, ratees also realize that a bad performance is difficult if not impossible to erase. Although everyone recognizes that it is only human to err, perfection or extremely high quality output is all that is accepted by certain raters. A past poor rating can become etched indelibly on the brain of a rater and unfairly influence all future ratings.

The previously mentioned problem of the almost universal desire to be "number one" in conjunction with the terrible connotation of being rated "average" almost spells doom to any measurement process. In any work situation, there is a "number one contributor" or a small group who perform in a manner that exceeds that of the remaining members. Even in an exceptional group, there are those who outperform or who make contributions that place them in a relatively higher position than others. It is highly unlikely and occurs very rarely that all those being measured deserve equal ratings.

The "Average" Issue

This rating problem becomes magnified when the unacceptability of being "average" is analyzed. The word "average," when describing performance, has a negative connotation to many people. In this respect, "average" actually means "mediocre," or less than acceptable. This, in turn, means that raters are faced with an emotional problem when rating their employees as average and then with a mathematical incongruency when rating the majority of their subordinates as "above average." Nowhere has this problem been more pronounced than in the rating of military officers. It is not unusual in a military unit to find 95 percent of all officers rated in a category identified to include the top 5 percent of those being rated, a mathematical impossibility. (In the military, if an officer is not rated among the top 5 percent, the likelihood of promotion is severely impaired.)

Long-Term Survival

A major emotional and intellectual issue related to performance ratings is that of individual concern with physical survival and future job security. Because managers at the highest levels are principally responsible for the long-term direction and growth of the organization, they have the best ideas of where the organization is heading and what the future may offer to them. They have the greatest visibility and mobility and the best opportunities to move into better jobs in other organizations. Normally, they have the most accumulated wealth to protect them from some kind of job-related adversity. These individuals are also the most immune to performance appraisals. To begin with, they are often exempt from the formal appraisal process because their performance is more related to long-term results, and most performance appraisal programs are designed to measure short-term results. Those involved in providing direction at the top of the organization also claim that their jobs are so complex and the situations in which they become involved vary so greatly that it is virtually impossible to describe their jobs, let alone measure their performance. The validity and usefulness of performance appraisal for these employees is considered to be highly questionable. Exemption from the formal appraisal process, mobility opportunities, and accumulated wealth combine to minimize emotional and psychological concerns connected with performance ratings. The paradox associated with this combination of factors is that the factors frequently create a short-term perspective with regard to job-related security, resulting, in turn, in short-term commitment to the organization. It also minimizes their commitment to the appraisal process.

On the other hand, lower-level managers and most technicians and operative employees have a limited view of what the organization's future offers to them, yet they often have the strongest ties to the organization. Performance ratings will directly influence their future lifestyles. To them, the future may mean the opportunity to seek a highly desired promotion, or to be accepted into a training program, or even to be excluded from a reduction in force (RIF). In any case, the decision made may be critically influenced by past performance ratings with the possibility that even one poor or unacceptable rating could result in an adverse decision for the ratee. This concern with the future and lifetime employment by many mid- and lower-level managers and operative employees has a direct bearing on their view of any performance appraisal program.

Abuse

In addition to all of the other concerns, many employees fear the physical and emotional abuse that may occur because of performance ratings. Although the great majority of employees want their contributions to be recognized, there are many times when they do not want their peers or co-workers to know how they have been rated or what they have contributed. This fear of peers has a number of foundations. Most basic is that of being recognized as a "rate buster," which allows management to set higher performance requirements or goals for all other workers. Second, the efforts of the good or exceptional worker may result in the loss of jobs of co-workers because improved work-unit output resulted from the contributions of the exceptional worker.

The results of most formal performance appraisals become public knowledge, even when administration policies stamp them as confidential or secret. This communication of the performance and rating received by some good workers may be perceived by them as a threat.

Another factor that may be considered a threat is competition. Some high achievers or even those with specific goals may not want their peers or co-workers to fully recognize what they are doing or how well they are doing it. These peers or co-workers may be considered competitors for some future opportunity, and the good performers may want to keep their co-workers' competitive feelings at a minimum.

The final fear many ratees have of any formal performance appraisal process is that the well written, precise operating policies and the well designed measurement instrument provide an aura of objectivity while actually permitting raters and the organization to operate in a subjective, highly biased manner. The more bureaucratic, logical, and rational in appearance the process, the more difficult it is to overcome any unfair, unwarranted ratings. This, in turn, makes it more imperative to neutralize or destroy the process before it can cause short- or long-term unfavorable consequences to the ratee.

RATER CONCERNS Some of the major behavior-influencing forces that can affect rater behaviors are:

1. Desire to be accepted.
2. Concern with job security.
3. Concern with self-protection.
4. Affiliation with those holding similar views or having similar qualities.
5. Limitations due to lack of prior education, previous experience, or developed skills.

Desire to Be Accepted

All human beings have both instinctive and learned behavior determinants regarding social processes. The need for social affiliation may be stronger and easier to observe in some individuals than in others, but each person requires some kind of social interaction, and underlying any successful interaction is a feeling of concern, comradeship, respect, and so on. When one employee rates the performance of another, there is a distinct possibility that this rating could damage the acceptance of one by another.

Concern with Job Security

All supervisors worth their salt know that their success depends on the cooperation, effort, and contributions provided by subordinates. If in the appraisal process they inappropriately (not necessarily inaccurately) rate certain employees, the performance of the entire work group (not just the inappropriately rated employee) may suffer. Most supervisors realize that the performance of their work unit and job security usually go hand in hand.

Concern with Self-Protection

Anyone who has ever worked with people realizes that the range of behaviors that people can demonstrate relative to some incident or issue defies the imagination. Performance appraisal can be very crucial to an individual. An individual's response to an unsatisfactory performance appraisal can range from absolute indifference to becoming so distraught that he or she could commit suicide or murder. Very few raters like to be in such a position and, although the chance for such drastic action is very unlikely, concern for violent ratee reactions often influences appraisal ratings.

Affiliation with Those Holding Similar Views or Having Similar Qualities

It is always easier to relate to people who have similar perspectives. The factors that influence perspective may relate to race, sex, national origin, religion, educational background, work experience, physical characteristics (height, weight, length of hair, etc.), place of birth, or location of residence. Factors that influence perception are innumerable, but it is easier to communicate and be with people who have similar views or even speak in the same manner. It is also easy to see that those who do possess such qualities will probably receive higher appraisal ratings than those who do not. These differences often do not arise because of specific, conscious action but may result in a subconscious minimization of unacceptable activities by an individual who is considered similar or who holds similar views and a subconscious negative overreaction to those who are dissimilar or who hold different views.

Limitations Due to Lack of Prior Education, Previous Experience, or Developed Skills

Although it is important to recognize the other four influencing forces, most organizations have fairly large limitations on what can be done to minimize these unsatisfactory influences. Education, experience, and skill limitations, however, are fertile grounds for organizational improvement.

Humans Who "Play God"

One of the first complaints voiced by many raters is, "I don't want to play God." Raters feel that they should not have to bear the brunt of the adverse effects resulting from the formal appraisal of performance. There are many reasons for this feeling, but one of the more critical is the incompatibility of being both a judge and a counselor. The immediate supervisor (the one who most frequently does the rating) must perform the role of both judge (appraising employee performance) and counselor (listening to employee concerns, observing employee behavior, and providing information that assists the employee). It is not easy to be both judge and counselor, but these roles must be performed by supervisors whose organizations operate a formal performance appraisal program. These roles frequently thrust supervisors into conflicting situations, and to be competent requires extensive knowledge of employee personality and lifestyle problems, job requirements, and work-unit and organizational goals and operations, as well as requiring the skills to work with this knowledge.

Although all supervisors (and most other employees) rate performance continuously, it is one thing to do it informally and quite another to do it formally. As long as the rating is simply spoken—something that occurs strictly between the rater and ratee and goes no further, there is little concern. Once it becomes a formal process and the rating becomes part of some permanent record system available to almost anyone, ratees recognize that penalties for poor performance can be inflicted in a number of ways over an extended period of time, and concern heightens significantly.

Abuse. Raters realize that at times they must give poor or unsatisfactory ratings and that this goes with the job. They also realize that a rating that is less than expected by the ratee can lead to significant emotional and physical abuse of the rater. Although it is certainly not a common occurrence, subordinates have been known to murder supervisors because of a poor rating, especially when it leads to discharge. More common is the late-night phone call with heavy breathing, or a disconnect when the call is answered, or the threatening or abusive call to a family member when the supervisor is not home. Damage to a car or personal property is also not unknown. Although these behaviors may occur only rarely, those who work with others know of the wide range of behaviors that humans may display under adverse circumstances.

Selective Perception. Raters also know that they can overcome the adverse impact of a poor performance rating by measuring only those dimensions or qualities of performance that will provide a rating approximate to or identical with one desired or one that is considered nonthreatening or acceptable to the ratee, the rater, and the organization. Because they are only human, raters will remember best what occurred most recently. They are also limited not by what they see, but by what they thought they saw—their perceptions. Problems related to differences between what is perceived to have occurred and what has actually occurred affect all who are involved in the actual measurement and rating of performance. An issue frequently overlooked when discussing human perception is that what a person perceives as reality actually *is* reality to that person.

Most supervisors recognize that their jobs are multidimensional. They must not only lead, judge, and counsel subordinates, but also train them. They are well aware not only that subordinates possess certain abilities that allow them to perform better in some areas than others, but also that a wide variety of conditions may exist or develop that will improve their performance in some areas and detract from it in others. Quite often, they have minimal or no control over these situations. Supervisors know that it is quite possible for *their* supervisors to select a specific behavior or performance dimension and "march with it." They also know that their subordinates' performance is multidimensional and that the same factors that can influence subordinate performance and the ratings they receive can be easily manipulated when performance is being rated.

Playing It Safe. Supervisors are particularly aware, especially at lower levels where their span of control may be quite large (15 to 25 directly reporting subordinates), that they are held accountable for the behavior and results of a group of employees whose behaviors and results can vary dramatically. (Through the selection and promotion processes, behavioral differences lessen when employees move upward through the organizational hierarchy. Those at higher levels will demonstrate greater similarities in behaviors and results achieved.) Supervisors at lower levels recognize that if they rate an employee as a poor performer, there is the likelihood that their own performance could be questioned by their supervisors. "Haven't you counseled with this person or given useful feedback?" "Have you provided the right direction or proper training to this poor performer?" "Are you providing a supportive environment for your work unit?"

In another case a supervisor may rate an employee as superior and identify some outstanding contributions of the ratee. A reviewing authority then questions the rater's (immediate supervisor's) abilities by asking, "Why didn't *you* think of that?" Hidden agendas held by supervisors, raters, or reviewers of ratings at higher levels in the organization are always threats to anyone being rated. For example, higher-level management knows that a new job is to be created and will be a promotion for the individual selected. For all practical purposes, the selected candidate has already been identified. Now, through the appraisal process, the selected individual is made to look more favorable than others in the selection zone.

To play it safe, a supervisor frequently provides a rating that is acceptable, average, proficient, satisfactory, or whatever is in reality the "average" rating—the rating most employees will receive. The only individuals who are hurt are those doing an excellent job, the outstanding contributors. This failure can be overcome to a degree by recognizing the efforts of these individuals in a number of informal ways that are available to most supervisors and valued by the ratee. By providing a rating that conforms to some central tendency statistic, the rater demonstrates a high degree of consistency. Many organizations reward behavior that promotes stability, that doesn't "make waves." By giving a similar rating to all or practically all employees, a rater can frequently stay out of trouble. However, this kind of rating behavior can frequently destroy the motivation of the "highly charged" employee.

Raters sometimes feel that the organization actually makes little constructive use of performance ratings. The positive value of performance ratings is then easily overwhelmed by the negative use, which is punishment. Employees who are being rated, and this group includes most raters, are quite insecure when it comes to the potential for unfair use of the rating or treatment they might receive because of performance ratings.

The Multidimensions of Performance

Another problem, one that is based in technology but becomes a distinctive human problem, is the lack of knowledge by the rater of the ratee's job and its requirements. Although a supervisor's intimate and extensive knowledge of the content and requirements of a subordinate's job is assumed to be a fact, this is often far from reality. At best, some supervisors may have only a limited knowledge of the responsibilities and duties of the jobs of incumbents. Possibly even a greater pitfall is that supervisors do not know or are not familiar with the standards that should be used to measure subordinate performance.

Even if the lack of job knowledge and performance standards is not serious, supervisors frequently do not know which activities of the job are more critical or more important. This means that they weight all activities of a job equally or assign a weight to a job component based on their own specific value systems. The weighting of the worth of the various dimensions of performance may have no relationship to reality and, quite possibly, may be distinctly different from that understood and considered by the ratee.

Opportunity to Observe

The physical impossibility of a rater's being available to observe all or even a significant sample of ratee behavior and workplace contributions is also a serious problem. The fewer opportunities a rater has to observe the ratee, the more dependent the rater is on inference and memory for identifying levels of past performance. Such dependency can frequently result in incorrect and unfair ratings. Many times, the supervisor (rater) has only a limited understanding of the quality of the employee's workplace behavior and how the employee's behavior supports or blocks improved work-unit performance and organizational productivity. Even when observations are made, employees are aware that they are being observed and the behaviors they exhibit are not typical of those normally demonstrated on the job; in other words, observation introduces another variable that may result in an incorrect rating.

Common Rater Errors

As just described, there is an almost unlimited number of reasons why raters make these kinds of errors. The first clue to understanding why these errors are made is to recognize that raters are human. They are subject to the same problems and forces that influence all human behaviors.

Some of the typical rating errors that contaminate performance ratings are:

HALO EFFECT: Rating an employee excellent in one quality, which in turn influences the rater to give that employee a similar rating or a higher-than-deserved rating on other qualities. A subset of the halo effect is the *logic error*. In this situation, a rater confuses one performance dimension with another and then incorrectly rates the dimension because of the misunderstanding. For example, an employee demonstrates a high degree of dependability (is never absent or late) and, from this behavior, a comparable high degree of integrity is inferred (would never use organizational property for personal use).

HORN EFFECT: Rating a person unsatisfactory in one quality, which in turn influences the rater to give that person a similar rating or a lower-than-deserved rating on other qualities. (Frequently, the term "halo effect" is used to include both the halo and the horn effects identified here.)

CENTRAL TENDENCY: Providing a rating of average or around the midpoint for all qualities. This is the most common and serious kind of error. Since many employees do perform somewhere around an average, it is an easily rationalized escape from making a valid appraisal.

STRICT RATING: Rating consistently lower than the normal or average; being constantly overly harsh in rating performance qualities.

LENIENT RATING: Rating consistently higher than the expected norm or average; being overly loose in rating performance qualities.

Rating errors can completely nullify the value of performance appraisal ratings for all organizational uses and, in fact, cause the organization to suffer a wide variety of penalties. For this reason, the kinds of injustices that occur when making central tendency, strict, or lenient rating errors must be identified. For example, the lenient rater hurts the superior performer. When the contributions or performance of these exceptional individuals are rated about the same as those who do less, there is always the possibility that their future performance will decline. In this case, the superior performer, the supervisor, and the organization all lose.

When employees are rated too strictly, the supervisor in effect lowers the ratings of his or her subordinates relative to the ratings received by workers in other work units who perform at similar levels. This can have a significant demoralizing effect on all members of the work unit.

Central tendency ratings again lower the ratings of the above-average workers and *raise* the ratings of the poorer performers. This kind of injustice can easily lead to lower organizational performance.

Two courses of action organizations frequently take to overcome rating errors are (a) requiring raters who give poor ratings to outline procedures for improving performance and/or initiate termination proceedings and (b) requiring raters who give high ratings to verify such ratings and make recommendations for promotion. These two approaches can often have an adverse impact in that they cause raters to commit central tendency errors; that is, the tendency to rate all employees as "satisfactory" or "average." An interesting point about central tendency errors is that it is far easier for supervisors to rate their best and poorest performers accurately. It is the large group of proficient, average workers who cause raters trouble in precisely describing and rating differences in performance. However, various organizational constraints frequently influence raters to rate all members of their work units similarly.

Other rating errors that are frequently made are:

LATEST BEHAVIOR: Rating influenced by the most recent behavior; failing to recognize the most commonly demonstrated behaviors during the entire appraisal period.

PERFORMANCE DIMENSION ORDER: Two or more dimensions on a performance instrument follow or closely follow each other and both describe or relate to a similar quality. The rater rates the first dimension accurately and then rates the second dimension similarly to the first because of their proximity. If the dimensions had been arranged in a significantly different order, the ratings might have been different.

INITIAL IMPRESSION: Rating based on first impressions; failing to recognize most consistently demonstrated behaviors during the entire appraisal period.

SPILLOVER EFFECT: Allowing past performance appraisal ratings to unjustly influence current ratings. Past performance ratings, good or bad, result in a similar rating for the current period, although demonstrated behavior does not deserve the rating, good or bad.

STATUS EFFECT: Overrating employees in higher-level jobs or jobs held in high esteem and underrating employees in lower-level jobs or jobs held in low esteem.

Errors that relate to personal qualities and characteristics can be described as:

SAME AS ME: Giving the ratee a rating higher than deserved because the person has qualities or characteristics similar to those of the rater (or similar to those held in high esteem).

DIFFERENT FROM ME: Giving the ratee a rating lower than deserved because the person has qualities or characteristics dissimilar to the rater (or similar to those held in low esteem).

Another kind of error frequently identified by performance appraisal researchers is one called *contrast effect*. This kind of error results when a rater measures a ratee against other employees he or she has recently rated or relative to the average performance of other members in the work unit or those performing in similar jobs rather than in comparison with established performance criteria. If the recently rated others were rated properly and their activities (behaviors) or results were correctly identified, the rater could be establishing credible performance behaviors or standards for measurement. On the other hand, if the individual received an undeserved higher or lower rating because the other rated workers were working at a lower or higher than expected level, or if the recently rated others were rated incorrectly and the rating errors can be attributed to the errors previously described in this chapter or to a lack of knowledge of performance criteria, then the present ratee is the beneficiary or victim, as the case may be, of rater bias or incorrect/inadequate knowledge of ratee performance. Remember, the best worker in a low-performing work unit is not necessarily an excellent worker.

REVIEWER CONCERNS The monitoring of appraisal ratings normally starts with the immediate supervisor of the rater. This person has the initial responsibility for identifying rating weaknesses, even inaccuracies. The ability to provide a good review of ratings requires some understanding of the work performed by the ratees, some knowledge of their personalities, and even a good recall of past ratings and the distribution of ratings given by the various raters whose ratings are being reviewed. Some organizations use a rating review board to improve their monitoring capabilities. Here, a select group of managers work together to ensure the proper operation of the appraisal process.

Time Constraints

The issue of time availability confronts the reviewer just as it does the rater. Both reviewers and raters have only so much time to perform all of the assignments required in their jobs. Rating employee performance and reviewing performance ratings, if done properly, can consume an extraordinary amount of time. Is it worth the effort? Here again, the critical issue regarding the use of appraisal data and information comes to the front and center. If the reviewers (and ratees and raters) feel that the organization is going to make minimal progressive use of the rating, why spend the time carefully reviewing each rating? Just sign on the dotted line and send it forward! Credibility and critical use of performance appraisal data and information must come from higher levels of management, or reviewers will take the course of action requiring the least effort.

Comparison Capabilities

In addition to time, another problem that is critical to a successful review is the ability to analyze the rating given by the rater by using a series of comparisons. This review requires a support system that can store, analyze, retrieve, and disseminate information in a quick and cost-effective manner, almost mandating the use of some kind of computer-based information system. Information useful to reviewers includes past ratings given by rater to ratee; the distribution of ratings given by raters; comparison of these rating distributions with those given by other raters; rating distributions received by select demographic profiles such as gender, race, or religious comparisons; comparisons between age categories (18 to 25, 25 to 40, 40 and over); kinds of jobs; levels of jobs; and multiple demographic comparisons (combination of sex, race, and age). When this kind of information is readily available to reviewers, they are no longer dependent on memory and all of the problems related to human recall. Chapter 8 provides a detailed discussion of the use of computer-assisted performance appraisal reports for solving these kinds of problems.

ADMINISTRATOR CONCERNS

Administrators who are responsible for the operation of the performance appraisal system are usually members of the personnel/human resources department. These individuals have often been the victims of past appraisal failures. Their experiences with previous appraisal programs frequently have caused them to become cynical or disenchanted with the idea that any such program could be successful. They, like raters and reviewers, believe it is another time-consuming exercise in futility that can lead only to trouble for all involved parties. They often feel that ratee, rater, and reviewer will practice some kind of collusion that will result in sabotaging the accuracy and thus the effectiveness of the appraisal program. This lack of trust in the system by those responsible for its overall administration will quickly promote a credibility gap throughout the organization.

Because they often fail to recognize the multitude of human concerns at every phase of the appraisal process, those responsible for component design and overall operation of the system do not always have sufficient job-related information about tasks, performance dimensions, performance standards, and performance goals to ensure a solid job-content foundation to the program. They do not provide sufficient training or see that training is provided to all involved parties. Ideally, training should ensure proper understanding of the system and provide sufficient skills or enhance those already demonstrated so that each group can perform its appraisal assignments properly.

Performance appraisal systems frequently omit vital components that could ensure successful operation. Lack of knowledge of the components to include in a performance appraisal program is a serious shortcoming of many involved in the administration of such programs for their organizations. Not only are vital components missing, but instruments are designed or placed into use that do not permit an adequate rating of different kinds of jobs. Some instruments are too specific, while others are too general; either approach may cause trouble. In addition, user requirements are neither understood nor recognized, and the output data and information are in such a form that their value to the specific users is drastically restricted. If, for example, those responsible for the design of training programs use rating information to identify training needs, but raters, for some reason, fail to accurately and comprehensively identify employee knowledge and skill deficiencies, the trainers receive minimal assistance from the rating outputs.

All of these problems affect the acceptance and credibility of performance appraisal. Administrators must know how to communicate to all involved parties the kinds of information they require in order to be responsible participants in the appraisal of performance. When forced into using a rating program that has critical design and operation flaws, inconsistencies, or errors in logic, administrators cannot communicate information concerning the inadequacy of the program. An example is the use of one form with the same performance dimensions to rate all employees. The form is used because it is easy to complete, provides a standard score, and requires minimal time for all involved parties. Such an instrument must have extremely general or universal performance dimensions. This forces the use of traits that probably do not adequately relate to the wide variety of work assignments performed by the ratees. In such a case, the administrators become severely restricted in what they can say. This leads to an unwillingness to tell the truth or hear the truth, and, in turn, is followed by cover-ups and less-than-honest appraisal actions.

The underlying issue here is that the trait-based performance appraisal instrument is, in reality, measuring and rating employee performance relative to organizational and work-unit values—those qualities that the organization prizes and wishes its employees to demonstrate. The instrument obscures, even prohibits, the accurate measurement and rating of job-content-related performance. This does not mean that these trait- or organizational-value-rating instruments are wrong but, rather, that they must be used to measure what they are capable of measuring—qualities or traits. Other instruments must be designed for measuring and rating job-content-based performance.

The impact of weaknesses or deficiencies in a performance appraisal program accumulates geometrically rather than linearly. This means that if ratees, raters, reviewers, and administrators have problems accepting the credibility of the performance appraisal program or the integrity of the rating instrument data, and do not, to the best of their abilities, provide valid performance information, the rating data become almost worthless to end users. These individuals are involved in organizational planning, compensation administration, training and development, and employee movement decisions. Users may give lip-service credence to the performance appraisal data output, but they design and operate their programs with little or no dependence on this output.

USER CONCERNS

It takes little time or effort for ratees, raters, reviewers, and administrators to become aware that little value or credence is given to appraisal rating scores. When legitimate users of appraisal data and information make minimal or no use of ratings, those most influenced by performance appraisal ratings—ratees and raters—will frequently do everything in their power to destroy or subvert the process. They will take this action for the reasons already mentioned in this chapter. Therefore, performance appraisal has no useful organizational benefits; it is only implemented to collect information to be used in a punitive manner, valuable for subjectively or unfairly punishing certain employees and, in turn, unfairly rewarding others.

Some of the problems rest with the users. They frequently demand information and data that are stable and have consistency, yet a good appraisal system may provide outputs that widely fluctuate. This variation in data may place additional burdens on users that they wish to avoid. They don't want to revise their programs and change preconceived ideas. Their inquiries and complaints about the lack of consistency of performance ratings only reinforce the raters and administrators in thinking that the users don't want to hear anything that is threatening to positions they have already established.

Properly designed and operated performance appraisal programs have the capability of providing threatening information to all groups involved in the process. If the organization has a basic norm of not communicating anything that is threatening, then an effective appraisal program is a threat in some manner to everyone in the organization, and it will be subverted or sabotaged to protect all parties.

IDENTIFYING HUMAN PROBLEMS

In developing workable solutions to performance-appraisal-related problems, a logical first step can be to ask a series of questions of those who influence and are influenced by the appraisal process. Asking the right questions, then obtaining honest, complete, and accurate responses from those who understand the questions will be a significant help to anyone attempting to solve the many enigmatic problems of performance appraisal. Responses to these questions, in turn, assist designers and administrators in recognizing the constraints within which they must function.

The following is a list of questions that should be answered by (a) top-level managers (the executives of the organization)—those responsible for the overall operation of the organization; (b) senior-level operating managers—those responsible for the effective and profitable operation of their major organizational units now and into the future; (c) reviewers of ratings; (d) raters; (e) ratees; and (f) administrators—those responsible for the proper operation of the performance appraisal system, including those having auditing, monitoring, and appeals responsibilities.

MAJOR DECISIONS

Technology: Understanding and Availability

Top-Level Management

1. What kinds of organizational performance appraisal policies should be established?

2. How will the organization know what each unit is doing and what contributions specific individuals are making?

3. What kinds of performance-related decisions should be made at each level?

4. What kinds of information are required by those first involved in critical, unusual, or risk-taking situations in order to respond wisely and properly?

5. What kinds of and how much information should be provided at each level to support effective problem solving and decision making?

6. Is it desirable to obtain "bottom-up" generated information? _____Yes _____No If yes, how should "bottom-up" information be developed and processed?

7. Should employees at all levels have significant input into decisions that affect them and their jobs? _____Yes _____No If yes, how is this kind of job-related information to be transmitted throughout the organization?

8. How are unit suboptimizing [1] activities recognized and identified?
9. What actions should be taken to stop suboptimizing activities?
10. How will the organization support and reinforce cooperative effort among all work units?
11. How should performance appraisal be tied to the strategic planning processes of the organization?
12. How should performance appraisal be tied to the shorter-term, operating processes of the organization?
13. Should variations between employee values and organizational values be recognized and measured during the appraisal process?

Operating Management
1. What actions are taken to recognize the degree of understanding and acceptance of work-unit goals?
2. What actions are taken to ensure the proper organization of work-unit activities?
3. What kinds of and how much organization and job/work-related information is provided to incumbents at varying levels and in different kinds of jobs?
4. What kinds of and degree of specificity and precision of performance standards are set to measure the effectiveness of all work-unit and incumbent activities?

Reviewers
1. How are differences in the performance of subordinate supervisory responsibilities recognized and measured?
2. How are subordinate raters trained, coached, and counseled to effectively present ideas, goals, and demands?

Raters
1. How is work organized for each ratee?
2. How are performance standards established for each ratee's job?
3. What kinds of training, coaching, and counseling do you provide to your ratees?
4. How are work schedules established for each ratee, and what influence do you have on the scheduling process?

---

[1] SUBOPTIMIZING: Achieving individual and work-unit goals that negatively influence or, in some manner, subvert the accomplishment of organizational objectives and goals.

5. How do you assist ratees in improving their performance?
6. How do you obtain sufficient quality information to resolve unusual problems?
7. How do you obtain sufficient work-related information to transmit to ratees to ensure that they perform their assignments in an acceptable manner?
8. How are novel methods or procedures developed to solve new or unusual problems?
9. How do you obtain higher-level management support as demonstrated through the acquisition of sufficient resources to accomplish assignments?
10. How does your supervisor emphasize the goals of your work unit?
11. How do you use the full range of ratee job knowledge and skills?
12. What does the organization do to improve your skills in measuring and rating employee performance?
13. What would you like the organization to do to improve your skills in measuring and rating employee performance?

Ratees
1. How do you receive sufficient information to enable you to properly perform your job assignments?
2. How do you know precisely what you are to do, how well you are to do it, and when it is to be done?
3. How do you determine whether or not your rater knows what you are doing and is capable of assisting you in improving your performance?
4. How does your rater communicate work-unit goals?
5. How do you acquire sufficient information to successfully respond to unusual work demands?
6. How do rules and regulations block you from solving job-related problems and performing in an effective manner?

Administrators
1. How do you determine what measurement instruments or procedures are best for your organization?
2. How do you determine who should do the rating, when the ratings should be made, the form the ratings should take, and the procedures used in rating employees?
3. What kinds of training do you provide to improve the performance of those involved in the appraisal process?

4. How are resource allocation decisions made?

5. How is job performance linked to short-term planning?

6. How does the organization make certain that policies, rules, practices, and procedures support successful job performance?

7. How do those who have the right to know acquire worker performance information?

Environment: Establishing Trust and Cooperation

Top-Level Management
1. Who should be privileged to know the long-term objectives and shorter-term goals of the organization?

2. How should the organization communicate its long-term objectives, shorter-term goals, and basic organizational values?

3. How much policy detail should be communicated?

4. To which levels in the organization should policies be communicated?

5. How much influence is desired, and how should it be exerted throughout the organization in the allocation of resources?

6. What actions will the organization take to improve job satisfaction and job interest?

Operating Management
1. How are unit and subunit goals communicated to work-unit members?

2. How is cooperation among work-unit managers obtained, supported, and reinforced?

3. What actions are taken to improve working conditions?

4. What actions are taken to improve worker job satisfaction?

Reviewers
1. How are all raters given equal opportunity to influence reviewers?

2. How are all raters given equal access to reviewers?

3. How are trust and confidence in subordinate ratings established and maintained?

4. How do reviewers grant equal receptivity to ideas and suggestions of subordinate raters?

5. How is cooperation among subordinate raters encouraged and maintained?

Raters

1. What kinds of organizationally established interpersonal processes assist and support you in providing training, coaching, and counseling to your ratees?

2. How do you establish and promote teamwork and cooperation among your ratees?

3. How do you obtain the trust and confidence of your ratees?

4. How do you become aware of ratees' problems that affect their performance?

5. What opportunities do you grant ratees to discuss their ideas, goals, and problems?

6. How do you follow through on ratee-identified ideas, suggestions, recommendations, problems, and desires?

7. How do you obtain support from peers and other professionals in helping you and your work unit achieve its goals?

8. How does your supervisor encourage cooperative peer relationships?

9. How do you improve working conditions in your unit?

10. How do you improve ratee job satisfaction?

Ratees

1. How do you get your rater to recognize, pay attention to, and accept your ideas, suggestions, and recommendations?

2. How do you get your rater to have trust and confidence in your capabilities to competently perform your job assignments?

3. What involvement opportunities do you have in influencing decisions that affect your performance?

4. What opportunities does your rater/organization provide to increase your job satisfaction?

5. How does your rater encourage cooperation among work-unit members?

6. What opportunities do you have for setting or influencing the setting of performance standards for your job?

7. How do peers/co-workers assist you in successfully accomplishing job assignments?

Administrators

1. What do you do to improve employee job satisfaction?

2. What do you do to improve the quantity, quality, and flow of information throughout the organization?

3. What kind, how much, and when should job and organization information be offered to employees?

4. How are unsatisfactory working conditions identified and how can these problems be resolved?

5. How is worker performance information kept confidential?

Uses: Rewarding and Penalizing

Top-Level Management
1. What uses should the organization make of performance appraisal data and information outputs?
2. How will job requirements and employee performance be recognized and rewarded through pay and other, similar kinds of compensation opportunities?
3. What kinds of growth opportunities will the organization provide to members at each level in the organization?
4. What opportunities will employees be given for job openings?

Raters
1. What influence do your ratings have on the various kinds of rewards provided to your ratees?
2. What do you do to assist your ratees to grow and develop?

Ratees
1. How does your rater/organization make effective use of your knowledge and skills?
2. How does your job performance assist you to advance, grow, and develop?
3. How does your organization establish a proper relationship between pay and job requirements? How does it work?
4. How does your organization establish a proper relationship between individual contributions and pay, bonuses, and other monetary awards?
5. How are career-development and career-ladders programs established and operated for members of the organization?
6. How do you achieve flexibility in performing assignments in a manner that you think is most effective and desirable for you?
7. How do you gain respect and recognition from the work you do?

Administrators

1. What do you do to relate job requirements to pay?

2. How do you link employee performance and results to pay increases, bonuses, and other kinds of rewards?

3. How is job performance linked to such employment decisions as promotions, demotions, transfers, layoffs, and terminations?

4. How is job performance linked to training opportunities?

5. How does the organization link job performance to employee status, respect, and recognition?

6. How does the organization maintain an active interest in career-development and career-path plans for its members?

7. How can current employees be given consideration for job openings?

Responses to these questions by these various groups of involved employees assist designers and managers of the performance appraisal system to recognize: (a) the degree of understanding of the process at all levels; (b) the usefulness and acceptance of performance appraisal at various levels; (c) the involvement in and support of the process by all involved employees; and (d) the information now available and the technologies now in place that support an appraisal program.

Throughout the remainder of this book, there will be many discussions concerning a wide variety of processes, procedures, and technologies involved in establishing and operating a performance appraisal program. However, it must be remembered that performance appraisal is first and foremost a humanistic process. It involves people formally observing, measuring, and rating others. This, in turn, stimulates all kinds of human phobias and behaviors.

Unlike mushrooms, which grow best under dark and heavily fertilized conditions, people grow, prosper, and interact best in an open, enlightened, and trusting environment. The remaining chapters describe the many requirements or, possibly better, opportunities available to organizations to illuminate the work demands made of employees and the expectations of all involved in work activities.

This book also recognizes human frailties and inconsistencies and maintains the thesis that if any program as controversial as performance appraisal is to survive, surveillance must be constant. From the moment they enter the organization and throughout their entire stay, employees must be informed that performance review and measurement are a condition of employment. The organization wants to treat all employees fairly. To accomplish this goal, it must know how well and how poorly each employee performs as a member of the organization. Covering up inadequate performance is unacceptable, and rewarding acceptable and superior levels of performance is the name of the game.

Chapter 2

Individuals and Groups Involved in Performance Appraisal

As mentioned in Chapter 1, a major barrier to effective appraisal of performance often occurs with the involved employees. Reviews of performance and follow-up ratings, in most situations, require analysis that depends on the human eye and brain. However, as Jacob Bronowski stated, the eye and the brain provide an *interpretation* of reality, not a view of *absolute* reality.[1] Related to the perceptual problems are problems that involve the human brain in storing, recalling, processing, and disseminating information. In addition to human intellectual and perceptual problems are those that relate to personal aspirations, expectations, and emotions. Acquiring credible performance information about employees who work at numerous jobs requiring a wide variety of knowledge, skills, and responsibilities in an almost limitless number of settings is a monumental assignment. It is difficult to conceive of a place or situation in which one instrument or one set of raters will be adequate to achieve performance appraisal objectives and goals for the organization.

To overcome deficiencies related to these issues, many organizations develop appraisal systems that link the ratee, various raters, and other review authorities into an integrative process. This chapter focuses on the basic groups involved in appraisal programs and processes and the characteristics of members of these groups that significantly influence the accuracy and usefulness of measurement and rating information. In addition to a review of *who* is involved, *when* appraisals should be conducted, and *where* they may be conducted, there is a discussion of the employee characteristics that further influence the effectiveness of appraisal programs.

---

[1] Jacob Bronowski, *The Origins of Knowledge and Imagination* (New Haven, CT: Yale University Press, 1977).

Although at this time many organizations do not have an appeals process, individuals who have responsibility for reviewing ratee appeals of ratings will probably become more common in the future. Chapter 11 discusses the operation and importance of appeals in a performance appraisal program. Two other groups that are found even less frequently than the appeals group are those responsible for monitoring and auditing the operation of the appraisal process. These groups are also certain to assume a more visible role in the future.

The final group involved in the appraisal system consists of those who have overall administrative responsibilities. The discussion of the use of computer collection, analysis, summarization, storage, and dissemination of compensation information in Chapter 8 centers on the administration of the appraisal program.

RATERS Who should be involved in the rating of performance? At first glance, this may appear to be one of the easiest of the measurement problems to resolve. A review of surveys of performance appraisal processes consistently indicates that, by far, the most frequently and commonly used rater is the immediate supervisor. It is unlikely that anyone would argue with this information. It is also unlikely that this situation will change in the future. In most cases, the immediate supervisor is the person who is closest to the worker; he or she knows what the worker should be doing and understands the constraints that impede performance or the activities and events that assist in providing higher-than-expected levels of performance. Possibly most important, the immediate supervisor is aware of the contributions the worker must make in order for the respective work unit to achieve assigned goals.

Although the immediate supervisor usually has this range of performance-related knowledge, it is almost impossible for any one supervisor to observe and measure the multidimensions of employee workplace performance or to be completely aware of the range of behaviors demonstrated by a subordinate and the impact of these behaviors on work-unit outputs. For this reason, observations and measurements by others must be brought into the system.

Among the various raters other than the immediate supervisor, possibly the most important additional rater is the ratee. The employee may have views, even perform work activities, that are not in line with those desired or considered acceptable by the supervisor. Permitting self-measurement of performance almost forces the supervisor and the subordinate to discuss their views on the demonstrated behavior of both parties and the rating of performance and to review and discuss current work activities and assignments.

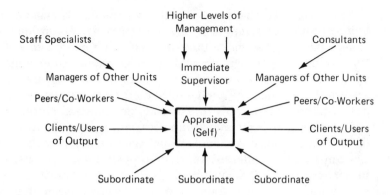

FIGURE 2–1. Raters.

In addition to self-rating, it may be necessary and useful to involve other individuals who have either witnessed or been influenced by the behavior of the employee. These individuals may include co-workers/peers, subordinates, other supervisors or managers who have had the opportunity to observe the individual at work, staff personnel specialists/consultants, committees, and, last but not least, clients (users of the employee's efforts who have the opportunity to observe personally the quality of that person's outputs). (See Figure 2–1.) It is important to recognize that the performance information from these other sources is not simply acquired to justify the accuracy of the rating of the immediate supervisor. These other individuals often observe behaviors or quality of output that the supervisor probably may not see at present or, in fact, may *never* see. It is also possible that these other people may be aware of the results of or feel the impact of a behavior that the supervisor could not predict from observation.

The use of more than one rater provides a more valid performance rating, reducing the opportunity for random error by correctly identifying and measuring more dimensions of performance and minimizing rater bias that is more likely to occur when using one rater. It provides a variety of rating considerations from different points of view. The result of involving other observers of performance in the process is an expanded view of the multiple dimensions of employee workplace performance.

Using multiple raters will require appraisal instruments with different performance dimensions. It is possible that some performance dimensions will be the same on all instruments. However, the major value of multiple raters is in the measurement of performance dimensions that are observable only to specific kinds of raters. Collecting these kinds of performance information entails the development of special performance rating instruments for each kind of rater. It is apparent that the *who* problem, like other performance appraisal issues, further complicates this already complicated problem.

In most cases, individuals who observe the behavior of an employee from different organizational perspectives or within varied work relationships observe different dimensions of workplace performance. This also means that it is very difficult to compare and reconcile the performance measurements of individuals who have different perspectives (both organizationally and individually). Even when raters with varying perspectives provide similar overall performance ratings, it is quite likely that these individuals are basing their ratings on different criteria or performance dimensions. There is absolutely nothing wrong with this approach. In fact, the use of multiple raters can provide a composite view of employee performance that would otherwise be impossible to achieve. However, when using multiple raters, organizations must recognize and be able to develop the performance dimensions that these raters with their different perspectives are actually observing, measuring, and rating.

The use of multiple raters provides an opportunity for various eyes and brains that are viewing, recording, and measuring various dimensions of workplace behaviors to provide inputs into the appraisal process. Simultaneously, it protects the ratee from the possibility of receiving an inappropriate rating because of a limited ability or opportunity to focus on a specific dimension of performance. It also provides multiple views of demonstrated workplace behavior that, if used in a nonthreatening, constructive manner, will be extremely valuable to employee personal growth and improvement in organizational productivity.

A 1977 study by The Conference Board revealed that almost 95 percent of the respondents stated that the immediate supervisor was a rater. Others identified as raters were self (about 13 percent of the time), groups or committees (about 6 percent), and representatives of the personnel department (about 6 percent). Representing less than 1 percent each were consultants (internal and external), peers or co-workers, and subordinates (zero percent by this study).[2]

---

[2] Robert I. Lazer and Walter S. Wikstrom, *Appraising Managerial Performance: Current Practices and Future Direction.* Conference Board Report No. 723, (New York: The Conference Board, Inc. 1977), p. 26.

This study also found that the raters' immediate supervisors reviewed ratings given by their subordinates about 70 percent of the time, with the personnel department performing reviews about 30 percent of the time and the rater's immediate supervisor's superior about 20 percent of the time.[3]

Immediate Supervisor

Because of close contact, most organizations feel that immediate supervisors are best able to appraise subordinates. The immediate supervisor is the one person who should know the responsibilities and duties of the jobs within his or her domain and how the outputs of these jobs assist in the attainment of unit goals. Furthermore, an effective supervisor is aware of subordinate strengths and weaknesses and is able to relate demonstrated subordinate performance to specific individual capabilities. Among all possible raters, it is the immediate supervisor who should have the greatest opportunity to observe the ratee's performance and to provide feedback on how well the employee performed relative to specific performance criteria or job standards. The immediate supervisor is the one person from whom most subordinates want to receive performance-related feedback. They feel confident that the immediate supervisor knows job requirements, established workplace procedures, and expected outputs. Because of the supervisor's knowledge and better understanding of unique personal qualities, the ratee feels more comfortable in discussing with the supervisor improved or preferred methods or changes in behavior required for satisfactory or superior performance. It is the immediate supervisor who is most influential in establishing a workplace environment that makes it possible for subordinates to gain a sense of satisfaction from the work that they do and to feel that their efforts have been recognized and that they have made valued contributions.

Most organizations want four major pieces of information from appraisals:

1. How well is the employee performing?
2. Is the employee ready for a vertical promotion or lateral transfer into a job with different knowledge, skill, and responsibility requirements?
3. What kinds of training and development programs could be provided to improve overall present and future employee output?

---

[3] Lazer and Wikstrom, *Appraising Managerial Performance,* p. 28

4. Should the employee be demoted or terminated?

In most cases, the immediate supervisor is able to provide relevant information for each of these four critical areas.

It is important to recognize that organizations do not have to implement a formal performance appraisal program to assist supervisors in identifying and rating the quality or level of performance of their subordinates. Supervisors who do their jobs adequately know how well or how poorly their subordinates are performing. In fact, formal performance appraisal may frequently be unnecessary if done solely to identify training needs and provide developmental support. An informal performance review program may be far more valuable and have a greater opportunity for success. With no formal recording of skill, knowledge, energy, or interest deficiencies, supervisor and subordinate can communicate in a far less threatening environment to solve both personal and job-related performance problems.

A major threat to instituting supervisor-based subordinate improvement programs that has been recognized for almost two decades is that when a supervisor formally recognizes personal deficiencies or weaknesses of a subordinate, the supervisor may also be significantly reducing the subordinate's opportunity for pay increases or promotions. The negative side of this approach, therefore, is that when training and development are part of an informal process, consistency and adequacy become major issues and monitoring the effectiveness of this crucial area becomes extremely difficult.

A major weakness of having only the immediate supervisor appraise performance relates to the personal issues that contaminate the appraisal process. Personal factors that contribute to contamination of appraisals are friendships, first impressions, stereotyping, and irrelevant or poorly understood performance standards. These factors can bias any rating.

Friendship. It is always possible for interpersonal relationships to bias a performance rating. In many cases, it is difficult to see a glaring deficiency in the performance of a friend and even more difficult to report it. However, when someone who is not particularly liked does one little thing slightly out of line, there is a tendency to be all too ready to initiate termination procedures. The friendship issue relates not only to specific individuals but also to groups. There is the possibility that the rater relates personally to a specific unit or group. (It may be a group that has always been particularly helpful and can be counted on to provide assistance when requested, a group of which the rater was once a member, and so on.) The rater who has a group affinity may rate members of that particular group higher than individuals in other groups who perform equally well.

First Impressions. Forming first impressions is a common human behavior. Individuals are prone to identify specific qualities or features of another person and quickly form an overall impression of that person from a very limited perspective by categorizing the person based on these qualities or features. Like friendships, first impressions are a typical personal bias that can contaminate appraisals. Most people develop an opinion about other people very shortly after meeting. Sometimes these first impressions are correct, and sometimes they are completely wrong. The issue facing raters is of not allowing first impressions to block out true recognition of what the person is and how he or she performs. First impressions can bias a rating either favorably or unfavorably.

Stereotyping. Stereotyping is a standardized mental picture that an individual holds of another individual because of that person's race, sex, national origin, or other distinguishing qualities. Stereotyping results in an oversimplified view of the individual and may block the establishment of a realistic description of the character or quality of the individual. Examples of stereotyping that appear to bias ratings in a favorable manner are the ratee's sex (male), race (white), age (30 to 35), tenure (5 to 15 years in the organization), even height (over 6 feet), weight (slender), and other physical characteristics.

Irrelevant or Poorly Understood Performance Standards. This issue becomes increasingly important the further removed one is from the job site. Although it is entirely possible for an immediate supervisor to appraise an employee on criteria that have lower or minimal weightings as compared with other criteria or even not to know or understand just what the performance standards are, this situation is more likely to occur with raters other than the immediate supervisor. Frequently, employees establish, with the approval of their immediate supervisors, certain workplace behaviors that are not in line with standing orders or operating procedures. When individuals other than those having knowledge of the changes see what appears to be an unacceptable behavior, they may rate the employee improperly because of their lack of knowledge of what the workplace standards or performance criteria actually are. This problem can also occur if the raters are not properly trained or if the performance criteria have not been properly defined through job analysis.

Other Contaminating Factors. Other factors that influence appraisal ratings, even though they have little or no relationship to actual job performance, are (a) membership in an elite unit and (b) an incumbent in a highly-prized job.

Rating Errors. Possibly the greatest contamination of ratings results from rating errors that were described in detail in Chapter 1. Chapter 10 specifically discusses the use of training for reducing these errors.

Supervisors of the Immediate Supervisor

Some organizations require supervisors at levels higher than the immediate supervisor to review and, at times, rate performance. A major reason for involving the rater's supervisor in performing the actual appraisal is the thought that this individual may have an even better understanding of what the employee should be doing to achieve a certain output. Supervisors on one or more levels above the immediate supervisor may be more aware of suboptimizing behavior and, by active involvement in the actual appraisal, may identify such activities and implement necessary changes.

From their vantage point, higher levels of management may focus on goal integration, methods used to achieve goals, unintended side effects from goal achievement, acceptance of responsibility, and job knowledge. On the other hand, the immediate supervisor may concentrate on results achieved or behaviors demonstrated by the employee with which he or she agrees or disagrees but which are not necessarily those most desired by the organization. In some organizations, the review function is accomplished by a rating review board. Members of a rating review board are normally higher-level managers in the organization. This board has responsibility for identifying performance behaviors that do not comply with established policies, regulations, and procedures.

Self-Appraisal

Self-appraisal has received support in recent years as more organizations have become involved in participative goal setting. A valid participative goal-setting program requires that the organization identify and subdivide objectives and goals and that involved employees develop their own goals that integrate with and support the achievement of work-unit and organizational goals. Setting goals and then analyzing successes and failures gained in goal achievement provide participating employees with valuable opportunities for self-appraisal. Self-appraisal is especially valuable for self-development and the identification of training and development needs. It permits the employee to assess personal potential and to verbalize his or her desires for lateral transfer or future promotions. On the other hand, individuals who have high dependency requirements or low self-esteem are poor candidates for involvement in self-appraisal programs.

A major problem related to self-appraisal is that the great majority of employees feel that they are average or above average performers. From a literal definition of the word "average," half of those being appraised are above average, and half are below average. Thus, when a supervisor appraises an employee as performing below average, there is a great likelihood that a conflict situation may arise. Having employees appraise their own performance encourages employees to verbalize actively their discontent with the appraisal. Although this is a problem frequently related to self-appraisal, in reality, it is a problem that relates to all appraisals. If self-appraisal brings into the open differences in ratee and rater perceptions, it is a valuable addition to the appraisal process. It is far better for employees to be able to voice their discontent than for them to suppress their feelings or to agree to a rating that they feel to be incorrect and unjust.

Regarding the issue that the "great majority of employees feel that they are average or above average," there are some legitimate answers to this problem. If an organization has existed for an extended period of time ("extended" must be defined by each organization), has done a careful job of screening job applicants, and has through performance requirements or normal attrition eliminated most individuals who have not met minimal job requirements, the words "average employee" may be misleading. Possibly a far better word or term would be "proficient" or "fully successful." This eliminates the need to relate to the numerical connotation of "average" by identifying worker performance with a more appropriate term.

Peers and Co-Workers

Although seldom used as raters, peers and co-workers have excellent insights into behaviors demonstrated at the workplace that either support or block improved work-unit performance. Figure 2–2 is an example of a rating instrument that could be used by peers for rating activities for which they may be the best observers. Peers and co-workers may also be valuable sources for identifying leadership skills and future potential. However, some very definite problem areas limit or even negate the use of peer appraisals.

FIGURE 2–2
Peer Performance Appraisal Rating Instrument

Peer-Observed Intragroup Performance Dimensions	Never	Seldom	Often	Frequently
1. Presents new ideas or new ways of carrying out procedures already in use.	1	2	3	4
2. Searches for and provides facts and information.	1	2	3	4
3. Clarifies issues and coordinates ideas and suggestions as well as activities of various groups.	1	2	3	4
4. Provides informal training.	1	2	3	4
5. Criticizes outcomes in constructive manner.	1	2	3	4
6. Recognizes, supports, and encourages others.	1	2	3	4
7. Acts as a peacemaker among individuals and groups.	1	2	3	4
8. Encourages participation by other, less active members.	1	2	3	4
9. Listens attentively to ideas and views of others.	1	2	3	4
10. Counsels others informally.	1	2	3	4
11. Displays a generally positive attitude on issues and discussions.	1	2	3	4
12. Exhibits modest behavior, but can be assertive when feels a view or opinion is worthwhile.	1	2	3	4
13. Volunteers services freely.	1	2	3	4
14. Minds own business.	1	2	3	4
15. Praises contributions of others.	1	2	3	4

Next to the relationship of employees with their supervisors, the most critical factor influencing job satisfaction is their relationship with peers. When peers perform appraisals, extreme care must be taken to ensure that the peer ratings do not damage co-worker social interactions. If this should occur, the costs involved in reduced job satisfaction might far outweigh the benefits gained from increased kinds and quality of rating data.

It must be remembered that the basic and overpowering need for security exists among practically all employees. Frequently, behaviors related to satisfying this need are not readily apparent, but they are demonstrated as soon as an individual feels that his or her security is threatened. Many individuals do excellent jobs of disguising security-satisfying behaviors even when they demonstrate such actions. The point here is that employees work for employer-provided rewards. Great competition for current and future employer rewards exists among members of a work group. Employees see employer-provided rewards as a discrete package, and, if someone else receives a desired reward, then it may be quite likely that these rewards will be unavailable to them. Employees have a very long-term perspective when it comes to working for employer-provided rewards. Reward aspirations and expectations may cloud how one employee perceives or identifies the performance of another.

For these reasons, it is quite possible that intragroup competition for employer rewards can raise individual levels of stress, accentuate the demand for self-protection, and encourage anxiety and hostility. Even though the high-performing organization needs some competition, activities that result in intragroup hostility and fears must be avoided if at all possible.

If an organization accepts the idea that peers can identify personal contributions as well as the strengths and weaknesses of their co-workers with considerable accuracy, and if that organization uses this information for reward purposes, problems may quickly arise. Once employees recognize that the organization is using information that they provided to make reward decisions that discriminate among its members, the informal organization will stop the flow of this kind of information. In retaliation, they may institute job-related behaviors that block the achievement of organizational goals.

An interesting observation about peer appraisals is that peers can provide information that is valuable for predicting workplace successes. However, research does not indicate that peers provide accurate assessment of workplace performance. A major reason for co-worker inability to judge performance accurately is that they look at jobs and employee outputs differently from the supervisors of those jobs. Peers frequently do not have sufficient information on co-worker job requirements and actual performance to determine level or quality of job performance. In fact, the very reason that organizations expend the time and energy to write and disseminate up-to-date and valid job descriptions, to promote goal setting, and to have the supervisor and subordinate sit down and mutually discuss goal attainment is to ensure that the supervisor and subordinate know and mutually agree on job requirements and performance standards. If organizations need to expend this much effort for the supervisor and subordinate to understand and agree to performance requirements, why should peers be expected to understand them? And, if they do not, how can they accurately identify job-related performance?

Many employees recognize that peers can identify personal strengths and weaknesses (most likely, weaknesses) better than any other members of the organization. There is a great likelihood that employees will accept peer analysis of particular deficiencies and will implement behavioral changes aimed at minimizing or overcoming these weaknesses. The issue is how peers can identify co-worker characteristics and how organizations can transmit this information to the affected individual without jeopardizing the employee's opportunities in the organization.

Telling employees that peer appraisal information is to be used only for counseling purposes by the supervisor is so much trivia. The more weaknesses identified by peers, the greater the chance that the supervisor will lower his or her esteem of that particular individual. Thus, this information has the potential of unfavorably biasing the supervisor. This process can operate just as well in reverse when a subordinate receives peer praise.

In spite of the competition for rewards and the opportunity for friendship and stereotypes to bias ratings, one idea that has been promoted may make it possible to use peer appraisals in a relatively nonthreatening manner. This possible, though not fool-proof, answer is the use of an in-house or external professional counselor as the only person to receive and review peer appraisals and to discuss them with each employee. The purpose of peer appraisal is strictly to assist the employee to become a more effective member of his or her work unit and the organization. This approach will minimize the need to appraise a peer unjustly because of common, desired rewards or to overrate a peer because of friendship. In fact, true friendship within this type of system may foster constructive criticisms that would never be identified under any other type of situation. Co-workers who would tend to be unjust raters would say nothing because their accusations could only hurt their cause, not help it. (If a criticism is unjust and is recognized as such in an open counseling session, the ratee realizes some individual in the group has these feelings. Although this may put an employee on guard, he or she at least knows what feelings are present in the workplace.) Even though counselors may be used for development purposes, it is still possible for supervisors to identify employee behaviors that significantly improve work-unit performance and are deserving of reward recognition.

Immediate Subordinates

Other seldom used but possible additions to the rater group are immediate subordinates. Although they tend to overrate their supervisor, they do identify his or her effectiveness in communicating job knowledge, interest in subordinates as individuals and team members, and skill in coordinating the subordinates' efforts into effective teamwork.

The major weakness of subordinate appraisal is lack of information regarding acceptable performance standards. Not understanding what their supervisor should be doing may bias the appraisal. Additionally, subordinates hold supervisors whom they perceive to have more influence throughout the organization in higher esteem. If subordinates find that their supervisor can gain special treatment either for themselves or their work units, there is the likelihood that they will appraise the supervisor's performance relative to this influencing ability rather than according to other and possibly more important demonstrated workplace behaviors (the halo effect in action; see a description of the halo effect in Chapter 1).

Committee

Using a committee for appraisal permits more than one person to have an immediate input. This approach allows various perspectives to be considered at one time. A strength of multiple raters is their ability to observe different behaviors. Committee members are usually managers one level above the employee being appraised and have had contact with the employee during the past appraisal period. The committee may also consist of managers at various levels who are aware of the employee's performance. However, just as committee appraisal may result in fair and just treatment, it may also result in a "kangaroo court." A committee appraisal can be influenced by the same contaminating factors that bias individual appraisals. Another weakness in using committees is excessive use of time.

Staff Personnel Specialists/Consultants

Well-trained specialists from the personnel department often assist in the employee appraisal. In most cases, when they are part of the appraisal process, they work together with individuals who have had the opportunity to observe the ratee's performance directly (e.g., in the field review method of appraisal discussed in Chapter 6).

One way organizations use this group of specialists is in assisting the immediate supervisor in rating his or her subordinates. This approach uses a specialist (internal or external) who is extremely familiar with performance appraisal processes in general and with the performance dimensions used to measure ratee performance in particular. The specialist will interview the raters (individually or in groups) and carefully explain each performance dimension and the rating scale or measurement process being used. He or she will then request the rater to provide a rating appropriate to the demonstrated and observed behavior of the ratee. This appoach minimizes conflict in understanding the measurement criteria and provides a more uniform rating by all raters who have contact with a common source of measurement explanation information (the specialist).

By providing an intermediary to assist the rater, various rating methodologies can be used at the same time. For example, a supervisor could first be asked to rank employees by a global criterion—performance—or through the use of various performance dimensions. This could be accomplished through some form of paired-comparison (discussed in detail in Chapter 6). Following this, the rater could then rate the employee using some kind of performance dimension, with an associated rating scale such as that described in Chapter 6. This kind of approach appears to provide extremely accurate ratings with a high degree of correlation between the ranking and rating techniques.

Multiple Supervisors

A number of recent additions to organizational design have placed more demands on performance appraisal ratings. These changes relate to structures known as matrix, task force, and project management organizations. These kinds of organizations normally have very specific and special assignments. Those directing the operations of the unit may be assigned to their jobs for the completion of the project, while most members work on a temporary and as-needed basis. Many team members may actually be reporting to two or even more supervisors. This complicates the appraisal process with regard to who is responsible for assigning a final performance rating and just how the rating is reviewed in comparison or in conjunction with peers and co-workers.

In many cases, the functional manager is responsible for the final rating. This, however, can lead to some serious difficulties for employees in these special assignments. Even when a special-unit manager rates the employee as superior, the rating may be given insufficient weight by the functional manager. This may occur because in some manner this manager resents or fails to recognize the true nature of the involvement of the employee on the special assignment. Similar to many responses to problems in this area, there does not appear to be any one proper or acceptable answer to the issue of multiple supervisors. One recommendation is that in these cases consultants or specially assigned staff members from personnel/human resources interview all supervisors in a multiple-supervisor situation and develop a final review and rating. What is certain is that organizations using such special units must pay extra attention to those involved in temporary or part-time assignments. They must be sure that their performance ratings adequately and validly identify the kinds and levels of contributions made.

Clients

Although this group is seldom used in appraising employee performance, there is no reason why organizations could not make use of the information clients are able to provide. Clients may be members within the organization who have direct contact with the ratee and make use of an output (good or service) this employee provides. Interest, courtesy, dependability, and innovativeness are but a few of the qualities for which clients can offer rating information. Clients external to the organization can offer similar kinds of information. Collecting information from clients, especially those outside the formal organization, places additional logistical demands on the administrative processes and also entails additional monitoring or policing requirements. The final decision regarding the collection of this kind of information is based on whether or not the value of the additional information is worth the added collection costs.

In summary, awareness and consideration of the following rater-related factors will assist in the successful design and operation of a performance appraisal program.

Factors that Tend to Improve the Accuracy of Appraisal Ratings

1. Rater has observed and is familiar with behaviors to be appraised.
2. Rater has documented behaviors to improve recall.
3. Rater has a checklist to obtain and review job-performance-related information.

4. Rater is aware of personal biases and is willing to take action to minimize their effect.

5. Higher levels of management are held accountable for reviewing all ratings.

6. Rating scores by raters are summarized and compared with those of other raters.

7. Rater focuses attention on performance-related behavior over which ratee has greatest control.

8. Rater's own performance ratings are tied to quality of rating given and performance of units.

9. Raters are trained in proper use of the system.

10. Performance factors are properly defined.

Factors that Tend to Decrease the Accuracy of Appraisal Ratings

1. Rater rates ratee only at times when administrative actions are contemplated.

2. Rater tends to inflate ratings when ratees receive scores and results of appraisals.

3. Rater tends to recall more behaviors known to be of particular interest to higher level managers, whether or not they are pertinent, when his or her ratings are reviewed by such authorities.

4. Rater is unable to express himself or herself honestly and unambiguously.

5. Appraisal systems, processes, and instruments fail to support the rater.

6. Rater is unaware of causes of rating errors.

7. Rater must rate employee on factors that are poorly defined.

RATEES A performance appraisal method used in the early stages of the Industrial Revolution was a rectangular piece of wood approximately two inches long and one inch wide that was painted a different color on each side and hung over the work station of each employee. Each day, the supervisor would turn the wood to the color that he thought denoted the employee's performance for the preceding day—black for bad, blue for indifferent, yellow for good, and white for excellent. [4]

---

[4] Robert Owen, "The 'Silent Monitor,' " in E. C. Bursk et al., eds., *The World of Business,* Vol. III (New York: Simon and Schuster, 1962), pp. 1350–1352.

Performance appraisal in the early part of the twentieth century also focused on operative employees. However, in the past two decades, there has been a trend toward eliminating performance appraisal among nonexempt, nonsalaried employees. (A possible exception is with nonexempt clerical and administrative personnel performing service-related assignments.) Frequently, when nonexempt employees are appraised, the rating is done in a perfunctory manner, and its main use is for approving a seniority or market adjustment pay increase. It is not uncommon to find over 95 percent of these nonexempt employees receiving an acceptable rating with a minimal amount of other information being provided. However, performance appraisal at the executive, managerial, and professional levels has become increasingly widespread.

One reason for the lack of interest in appraising nonexempt employees is the inability of organizations to develop valid and workable measuring instruments. Another reason is the strong allegiance of the operative levels to seniority. Many organizations consider their nonexempt, operative jobs to be highly procedural and technically oriented, and they think that all that is necessary to appraise the performance of the operative is to measure output. If this were true, the idea of not appraising the performance of lower-level employees might be valid. Often, however, this is not the case; even when the job requires that the employee follow specific procedures, 100 percent performance goes far beyond faithful performance of a list of duties.

Acceptable employee performance at all levels has elements that are difficult to specify. Employee contributions that affect output quality, reduction in costs, and the identification and solution of nagging problems are evident at every level. Measurement of these contributions requires some form of appraisal. Acceptance of seniority as the only criterion for rewarding performance is not only unacceptable but also wrong. This does not mean that seniority should not be recognized; it does mean that seniority and on-the-job performance are not the same thing and may not have a direct relationship. It is almost impossible to operate an organization that places a high value on human talent and individual differences without having a system for appraising performance.

By this time, it must be apparent that the performance appraisal system is complex and has many subparts or subsystems. Moreover, to many readers, its demand for increased structure is nothing more than a bureaucratic nightmare that can easily lead to more serious threats to employees. This increased structure may make it more difficult to hide the truth, but if the truth is threatening and the increase

REVIEWERS

in structure causes greater concern for survival, then those who seek to hide the truth will go even further underground and become more devious.

Employee performance can be and frequently is a most threatening issue. All kinds of emotional issues begin to appear with the rating of performance. Self-esteem, friendships, lack of valid job-content and results-related information, insufficient resources, and unfair distribution of resources are factors that influence these emotional issues. For most ratees, a situation will occur (sooner and more frequently than often thought likely) in which the appraisal process poses a distinct threat. Everyone involved in the appraisal must recognize that a performance appraisal rating by the immediate supervisor (or other ratings if more than one rater is involved) is not the end of the world. There must be confidence that performance ratings are being reviewed by other parties with various levels of authority and that no one will receive unfair treatment because of a performance rating. Past acceptable or good performance will be on record and will be a significant input to any management decision in which employee performance plays a part. At the same time, a record of unacceptable past behavior will instigate action on the part of management that could lead to demotion, even termination.

Review of performance appraisal ratings includes the following steps:

1. Supervisor-subordinate review.
2. Higher levels of management review.
3. Personnel department review.
4. Monitoring, auditing, and appeals.

Review of ratings by a supervisor (and others) should begin with the performance review or interview between the immediate supervisor and the subordinate. The next step in the process is usually a review of ratings and any ratee comments by the supervisor of the rater. There may be others in higher levels of management involved in the review process, but the next step is for the personnel department to maintain a longitudinal history of employee performance ratings and supervisory rating distributions, linking supervisory ratings to the measured performance of the work unit of that supervisor when possible. This personnel department information then should be made available and used by all parties influenced by performance ratings.

The final three steps of the review process are frequently omitted in many performance appraisal programs, but they must be included within a comprehensive performance appraisal system. These steps are (a) the right of each employee to appeal a review that he or she feels to be unsatisfactory, (b) monitoring by appropriate work-unit groups to ensure proper operation of the performance appraisal programs, and (c) auditing of the entire appraisal system by a unit that reports to the top level of management to assist those in key policy, planning, and strategy-making positions to perceive how well the entire system is operating.

The response to the claim of unnecessary structure and increased bureaucratization is that employee performance is a complex problem relating to employee survival and growth both on and off the job; organizational planning and the achievement of organizational goals is also an extremely complex process. These review steps are necessary to ensure honest and accurate application of the appraisal system.

Planning cannot be left to chance and, for the great majority of organizations, will not occur by chance. To promote and protect both individual security and organizational survival, constant, formal, and just reviews of employee behavior are essential.

Supervisor-Subordinate Review

Possibly the most difficult part of the entire appraisal program to implement is that of requiring a supervisor and subordinate to carry on meaningful performance-related dialogue. In many situations, such communication is not conducted or is conducted in such a manner that the perceived views of performance-related behaviors of each individual are not discussed in any meaningful way. The dialogue becomes more difficult the lower one moves into the organizational hierarchy. This relates to previously identified problems such as poorly identified job-content-based requirements and standards, the wide variety of subordinate behavior patterns, and the selection of lower-level managers for their technical competency and not necessarily for their interpersonal skills. The chapters that focus on training (Chapter 10) and interviewing (Chapter 9) relate to improving the interpersonal dynamics between supervisor and subordinate.

The entire performance appraisal system must be designed to reinforce and support supervisor-subordinate dialogue. Procedures must be implemented that ensure adequate and accurate descriptions of job-content requirements and performance standards. All employees must be informed of and understand why they are doing what they are doing and how their contributions lead to the successful operation of the organization. All employees must recognize the relationship between workplace performance and organizationally provided rewards. Supervisors must recognize the support and direct involvement that higher levels of management and other support units will provide when involved with the unsatisfactory performer. All supervisors must be provided with training opportunities that enhance interviewing skills and improve interpersonal dynamics. (It is the opinion of the author that possibly the single most important training opportunity to be provided to managers is that involving the improvement of interviewing skills.) Last, but not least, supervisors must recognize that they must review their perceptions of demonstrated employee workplace behavior and the ratings they make. This face-to-face dialogue is, in itself, threatening and extremely discomfiting to many individuals, but, like many other interpersonal actions, the more frequently it is performed, the less threatening it becomes. With well designed, properly implemented interviewing training, a supervisor will be more skilled in performing this critical performance appraisal assignment.

Higher Levels of Management Review

An important part of the performance of any manager is how well or how poorly he or she observes, rates, and reviews the performance of subordinate personnel. The review of the documentation and ratings provided by subordinate managers should be one of the most powerful insights as to what is occurring in subordinate work units and the overall performance of the immediate subordinate manager. This kind of review provides managers with an insight into the support subordinate managers may need both from a technical and interpersonal perspective and also from the perspective of the allocation of available resources.

It is also very important to those being rated that higher levels of management are fully aware of the contributions they are providing and of any unfair treatment that may exist. Awareness of individual performance must be pushed as high as possible through the ranks of management. This is a formalized procedure in which employees become recognized as unique individuals who provide a range of contributions, and not simply as social security numbers or job titles.

Personnel Department Review

Although the personnel department has always had the responsibility for maintaining personnel records, the changing role of the personnel department and the availability of computer-based information systems (CBIS) are having an important influence on personnel department activities relative to performance appraisal. The opportunities available through CBIS for data collection, analysis, summarization, storage, and dissemination have completely transformed the performance appraisal process. In the past, the costs involved in storing, retrieving, and comparing performance data frequently resulted in appraisal data being oversimplified. As a result, minimal use could be made of the data.

The ability of CBIS to perform various data manipulation activities makes it possible to store and compare multiple dimensions of performance over extended periods of time for one employee. The CBIS also enhances the opportunity to compare the performance of individuals performing dissimilar jobs or similar jobs within varied work environments. Rating behaviors of supervisors can be tracked and early warnings can be made available to indicate potential areas of unjust, possibly illegal, discrimination. Supervisor ratings can be analyzed by race, sex, national origin, age, seniority, and even kind of job. Distributions of supervisor ratings can also be analyzed relative to the performance of the specific work units. This kind of analysis of work-unit performance can, in turn, provide a standard for determining the adequacy or acceptability of a distribution of rating scores for a specific supervisor (rater). Such unacceptable rating behaviors as central tendency, halo effect, strictness, leniency, even latest behavior or first impressions can be identified for the information of both the rater and those responsible for reviewing raters' ratings, and this can lead to action to overcome these unacceptable rating behaviors. Rating information that assists each worker to relate his or her performance to other members can also be a valuable product of the use of CBIS in the appraisal process.

Using CBIS to monitor performance ratings will normally be more valuable to the large organization where there are many raters and ratees using comparable rating instruments and procedures. However, the monitoring of rating scores from both a rater and ratee perspective can be of value to any organization.

Personnel department review and closer contact with performance appraisal information will certainly assist personnel staff to develop and implement training programs that will improve organizational and individual performance. It will assist in mapping individual strengths and weaknesses and improve the implementation and operation of a skills and interest inventory of all personnel. Chapter 8 further discusses the role of administration in the performance appraisal system.

Monitoring, Auditing, and Appeals

Monitoring, auditing, and appeal components are missing or are conducted in a very limited manner in many performance appraisal programs. When considering the potential for subjectivity and how critical performance appraisal data can be to the current and future work opportunities for the appraised employee, it is difficult to conceive of an appraisal system that would operate as intended for any period of time unless it were carefully monitored and audited and unless employees had an opportunity to appeal unacceptable ratings.

Monitoring. A fully functioning monitoring component provides internal surveillance and proper operation. It is a continuous process that identifies problem areas and is a starting point for making changes as needed. A well designed and properly managed monitoring component will identify incorrect actions, errors, inaccuracies, or inconsistencies in the entire system. Because of the sensitive nature of appraisal data, all action necessary must be taken to ensure consistency of application and fair and impartial treatment. The monitoring process will normally include some personnel staff assistance in addition to members of the work unit who have monitoring responsibilities. Personnel staff can assist those responsible for monitoring operations by providing training and other support in improving skills in identifying problem areas or things to do to resolve errors and inconsistent applications.

The ratee plays an important role in appraisal monitoring. By providing the employee with feedback on rated performance and possibly some kind of comparison data, ratee participation in the monitoring process may be one of the first and possibly more accurate indications of some unsatisfactory condition.

The extent of monitoring in many existing appraisal programs consists of review of appraisal ratings by the rater's immediate supervisor, very occasionally by higher levels of management ranging to the chief executive officer, and, to a varied extent, by staff personnel specialists. Once an organization has in excess of 500 to a thousand employees, it becomes unlikely that the highest levels of management actually become involved in the review of appraisal ratings, although it *does* occur. It is extremely important that the immediate supervisor of those supervisors who are rating subordinates review the rating and other measurement information to ensure consistency, accuracy, and credibility of ratings among the subordinate supervisors. For the most part, these reviewing supervisors are the individuals who can best differentiate among the performance of subordinate work units. They should be the first to recognize an incongruence between rating distributions within a work unit and the overall performance of the work unit.

With the capability of the CBIS to provide past ratings of a specific individual and historical comparisons of rating distributions among supervisors and work units, probes can be directed toward work units, supervisors, and individuals in which ratings appear to be inconsistent or out of line with other kinds of organization- or work-related information. In particular, attention can focus on ratings that appear to discriminate according to race, sex, religion, age, and national origin rather than demonstrated performance.

Auditing. The auditing component of the performance appraisal system differs from monitoring in that monitoring is an ongoing internal review operation, while auditing is conducted by a completely independent unit that performs its activities at unannounced, irregular intervals. The auditing unit normally works under the direct authority of top management to review operations of the organization and to ensure compliance with established policies, procedures, and rules. To accomplish its assignment, the auditing unit must be capable of uncovering subversive tactics, misleading operations, or other actions that, if permitted to continue, could discredit the entire appraisal system. Specific instructions should be provided to the auditing unit, describing the timing and approach to the audit, the extent of the audit, the procedures to be followed, and reports to be issued.

An auditor's report should identify problem areas and significant weaknesses in current operations and specify follow-up actions to be taken. This report should be sent to top management for review and then to the appropriate individuals for further review and responses to any comments or directives from top management. True top management support of an appraisal program requires active involvement in the auditing process. If involvement is not forthcoming at this stage in the appraisal process, espoused top management support, which is so critical to the successful operation of this vital and extremely sensitive system, is nothing more than a sham. The use of CBIS for monitoring and auditing of the appraisal system is further developed in the discussion of the computer-aided performance appraisal (CAPA) in Chapter 8.

Appeals. Another essential component of the appraisal system is the appeals process. Again returning to the basic concerns of subjectivity, bias, and the extremely important impact that appraisal data have on the working and personal lives of the employees, this relief valve— the appeal—must be part of the performance appraisal system.

The appeals process must be viewed by employees as a nonpunitive device. It must be seen as a valid and open forum in which any grievances related to the performance appraisal system can be aired. The appeals must be heard and reviewed by individuals who can arbitrate and make judgments in a nonbiased manner. Those involved in listening and making decisions on an appeal must be able and willing to recognize both appellant and management points of view and have the authority to make a fair decision. Most importantly, employees must recognize that an appeal will not be followed by some kind of future punitive action. Appeals information can be fed directly into both the monitoring and auditing processes. The kind and quantity of appeals are excellent sources of information on appraisal problems and issues. There is a further discussion of monitoring, auditing, and appeals in Chapter 11.

THE TIMING OF APPRAISALS

It has been common practice to perform a formal performance appraisal once a year. The proponents of the annual appraisal state that, if held more frequently, formal appraisals tend to become mechanical, worthless procedures. A semantics problem arises here regarding the meaning of the term *formal appraisal.* If it means completion of a special form, then this consideration may have some validity; however, if it applies to the entire process, then it is probably incorrect. All of the problems relating to the ability of the human brain to store and review all kinds of information about the behavior of others over a period as long as one year are well known. The most recent behaviors, especially if they vary significantly from the norm, will probably have the greatest influence on an annual rating. It is difficult in this fast-moving, dynamic world to remember accurately what transpired 60 days ago, let alone to search for and accurately reflect on the behaviors demonstrated over a 365-day period.

Many procedures, some formal, some informal, have been identified and, in fact, widely used to assist the human brain in remembering behaviors of others over an extended period of time. Possibly the most important is the use of a "little black book" in which the supervisor records brief summaries of what was observed. A formal adaptation of the "black book" is the completion of some kind of a critical-incident form by the supervisor. An example of such a form is given in Chapter 10 in the discussion of documenting workplace behavior. This form provides an outline for the supervisor to describe a particularly good or poor behavior that can then be reviewed when making the formal appraisal or documenting information to support a specific rating. The same form may also be given to employees to document their own behaviors and to support their views when involved in performance reviews with their supervisors. In this way, the recording of behavior is a two-way, aboveboard operation.

Because of the rapid degeneration of behavior-related information stored in the brain of the rater and ratee, and also because of the selective memory or recall of performance information by involved parties, the best answer regarding when to appraise is to shorten the formal periods for review of performance. Although it may be impractical and unnecessary to review performance formally on a daily, weekly, or even monthly basis, the administration of a bimonthly or quarterly formal appraisal is possible and desirable. What at first may appear to be another bureaucratic burden may, in reality, assist in overcoming many of the interpersonal barriers related to performance appraisal. Most people do not like surprises; this is one of the important emotional issues that a well designed appraisal system must minimize. Taking away from the rater the pain of providing bad news and eliminating the shock frequently experienced by ratees is possible through more continuous dialogue between rater and ratee.

As all employees get used to having their performance reviewed and rated on an on-going basis with an improvement in the accuracy of the rating, defensiveness on the part of both raters and ratees may begin to diminish.

The bimonthly or quarterly formal ratings may be summarized in an annual rating if the administrative procedure of the organization requires some kind of an annual summary. But if performance appraisal is to be used as a basic part of the planning process, informal reviews of performance and the identification and discussion of performance-related problems should be a consistent and on-going operation. Formal reviews, however, are still required to ensure that this sensitive and critical process is being implemented in a manner consistent with organizational planning and control requirements.

When an organization permits a supervisor to rate a subordinate on completion of an exceptional piece of work, and the rating is then tied into an immediate pay adjustment, that ratee receives this desirable reward more often than other employees. Employees in the lower half of a pay grade may also receive performance reviews more often than those in the third and fourth quartiles of a pay grade. This permits the lower-paid employee to move more rapidly to at least a market rate of pay.

Annual Formal Reviews

Organizations have two basic timing opportunities available for the formal review of performance. They are anniversary date reviews and a common review date for all employees.

Anniversary Date Review. The anniversary date of an employee may be the date of hiring, but, far more likely, it is the date the employee entered his or her current job. By reviewing an employee's performance and providing a rating on the employee's anniversary date, the rater is not overwhelmed by the requirement of reviewing a large number of employees at one time. This process removes the sting or minimizes widespread ill feelings that may result when all employees receive their reviews and ratings at the same time.

Common Review Date. Even after recognizing the problems that arise when supervisors are required to review all immediate subordinates at one time, more organizations are turning to a common date for reviewing and rating employee performance. A major reason for this change is that if comparisons are to be made among employees for such purposes as sharing merit increases or for promotions, it is important that the internal and external forces that may influence employee performance receive equal recognition. The influence of internal and external forces is especially important when some form of goal setting and goal attainment is a critical part of the appraisal process. If performance is formally reviewed and measured bimonthly or quarterly, the final review consists only of the bimonthly or quarterly review and the summary of previous ratings. If the periodic review is conducted according to defined practices and procedures and if ratings are already stored in the computer, the final review is not so traumatic and time-consuming as the annual review that is now so much a part of the practices of many organizations.

Completion of Major Assignments or Projects or Significant Job Changes

Employees assigned to special projects should have their performance reviewed upon the completion of the project regardless of the relationship to some established annual review date. This same approach may be applicable to the completion of notable or significant activities that are not part of the normal work of an employee or when duty or even responsibility changes are made in job requirements. In these cases, it may be wise to rate the performance of the employee on past assignments as soon as possible after changes have been made.

TIMING OPPORTUNITIES Figure 2–3 identifies timing opportunities for review and rating plans.

LOCATION OF APPRAISAL INTERVIEWS The great majority of performance reviews are conducted in the rater's office, where the rater has access to a variety of information that assists in recalling behaviors and results over the current appraisal period. One major organization has experimented with conducting

---

Predetermined Time Periods

1. Daily or weekly informal performance reviews.
2. Bimonthly or quarterly performance or goal achievement reviews.
3. Semiannual formal performance reviews and ratings.
4. Formal rating upon anniversary date of employment or entry to job or established common review date.
5. Specified periods during probationary period:
   a. 30 days after entry into job;
   b. 90 days after entry (may include next level of management at interview); and
   c. 180 days (or near end of probation period). Identify retention, separation, or request extension for further training or job experience.

Work-Related Time Periods

1. Upon completion of observable and measurable work cycle.
2. During a period of declining performance.
3. Upon conclusion of an exceptional performance.
4. Prior to transfer to another work unit or division.
5. Prior to termination.
6. Upon significant changes in duties or responsibilities.

FIGURE 2–3. Guidechart for Timing Appraisals.

group reviews at a location away from the work site to eliminate the interruptions that are bound to occur when the raters are in their own offices.

This procedure requires that the raters bring any kind of behavior and results documentation with them to the off-worksite location. A group leader (personnel specialist/consultant) then reviews and describes each performance dimension for the raters. (These raters will be reviewing subordinates who are performing the same kind of work assignments.) The raters measure incumbents in the same job by one dimension at a time, and they all have the same opportunity to hear what the performance dimension includes or relates to and to ask questions to clarify unresolved issues. This technique does add another cost to the appraisal process, but if it improves the accuracy of the ratings, it may easily be worth the additional cost.

INFLUENCE OF EMPLOYEE CHARACTERISTICS ON RATINGS

Any discussion of appraisal procedures and operations must underline the obvious. It is critical that differences in employee characteristics and the ways these differences influence the design and output of any appraisal program be recognized and understood.

Over the past 25 years, an extensive amount of research has been conducted to develop a better understanding of the influence individual rater and ratee characteristics have on appraisal ratings. This research has been investigating not only the unique individual qualities but also the possibilities of variations in results when raters and ratees have significantly different characteristics and qualities.

Rater–Ratee Characteristics and Qualities

Those involved in the design and administration of performance appraisal programs must be aware of the following demographic characteristics of both raters and ratees:

Sex

Age

Race

National origin

Disabilities

Physical characteristics (height, weight, etc.)

Years of formal education

Years of job experience

Level in organization

Kind of job

Employment status (permanent or temporary, full-time or part-time)

It is quite likely that individuals with varying demographic characteristics will view and relate to performance measurement and rating programs differently. It is also possible that when a rater has one set of characteristics and the ratee has another, these differences may be the overriding influences on ratings received, while workplace performance takes second place. This has always been an important issue in assessing the accuracy of performance measurement. A basic concern is that unfair performance ratings can negatively influence employee job satisfaction and morale and lead to reduced levels of performance.

Today, additional areas of concern relate to the possibility that such measurement behaviors could result in violation of state and federal legislation, which, in turn, could bring about costly lawsuits. There must be an awareness and constant review of appraisal procedures to minimize the occurrence of such dysfunctional activities.

Although research does not provide explicit or unequivocal findings relative to differences in ratings caused by varying demographic characteristics, it is easy to believe that similar characteristics may lead to higher ratings while dissimilar characteristics may lead to lower ratings. When there are extreme differences in employee characteristics—such as having raters of predominantly one age group, sex, or race and ratees of another age group, sex, or race—inappropriate performance ratings may be forthcoming.

In addition to these demographic characteristics, personal qualities can play a significant role in the quality of appraisal ratings. Research has focused on such qualities as:

Cognitive complexity

People orientation

Production orientation

Free spirit

Physiological health

Emotional stability

Psychological state

These various qualities can certainly influence both rater and ratee appraisal behaviors. Individual interests, values, motives, and attitudes can temper the ability to observe and accurately rate performance. From the early pages of this book, the issue of subjectivity has been recognized as one that will always exist and can harm any performance appraisal program. There is no way to rule out these employee personality factors. What organizations can and must do is to

1. Be aware of how these factors can influence employee ratings.
2. Monitor the appraisal program to identify when and where these influences may be operating.
3. Provide information through training and other communication programs to assist all employees in minimizing such negative influences.

ORGANIZATIONAL CHARACTERISTICS

Employee differences are not the only issues that affect the design and operation of an appraisal program. Performance appraisal specialists must also be aware of how organizational characteristics can influence the accuracy of performance ratings. Some of the most significant organizational characteristics are:

Organizational design (number of levels, use of project management, task forces, or matrix organization)

Number of employees

Number of different divisions, departments (work units)

Geographic distribution of work units

Different kinds of work performed

Organizational philosophy and value system

Managerial span of control

Use of appraisal rating information

Influence/status of certain positions

When designing performance appraisal procedures and rating instruments, it may quickly become apparent that both procedures and instrument design must be different for different classes of jobs. In other words, an appraisal program for operative employees may be significantly different from one designed for senior management. In turn, a senior management program may be different from one to be used for operating managers, and these programs may vary from one for professional personnel.

The first and foremost issue is not uniformity of techniques, procedures, or instruments, but validity of performance ratings. Not only may one organization have to use different approaches for measuring and rating employees in different groups, but a program that works for one organization may be a complete dud for another organization. The point is that the design and administration of a performance appraisal program must be tailor-made to fit the many unique employee and organizational characteristics and qualities.

An organization that provides employees with considerable information on their job requirements, feedback on their performance, and even opportunities to design their jobs and establish their own work schedules will most likely use an entirely different set of operating procedures and even design rating instruments differently from an organization that maintains a cloak of secrecy on most operational information and operates within a strict bureaucratic environment. The use of appraisal rating information when making organizational decisions that have an impact on the timing and amounts of pay adjustments, merit pay allocations, opportunities to attend desired training programs, selection for higher-level jobs, and even lateral transfer or demotion or termination will have a strong influence on appraisal program design and operation. If past organizational behavior has been extremely authoritarian and the decisions resulting from performance appraisal are viewed as more of a punishment than a reward, then employee responses may relate closer to "a cover your rear" attitude than one that considers "honesty to be the best policy."

Chapter 3

The Linking-Pin for Planning

Many leaders of top organizations have stated and continue to state that their employees are their most valuable resources. If this espoused theory is to come into line with practice, then major changes have to be initiated in the performance appraisal programs of organizations. It is no longer possible (in fact, it hasn't been for some time) to implement and administer an appraisal program and expect it to succeed when a major output is its threat to the survival of lower-level managers and workers. When organizations begin to recognize that performance appraisal is a critical part of the planning and control functions, a first step will be taken toward the establishment of a workplace environment in which employees at all levels will have the opportunity to influence organizational objectives, assist in their achievement, and take their rightful places as the most important resource of the organization.

A performance appraisal system has considerable front-end costs and continuous operational costs. Defining job requirements that can be linked step-by-step to the organizational mission and objectives is a time-consuming and thought-provoking process. It requires considerable verbal efforts and skills; it requires a willingness to provide information many top-level managers are not willing to divulge. They are not only unwilling to pass on through the ranks what they consider to be extremely confidential information, they are also unwilling to spend the time and effort to verbalize these strategic requirements and movements of the organization so that they can be translated downward through the organization. Figure 3–1 identifies the major events that must occur to permit the flow of critical performance-related information.

Many respected researchers on human behavior recognize the need for power as possibly the strongest drive possessed by successful top managers. Research has also identified information as one of the most

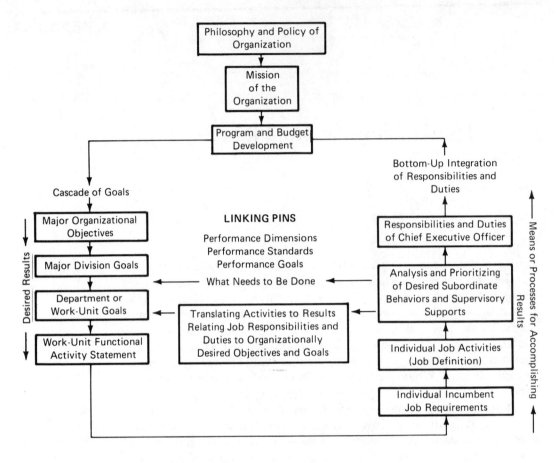

FIGURE 3–1. The Framework of a Performance Appraisal System.

valuable tools of the powerful. Performance appraisal is a powerful information-providing tool. At the same time, in order for performance appraisal to operate properly, a large amount and a wide variety of information are required. The communication of information becomes the lifeblood of a performance appraisal system. If top management wishes to release the power held within performance appraisal, it must be willing to share that power with all those whose destinies are influenced by this system.

Establishing a productive workplace environment that promotes trust among all employees must include the transfer of information that certain individuals and groups have felt, in the past, to be too threatening to communicate. It is folly to think that the personal threats related to employee performance can be eliminated through the completion of some document or the establishment of some process, but the steps involved in implementing a performance appraisal system just may be the best first step available to management. Figure 3–2 identifies the steps and the factors that influence them in establishing a performance appraisal system.

In 1915, a delegate to a convention of the National Education Association stated that performance appraisal was demeaning, arbitrary, perfunctory, and superficial. If an organization is to operate a performance appraisal program that improves its productivity and does not have a 1915 impact, it must meet a variety of demands.

The design, development, and operation of a performance appraisal system that meets organizational demands and is accepted by employees at all levels must be firmly based in the foundation of the organization. The philosophy, policy, and mission form the foundation of the organization, and it is within this base that strategic planning develops. Here, long-term objectives are defined and established, and it is in the long-term objectives that the performance appraisal process truly begins and ends.

Top management is responsible for the achievement of organizational objectives as each succeedingly lower level of management is responsible for the accomplishment of the respective goals of their work units. If all of the work-unit goals are to interlock successfully and totally support the attainment of the objectives of the organization, the goal-setting process, above all, must be orderly. To maintain order and harmony among the wide variety of work-unit goals that, in aggregate, form the objectives and goals of the organization, top management must always be in complete control of the process. To understand how objectives and goals develop, it is important to recognize the continuing influence of the strategic planning process on the success of the organization.

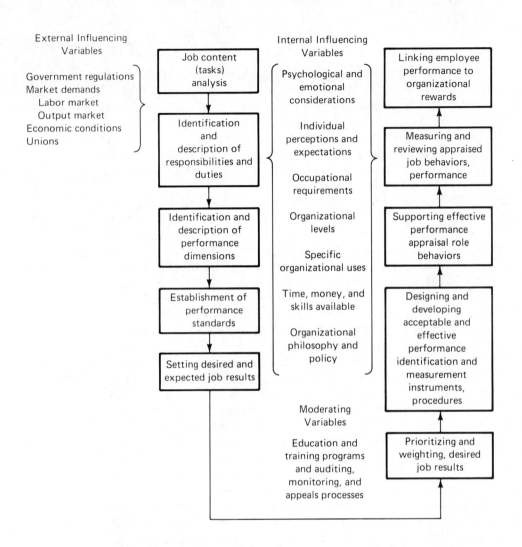

FIGURE 3–2. Sequential Performance Appraisal System Component Relationships.

60

A primary responsibility of senior management of any organization is to provide adequate guidelines that assist all members in performing their assignments in a way that guarantees survival not only for today and tomorrow but for the many tomorrows that lead into the distant future. The strategic responsibilities of the leaders of contemporary organizations relate very closely to the concepts of strategy as developed and practiced by military organizations for thousands of years. Military leaders develop strategic plans that identify the major overall reasons and purposes for the military operation. In addition, they specify the general nature of the actions to be taken and the results to be achieved by their tactical leaders so that the grand design of the organization can be accomplished.

STRATEGIC PLANNING

This is also the purpose of strategic planning from the perspective of contemporary organizations. Top executives establish the philosophy and mission of the organization. These broad, general outcomes are then divided into functional-unit objectives and eventually are translated into assignments for specific individuals. In this stage of the planning process, the long-term strategic plans evolve into the shorter-term tactical plans and operations of the organization.

The major components of the strategic or long-term plans include (a) organizational philosophy, (b) organizational policy, (c) organizational mission, (d) organizational objectives, and (e) organizational strategic operations and budget.

Organizational Philosophy

The philosophy of the organization defines the beliefs or value system top management expects all members to follow in performing their assignments. This expression of approved concepts and attitudes adds stability and consistency to the actions taken in achieving the mission of the organization. An effective philosophy statement clearly informs each employee of the limits of acceptable behavior. Whenever possible, the organizational philosophy should be in writing. It should express the values of those responsible for establishing and directing the organization. It should be sufficiently explicit to ensure that all members of the organization know what ought to be done and how to behave when solving problems and making decisions.

Organizational Policy

Policies provide guidelines for acceptable behavior relative to specific operational areas of the organization. Organizational policies develop because top management recognizes that the various functional and operating work units of the organization require different kinds and amounts of freedom to accomplish their specific objectives and goals. To grant employees in these varied work units sufficient freedom of action within certain limitations, top officials establish organization-wide policies and subpolicies that relate to specific subject areas (e.g., organizations frequently have a set of policies that defines acceptable performance appraisal behavior of all personnel).

Organizational Mission

In some cases, the mission of the organization is a group of ideas or dreams firmly locked in the brain of the founder. At best, the remainder of the work force has only the slightest glimmer of the long-term reasons for the existence of the organization other than its ability to provide an output that is desired by its consumers and to continue to provide income for all of its members. An organizational mission statement describes in writing the long-term outcomes the senior managers of the organization expect to achieve. The mission statement is the first step in providing orderliness for organizational practices. Although by necessity the statement articulates in fairly general terms the reasons for the existence of the organization, it acts as a guidepost or lighthouse that directs widely diverse organizational activities toward a common end.

Organizational Objectives

The establishment of broad organizational objectives is the first step in articulating the values and philosophy of the organization. They permit the description of desired organizational results in more precise and specific terms than those defined in the mission statement. These results may include quantity, quality, and time standards that provide a better definition of expectations. They provide the foundation for the objectives and goals of the many work units that comprise the organization. (The words *objectives, goals,* and *targets* may be used synonymously. In this book, however, the word *objective* has a broader and longer-term perspective, while the word *goal* is used to define a narrower, shorter-term desired end result. It may be considered a subobjective.)

Organizational Strategy and Budget

The strategic plans of the organization identify the actions the organization wishes to take to accomplish its objectives. The fundamental planning tool that formalizes these actions is the organizational budget. The budget brings the world of dreams and aspirations to the often hard and even cruel world of reality. The organization's budget informs all members of the resources available to accomplish its intended objectives. It defines in quantitative terms the priorities set by top management and the support each work unit can expect to receive to accomplish its assignment.

A TOP-DOWN OPERATION

The development and implementation of the strategic components of the planning process are the responsibility of top managers. They may request information from employees at subordinate levels as to the adequacy, acceptability, and usefulness of the composition of these components and they may use lower-level support personnel to actually develop the components, but it is the ultimate responsibility of top management to approve the strategic plans and enforce their implementation within the organization.

To ensure a consistent and supportive relationship between the longer-term objectives of the organization and successive sets of work-unit goals, longer-term objectives have to be redefined into shorter-term organizational work-unit goals. Care must be taken at the very top levels of the organization to ensure that the longer-term strategic considerations and the shorter-term operating requirements are compatible and reinforce each other. It is important at this stage that there be explicit and easily recognizable separation of the longer-term objectives and the shorter-term goals. It should also be easy to recognize how current operations fit into and support the achievement of the longer-term objectives.

Since organizational planning must coordinate and integrate the many diverse functions and specialized work units included within the organization, it must initially be a highly centralized, nonnegotiable, top-down operation. This does not mean that the dynamics of change and the pressures emanating from untold internal and external forces that affect the planning process as each employee performs his or her work assignments will be ignored. In order for the strategic plans to be successful, they must take into account the constant changes occurring inside and outside the organization that directly influence organizational activities. These influences must be recognized by those responsible for the centralized planning activities of the organization. The major problem here is that the planners are seldom those who first recognize the importance of changing conditions or situations. It is far more likely that particular individuals performing specific work assignments directly affected by the condition will first feel the impact of the change. For this reason, these individuals must have direct contact with the strategic planning activities.

TACTICAL PLANNING While strategic planning centers on the accomplishment of organizational objectives, tactical planning focuses on the achievement of the goals of the many specialized work units of the organization. Developing a link between the activities performed by each jobholder and the mission and objectives of the organization requires a series—and in cases of large, diversified organizations, a rather lengthy series—of work-unit and subwork-unit goals. These work-unit goals are then translated into work-unit activities that are bundled together, forming jobs. Workers with certain sets of knowledge and skills are then selected to perform these job activities, which are frequently identified as responsibilities and duties. This translation and retranslation process must be performed in an orderly manner if the lower-level work-unit goals are to be consistent and support the goals of the next higher work unit and, in turn, the overall objectives and goals of the organization.

The major components of shorter-term tactical planning are (a) work-unit objectives and goals, (b) the work-unit function statement, (c) work-unit budgets, and (d) individual job assignments.

Work-Unit Objectives and Goals

The translation and retranslation of organizational objectives into work-unit goals at succeedingly lower levels of the organization require an appreciation of the challenges facing anyone involved in the communication of concepts, programs, and procedures. This downward restatement of work-unit goals may, at first, appear to take the form of an extrapolation, but this depends on the realism and honesty that is part of the initial establishment of organizational objectives. The reformation of work-unit goals is part of the total planning process and assists not only in establishing goals but also in defining the appropriate tactics for each work unit.

Work-Unit Function Statement

The work-unit function statement is, in essence, the charter for the work unit. It describes in general terms the activities to be performed by the work unit to accomplish its established goals.

Work-Unit Budgets

In a process similar to the translation of organizational objectives into work-unit goals, the organizational budget becomes redefined into applicable work-unit budgets. The budget process may not go through as many iterations nor be as finely tuned as work-unit goals, but the budget at whatever level it stops tells each work unit and its members in very specific quantitative terms the funds available for acquiring the resources to assist them in achieving their assigned goals.

Individual Job Assignments

The final step in the top-down planning process is the bundling of work-unit activities into sets of responsibilities and duties to be performed by a specific incumbent. The identification and description of responsibilities and duties are discussed in detail in Chapter 4.

OPPORTUNITY FOR BOTTOM-UP COMMUNICATION

The top-down, nonnegotiated process does not eliminate the opportunity for participation in goal setting. That opportunity occurs when those who have some voice in the allocation of resources and the development of the budget can identify their resource requirements and the goals they feel they or their work units can achieve within the constraints set by the budget. This occurs with the setting of individual performance goals. The performance goal of a particular work unit will be a significant part, if not the total set, of the performance goals of the manager of that unit.

Through the development of a channel of communication that moves upward, managers of succeedingly higher levels become aware of the problems and issues facing their subordinates. When the full force of these issues is placed in front of the executives responsible for the achievement of organizational objectives, they can make the necessary changes in these objectives that, in turn, result in changes in the goals of the affected work unit.

This kind of upward communication enables top managers to make changes in organizational assumptions, objectives, and policies. Through this upward flow of information, managers at succeedingly higher levels learn about processes, procedures, or operations that no longer work and are inhibiting the achievement of organizational objectives and goals. This is almost the only process that will tell the top executives that "the skywalk is not safe and could collapse," or "the gas tank is in a poor location," or "we are not contacting the right people in the client's organization to sell our product," or "the raw materials we are purchasing are not meeting established standards."

All too often, top managers insulate themselves from the day-to-day operations of the organization. They don't want to hear about the "brush fires" and "nit-picking" human problems facing those in the here-and-now environment. When top management exhibits this kind of behavior, subordinates at all levels almost always hide the truth. Hardly anyone wants to be the bearer of bad news.

Many of the disasters that eventually engulf organizations and cause their decline or even demise start with problems that could have been identified by lower-level employees and would have been communicated upward if the involved employees either had not felt threatened or had felt that higher levels of management were truly interested in what they had to report.

PLANNING AND BUDGETING

The bottom-line result of planning is a budget. The budget identifies and defines how the organization will spend its money for the coming planning period. For organizations that do not have a formal budget, there is, in reality, an after-the-fact budget behavior. In this situation, actual expenditures for the past period can be summarized and a budget-in-use created. This after-the-fact kind of budget permits those with expenditure authority to have practically unlimited control (within available resources) over how and where funds are used. This negates the primary reasons for the existence of the budget—that is, to ensure that resource allocation supports and reinforces organizational objectives and goals, that expenditure information is brought into the open for review and analysis, and that order and structure are provided to expenditures.

Budgets are written plans expressed in terms of dollars, or units, or both. From organization to organization, they vary considerably by degree of complexity and detail. Among organizations, however, the major operating budget does have these common features:

1. It is an annual statement of resources to be made available to meet organizational objectives and goals.
2. It identifies the kinds and amounts of resources to be made available to the various work units.
3. It usually includes a capital equipment budget, an operating budget, and a cash budget.
   a. The capital equipment budget details the goods, equipment, and buildings to be acquired that will be used for more than one year.
   b. The operating budget identifies the operating revenues and expenses for the budget period.
   c. The cash budget provides an estimate of monetary flow or working capital required for the given period.

To ensure that the resources provided and allocated in the budget support the attainment of both the long-term objectives of the organization and its shorter-term annual goals and those of its various work units, budget preparation theoretically should involve input from all work units.

For this reason, the budget development process should follow closely behind the setting of organizational and work-unit goals. It is in the formulation of the budget that work-unit managers inform their immediate supervisors of the resources they will require to achieve forecasted end results. Resource estimates must be developed in conjunction with organizational and work-unit goals. These work-unit estimates then move back up the organizational ladder, and the accumulated estimates result in the final organizational operating budget.

A major problem with budget formulation links directly to a problem previously identified in goal setting. That is, the communication of organizational objectives and goals downward through the organization is performed in such a manner that each subordinate work unit does not truly recognize and understand what it must do to actively support and assist higher-level work units and the organization in achieving their goals.

In addition to the barriers that block the downward flow of goal information, other barriers block the upward flow of goal-achievement information that identifies problems encountered by specific work units and individuals. These same barriers will, in turn, inhibit communication of information regarding the need for different or additional resources to achieve specific goals.

If the goal, budget, and resource allocation processes are to be linked together in a supportive manner, the complete loop of goal and budget information must operate from the top-down movement of organizational goals to the bottom-up movement of performance goals, influencing the design of organizational budgets so that the additional resources required to bring performance goals in line with organizational and work-unit goals are made available. When required resources cannot be provided, then it may be necessary to review organizational objectives and make necessary adjustments. (See Figure 3–3, The Goal-Setting Budget Process.)

Resource Negotiation and Budgeting

For many jobs, the incumbent has minimal input or influence on the assignments to be performed. The incumbent receives certain well defined inputs, processes these inputs, and provides an output that becomes an input to another employee. Possibly the only choice available to the employee is the selection of the procedures to be used in

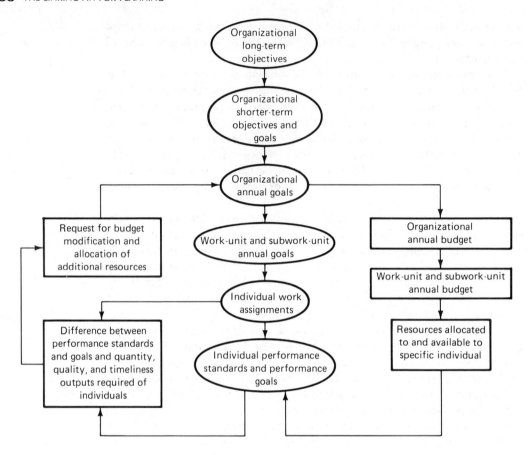

FIGURE 3–3. Goal-Setting Budget Process.

performing job assignments or in the sequence and time to be allotted to each procedure. This does not imply that a person performing such assignments may not have important information to provide to management. Situational changes and variations in quality of inputs, organizational resources being used, and factors influencing performance of these workers must be communicated upward so that changes in job assignments can be made if necessary to meet these contingency demands.

What must be recognized is that these individuals have little or no opportunity to negotiate for the resources made available to perform work assignments. Recognizing the opportunities available for negotiating for the allocation of resources available to a work unit becomes extremely important when determining how individual performance is to be measured. Those incumbents who have minimal or no opportunity for input in the resource allocation process will most likely have their performance measured against well defined, preset performance standards. When an employee has the opportunity to negotiate with higher levels of management on the resources available for the successful completion of job assignments, then attention may focus on goal achievement.

In its most basic form, negotiation occurs when determining the procedures, timing, sequencing of activities, and amount of time to be made available for achieving an identified result. In jobs where the incumbent has a significant amount of latitude in the procedures to be used in performing job assignments, this is a valid and critical part of goal accomplishment.

When an employee negotiates for the allocation of available resources or even participates in determining procedures to be used for achieving a desired result, an implied contract is being established. This contract, in addition to the contractual considerations established in the job description, defines certain requirements both parties are agreeing to accept. As in any contractual obligation, both parties are stating that they are able and willing to meet these established obligations.

The negotiation process provides management with an early and important view of the achievability of the established work-unit and organizational goals. Higher levels of management should be receiving feedback at this early stage in the goal-setting/budgeting process to review and, if necessary, modify the top-down established goals of the organization.

If the negotiations on the need for certain kinds and amounts of resources lead to disagreement or acceptance by the subordinate under some kind of reservation, higher levels of management must be ready to (a) acquire additional resources, (b) reallocate current available resources, (c) mandate the achievement of performance goals with those resources that are currently available, or (d) change the top-down directed objectives and goals.

Acquiring Additional Resources. In setting performance goals and comparing them with the results expected to meet the work-unit established goals, it may be obvious to the work-unit manager that additional resources are required. In developing a case for additional resources, the individual making the request can document it with the performance goals and the established performance standards for each incumbent in the work unit. In this manner, a logical and rational defense can be established using job content, employee skills, interest, and opportunities for identifying what can be done with current available resources, what can be done if additional resources are made available, and, possibly most important, what deficiencies will occur relative to currently established work-unit goals if additional resources are not made available. Now, higher levels of management have a clear understanding of what they must do to bring organizational and work-unit goals in line with operational realities.

Reallocating Currently Available Resources. After reviewing the performance goals of each subordinate, the supervisor may be able to identify resources that can be shifted from one individual to another or from one subordinate work unit to another. If the supervisor has the authority to shift resources within his or her area of responsibility, this shifting or reallocation may enhance the overall performance of the involved work unit. Even though some units or individuals may be adversely affected, other units or individuals may be even more positively influenced, leading to improved performance of the larger work unit.

Mandating Achievement of Performance Goals. After reviewing established performance goals and recognizing unacceptable discrepancies between them and the required goals of the work unit, the supervisor may simply mandate the achievement of goals that support those established for the work unit. The mandate may be to work more hours, or to make better use of time when working, or to share available equipment by changing scheduled work hours, or to improve skills, or possibly to terminate those who are not producing and hire those who can get the job done. These and other such options may not always be preferred courses of action, but they are quite often the only options available. The mandate option always has the associated risk that those working under the mandate will appear to be providing acceptable results, but, in the longer term, will be found to have been performing in such a way that the profitability and the success of the work unit and the organization have been damaged.

Changing Work-Unit Goals. As requests for additional resources get pushed up the organizational hierarchy, it may become apparent that the already set top-down goals are unrealistic. For whatever reason, the available resources, in combination with all of the internal and external factors that influence every incumbent, may be insufficient for the organization to meet its targets. Now arrives a moment of deep soul searching. Are those desired end results unrealistic? Is it possible to lower desired end results without damaging the organization? Would it not be more damaging to recognize the failure to achieve an established goal a year or two in the future?

Many factors influence the making of decisions that are in the best interest of the organization. In the great majority of cases, the old adage that honesty is the best policy will be a guide to follow. Also, it is usually better to relay bad news right at the start than to hide it and let it fester and cause a worse scene some time later.

Combination of Two or More Options. The entire process of relating performance goal deficiencies to work-unit expected results will probably take two or more of the options listed here. Just what approach is best for the involved individuals, the work unit, and the organization will depend on a complete understanding of all the facts and issues. The better the job of collecting, identifying, and analyzing all information at each stage in the planning process, the better the chance that the resource allocation decision will be for the overall good of the organization.

Budget and resource allocation goes hand-in-glove with planning. In many operating performance appraisal programs and in discussions of performance appraisal, it is difficult to see the mechanical linkages between performance appraisal and the budget-resource allocation processes.

A planning process that effectively links the short- and long-term plans must involve top management solicitation of inputs into the budget process from lower-level managers and even operative employees. Although the term nonnegotiable does not mean that inputs are not solicited, are not welcome, and are not recognized as crucial in the development of the budget. If organizational objectives are to be realistic and achievable and if budget allocations are to support the achievement of these objectives, employee inputs at as low a level as possible must be solicited. The nonnegotiability of the objective/goal-setting process simply underscores the fact that it must be orderly. It must be disciplined, and changes in organizational goals must start at the top and flow down through the entire length of the organization, so that all employees are on the same track, moving together to achieve common organizational objectives and goals.

This discussion of resource negotiation underlines the point that in fact supervisors and subordinates do not negotiate over goals; they negotiate over *resources*. Here, in this part of the planning process, theory meets reality, and such questions as these begin to be answered:

1. Are these the activities this jobholder must perform?
2. Is the current job workload estimate accurate?
3. Are the resources available to do the job?
4. Is the employee able and willing to perform the assignment in an acceptable manner, given the resources available?

When differences begin to surface between work-unit goals to be achieved and the results work-unit members state they can provide, work-unit supervisors have the opportunity to identify resource requirement problems. They must then be able to identify both short- and long-term problems that block the achievement of the goals of their work units and begin negotiating with higher levels of management for additional resources, for the right to reallocate available resources, or even for changes in work-unit goals.

It is certainly possible that involvement in the budget process could lead to increased organizational structure and rigidity, forcing more sophisticated game-playing and hiding threats by going deeper underground—becoming the mole that destroys the foundation of the organization. This will occur if management uses the goal-budget process as a manipulative tool to deceive workers. If, however, the goal-budget process is to permit and encourage employee participation, logical and rational approaches must be presented in answering the who, why, what, when, where, and how problems presented by workers at every level. Bidding for resources requires up-front and on-the-table discussion. Employees have the opportunity to see where the resources are going and what results are to be achieved with the allocated resources. The employees may still not agree with the allocation process, but deadly issues involving secrecy and cover-up are no longer paramount.

Negotiation for available resources requires the confrontation of issues by all involved parties. It provides a splendid opportunity for situation changes to be recognized, for risky issues to be brought forward, and for automatic responses to give way to thoughtful concern about issues and underlying assumptions. Tying resource allocation to specific job results reduces the need, even the desire, to distort information. It does not mean that people will not continue to be unrealistic in the results they feel they can achieve given certain kinds and amounts of assistance.

Negotiation for limited available resources requires tough and well-thought-out reasoning. Hiding the truth does not benefit either party. Sooner or later personal agendas come into play. Rational, logical, and systematic analyses link resource requests to identified end results. Weakness in logic between intentions and possible results must be considered in a candid, forthright manner. The entire process promotes conscious awareness, constant self-questioning, and positive confrontation. It limits the opportunity to shift the blame for the failure to achieve identified results. From an organizational perspective, the resource negotiation process facilitates detection of failures or, at least, problems within its basic assumptions, policies, objectives, and strategies.

ORGANIZATIONAL INFLUENCE AND RESOURCE ALLOCATION

The allocation of resources becomes a major focus of organizational activity. Here, the real political battles are fought. Money is a limited resource even for the wealthiest organizations. For example, which division, department, or unit will receive funds for new capital investment (new facilities, new machinery), new or expanded research and development capabilities, or development and introduction of a new product or service? This competition for resources eventually ends in such grass roots debates as what new jobs should be created, who should receive pay adjustments, how much the adjustments should be, and the appearance that the adjustments should take (change in base pay, cost of living, merit increase, stock acquisition, etc.).

Those who win budget skirmishes and battles exhibit to all members of the organization their influence and negotiation prowess. The final allocation of resources for the budget period is a major indication of just exactly who are the true leaders of the organization.

Seldom, if ever, can all requests for resources be satisfied. Almost always, there will be winners and losers. To reduce the negative impact of being on the losing side, it is critical that there be a direct connection between organization and work-unit objectives and goals and the budgeted allocation of resources to each work unit and, eventually, to each individual. It may be unlikely that even the best designed and most wisely explained rationale relating organizational objectives to the final budget will sit well with all members, but the more logical and orderly the process, the easier it will be to "sell" the budget. The word *sell* may appear to be inappropriate in this context, but a major reason for everything discussed in this book is to get all employees working together, supporting each other, and exerting all efforts possible toward the achievement of organizational objectives.

This is only possible when employees truly understand what the objectives of the organization are or, possibly more important, how their assignments contribute to the achievement of these broad objectives. (It is quite possible that some workers will take on faith alone the idea that the work they do will assist the organization in attaining whatever it is out to accomplish; on the other hand, there are many "doubting Thomases" in every organization.) Employees must also recognize the fairness in the requirements of their jobs and the rewards provided for services rendered. What this means is that management at every level in contemporary organizations must minimize the simpler and more expedient behavior of answering the common question "Why?" by stating "Because I told you so," and engage in the more difficult and, at first glance, more time-consuming action of actually explaining why a certain behavior is required of subordinates and why certain actions were or are to be taken by higher levels of management. The allocation of resources raises all kinds of "why" questions.

ESTABLISHING PERFORMANCE GOALS AND DEFINING RELATED ACTIVITIES

The final step in the objective/goal-setting process is the establishment of performance goals by the individual (or possibly work group) responsible for their achievement. In setting performance goals, there is an interesting reversal of procedure from the top-down, nonnegotiable process described earlier in this chapter. This reversal frequently goes unrecognized and a critical step is omitted, which may easily lead to the failure of any goal-setting program.

The bottom-up negotiating process begins with a work-unit function statement that leads to the development of jobs within that work unit. This results in the definition of job responsibilities and duties. The job definition is impersonal and identifies the requirements that must be performed by anyone occupying that job. The transition process that assists in identifying the personal qualities and situational factors that influence the job requirements to be performed and the manner in which they are completed involves the development of performance dimensions and, finally, the setting of performance standards. The reversal of the process with regard to the establishment of performance goals occurs in the following manner.

The performance goals, which are the final step in the goal-setting process, are in reality performance standards. As mentioned early in this chapter, to be useful performance goals must be identifiable, observable, measurable, and, if at all possible, expressed in quantitative terms. This is also an acceptable definition for a performance standard. After setting the performance goals, those involved in the process—normally a supervisor and an immediate subordinate—must (or at least should) identify and describe the activities that will be carried out during the time interval set for achieving the goal.

The performance goal identifies a desired result related to a critical or major activity that must be accomplished if the incumbent is to be considered successful in the performance of the job. The activities that identify what the subordinate will do in attaining the performance goal become an additional set of duties or a subset to the regularly assigned duties that would normally describe that responsibility area.

In many goal-setting programs, members involved in the process often become so dedicated to setting the goals that they forget to identify and describe the activities that will transpire in the accomplishment of the performance goals. Or, the activities are set in such a cursory manner that they become useless for providing direction for future effort or for reviewing past efforts in order to clearly identify areas of successes and failures. It is in the activity identification of the goal-setting process that the obligation and a well defined procedure for reviewing the obligation are crystallized. Without this step, goal setting may easily result in so much hot air or worthless scribbles on a piece of paper.

An application of goal setting that has enjoyed a significant amount of publicity over the past 25 years is management by objectives (MBO). Management by objectives or its acronym, MBO, is a familiar term to most people involved in the field of management. MBO has been defined as a process that joins the planning, doing, and control functions of an organization. It operates basically in this manner:

MANAGEMENT BY OBJECTIVES (MBO)

1. The overall organizational mission and objectives are established and communicated downward through the organizational hierarchy.
2. Supervisors and subordinates analyze the organizational objectives from the perspective of their work units and jobs and establish goals for their respective work units.
3. Supervisors and subordinates rank goals in order of importance and then, in turn, mutually agree on the accomplishment of specific goals that are observable, defined in measurable terms, and have a time constraint.
4. Plans are developed that describe the actions that will be taken to achieve the identified goals within the constraints of available resources.
5. Supervisors and subordinates monitor progress through the goal achievement period and, at the end of the period, measure the degree of goal achievement in a performance review session.

MBO has been touted as a process that can successfully integrate organizational and work-unit goals and organizational and individual goals. In addition, it provides a means for analyzing organizational requirements and the organization's capacity for meeting changes in demands.

MBO exploded into the management world through a book, *The Practice of Management,* written by a foremost author on management concepts, Peter Drucker. Over the past 25 years, it has received much publicity.

Since Drucker provided his cure-all for the management world, many twentieth century medicine men have been bottling and selling his famous elixir. These modern-day witch doctors claim that if management will implement this panacea called management by objectives, many of the performance-related problems in the organization will disappear.

The major problem with these hucksters of Dr. Drucker's magic potion is that they truly don't understand what Drucker was saying, or they have implemented their own formulas under the Drucker label and have sold a product that seems more palatable to the user seeking assistance. Unfortunately, there are some basic inconsistencies and flaws in the concepts and processes that form the foundation for these pseudo MBOs, as well as a significant fuzziness in the participation-negotiation process described by Drucker and other advocates of MBO. The result is that now, almost 30 years later, organizations are frequently no better and no wiser from the insights provided by the promoters of MBO.

"Management by Objectives and Self Control," a major chapter in Drucker's book, describes in some detail the process of involving management at succeedingly lower levels in the organization in setting objectives and increasing the opportunities available for managers at these succeedingly lower levels in the hierarchy to direct their own work activities.[1] Drucker described as critical to the success of an MBO program the need for managers at all levels to understand the objectives and goals of the organization.

In 1954, Drucker had concerns that employees (management and nonmanagement) at lower levels in the organization did not recognize and understand the objectives and goals of the organization. This concern is still relevant and just as valid. The powerful forces of misdirection identified by Drucker "in the specialized work of most managers; in the hierarchical structure of management; and in the differences in vision and work and the resultant insulation of various levels of management . . ."[2] continue to destroy teamwork and result in friction, frustration, and conflict.

If one is to believe that Drucker had something substantial to offer to managers in all kinds of organizations and if one recognizes the

---

[1] Peter Drucker, *The Practice of Management* (New York: Harper & Row, 1954), p. 131.

[2] Drucker, *The Practice of Management,* p. 122.

extensive publicity and promotion provided to his concept of MBO, then it becomes difficult to understand why MBO has had such a minimal impact on improving the performance of American organizations.

A possible reason for its lack of success follows. First, the management of far too many organizations has been unwilling to take the time and accept the costs necessary to communicate to every level in the organization exactly what the objectives and goals of the organization are and the contributions that each work unit and each worker must provide in order for the organization to achieve these objectives and goals. Second, there has been wide-scale misunderstanding about the entire issue of participation and negotiation in goal setting. Those involved in selling the concept of MBO to managers have failed to communicate this additional message from Drucker: "Higher management must, of course, reserve the power to approve or disapprove these objectives"—those developed and set by each manager.[3]

An important point, frequently forgotten by those describing or selling MBO, is that objective/goal setting that originates with the mission of the organization is, first and last, a top-down nonnegotiable process. This is not where participation and negotiation in goal setting occur.

The participation process is only viable when each manager understands the exact goals of his or her work unit. Only then is it possible for the work-unit manager to recognize internal and external factors influencing the work situation; to review subordinate work assignments, performance standards, and, when set, performance goals; and to accept or make modifications required by the goals of the work unit.

The final and possibly most crucial step in the entire process occurs in the negotiation over resources to be made available to accomplish established performance goals. It is here that goal viability and goal acceptance come to life. If either the supervisor or subordinate is unable or unwilling to provide the resources necessary to accomplish the desired (performance) goals, the entire process is a sham.

When the supervisor and subordinate take the extra, critical step of identifying the activities each individual will perform to ensure accomplishment of performance goals, the opportunity for employee involvement in management decision processes moves a giant step forward from fable to fact. Although there have been thousands of articles and books written over the past 30 years extolling employee participa-

PARTICIPATION AND NEGOTIATION

---

[3] Drucker, *The Practice of Management,* p. 129.

tion, much of what has been written is so much rhetoric. Practically all employees want some opportunity to participate in organizational decisions. The truth is that, for many employees, participation centers around decisions involving when, where, how, and with what they will do their jobs. Here, performance standards and performance goals begin to take form. Many employees have little to say about how they do their work, when they do it, and the tools and support available to assist them in their work assignments. In these cases, the setting of performance goals usually has little or no meaning if implemented and is, therefore, not worth the time and effort expended. In such cases, performance standards are set, including attendance and quantity, quality, and timeliness of output. If the standards are met, the relevant behaviors are acceptable; if the standards are not met, some kind of action must be taken to modify and improve undesirable behaviors.

If, however, employees do have some voice in negotiating for the kinds and amounts of resources available and the extent of use of these resources in performing their jobs, then it is quite possible that the setting of performance goals is a practical and worthwhile procedure. Possibly the most important resource available to employees is the control they have over how they spend their time. The more control they have, the greater the value of performance goals.

This may be why MBO has had its greatest success in the sales units of organizations. Not only is it easier to document the success of sales personnel behaviors through the use of numerical indicators, but also sales personnel have more freedom to make decisions on how they use their time than almost any other employees in the organization.

A number of years ago, a sales division of a major pharmaceutical manufacturer made extensive use of an MBO program to direct and appraise the performance of its members. The national sales force had the organizational structure shown in Figure 3–4.

Although there are five levels in the hierarchy shown, the communication channels between levels are open and extremely interactive. The relationship between corporate sales goals and those of each succeedingly lower level are clearly identified and well understood. Information on new products, competitors' intrusions, and changes in channels of distribution flow quickly up and down the ladder. A significant amount of time (approximately 50 percent of the district manager's and 30 percent of the regional manager's) is spent in direct face-to-face contact between the regional and district managers and the territorial representatives. During these contacts, the managers provide teaching, leading, and counseling services. At least 25 percent of this time is spent reviewing performance goals. The goal-setting activity takes the form shown in Figure 3–5.

At the grass roots level, the district manager and his or her territorial representative review the feasibility and acceptability of the goal for that specific individual. Problems that cannot be resolved between the district manager and the territorial representative are moved up the hierarchy to a point where they can be resolved. Following the identification and resolution of major goal-related problems, the district manager and territorial representative set performance goals. These goals seldom exceed three; sometimes only one performance goal is set. The goals are reviewed every two months, goal attainment is measured, and one or more new goals may be set. The setting of performance goals follows this process:

1. The district manager and territorial repesentative review performance goals to be achieved by the representative and select one or more for particular attention during the next 60 days. An example may be "increase average completed calls from 4.8 to 5.7 per day over the coming two months."

2. Next, the district manager and territorial representative brainstorm (have an intense discussion involving acquired knowledge and skills and possibly innovative approaches) to determine how to achieve the performance goal.

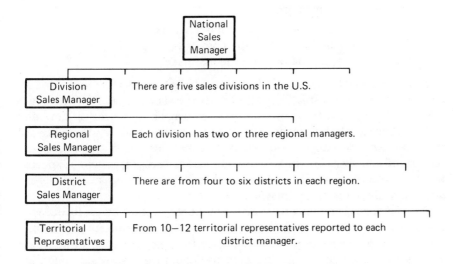

FIGURE 3–4. Organizational Structure of Sales Force.

Corporate sales objectives determined

↓

Each division share of corporate sales objectives set

↓

Division goals divided into regional sales goals

↓

Regional goals further divided into district sales goals

↓

Sales goals established for each territorial representative

FIGURE 3–5. Goal-Setting Activity for Sales Force.

The attainment steps identified to achieve the increase in completed calls could include the following specific activities. (In reality, these activities become an additional list of duties or possibly a subset of duties to be performed in addition to normal requirements.)

1. Purchase an alarm clock and set it for 6:15 A.M. and then get moving instead of waking at my normal 7:00 A.M. Then, I'm on my way to making my first call by 7:45 A.M. instead of 8:30 A.M.

2. Spend some time each weekend to plan all calls for the coming week. Make an extra effort to identify the best time to call on each account to improve my chances of seeing the client. Route the calls to minimize travel time.

3. Evaluate the accomplishments of the day each night and, if necessary, reschedule the calls for the coming day. Add or change calls and routes depending on the progress made that day.

From this brief scenario, it is apparent that the performance goals are specific and relevant. They should also be stimulating and achievable. The secret of success in using this approach, however, is not the performance goals, but rather the attainment steps. When the district manager and territorial representative can establish an accepted stream of conversation in which each party recognizes and respects what the other is saying, where both talk and listen, many useful and valuable ideas come forward.

The developed and agreed-to attainment steps, like the performance goals, are put into writing. (Chapters 4 and 5 describe in detail the identification and description of job activities, performance standards, and performance goals). At the next performance review session, the first issue is to identify the degree of goal achievement, but this is not the primary thrust of the review session. Attention focuses on *what* the territorial representative did relative to the degree of goal attainment. If goal attainment was successful, what particular activities did the representative perform that assisted in successful performance? Perhaps it was some activity not previously identified, possibly a serendipitous action (in the process of doing one thing, something not even considered occurs, but because of the awareness established in the initial thrust, the new find is observed and recognized as a valuable aid). Maybe the goal was not met. Why not? Did the representative perform all the attainment steps? If yes, then possibly some critical activity was not identified and not performed or possibly factors beyond the control of the representative are blocking achievement. The essence of the attainment step process is, "*What* can each of us do to help each other and where can improvements be made?"

A review of the entire goal-setting process from the establishment of corporate sales goals to the identification of individual attainment steps has these major parts:

1. Organization and subunit sales goals are precisely identified and described and related to each other in a logical and orderly manner.
2. Performance standards are established that describe as precisely as possible quantity, quality, cost, timeliness, and other significant dimensions of measurement.
3. Individual performance goals that in reality are desired, self-set standards are established and then ranked in order of importance.
4. Resources required to achieve goals and resources available are identified. (This establishes possible constraints for future actions.)
5. Action plans are developed that describe what will be done to achieve specified performance goals and how available resources can be used.
6. During periodical review sessions, goal achievement is measured and actions taken are reviewed and analyzed to identify possible reasons for goal attainment successes and failures.

There are four very critical reasons why MBO has adapted so well to a sales organization. First, a major portion of sales personnel performances can be measured in quantitative terms. (This does not imply that there are not some significant results that may only be able to be measured in qualitative terms; for example, developing an interest and appreciation of products among those who currently are not customers or acting as an early warning indicator of market trends and new products developed by competitors.)

Second, the major resource required of a sales person is his or her time. How well and how skillfully these individuals use this resource is primarily their responsibility. Although it may appear that the negotiation over goals to be achieved relates primarily to such dimensions as quantity, quality, and time, the most vital participative discussions truly focus on how these professionals use the time they have at their own disposal and how skillfully they function in the actions they take during the time they allot to goal attainment.

Returning to the interaction between the district manager and the territorial representative in the performance goal-setting/attainment-step identification example, the real participation occurs in the identification and description of the attainment steps. The activities identified here are often far more specific and personal than those found in the job definition—the responsibility and duty statements of a job description. If the discussion is to be successful, both sides truly have to get at the heart of the discussion—negotiation over resource allocation.

In this case, the critical resource of the territorial representative is his or her time and how the individual will allocate available time toward the pursuit of achieving certain identified performance goals. The supervisor or district manager must identify commitments he or she will make that will assist the subordinate in successfully accomplishing the established goals. This commitment may include certain amounts of his or her own time, training opportunities made available to the subordinate, facilitating access to certain clients, and additional sales support ranging from providing specialists who have certain skills or contacts, to assisting in closing a sale, to furnishing better or more sales and promotion aids.

This process enables the supervisor to understand more fully the personal, organizational, and situational problems facing the subordinate and, in some kind of mutually supportive behavior, to assist that individual in developing solutions that overcome or minimize the negative aspects of these problems. Possibly the most important resource allocated in this process is the teaching, leading, and counseling skills offered by the supervisor.

At first glance, it may appear that participation and negotiation over performance goals are the same thing. It is quite likely that there is some negotiation at the participation stage, but it is in many cases a very limited part of the entire participation–negotiation process. The heart of negotiation occurs when supervisor and subordinate precisely identify and describe the resources each will make available to ensure successful performance goal completion. It is here that the "meeting of minds" occurs that, in 1954, Drucker emphasized as so critical to the success of management by objectives and self-control.

1. Organizational and work-unit goals are identified.
2. Performance standards are established for each job.
3. Supervisor and subordinate *participate* in the development of performance goals.
4. Supervisor and subordinate discuss the availability of resources required for accomplishing established performance goals.
5. Supervisor and subordinate *negotiate* over allocation of available resources.
6. Performance goals are redefined (if necessary) in line with available resources.

PARTICIPATION–NEGOTIATION IN THE SETTING OF PERFORMANCE GOALS

Like the dimensions of performance, which are many and varied, performance goals come in many kinds and shapes. In this chapter, performance goals have related primarily to those that come directly from job content requirements and evolve from the downward transformation of organizational goals to specific work-unit goals. They are primarily short-term or tactical in design. There are performance goals, however, that relate in a less direct manner to the achievement of personal and organizational goals and are longer term in nature. These relate more closely to the strategic objectives of both the ratee and the organization.

KINDS OF PERFORMANCE GOALS

These kinds of goals may relate to individual growth and development and involve long-term training programs, assignment of additional responsibilities, and possible lateral transfer or upward movement into new jobs that advance career aspirations.

Goals may also be innovative in nature, with the individual developing new ways of doing things or new kinds of technology that may promote both the short- and long-term growth of the organization. The innovative goals usually address a problem of which the innovator is aware and for which he or she feels that a practical, useful, and valuable solution to the problem can be developed.

In moving from specific short-term, job-related goals to longer-term job and personal goals, the measurement of goal success moves from quantitative to qualitative terms. Quantitative goal definition provides criteria for measuring efficiency of effort. It assists in identifying how well available resources have been used in achieving certain results. It may not, however, provide the entire measurement story. Qualitative definition of goal achievement may be the only criterion available to measure successful attainment of certain kinds of goals—the overall effectiveness of the related action. This is especially true in moving up the organizational ladder and relating to goals that are not firmly rooted in job content requirements. In addition, as the time frame for goal achievement lengthens, interim analysis frequently can only relate to qualitative measures of success. Once again, the old nemesis—subjectivity—raises its potentially ugly head. As mentioned early in this book, subjectivity will always be an issue in performance appraisal. Qualitative standards provide the appraisal process with guidelines for setting limits for analysis and discussion. They assist in keeping all involved parties on the same course, where the efforts are directed toward the achievement of goals common to the individuals, their work units, and the organization.

Group-Set Performance Goals

Earlier in this chapter, there was a discussion concerning the inadvisability of having individuals set performance goals when they have little or no control over the resources available for accomplishing their job assignments. There is a qualification to this statement, and that relates to the opportunity for groups of employees who must work together in some tight, lock-step process to discuss and participate in the results required of their work groups and set performance goals for the group. Although each member may still have minimal influence on the activities to be performed in a particular job, as a group they may be able to assign individuals to particular activities; schedule the flow of work; review quality; and make other job- and group-related decisions that can have an impact on the quantity, quality, and timeliness of output. As a group they can negotiate with their supervisors for resources and make their own determinations on just how their most valuable resource—their time—is used in productive group output.

ACTIVITY TRAP VS. GOAL DECEPTION In the 1960s, a number of promoters of MBO criticized activity-oriented approaches to performance appraisal. They supported their views by raising an issue called the activity trap. Their line of reasoning was that by focusing on what workers do and not on the results they achieve, the activities become an end in themselves. The reason for taking the actions is soon forgotten, and minimal or no contributions are made toward the achievement of work-unit and organizational goals.

There is no doubt that the "activity trap issue" is still alive and continues to be a problem. However, an overemphasis on goals can also lead to unsatisfactory results. The twin to the activity trap is goal deception. Just as overemphasis on activities without tying these activities to desired work-unit and organizational goals can lead to unsatisfactory performance, overemphasis on goals can lead to suboptimizing workplace behaviors—accomplishment of individual work-related goals that, in turn, lowers or minimizes the chance for accomplishment of higher-level or other worker or work-unit goals.

Some of the behaviors that occur when goal achievers use the goal-setting process to deceive are:

1. Overemphasis of areas where goals are monitored and deemphasis of areas where goals are not set or where goals tend to be more vague or qualitative in nature.

2. Setting of goals that are relatively easy to achieve and unwillingness to be involved in goal-achievement areas where greater risk is involved and the chance for failure increases.

3. Inordinate amounts of paperwork, making the process another bureaucratic jungle.

4. Inappropriate and inefficient use of available resources.

The guile involved in goal setting can be as dysfunctional to the organization as activity expended with no useful end result. The solution here is twofold. One, activities and results must be linked, and two, activities and results must relate to coordinated effort that assists the organization in being successful in both the short and long terms.

Chapter 4

Establishing a Job Content Foundation

To ensure that the measurement of employee performance has a foundation solidly based on job content, an initial step required in the appraisal process is the development of a comprehensive and accurate definition of job requirements. Comprehensive and accurate job definition means identification and description of all activities that are critical to the successful completion of job assignments, elimination of activities that are inconsequential or that should not be part of the job, and ordering or weighting of activities to indicate the relative importance or worth of these critical assignments.

In the late 1960s and throughout the 1970s, enforcement of equal employment opportunity laws focused on the job-relatedness of a wide variety of personnel decisions. The actions of government agencies responsible for enforcement of these laws, in turn, influenced organizations to review their job analysis practices to see how well they were describing their jobs. For most organizations, job analysis means the laborious practice of collecting job content information through the use of questionnaires, interviews, or observation (in any combination) and then processing this information into job descriptions. The process is costly and fraught with errors, and the results are seldom worth the cost. To minimize expenses and hasten the entire process, those involved in job analysis and writing job descriptions frequently resort to the use of existing job content information wherever it can be found. When using information collected in the past or information collected by other organizations, the analyst-writer becomes susceptible to past errors and fails to identify accurately, completely, and precisely the content of jobs under review and to recognize changes that may have occurred in job requirements. These mistakes combine to cause considerable grief to all parties who, in some way, depend on accurate and current job content information.

Many managers and human resource specialists have recognized for some time the need to drastically overhaul their job analysis programs. As far back as the 1930s, government officials in the U.S. Employment Services began to develop new and better procedures for identifying the work performed within occupations and classes of jobs. The work of these pioneers in job identification and description provides to this day a primer on, first, how to collect job content information and, second, how to describe it. This chapter recognizes the value of existing job analysis processes. It provides additional insights and describes procedures useful for improving the accuracy and precision of defining jobs. It also describes how to move forward from a technology based in the 1930s to a technology based in the computer-oriented world of the 1980s.

THE BEDROCK FOR PERFORMANCE APPRAISAL

The behaviors exhibited by employees in the performance of their jobs are the results of many complex interactions that are frequently hidden and, many times, unknown. The establishment of position descriptions, as described in this chapter, provides a solid and observable foundation for supervisor, subordinate, and all other interested parties for identifying and measuring job-related behaviors. The prior chapters have described a number of the major forces that influence and, in turn, are influenced by employee behaviors. Figure 4–1 identifies the various layers of factors that provide a sometimes solid and other times very shaky foundation for the performance appraisal system. The firmness of the organizational layers that form a foundation for employee performance will certainly influence demonstrated employee behavior. However, even under the most turbulent of conditions, a well written position description can protect both employees and employers.

Currently, as in the past, most descriptions of work for an employee take the form of either a job or a class description. In most cases, the only time position descriptions are written is when the class or job is held by only one individual and if the description, by whatever title it may have, accurately describes what that person is doing.

One reason position descriptions are not written relates directly to cost. The time required of the incumbent and analyst to collect and analyze position content information and the skills required to write precise and accurate statements that describe work activity are a cost many organizations are unwilling to accept. Another reason is that most personnel/human resources practices do not require as precise and accurate a description of *what* the jobholder does as is required in the appraisal of performance. Employment, training, personnel planning, and even compensation activities can be successfully performed with fairly broad descriptions of work requirements; but when an organization wishes to measure and rate the performance

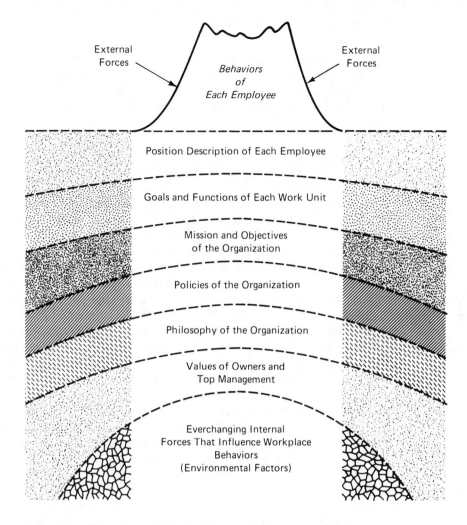

External
Forces

External
Forces

*Behaviors
of
Each Employee*

Position Description of Each Employee

Goals and Functions of Each Work Unit

Mission and Objectives
of the Organization

Policies of the Organization

Philosophy of the Organization

Values of Owners and
Top Management

Everchanging Internal
Forces That Influence Workplace
Behaviors
(Environmental Factors)

FIGURE 4–1. Factors Influencing Employee Behavior.

of an individual, it must know exactly what the person is supposed to be doing, what the person has been told to do, and just how he or she has behaved while performing the assignment. Any doubts, any gaps in this process can quickly lead to the repudiation and demise of any performance appraisal program.

Glossary of Key Words and Terms

Integrating the individual into the world of work begins with a valid and useful understanding of *what* the individual must do to accomplish assignments successfully. What at first glance appears to be a simple task—telling the individual what is required—quickly becomes mired in the quicksand of words. Selecting words that accurately describe what must be done and that have a common meaning to the supervisor, subordinate, and all other parties who influence or are influenced by the job is a difficult task. Those involved in describing work and job requirements quickly realize that they can be tyrannized and intimidated by these words. The result is that their efforts often provide a far from acceptable product.

This chapter focuses on the use of words and terms that have specific meanings and common understanding and are combined in a manner to provide precise statements that describe job activities. This approach to job content analysis forms the basis for a valid and accurate description of a job. Using the following definitions of crucial job-analysis-related words and terms will facilitate the communication of job content.

ACTIVITY: A broad, general term that includes any kind of action, movement, or behavior required of an incumbent in performing job assignments. The word *activity,* as used in this book, has a *generic* meaning. It covers or relates to any kind of an action taken by an employee.

TASK: A basic work activity that has identifiable and definable starting and finishing points and is recognized, understood, and accepted as a part of the job by the incumbent and appropriate supervisors. A task statement describes what the incumbent does and, normally, why the incumbent does it, and possibly indicates guides and work aids used in performing the activity.

MAJOR ACTIVITY: This term relates to an important or critical area of the job. Together, major activities describe all or almost all of the job. They organize the job into broad yet distinct categories. They identify what the incumbent is to be held accountable for in the performance of job assignments.

RESPONSIBILITY: A statement that describes relatively broad but significant job activity areas that, if not performed, or if performed in a less than acceptable manner, could result in an unacceptable performance of the job. These statements are written with sufficient clarity and precision to ensure proper identification of environmental conditions within which that responsibility is performed and the knowledge, skills, and abilities required of an incumbent performing that responsibility. Together, all of the responsibility statements should completely describe the scope of the job. Each responsibility statement should be as unique or as mutually exclusive as possible.

DUTY: A job task that further describes the actions occurring within a specific responsibility. Duties may be considered as subresponsibilities, and a set of duty statements provides a relatively complete and comprehensive view of a responsibility.

JOB DEFINITION: A set of responsibility and duty statements that accurately, adequately, and precisely describe the activities performed by a jobholder.

(Responsibilities are similar to major activities, and duties are similar to tasks. The reason for two sets of words/terms that have similar and at times identical meanings is that they do *not* have similar use, and the uses will become distinctly different when computer technology becomes available in this area. Major activities and tasks are the direct output or product of job analysis. Frequently, a number of incumbents performing identical or very similar kinds of work will provide major activity and task information. From their inputs, inventories of major activity and task statements are developed. The next stage in the description process is the translation of these major activities and tasks into job definition responsibilities and duties. This process is described later in this chapter.)

BEHAVIOR: An observable activity exhibited by an employee in the performance of a job assignment.

POSITION: Responsibilities and duties performed by one member of an organization. (There are as many positions as there are employees—in fact, there may be unoccupied positions, meaning that there are more positions than employees in the organization.)

JOB: A set of responsibilities and duties that are sufficiently similar in the kind of work, knowledge, and skills required of an incumbent and the conditions within which the work is performed and that are grouped under one job title. A job may be performed by one or more employees.

CLASS: A group of jobs sufficiently similar as to kinds of subject matter; education and experience requirements; levels of difficulty, complex ity, and responsibility; and qualification requirements of the work. (It is possible to have a single-job class.)

CLASS-SERIES: A grouping of job classes having similar job content but differing in degree of difficulty, complexity, and responsibility; level of skill; knowledge; and qualification requirements.

OCCUPATION: Two or more jobs, classes of jobs, or class-series that require similar knowledge and skills that may vary by scope or complexity. Normally, performance in a job requiring a lower-ordered set of knowledge and skills would prepare the jobholder for the next higher or highest level jobs included within the occupation. Occupations are usually represented in a variety of organizational settings. There is a broad variation in the grouping of jobs within an occupation. The variety of jobs within an occupation depends significantly on individual choice; that is, the occupation can be made as broad or as narrow as desired. The term *family*, when used in this context, has a meaning synonymous with *occupation*.

OBTAINING JOB CONTENT INFORMATION

To develop and implement an appraisal program that has a good chance of success and validly relates to the work of the employee and his or her behavior, it must have a foundation established in the job itself. This chapter describes how to obtain major activity and task information and moves through a series of transformations that assist in developing job responsibility and duty statements that accurately and precisely describe job content.

The Position/Job

Most organizations use a job or class description as a written record of what an employee does on the job. A fairly broad description of what an employee does provides sufficient information for most personnel-related practices. Since these two kinds of descriptions are broader in scope or more general than a position description, they may include activities that a specific incumbent may not perform. In addition, since these descriptions relate to what two or many more incumbents are doing in general, it is difficult to precisely identify and order by importance those activities that are most important or critical in the performance of a specific job. Finally, because individuals performing in the same job or class of jobs may be working under quite different output demands and environmental conditions, it is not appropriate, or even possible, to effectively group tasks within specific major activities. Both major activities and tasks could vary in form, which would make a significant difference when identifying and describing the kind of performance expected from an individual.

This chapter describes the process that leads to the writing of a position description—an accurate and current identification and description of what a specific individual is doing. Because the word *job* is so much a part of the vocabulary of this field and is commonly recognized by all workers, its meaning, as used in this chapter, is synonymous with the word *position. Position = Job.*

Obtaining major activity and task information begins with an analysis of existing jobs. The first step is to request a respondent to identify the activities of the job.[1] Specifically, the respondent is asked to identify and describe the major activities and tasks that must be performed to successfully complete job assignments. Frequently, this request for job content information asks the respondent to identify the *activities* or *tasks* or *responsibilities* or *duties* or *functions,* and so forth. The ambiguity related to the use of these words begins with job analysis and continues throughout the entire performance appraisal process. The glossary of words and terms presented earlier is intended to reduce the possibility of ambiguity.

MAJOR ACTIVITY AND TASK ANALYSIS

Information about the job can be obtained through the completion of a written questionnaire by the incumbent, or someone intimately familiar with the job, or an analyst observing the job or interviewing an incumbent or group of incumbents. In this process, responses to two very important questions can assist in identifying and describing job content.

1. What are the major or most important things you do in the performance of your job? *Major* or *most important* means the general activity areas of the job that, if not performed or if completed inadequately, would result in a less than acceptable performance of your job.

   To enable respondents to easily understand what is meant by a major activity, it may be useful to provide examples of general areas of work where a major activity is performed. Some of these are:
   a. Provides an observable and measurable output.
   b. Maintains equipment.
   c. Directs the efforts of others.
   d. Plans or schedules the work of others.

---

[1] This chapter identifies the respondent as the provider of job content information. Normally, the respondent will be the incumbent, but it is quite possible that the respondent could also be the immediate supervisor or other employees who are intimately familiar with the job.

e. Improves worker performance.
f. Trains others.
g. Coordinates the work activity of and with others.
h. Conforms to established legislative mandates, policies, and rules.

2. What are the tasks that further describe the kinds of things done in performing each major activity?

After obtaining major job activity information, the respondent is asked to place on one sheet of paper the first of the major or most important activities that were identified in response to Question 1, and a list of tasks is developed for that major activity.

To further assist the respondent in answering Question 2 as completely as possible, the following request can be made:

Think of the things you do when you first arrive at work; then list each task as it occurs in chronological order within the already described major activities.

An additional request for more information is:

Please list tasks that you perform on a less-than-daily basis, that is, once or twice a week, bimonthly, monthly, quarterly, semiannually, or annually, and identify each task according to how frequently it is performed.

It may also be useful to provide an example of a major activity and its related task:

Major Activity: Performs secretarial services for manager of marketing.

Task: Types letters to complete correspondence, following standard office practices.

After providing task information, the respondent should be requested to give the following information:

3. Review the tasks you just described. Are there any tasks you are now performing that you think you should not be performing? Please identify these tasks and briefly describe why you think you should not be doing this work.

4. Review the tasks you just described and identify tasks you are not now performing that you think you should be performing. Please describe briefly why you should be performing these tasks.

Answers to these two questions are critical because they assist in identifying possible missing tasks and tasks now being performed that are truly unnecessary or the places where there is duplication of effort. These answers may be a first indication of incorrect assignment of tasks, or possibly even of major activities.

When collecting this kind of activity information directly from an incumbent, the immediate supervisor of that incumbent should review the task list for accuracy and adequacy. The supervisor doing the review can note any disagreement, list tasks to be eliminated, or list tasks that the incumbent failed to include. *A warning:* In any review conducted by a supervisor or any other review authority, the incumbent's comments are never erased or crossed through, but notes can be made that identify disagreement with a specific input. The reason for this is that the list and the comments all become part of a formal documentation that may be used for a wide variety of personnel-related actions and may, at some future time, be critical in a legal defense of an action taken that is based on identified and defined job content.

A useful format for providing any kind of activity information is:

Action Verb + Object + Additional *why* and *how* Information.

Figure 4–2 is an example of a task identification form that can be used either by an analyst in interviewing an incumbent or as part of a questionnaire to be completed by an incumbent.

Writing Activity Statements

All activity statements are written in the same format. The statement *always* begins with an action verb that describes as precisely as possible *what* is happening. The verb tense is third person present. The unstated subject of the verb is the "job title." As in the example just provided, the statement could read, "(Secretary) *types. . . .*" Following the verb is the object that identifies what the action relates to. The object may be a word or a group of words. A more complete description of the action may require further words that describe the *why* and *how* of the action: "(Secretary) types *letters to complete correspondence, following standard office practices.* In other words,

Action Verb (Word) + Object of the Verb + Words or Terms that Further Describe Action Taken = the Activity.

In writing any kind of an activity statement, it is possible to use compound verbs and compound objects. The only warning or rule to

Position _____

Date _____

Interviewee _____

Interviewer _____

Does What? (Action Verb)	To What? (Object)	Why Is It Done? (Explanatory Words and Phrases)	How Is It Done?	Using What? (Machines, Equipment Tools, Work Aids)
Task #1				
Task #2				
Task #3				
Task #4				
Task #5				
Task #6				

FIGURE 4-2. Task Identification Form.

follow is that these compound verbs and objects must naturally reflect job-relatedness and, under almost all circumstances, join together as part of one sequential or coordinated action. Statements may also take this form:

Verb + Object, Verb + Object, Verb + Object, etc., + Necessary Modifiers.

This kind of sequential relationship where one activity fits into the next must result in a meaningful output that is easier to observe and measure than each separate activity. If this is not the case, then it would be far wiser to split the verbs and objects into separate activity statements.

The secret to writing good or effective activity statements centers on the writer's ability to clarify the initial information collected from the incumbent to identify the essence of the job—the major reasons for its existence. Each statement must clearly and accurately identify an essential area of job activity.

Developing Inventories of Major Activity and Task Statements

Using the major activity and task statements provided by the respondents through the questionnaire or interview or other means, the analyst develops an edited list of *occupation-oriented* major activity and task statements. This is accomplished by first reviewing and combining the output from the analysis of jobs that would normally be found in the same occupation. To compile a well written and complete master list of occupational major activities and tasks requires a combination of knowledge of jobs under study and editing skills. In the editing process, the first requirement of an analyst is to search for the most appropriate verb to introduce the major activity or task and then to use the most suitable object and additional modifying words and terms to achieve the most precise and accurate description. The analyst should also make certain that the major activity and task statements for each occupational inventory are written at the same level of detail. If upon review it is found that they are not, effort must be made to divide or rephrase the statements that are too ambiguous and to broaden the statements that are too specific. When analyzing and possibly rephrasing major activity and task statements provided by incumbents and supervisors, job analysts must also make certain that they

1. Do not have more than one statement that is actually describing the same or almost the same action.

2. Have sufficient statements to minimize the opportunity for a deficiency to occur (failure to have sufficient statements to adequately describe a specific position or job within the occupation).

3. Do not include a major activity or task that could lead to contamination (providing information on things that do not occur in positions or jobs in the occupation).

4. Avoid writing statements that cause distortion (using words or terms that make the major activity or task appear to be more or less important than it actually is within an applicable position or job).

Although much effort goes into the writing of major activity and task inventories, changes will occur that must be recognized and described. Modifications, additions, or deletions to major activity and task inventories occur because of changes in technology, organizational demands, and raw material inputs.

With the final editing of the occupational major activity and task statements and action word glossary (discussed later in this chapter), a significant amount of the time-consuming development work is over. In the future, as jobs change, new major activity and task statements can be added as necessary, or existing statements can be removed, revised, or modified when more descriptive verbs, objects, and other modifiers are identified. Action word glossaries can also be updated and refined.

These efforts may appear to be unduly time-consuming and quite costly. Before making this assumption, however, and dismissing this stage as an unnecessary part of the performance appraisal system, it may be helpful to review how computer-based information processing can provide accurate and comprehensive information that can be stored and processed for availability at some later time. The computer-stored information may consist of:

1. A complete list of occupation-oriented major activity and task inventories.

2. Action word glossaries for each occupation that precisely define what the verb means when used in the context of that occupation.

3. An action word glossary for the entire organization that identifies different meanings for the same word when used in a variety of organizational settings.

4. Activity worth dimensions and rating scales that permit easy access and operation by all involved in activity worth measurement. (This subject will be discussed later in the chapter.)

This information can then be placed on tapes or other word processing or computer-applicable data storage devices. The information can be recalled by anyone having access to a terminal (cathode ray tube and keyboard).

Through the interaction between the incumbent and the computer-based inventories, changes can be recognized and resulting activities defined or redefined. The computer will facilitate this change-recognition process on an on-time basis at minimal cost. Instead of reinventing the wheel—writing new job descriptions—job analysts can be constantly reviewing the process and searching for better or more appropriate ways of defining jobs.

The process described in this chapter involves greater start-up costs but significantly lower maintenance charges than most current approaches. The approach used by most organizations today requires substantially lower start-up costs, but maintenance is a constant drain, and the result of such reactive behavior is job content identification and description that is far from adequate. The tedious, costly job analysis overhaul and the concern with out-of-date, obsolete job descriptions may shortly be part of the past, sad history of human resources management.

The analyst must use his or her writing and editing skills to select the best or most appropriate words and terms to describe what is occurring. Precision in writing and gaining better understanding of the activity statements can be enhanced through the development and use of an occupational glossary of action verbs.

Organizational and Occupational Glossary of Action Verbs. Over the years, various authors, including this author, have developed extensive glossaries of action verbs that are commonly used to describe the things employees do in performing job assignments.[2] The tyranny of words begins with the selection of the action verb. Here also is where the "cheating" starts. It is all too easy to look at a previously written job description and pick a seemingly appropriate word such as *directs, plans, researches, reviews, handles,* or *coordinates.* However, these words frequently are not precise enough to accurately describe what the individual is doing. The search for the best word can be time-consuming and, at times, nerve-wracking. The final, edited copy of accurate and precise major activity and task statements cannot be left to the hands of amateurs—not even incumbents or immediate supervisors. A serious mistake made by many managers, even person-

---

[2] See Richard I. Henderson, *Compensation Management: Rewarding Performance,* 3rd ed. (Reston, VA: Reston Publishing Co., 1982), Action Word Glossary, pp. 511–521.

nel specialists, is to request the incumbent or his or her immediate supervisor to write a description of the job under study and then expect to receive an acceptable and final draft of a job description. At best, this is a "cop out," and at worst, a shabby deception. Most employees *cannot* write an adequate and useful description of their jobs. The reasons are numerous, but here are some of the major ones:

1. Most people do not like to write.
2. Many people have a limited command of the English language.
3. Incumbents and supervisors may be so close to the job that they truly do not recognize all that is occurring, or they may assume that others recognize job activities that, in reality, are undetected.
4. Job or position descriptions must be written in a uniform manner, and the words used must have a common understanding. Statements describing jobs at the same level must be consistent as to the degree of specificity. These factors alone require the use of highly-skilled specialists in this foundation stage of performance appraisal.

To add to the confusion, the subjectivity problem in performance appraisal has its roots in the meanings of the action verbs. Verbs are words; words are not nearly as precise and uniformly understood as numbers. There is a certain amount of ambiguity or vagueness within almost all verbs. Verbs may have a variety of meanings as to level or degree of action. These differences in meaning can easily result in significant variations in interpretation of the work to be performed and the expected outcome.

To ensure common understanding, action verbs must be defined both from a broad organizational context and, more precisely, from an occupational view. It is critical that the incumbent, supervisors, and any other individual reviewing inventories of major activities and tasks or job definitions that contain responsibilities and duties have a common interpretation and understanding of the meaning of the key word—the action verb. To accomplish this goal, an action verb glossary can be developed that precisely describes the meaning of the verb as used in the context of a specific occupation or family of jobs.

The occupational glossaries can then be combined into an organizational glossary that will be readily available for all parties involved in either writing or reviewing major activity and task statements and job definitions. When the occupational glossaries are combined into a single glossary for the organization, some verbs will have a number of different meanings. Unless these different occupational meanings are recognized, action verbs can cause severe cases of misunderstanding. The following steps can be taken to develop an action word glossary:

1. Group all job analysis major activity and task listings by occupation.
2. Develop a complete list of all action verbs used in statements that describe all jobs within each occupation.
3. Use a dictionary and other appropriate glossaries to define verbs.
4. Review verb definitions with individuals who are capable of stating whether or not the definitions are adequate and fully understanding whether or not possible revisions or additions would improve their descriptive qualities within the occupational setting. Organization- and occupation-specific jargon may be used as long as the words are widely and clearly understood.

Hints for Writing Activity Statements

After the action word glossary is developed, there are certain requirements that apply to the writing of all kinds of activity statements. These requirements may be met by taking the recommended actions that provide answers to the following questions:

1. Is the verb selected the most descriptive verb possible? If there is any question, continue to search for a better, more appropriate verb.
2. Does the statement require the use of more than one verb? If it does, check to see whether or not it is possible to use one verb that carries within it the meaning or action transmitted by the compound verbs.
3. Does the statement involve a sequential relationship of verb + object, verb + object, verb + object, etc., plus *why* and *how* information? If it does, the sequential actions may be combined into one or more comprehensive verb + object with the same common *why* and *how* modifiers.
4. Does the statement consist of a single verb + object with compound modifiers? If it does, it may be useful to divide the single statement into two or more statements, each with its own *why* and *how* modifiers.

Structured Job Analysis

Over the years, the term *structured job analysis* has been applied to various kinds of inventories of work activities. At times, these inventories have been given such titles as *worker-oriented task inventories* and *job-oriented task inventories.* Worker-oriented task inventories describe *how* people do their work, or the behaviors required to perform the job, while job-oriented task inventories describe *what* is done. Some of the specific inventories developed over the last 10 to 15 years are PAQ, CODAP, JAQ, and FOCAS.

PAQ. The Position Analysis Questionnaire (PAQ) was developed by three industrial psychologists at Purdue University.[3] The PAQ is called a worker-oriented task inventory. The reason for this title is that 187 out of the 194 statements that make up the PAQ are considered to be behaviors demonstrated by workers performing a wide variety of jobs.

The PAQ consists of 194 statements that are grouped within 27 division job dimensions and five overall job dimensions. These 32 dimension are further grouped within six major divisions: information input, mental processes, work output, relationships with other persons, job content, and other job characteristics.

When completing the PAQ instrument, respondees rate each of the 187 behaviors against certain identified scales. For example, the dimension *job demands* is described by the behavioral statement, "specified work pace (on continuous assembly line, etc.)." The respondee would rate this behavior in terms of how important the behavior is to the total job. The possible responses are: N—Does Not Apply; 1—Very Minor; 2—Low; 3—Average; 4—High; and 5—Extreme.

From approximately 15 years of research, PAQ researchers claim that this instrument is able to relate a job under study to a specific job family and identify applicable tests for selecting applicants for these jobs and for evaluating job worth.

CODAP. For over two decades, the Air Training Command of the United States Air Force has been developing task inventories for Air Force specialties. This program is called the Comprehensive Occupation Data Analysis Program (CODAP). In this program, task inventories have been developed for approximately 216 out of the 240 Air Force specialties. (An Air Force specialty is very similar to an occupation). The 240 specialties cover thousands of different kinds of jobs. CODAP could be considered a job-oriented task inventory. An example of a typical task listed in a CODAP inventory is the computer systems specialty, "Change or align paper in printer." A respondee would first check whether or not this task is currently being performed, then

---

[3] Ernest J. McCormick, Paul R. Jeanneret, and Robert C. Mecham, "A Study of Job Characteristics and Job Dimensions as Based on the Position Analysis Questionnaire (PAQ)," *Journal of Applied Psychology,* August 1972, pp. 347–368.

rate the task on the "average time spent" scale that ranges from 1 to 9, with the terminal intervals identified as

1—Very Small Amount

.

.

.

9—Very Large Amount

This particular inventory lists 577 task statements.

JAQ. Job Analysis Questionnaire is a job-oriented task inventory that provides specific job task, job environment, and job knowledge information. In a project for Northern States Power, Jerry Newman and Frank Krzytofiak identified 598 task items, 30 job environment items, and 130 job knowledge items that were relevant and useful for describing 1700 exempt positions.[4]

FOCAS. Control Data Corporation has been working for about 10 years on a task inventory program called *F*lexible *O*ccupation *A*nalysis *S*ystem. This program also could be classified as a job-oriented task inventory. Currently, six of the 16 major job families—occupations—within the corporation have had inventories developed. The number of tasks listed under FOCAS range from 258 for the engineer occupation to 450 for the computer occupation.

Other Inventory Programs. A wide variety of other organizations have been working on inventories. V-TECS, a unit of The Southern Association of Colleges and Schools, has been working for almost 10 years to develop task listings that will assist vocational education schools in designing educational programs that provide the knowledge and skills their students will require to successfully perform assignments when they go to work. Over the years, V-TECS has developed 115 inventories that they call catalogs. Each catalog consists of one or more job titles listed in the *Dictionary of Occupational Titles.*

Other organizations and associations have generated inventories for data processing jobs, jobs in the clerical-secretarial field, and for police officers and firefighters. Much of the work in this area has not been widely communicated, but dozens of occupational inventories have already been developed and put to some use. There will un-

---

[4] Jerry Newman and Frank Krzytofiak, "Quantified Job Analysis: A Tool for Improving Human Resource Management Decision Making," A paper presented at the Academy of Management Meeting, Orlando, Florida, August 15, 1977.

doubtedly be significantly more attention given to this area before the end of the decade.

Linking Inventories to the Computer. The process previously described in this chapter for obtaining job information, or one quite similar to it, can be used to develop task inventories. Once inventory task listings are developed, they can be placed into files for word processing. With the integration of word-processing capabilities into a wide variety of computer-based applications, interactive processes can be established. Major activity and task inventories and glossaries can be placed on word processors linked to computers. Employees with access to a terminal (within a few years, this will be a significant percentage of all employees) will be able to recall relevant activity inventories and select those major activities and tasks that best describe what they do.

If there are problems with the verb—the meaning of the verb relative to the action taken in the context of the specific occupation—the incumbent can request a glossary of verbs in an occupational mode. This provides a definition that, as precisely as possible, describes the meaning of the verb.

The selections made by the incumbent can be stored and grouped and, upon receipt of specific instructions, provide a hard copy of the results. Both the supervisor and subordinate can review the document and make necessary changes. They can both search for missing activities, either major activities or tasks, or possibly restate the activity in a manner that improves the description of the position. They can then review the hard copy, make any changes they think necessary, and, if they require the help of a personnel specialist, they can request such aid through the computer terminal or other communication device. This entire process will take the supervisor and incumbent out of the activity writing business. They will, however, make modifications, additions, or deletions as necessary. Through their on-line connection to job analysts or inventory development specialists, they will be able to identify where changes must be made, not only regarding their specific positions, but where changes are to be made in the computerized inventories and glossaries. Constant updating of position descriptions and occupational inventories and glossaries will negate the need for massive job analysis programs when current position/job descriptions and occupational inventories are out of date.

Supervisor and subordinate will add *why* and *how* information to the basic *what* and *to what* terms that are universally applicable to the occupation. It is the addition of the *why* and *how* information to the task statement that makes it truly unique, that provides the descriptive material necessary for a position description. Once again, the supervisor and incumbent jointly review these inputs. They discuss differences in requirements or possibly differences in perception. This process leads to a much-improved mutual understanding of what the job is and what the job is *not*. The computer-based process eliminates the drudgery (for most people) of thinking, reviewing, and attempting to describe what the individual does.

Moving from Inventories to Position Definitions. The writing of a position/job definition requires nothing more than a selection from major activity and task inventories that result in a draft list of responsibilities and duties. Major activities and task statements are used for establishing occupational inventories. Responsibilities and duties are the end product that defines the work assignment of a specific position or job.

Understanding what the position requires is the first step in gaining acceptable performance from the incumbent. Before an individual can accept the responsibility for performing a particular assignment, that person must know exactly what the assignment is, the standards to be met, and any constraints that limit the actions to be taken. It is this understanding that can lead to an honest, healthy working relationship between the supervisor and subordinate.

To provide a solid foundation for the performance appraisal system, the position definition must assist in responding to these questions:

1. Is the incumbent doing what he or she is supposed to be doing?
2. Does the incumbent know what he or she must do?
3. Does the supervisor know what the incumbent is doing?
4. Does the incumbent know why he or she is doing what he or she is doing?
5. Does the incumbent recognize how his or her contribution leads to the success of the work unit? The organization?
6. Does the incumbent recognize the limits within which he or she can perform? (Must do this; can't do that!)
7. Does the supervisor or other organizational member provide support for improving performance?
8. Is the incumbent aware of the rewards available for making certain kinds and amounts of contributions?

The kind of interaction and agreement just described will minimize, if not, in the great majority of cases, eliminate such unacceptable statements as, "I didn't know I was supposed to do that," or "Why didn't you tell me you were doing this?" or "You never told me *this* was more important than *that*," or "Why didn't you do that?"

To be useful, a position definition must describe in an orderly and logical manner what an incumbent must do to be a successful performer. Once top management recognizes the role the position definition plays in gaining an accurate and complete understanding of what each person is doing, it can appreciate the reason for granting the expenditure of funds to provide these documents.

THE POSITION DESCRIPTION

The position is a series of assignments a person is hired to perform. These assignments require that the incumbent have some kind of knowledge and skills ranging from pushing a broom, to influencing hostile individuals to accept a distasteful concept, to creating a new technology, to inventing a new product that will benefit the organization. In addition, position assignments are performed under a wide variety of conditions. The unique physical, psychological, and emotional demands placed on an incumbent must also be recognized and described as precisely as possible.

Position Title

To start the identification process, it may be useful to look at the position as an empty circle. The first step in the description process is to provide a title to the circle that aptly describes what that set of activities as performed by the incumbent contributes to the organization (Figure 4-3).

Many organizations recognize that a title carries status and can have a positive influence on an employee's workplace behavior. Every effort must be made to establish a legitimate and realistic title that provides the maximum possible amount of dignity and status to the incumbent.

Position Title

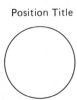

Figure 4–3.

Position Summary

The next step in the identification and description process may be the writing of a brief summary of the position. The summary consists of from one to three, possibly as many as five, sentences that concisely describe the distinctive features of the position, the reasons for its existence, and the unique contributions it makes. In most cases, a summary sentence will contain approximately 12 words.

Responsibilities

With the establishment of responsibilities, the position becomes subdivided into specific categories or component parts. In this example, the position has four responsibilities (Figure 4–4). It is at this stage of the process that the art and skill required for writing quickly become apparent. As the summary becomes further enlarged through the re-

Figure 4–4.

sponsibility statements, the problem of detail and specificity occurs. Responsibility statements must certainly have far more detail than a summary paragraph, but the amount of detail that is sufficient is a major problem. The scope and specificity of the responsibility statement will vary according to the scope and complexity of the position. Before describing the "detail problem," it may be useful to continue to the next step in the process.

Duties

Duties further describe a responsibility. The position pie and its major slices of responsibilities are further divided into duties (Figure 4–5).

The duties explain in more detail what actually occurs in the performance of a responsibility. Duties typically not only describe *what* is

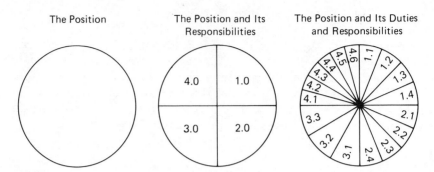

FIGURE 4–5.

done, but further describe the *why* and *how* that provide more individuality and uniqueness to the position description. They establish the foundation for the setting of performance standards, which is the subject of Chapter 5.

Responsibility Statements

After the summary has been reviewed for initial direction, the following three statements provide additional ideas for writing responsibility statements:

1. The responsibility statements must provide more detail than the position summary.
2. Each responsibility must describe a significant part of the position.
3. Together, the responsibility statements describe the reasons for the existence of the position—the major work areas of the incumbent.

After developing a list of responsibility statements, the position description writer must then review the total package and answer these questions:

1. Do these statements adequately describe the purpose of the position?
2. Are there any responsibilities missing?
3. Are there responsibilities that can be omitted?

FIGURE 4–6.
The Classification Process

Position Title	A hint. Depends on reader knowledge and perception.
Position Summary	A thumbnail description. Gives slightly more information, but considerable ambiguity continues to cloud what is happening.
Position Responsibility	More precise description of what is occurring. Begins to present a clear picture of what the position is all about.
Position Duty	Describes in detail what is occurring. These are activities that occur with some regularity.

4. Are there two or more responsibilities that can be combined and made into a more useful statement?

5. Is it possible to clarify or improve the statement?

The same general areas used for identifying major activities that are described on pages 93–95 are also valuable for identifying responsibilities.

Duty Statements

After the responsibility statements are completed, each statement should be analyzed separately, and a list of duties should be developed for each responsibility. The classification process is continuous, from the broad and relatively vague to the narrow and precise (see Figure 4–6).

Now a question arises. Is there a specific limit to the number of responsibility and duty statements? The answer is *yes*. Over the years, researchers in a wide variety of disciplines have recognized some common constraints to human activity that probably have their foundation

---

[5] Edward N. Hay, "The Application of Weber's Law to Job Evaluation Estimates," *Journal of Applied Psychology, 34,* 1950, pp. 102–104; George A. Miller, "The Magical Number Seven Plus or Minus Two: Some Limits On Our Capacity For Processing Information," *The Psychological Review,* March 1956, pp. 81–97. The works of Hay and Miller are described in much greater detail in Chapter 6.

in the very design of the human brain. In this case, the research relates to the magic number 7.[5] Whether it is 7 ± 2, or 7 ± 4, depending on scope and complexity, most positions will require from three to seven—possibly (though infrequently) as many as nine to eleven—responsibility statements to completely describe them.

In most cases, anywhere from three to seven responsibilities are sufficient to adequately describe most positions. In the same vein, three to seven duties are usually sufficient to describe a responsibility. This holds true for both the simplest and the most complex positions. The reason for this is that responsibility and duty statements become broader and more abstract as they describe activities performed by individuals in positions requiring a wider range or scope of work. The responsibility and duty statements for an office messenger, a janitor, or a data entry operator will be in very precise terms. On the other hand, in moving up the organizational ladder, responsibilities and duties are defined in more general terms. Figure 4–7 is an example of a position definition for a top executive of an organization. Figure 4–8 is a position definition for a first-line manager. A review of the two position definitions reveals that:

1. The higher the level of the positions the more complex are the position requirements and associated incumbent activities.

2. The more complex the requirements and activities are, the more difficult it is to describe them in clear, unambiguous terms.

3. The more complex the activities are, the more difficult it is to identify relevant activities that are observable and measurable in quantitative terms, although qualitative measurements are certainly applicable.

4. The higher the level of the position, the greater the likelihood that the way identified position activities are performed will vary significantly among incumbents.

5. As positions increase in importance, the cognitive and affective domains become more important, and the psychomotor domains become less important.

   COGNITIVE DOMAIN: Intellectual pursuits characterized by thinking, reasoning, and understanding skills.

   AFFECTIVE DOMAIN: Feelings and emotional pursuits characterized by interests, attitudes, openness to change, and appreciation of differences.

   PSYCHOMOTOR DOMAIN: Physical pursuits characterized by motor skills involving synchronized and coordinated movement of hands, arms, legs, torso, head, and eyes.

1.0 Commits unit to new courses of action.
 1.1 Allocates resources to individuals and projects that will have the greatest impact on the achievement of organizational goals.
 1.2 Directs activities of unit to adapt to changing environmental conditions.
 1.3 Recognizes disturbance issues and redirects efforts to minimize resulting ill-effects.
 1.4 Negotiates issues that may or will have a negative impact on organizational performance.
2.0 Monitors, collects, and transmits information for work unit.
 2.1 Scans environment, interrogates liaison contacts, and receives unsolicited information.
 2.2 Disseminates privileged information among subordinates.
 2.3 Passes information between subordinates who do not have readily accessible communication channels.
 2.4 Sends information to people outside the organization for subordinates.
3.0 Maintains interpersonal relationships with individuals both external and internal to the organization.
 3.1 Directs efforts of immediate subordinate/own staff personnel.
 3.2 Encourages all employees to coordinate efforts in order to meet group, unit, and organizational goals.
 3.3 Acts as a liaison with individuals outside the vertical chain of command.
 3.4 Performs assignments of a ceremonial nature.

FIGURE 4–7. Responsibilities and Duties of the Job of an Executive. (Paraphrased from Henry Mintzberg, ''The Manager's Job: Folklore and Fact,'' *Harvard Business Review,* July–August 1975, pp. 49–61.)

Writing A Position Description

To those who do not have or will not have in the near future computer-based major activity and task inventories, the process of writing a position description is similar if not identical to that currently required for writing job descriptions. The processes previously described for collecting major activity and task information can be used in an identical manner for directly gathering responsibility and duty information. The only difference is that the analyst edits the information provided by the incumbent (through a completed questionnaire or interview) and writes a position description.

1.0 Plans and schedules work assignments.
  1.1 Establishes and reviews group and individual goals.
  1.2 Sets workplace methods and procedures.
  1.3 Schedules daily work assignments.
  1.4 Coordinates work activities with related work group.
  1.5 Ensures that subordinates have necessary equipment and material.
  1.6 Establishes and maintains records and reporting systems.
2.0 Monitors performance to ensure acceptable levels and quality of output.
  2.1 Observes employee performance at work site.
  2.2 Compares individual performance to group norms.
  2.3 Compares actual performance with present performance standards.
  2.4 Conducts specified number of quality inspections.
  2.5 Investigates accident and damage claims.
  2.6 Resolves grievances and informal problems.
3.0 Develops employees and maximizes performance potential.
  3.1 Reviews records to identify low performers.
  3.2 Instructs employees on preferred procedures.
  3.3 Schedules formal training programs.
  3.4 Detects through observation unsafe work practices.
  3.5 Inspects equipment for safe working conditions.
  3.6 Appraises employee performance.
  3.7 Provides training to correct knowledge- and skill-related deficiencies.
4.0 Schedules employees to ensure work coverage within guidelines prescribed by government legislation, corporate policy, and union contract.
  4.1 Assigns hourly tours to provide appropriate job coverage.
  4.2 Develops weekly work schedule to ensure 8 hours per day and 40 hours per week work load.
  4.3 Establishes holiday and vacation schedules.
  4.4 Rotates work to allow for equal distribution of various types of work assignments.

FIGURE 4–8. Responsibilities and Duties of the Job of a First-Line Manager.

The position description provides a word picture of what the incumbent is doing. The skill exhibited in the use of words and their combination is similar to the skill of the artist in conceptualizing and combining various colors and different strokes to create a valuable picture. Writing a good position description, like painting a good picture, is hard work. It cannot be done by everyone. The results of the effort, however, can be most rewarding to those influenced by the position description.

Processing Incumbent-Provided Activity Information. After receiving the completed questionnaire, the analyst reviews the list of activities provided by the incumbent and identifies the *major activities.* The analyst then transfers these major activities to one or more sheets of paper. These transferred major activities now become responsibility statements, and the analyst is in the first stages of developing a position definition. The analyst then identifies each responsibility by a specific code, that is, 1.0, 2.0, 3.0, and so on. In pen or pencil of a different color than that used by the respondent (incumbent), the responsibility number is placed next to the activity on the original list and becomes an "address" that identifies (a) the recognition and use of the activity and (b) the location of the activity in the position definition. This same process is continued for identifying responsibilities and duties until all original activities have been recognized through some responsibility or duty in the position definition. The code for duties would be 1.1, 1.2 . . .; 2.1, 2.2 . . ., and so on.

The only caution here is that when an activity location is changed with respect to a specific responsibility or duty in the draft position definition, the code must also be changed on the list provided by the incumbent. The reason for doing this kind of detailed checking is to be sure that all activities identified by the incumbent have been recognized. The code shows where they are located in the position definition. It is entirely possible in this transformation process that two or possibly many more incumbent-identified activities will be described through the use of one responsibility or duty statement. It is also possible that an incumbent-identified activity may require two or more responsibility or duty statements to ensure an adequate description.

A challenge facing any writer of responsibility and duty statements is not only to use the most descriptive action verb possible when describing a responsibility or duty, but also to attempt to initiate duty statements with verbs that are different from the one used in the specific responsibility. The use of verbs in the duty statements that differ from the verb in the responsibility statement further clarifies the responsibility statement. It assists in reducing the ambiguity and vagueness of the broad-scoped responsibility statement. (This relates to the problem of defining a word by using the same word in the definition.)

After completing an initial draft of the responsibility and duty statements, the writer is ready to analyze each set of statements and make any changes deemed necessary. The first step in the analysis and editing process is to be sure that the duty statements describe the major parts of the responsibility—each one a significant activity area of the responsibility. Together, all of the duty statements should adequately describe the specific responsibility. The output of a duty should contribute to the successful completion of a responsibility. Next, the analyst may determine whether or not a responsibility statement has what appears to be an excessive number of duty statements. If it does, it may be necessary to write an additional responsibility statement or divide the existing statement into two or more responsibility statements, placing the appropriate duties with each one.

Analysts must constantly struggle with the problem of too much or too little detail. In writing a position description, responsibility statements must be written at the same level of detail. The same rule applies in writing duty statements. A responsibility statement that is too broad will tend to be too abstract and will probably have too many duty statements attached. A responsibility statement that is too narrow will be too specific and will frequently have very few related duty statements. When this occurs, it is quite possible that this statement is a duty and should be assigned to another responsibility or rewritten in a broader form. Additional checks for the appropriate relation of duties to responsibilities are discussed later in the sections of the chapter that discuss knowledge, skills, abilities, and environmental conditions.

Rank-Ordering Responsibility and Duty Statements

A major point emphasized in this chapter is that position descriptions must be tailor-made. "Canned," ready-made job descriptions are of little value other than for providing insights to the typical or common tasks performed by incumbents in jobs or classes of jobs. The activity analysis, even the transformation of activity information into responsibility and duty statements, is not a new idea. One point that may differ from or add to the normal practice, however, is the listing of responsibilities and their applicable duties by order of importance within the position definition. This not only provides a significant opportunity for employee involvement, but truly centers on the unique qualities or features of each position in the organization.

Rank-ordering responsibilities and duties by importance must involve incumbents and other employees who are intimately familiar with the position. The involvement of these individuals permits those most knowledgeable of position content requirements to have a significant voice in the final product, which is a listing and ordering of the responsibility and duty statements. Incumbent involvement may take this form:

A draft of the ordered and edited responsibility and duty statements is returned to each incumbent. The following cover letter is sent with the draft of the position definition:

> Through your past efforts in providing activity information, we have been able to develop this set of job responsibilities and duties. The responsibilities are the major activities you perform on your job. They are listed as 1.0, 2.0, etc. The duties are the subresponsibilities or activities that amplify or further describe the activities you perform in completing an assigned responsibility. They are identified by the number .1, .2, .3, etc.
>
> Would you please review this list of responsibilities and duties. Are there any activities you perform that have not been included in this list that you believe should be included? Please list these missing activities in their most appropriate location. Next, review the list for any activities that are not performed by you or that are so inconsequential that they should not be listed. Strike through these unnecessary activity statements. Now, review the responsibility statements and place a *1.0* by the statement you think is most critical for overall successful job performance. Then, place a *2.0* by the second most important responsibility statement and complete this numbering process for all the responsibility statements in your job. The same process must be followed in ordering the duty statements within each responsibility. This input enables you to inform us as to how you view the relative importance of the things you do.
>
> Review this list of activities with care. They not only assist management in determining the overall worth of your position to the organization, but they also provide the basis for establishing the standards you will be expected to meet.

Here, once again, at this early but important phase of the performance appraisal process, employee participation is sought and used. The incumbent not only provides activity information, but has a voice in the various stages of the review to ensure that the transformation process from an unstructured list of activities results in an accurate and understandable description and ordering of responsibility and duty statements.

Activity Worth Dimensions and Rating Scales. In addition to the pragmatic, empirical knowledge of the incumbent and supervisor in rank-ordering responsibilities and duties, it is also possible to use activity worth dimensions and rating scales. Here, once again, the computer and data-base management come into focus. Using activity worth dimensions can be done rapidly and at minimal cost when incumbents have the opportunity to interact directly in the rating process through the use of a terminal. The ratings resulting from the use of the activity-worth dimensions can be used in conjunction with the previously discussed pragmatic approach for the final ordering of responsibilities and duties.

The following activity worth dimensions may be used for this purpose. It is possible, however, that an organization may wish to develop other activity worth dimensions. The five activity worth dimensions provided here are: frequency, duration, criticality/consequence of error, extent necessary upon entry to the job, and relationship to overall successful job performance.

After the activity worth dimensions are identified, scales must be designed for measurement purposes. The basic design features of a scale are the number of intervals to be used and the description provided for each interval that assists raters in making the most accurate inferences between responsibility and duty statements and the level of the specific dimension under review.

The number of intervals within a scale used to measure each dimension may vary according to individual choice and values. The greater the number of intervals, the larger the possible variation in final rating scores. The fewer the intervals, the greater the likelihood of a smaller dispersion of scores. The other side of this coin focuses on how precisely differences can be noted with any accuracy by a rater. There may be some who argue that only a three-interval scale can be used with any reliability, while others may opt for a nine or even a 99-interval scale. The following are examples of activity worth dimensions and rating scales using different numbers of intervals and descriptions for each interval, which assist a rater in using the most appropriate interval.

Three-Interval Scale Example: [6]

1. *Frequency:* How often is this activity *typically* performed on the job?
   1 = Less than for most other activities.
   2 = About the same as other activities.
   3 = Substantially more often than other activities.
2. *Duration:* During a typical work day, how much time is normally spent performing this activity, as compared to other activities?
   1 = Less than for other activities (below average).
   2 = About the same as for other activities (about average).
   3 = More than for other activities (above average).

---

[6] These scales were developed by Kathleen Robinson, Consultant, Atlanta, Georgia.

3. *Criticality/Consequence of Error:* If this activity is not performed, or if it is performed poorly, how damaging will the consequences (results) normally be to the public, to the department, and/or to the organization?
   1 = Very little damage.
   2 = Moderate damage.
   3 = Considerable damage.

4. *Extent Necessary upon Entry to the Job:* How necessary is satisfactory performance of this activity at the beginning of employment?
   1 = Not necessary; activity can be learned after hiring.
   2 = Desirable, but not essential for hiring (places new hire at distinct disadvantage if unable to perform).
   3 = Necessary; new employee *must* be able to perform this activity at a satisfactory level upon entry into the job (after normal orientation).

5. *Relationship to Overall Successful Job Performance:* How critical is satisfactory performance of this activity for *overall* successful performance?
   1 = Not very critical for overall successful performance.
   2 = Moderately critical for overall successful performance.
   3 = Extremely critical for overall successful performance.

A nine-interval rating scale for frequency and duration could take the following form:

1. *Frequency:* How often is this activity typically performed on the job?
   1 = At least once a year.
   2 = At least once each six months.
   3 = At least once each quarter.
   4 = At least once each two months.
   5 = At least once a month.
   6 = At least once each two weeks.
   7 = At least once a week.
   8 = At least twice a week.
   9 = Daily

2. *Duration:* Time spent in performing the activity.
   1 = Less than 30 minutes.
   2 = 31 minutes to one hour.
   3 = Over one hour to two hours.
   4 = Over two hours to four hours.
   5 = Over four hours to eight hours.
   6 = Over eight hours to 16 hours.

7 = Over 16 hours to 32 hours.

8 = Over 32 hours to 40 hours.

9 = More than 40 hours.

In the CODAP of the U.S. Air Force, the primary dimension used to measure tasks is Time Spent on Present Job. Incumbents completing a CODAP job inventory respond to a nine-interval scale for each task they perform. The nine-interval time-spent scale is as follows:

1. Very small amount.

2. Much below average.

3. Below average.

4. Slightly below average.

5. About average.

6. Slightly above average.

7. Above average.

8. Much above average.

9. Very large amount.

Incumbent responses to this scale are transformed to percentage of time spent on each task. The data generated in this ordinal scale are processed as if the scale were a ratio scale. (There is an extensive discussion of scale design in Chapter 6.)

Using the activity worth dimensions and rating scales or the results negotiated between the supervisor and incumbents, the responsibility and duty statements are listed in sequential order of importance. The first responsibility listed is the most important; the second listed, the second most important; and so on. The duties listed under a specific responsibility also follow an ordering by importance or worth. The actual value assigned to a responsibility or duty through the use of activity worth dimensions and rating scales provides a quantitative basis for determining the relative order of the responsibility and duty statements.

For some positions, however, the most appropriate ordering of responsibilities and duties follows a sequence of occurrence. In positions in which the incumbent must follow a specific order of activities, it is easier for the incumbent to (a) identify activities performed by reviewing a daily routine and (b) evaluate the completeness of the description by reviewing the activity statements as a checklist. Most positions do not, however, follow a strict routine; they vary according to changes that occur or influence work assignments.

The ordering of responsibility statements requires a certain amount of judgment. To improve the quality of judgment in determining which responsibility is most valuable or critical to the overall success of the position, those making the judgment must combine information from a number of sources. One important source certainly is the overall score received by each duty included within a responsibility. Conditions of employment can also provide information that will be helpful in ordering the responsibility. (These are discussed later.) Since conditions of employment are identified after the completion of at least the first draft of the responsibility and duty statements, the ordering process may require two or more iterations.

In the process of ordering responsibility and duty statements, it may be possible that two individuals who perform in what have been identified as the same positions do not consider the ordering of the responsibilities and duties to be the same. This provides documentation supporting the concept that seldom are two positions identical. A point stressed in this chapter is that if performance appraisal is to have a specific meaning to each employee, it must be based on the work as it is being performed by that person. The great majority of positions cannot be made uniform; they cannot be completely standardized. Although some kind or amount of standardization may be acceptable for certain human resource activities (e.g., testing, orientation, training), when it comes to performance appraisal, application of broad-scaled, uniform standards of measurement may be disastrous and lead to the demise of a performance appraisal program. Once again, the computer and its word-processing capabilities become valuable. With word-processing capabilities, the incumbent and supervisor can quickly and easily reorder responsibility and duty statements (in addition to adding to, deleting, or changing specific responsibility and duty statements), and the computer can provide an instant hard copy of the new position description or the position definition. In this manner, the incumbent and supervisor are working from a current and accurate position "contract."

Conditions of Employment

Following the initial identification, description, and ordering of responsibilities and duties, information regarding conditions of employment can be collected. Using each responsibility as a center of focus, specific information can be requested; or, possibly, review information already collected can be used to identify and describe:

1. Environmental conditions within which the responsibility is performed.
2. Knowledge, skills, and abilities required of an incumbent to perform the responsibility at
   a. Minimally acceptable levels (entry into the job); and
   b. Proficient levels (fully qualified incumbent).

Environmental Conditions. This area is often titled or classified as *working conditions.* In the past, it normally centered on the physical demands and physical hazards the employee encountered when performing job assignments. Today, additional factors have been added that describe the psychological and emotional demands an employee must face.

In appraising employee performance, the rater must be aware of and able to accurately identify the kind and degree of physical, psychological, and emotional conditions that may, in some manner, endanger the health of the employee. Unusual working conditions such as extreme temperatures, excessive dust, dampness, toxic elements, heights, and depths have been recognized for many years. Today, attention also focuses on stressful conditions that may result in anxiety, frustration, fear, alienation, and hostility. It must be apparent that failure to recognize the existence of these conditions could result in a far from adequate appraisal of performance.

Although it often appears that positions are becoming simpler, the opposite is actually the case. Not only are work requirements becoming more demanding, but the relationship between employee performance and organizational productivity is also increasing in complexity. Computer-assisted machines are replacing humans where there is an emphasis on repetitive physical labor. Software that directs these machines accommodates a certain amount of flexibility in assignments and can quickly react to changes in input data. Human labor, however, is required to operate and repair these sophisticated machines. Many of the positions in contemporary organizations require the incumbent to act as an interface between different groups of these computer-driven machines. With the advent of this high-technology world, the work force is called on to perform less physical work, but the speed and number of interactions and the accuracy demanded in every phase of operations require workers to have significantly higher levels of knowledge and skills and a broader understanding of the reasons or causes of the interactions that influence their assignments. Workers have less time to make decisions, must consider more alternatives in the decision-making process, and frequently have less control over what they do than workers did prior to the computer revolution. This has resulted in emotional and psychological stress, which is replacing physical stress at the workplace.

Knowledge, Skills, and Abilities (KSAs). Knowledge, skills, and abilities may be defined as follows:

KNOWLEDGE: Prerequisites for thinking and action required to perform assignments necessary to produce acceptable output.

SKILL: Demonstrated level of proficiency of an ability.

ABILITY: A natural talent or acquired proficiency required in the performance of work assignments.

Although KSA information is typically collected for establishing minimum job qualifications and for developing minimum hiring requirements, this kind of information can be developed to identify requirements normally expected of a fully proficient employee. It also assists in test design and test validation. To acquire this kind of information, the analyst may have to return to the supervisor or discuss the KSA requirements with other personnel specialists. Individuals responsible for the design of testing and selection instruments or those involved in recruiting and hiring may be an excellent source of information. Questions relating to KSAs can also be directed to an incumbent.

Performance appraisal usually provides information on employee potential, additional training requirements, and even areas of interest. Providing KSA information to the rater not only increases the scope and value of the performance review, but also opens the rater's eyes to important job-related factors that may be missed when focusing only on results.

Comparing Conditions of Employment. It must be noted that the environmental conditions and KSA identification processes are performed only for each responsibility, *not* for the assigned duties. This now permits the use of one of the first of many checks and balances that must be built into a performance appraisal system. If the duties truly fit within an identified responsibility, they should be performed essentially under the same kinds of environmental conditions and require the same kinds of KSAs. After developing the environmental conditions and KSAs for each responsibility, each duty assigned to a responsibility should be compared to the conditions of employment established for that responsibility. If they match, this is further evidence that the assigned duties support the specific responsibility. If a duty doesn't match, it indicates that

1. The condition of employment may not have been adequately described and requires further clarification.
2. The duty does not fit within its assigned responsibility.
    a. If this occurs, the first action is to see whether or not the duty would fit better under another responsibility.
    b. If this is not a satisfactory solution, the next alternative is either to develop the duty as a new responsibility and identify its own conditions of employment or to use the duty as a basis for establishing a new responsibility.
    c. At this stage, it may be useful to review the initial task analysis to see whether or not certain tasks can be identified as duties that further describe this additional responsibility.

A TOOL FOR PLANNING, OPERATIONS, AND CONTROL

Accurate and current position descriptions provide supervisors with a most valuable tool for planning, operations, and control. Possibly, the first thing a supervisor can do with these current and accurate position descriptions is to place them into a "living" organization chart. After reviewing the position definition section (responsibility and duty statements), the supervisor can begin answering these questions:

1. Are there work-unit goals that are not met or will not be met because certain activities are not being performed by any work-unit members?
2. Can work-unit activities be reassigned or redistributed to take better advantage of member time, knowledge, skills, efforts, interests, and desires?
3. Are there activities now being performed that are unnecessary or inconsequential and can be eliminated because the work is being duplicated elsewhere or has outlived its usefulness and will have little or no impact on the success of the work unit or the organization?
4. What are the strengths and weaknesses of each member? What support does each member require?
5. What can be done to improve member cooperation and coordination?

Good and workable answers to these kinds of questions can only be found when supervisors know what their subordinates are actually doing and what they are supposed to be doing. A work setting based on a solid position description will facilitate supervisor-subordinate communication and foster the setting of performance standards that will benefit the subordinate, the supervisor, and the organization. A position description that provides a clear understanding of what needs to be done and what is actually happening can improve employee and work-unit performance and lead to the establishment of a no-nonsense, trusting workplace environment.

Non-Position Content-Related Contributions

Opportunities frequently arise for employees to either support or block improved organizational productivity. These actions frequently have no direct relationship to position content. They relate more to an employee's workplace behavior and to *how* assignments are completed rather than to the assignments themselves. These actions seldom appear in a position description, nor should they.

These activities relate mainly to the interpersonal dynamics occurring at the workplace. A major benefit derived from work is social interaction. On their own, many individuals demonstrate the interest and put forth the effort to enhance the social relations and quality of work life of all employees in their work unit, and often the value of their efforts extends beyond the boundaries of the work unit. Although these activities do not have a position-content base, they may contribute significantly to organizational effectiveness. When measuring employee performance, it is important that these contributions be recognized. From a positive side, examples of contributions that are made in an unofficial capacity are as:

1. Self-appointed social director—the person who bakes the birthday cake, or organizes the work group to recognize a special event, or supports other employees in time of need or distress.

2. Spokesperson—the individual who recognizes problems that exist at lower levels in the organization that formal processes appear to be incapable of resolving and who has the courage or opportunities to present issues to levels where suitable actions can be taken.

3. Interpreter—the person who is aware of and understands what is happening and is able to explain the actions or messages from higher levels in the organization in words that the other group members understand.

4. Expert or reference source—the person who has an exceptional or broad range of knowledge, skills, or experiences and can be counted on to provide the necessary support when a problem or need arises. He or she provides information of value to the other employees that the formal structure is incapable of providing or unwilling to offer.

5. Trainer—the person who trains employees to perform current assignments or expands knowledge and skills that enhance the future value of the employee (to himself or herself and to the organization).

6. Orienter—the person who orients employees (new, even old members) as to acceptable behaviors and the opportunities the organization makes available to its members.

There are dozens of similar examples that others come into contact with constantly. When performed in a positive manner, these contributions lead to group cohesiveness and improved work-unit morale, coordination, and efficiency. When not recognized formally, these activities will be recognized in some other manner. This may occur when a rater measures a subordinate higher in a job-content-based performance dimension or series of these kinds of dimensions than otherwise deserved because of these informal workplace contributions. The result may be the first wedge in destroying the credibility of the rating program. Better results can be achieved if these informal contributions are recognized formally and the contributors know exactly what influence their contributions have on their overall performance ratings. Figure 2–2 in Chapter 2 provides a way of measuring non-position-related performance behaviors. The content in this figure could be used as a basis for designing a work-unit/organizational values rating instrument.

The negative side of this issue is just as relevant. Take, for example, the individual who is forever making "oral potshots" at the supervisor or organization but, in all other respects, performs in a proficient manner. A job-content-based rating instrument does not permit the rater to recognize the derogatory or morale-influencing statements made by the ratee. The rater then downgrades the ratee on certain job-content performance dimensions. The rating is false and unjust, and, again, the entire rating program is placed in jeopardy.

Possibly, a far better way to recognize these non-job-related but critical work-unit and organization-related behaviors is to return to the trait-rating instruments still commonly used by many organizations (even though such instruments have incurred the wrath of many federal court judges involved in civil rights cases concerning adverse and biased treatment of plaintiff-employees). These trait-rating instruments do, in some manner (all too often crudely and unacceptably from an employee and court perspective), recognize qualities or values that the organization highly prizes.

The first thing to be recognized in using such an instrument is that it provides minimal support for the accurate measuring and rating of job-content-related performance. Second, when using a trait-rating instrument, the organization must carefully analyze its philosophy and identify those values it prizes and wishes its members to observe and demonstrate. Third, the organization must recognize that behaviors related to these values may take different forms at different levels and in different functional areas. This means that the values must first be defined from an organizational perspective and then defined operationally in terms that have a useful and valid meaning to those who will be rated against these values. Traits and trait ratings are discussed in both Chapters 5 and 6. Fourth, if employees are to be measured against these values, it is essential that the meanings of these values be communicated to all employees in understandable terms. For example, if dependability and cooperation are highly prized qualities, employees must know exactly what dependability and cooperation mean with regard to their workplace-related behaviors. The process for identifying and describing these specificly valued workplace behaviors takes a form similar to the development of job-related responsibilities and duties.

From the organization's philosophy, it should be possible to identify highly prized values. Then, through a series of iterations, these values are redefined in more precise and specific terms. The final step in this iterative process is the description of these values in terms appropriate to valued behaviors demonstrated by the employees in a specific work unit.

What must be recognized is that trait-based rating instruments in themselves may not be bad or wrong. To make them useful and to minimize the unfair treatment of employees, trait-related actions must be recognized, identified, described, and documented just as precisely as are job-content-related behaviors.

Chapter 5

Performance Dimensions, Performance Standards, and Performance Goals

The identification of relevant performance dimensions follows the description of job responsibilities and duties. Secure in the knowledge that the job has been precisely and adequately defined and that deficiency, contamination, and distortion problems have been either eliminated or reduced to an acceptable level, it is now possible to identify and describe the qualities to be used to measure performance.

Performance dimensions are those qualities or features of a job or the activities that take place at a work site that are conducive to measurement. They provide a means for describing the scope of total workplace activities. While responsibilities and duties provide a depersonalized description of a job, performance dimensions permit the descriptive process to take a situational and personalized route. A performance dimension may take one or more of three different forms. It may be a responsibility or duty, a behavior, or a trait. Each form permits the development of a solid bridge that carries the appraisal process from impersonal job content requirements to the extremely personal actions exhibited and results achieved by each incumbent.

Performance dimensions integrate the established requirements of the job with the specific knowledge, skills, efforts, and desires of the incumbent and the demands placed on the job through changes in environmental conditions. This integration process frequently requires that the performance dimensions be more dynamic than the work activities from which they evolve. To ensure a valid measurement of performance, a set of performance dimensions for a specific job must meet the same three tests required of responsibilities. There must be sufficient dimensions to eliminate any chance of *deficiency,* in terms of covering the most important aspects of the job or even non-job-content-related workplace activities such as baking a birthday cake; dimensions must not be included that would result in *contamina-*

tion of the performance measurement, that is, the inclusion of extraneous factors that are not important for overall successful performance; and dimensions must be weighted to minimize *distortion* that occurs through improper or unacceptable emphasis.

A problem with the classification of performance dimensions by responsibilities and duties, behaviors, and traits is that it is not easy to keep a specific dimension cleanly and clearly within the parameters of a particular area. The use of words is once again a problem, and with ambiguity that could result from the potential for overlap among the three ways of classifying dimensions, it is certainly possible that a dimension classified as a behavior could just as easily be identified as a responsibility or duty or trait. The important point is that these three descriptors of activities emanate from the job and other work-related activities and that the same statement can be called by any one of the three terms. A review of the three basic areas assists in clarifying what a performance dimension is and the role it plays in the performance appraisal process.

RESPONSIBILITY- AND DUTY- BASED PERFORMANCE DIMENSIONS

It is possible that a responsibility or a duty could be transferred "as is" into an activity-based performance dimension. While a responsibility or duty statement primarily describes *what* is to be done, the emphasis in the performance dimension begins the shift to *how* it is to be done. To be useful as a basis for measurement purposes, the performance dimension must be sufficiently narrow and precise in description to minimize any opportunity for ambiguity to occur. When ambiguity does occur, it frequently results in a wide variety of interpretations that may easily culminate in human barriers that block successful appraisal of performance.

Actions identified and described through the job-analysis process can also be used to establish performance dimensions. The transformation from responsibility and duty statements into performance dimensions focuses primarily on the changes or modifications occurring in these activities because of the specific qualities of the incumbent or the demands established by the situation.

BEHAVIOR- BASED PERFORMANCE DIMENSIONS

In the 1960s, behavioral scientists interested in improving the effectiveness of performance appraisal programs focused a significant amount of interest and attention on identifying and describing employee work-related behaviors that would be amenable to observation and measurement. As a result of their work, a new approach for measuring employee performance was introduced to the world of work. This approach includes the identification and description of behavior-based performance dimensions and the development of scales for measuring them. The titles used for these measurement or rating scales are BARS (Behavioral Anchored Rating Scales), BES (Behavioral Expectation Scales), and BOS (Behavioral Observation Scales). The development and use of rating scales are discussed in detail in Chapter 6.

Behavior-based performance dimensions are defined as sets of related behaviors or distinctive features necessary for performance. An example of a performance dimension in behavioral terms is:

Application of Knowledge: Analyzes work and sets initial work priorities before involving others in the work process. Identifies critical work issues, information needed, whom to contact, and when to make requests to complete assignments on schedule.

When measuring performance through the use of behavior-based performance dimensions, there should be sufficient dimensions to cover completely all essential behaviors of the job. Each performance dimension should be essentially independent of every other dimension, but, collectively, all of them should cover the major behaviors required in successful job performance. This coverage is essential if an appraisal instrument using behavior-based performance dimensions is to have content validity. (The subject of validity is covered in Chapter 11.)

The identification of behavior-based performance dimensions is derived directly from analysis of job content and job behavior. The analysis of job content as discussed in Chapter 4 focuses on the establishment of job responsibilities and duties. This analysis includes the identification of the knowledge, skills, and abilities necessary to perform the job and the environmental conditions existing at the workplace. The analysis of job behavior, however, focuses on specific employee behavior that can be observed, defined, and measured while the job is being performed. These types of analyses identify those behaviors that are critical to effective job performance and that comprehensively describe job requirements.

Jobholders and supervisors who are familiar with the job identify the performance incidents and critical behaviors required for performance. From a broad list of such incidents, knowledgeable job performers, supervisors, skilled staff specialists, or other subject-matter experts identify those job behaviors that are similar in content and cluster them under specific performance dimensions. An issue that arises when grouping performance appraisal factors or dimensions is whether they are equal in importance or should be weighted differently. Resolving the weighting issue is one of the most difficult problems facing designers and administrators of a performance appraisal program.

FIGURE 5–1.
Performance Dimensions

Flanagan (1949)	Sears (1976)	Latham and Scott (1975)
1 Proficiency in handling administrative detail.	1 Technical knowledge.	1 Work performance.
2 Proficiency in supervising personnel.	2 Application of knowledge.	2 Job commitment.
3 Proficiency in planning and directing action.	3 Administrative effectiveness.	3 Interactions with others.
4 Proficiency in technical job knowledge.	4 Work relations.	4 Planning, organizing, and setting priorities.
5 Acceptance of organizational responsibilities.	5 Response to superiors.	
6 Acceptance of personal responsibility.	6 Directing subordinates.	
	7 Personal commitment.	

In 1949, John C. Flanagan, a pioneer in this field, identified six performance dimensions.[1] In a study conducted from 1972 through 1976, psychological researchers of Sears, Roebuck and Co. identified seven dimensions that compare to those established by Flanagan.[2] G. P. Latham and R. R. Scott identified four dimensions in 1975.[3] The dimensions are shown in Figure 5–1.

The common features exhibited by the dimensions described by these researchers are the broad, universal area they cover. To be useful for measuring the performance of most jobholders, these universal dimensions must be further defined, either through a series of more specific and precise behavior-based performance dimensions or

---

[1] John C. Flanagan, "A New Approach to Evaluating Personnel," *Personnel,* January–February 1949, p. 42.

[2] Robert H. Rhode, *Development of the Retail Checklist Performance Evaluation Program* (Chicago, IL: Sears, Roebuck and Co., 1976), pp. 26–37.

[3] G. P. Latham and R. R. Scott, *Defining Productivity in Behavioral Terms,* (Tacoma, WA: Weyerhaeuser Company, 1975), pp. 13, 14.

through the development of a performance dimensions profile that would describe in behavior-relevant terms how these universally described dimensions would appear to an observer viewing an individual performing a specific dimension. The performance dimension profile would include a series of behaviors that would completely or adequately describe a range of behaviors from superior (or outstanding) to acceptable to completely unacceptable. The profiling of performance is further discussed in Chapter 6 in conjunction with the development of measurement instruments.

In 1949, in his work on improving the quality of performance dimensions, Flanagan identified an approach called the *critical incident technique* (CIT), which provides appraisal information based on actual job performance.[4] The CIT requires the systematic observation of actual job performance and behavior. These observations provide information that helps to identify and define *critical* job requirements. Flanagan defined such a requirement as a duty the jobholder must perform in order to be considered an effective (or successful) or an ineffective (or unsuccessful) job performer. (*Note:* Flanagan's definition of a duty is very similar to the definition of a responsibility as presented in this book.)

Flanagan recommended the following procedures for obtaining critical incident information:

Those individuals observing and reporting critical incidents are normally supervisors or associates of the employee involved in the incident. The incident must relate to an important aspect of the work and must describe an *actual* behavior "which is outstandingly effective or ineffective with respect to the specific situation." [5] Often, incidents are collected by asking supervisors or incumbents to think of the best and poorest employees they have known, then to think of the things these employees did that made them so good (effective) or so bad (ineffective). Then, based on this personal knowledge of the employees' work (i.e., observation), they write a description of the incidents.

The first output of the critical incident technique is the identification of incidents, which are identifiable, observable, and measurable behaviors that can be described in one sentence or a single paragraph. Information for writing the critical incidents may be gained through personal interviews, personal observation, a questionnaire, or any combination of the three. By analyzing all job activities, employees identify those behaviors that lead to job success or failure. From these lists of behaviors, specialists identify those that cover or fully describe a specific performance dimension. Behavioral analysts collect inci-

---

[4] Flanagan, "A New Approach," pp. 35–42.

[5] Flanagan, "A New Approach," p. 42.

dents; then, through the use of factor analysis, a statistical procedure, or some empirical approach, they analyze the incidents and group them with those having similar content in the more global performance dimensions. In the empirical approach, the analyst categorizes incidents that are related to each other or places them within a specific performance dimension. Frequently, a number of individuals who are familiar with the job duplicate the same approach and then compare their analyses. When there is disagreement on the placement of a particular incident, it is not accepted.

When supervisors or specialists review critical incidents for validation purposes, they answer questions such as the following:

1. How important is this incident in your unit of authority?
2. Is it observable to the degree that you can rate an employee on it?
3. Does it contribute to effective job performance?
4. Does each employee have a relatively equal on-the-job probability of demonstrating the described incident?

The acceptance or rejection of performance incidents depends on a review by two or more sets of qualified observers who are knowledgeable about the job and who are observing the same job behaviors. These raters must agree about the importance of the behavior and the frequency of its occurrence.

The identification, validation, and weighting process in the CIT may take the following approach:

Step 1: A group of jobholders and their supervisors identify performance incidents (job-related behavior) required in the performance of the job under review.

Step 2: A second group of jobholders (performing the same job) and their supervisors review the performance incidents and assess the degree of job relevancy of each incident. The resulting relevancy rating scale may take this form:

Relevancy Rating Scale	*(Lowest Number = Highest Relevancy Rating)*
1	Extremely relevant
2	Very relevant
3	Somewhat relevant
4	Irrelevant

Step 3. A third group reviews and analyzes relevant performance incidents, combining those that identify the same behavior or that are so similar as to be difficult for most people to perceive as being different. The performance incidents now become the performance elements.

Step 4. The elements are weighted as to their worth in the performance of the total job.

Step 5. A final review ensures that each identified, relevancy-scored, and weighted performance element ties directly to the performance dimensions of the job.

When performance appraisal instruments use a list of performance elements for describing a behavior-based performance dimension, the list of elements is called a *performance profile.* In Figure 6–2, the performance dimension is "training," and the groups of performance elements that describe various levels of the quality of training form a performance profile. This area is reviewed in greater detail in Chapter 6, which discusses the various procedures and approaches available for developing instruments useful for measuring performance.

Additional insights on how to implement and use the CIT are provided through the work of Gary P. Latham.[6] In a report, Latham and R. R. Scott identified three questions that must be answered to establish incident quality: [7]

1. What were the circumstances surrounding this incident? (Background or context)
2. What exactly did this individual do that was so effective or ineffective? (Observable behavior)
3. How is this incident an example of effective or ineffective behavior? ("So what?")

In one study, Latham and Scott interviewed 28 operators and five supervisors.[8] These 33 individuals were asked to think about the past six to 12 months and describe specific incidents that they had actually observed. Latham and Scott defined an effective behavior as one that the observer believed would contribute significantly to the accomplishment of the objective. Ineffective behavior, if occurring repeatedly

---

[6] Gary P. Latham and Kenneth N. Wexley, *Increasing Productivity Through Performance Appraisal* (Reading, MA: Addison Wesley, 1981), pp. 48–51.

[7] Latham and Scott, *Defining Productivity,* p. iv.

[8] Latham and Scott, *Defining Productivity,* p. 2.

or even once under certain conditions, would cast doubt on the competency of the individual performing the assignment.

A less rigorous procedure available for identifying critical incidents is to have experienced employees review a list of job responsibilities and identify examples of "good," "average," or "poor" behavior with respect to each responsibility.

Critical incidents relating to a specific job can be collected over time. They can be classified under more general categories that relate closely to major job performance requirements. These major categories are behavior-based performance dimensions.

As presented here, the critical incident technique provides an analysis of work that may best be titled *behavior analysis*. This title assists in differentiating the procedure from the more commonly used activity-based job analysis, which is described in Chapter 4. To be most effective, a behavior analysis should follow the completion of a successful job analysis. Another way of comparing job analysis and behavior analysis is that job analysis describes the *what* of the job, while behavior analysis further describes the *what* by identifying various ways or *how* the *what* is done.

TRAIT-BASED PERFORMANCE DIMENSIONS

The use of employee traits as dimensions of performance became part of the "world of work" with the advent of the "scientific management" movement at the turn of the century. Commonly used employee traits are those characteristics firmly anchored in human behavior—distinguishing qualities of character—that manifest themselves on the job and influence performance. Although there are literally hundreds of traits available for appraising performance, some of the most commonly used are:

Acceptance of responsibility	Courtesy	Judgment
Adaptability	Dependability	Leadership
Appearance	Effort	Loyalty
Application to duty	Honesty	Personality
Attendance	Industriousness	Punctuality
Attitude	Initiative	Resourcefulness
Conduct	Integrity	Self-control
Cooperation	Intelligence	Sincerity

The problem with these personal qualities or traits and a wide variety of others is that they often have little in common with job content and job performance. In addition, a rater can interpret them in almost any way desired. Even with care, human perception will vary significantly among individuals; and, when involved in the rating of employee performance, variations in rating because of differences in perception or understanding of the traits can destroy the validity of the program. Another weakness of all trait-rating instruments is that a high rating does not necessarily correlate with good job performance.

Traits have traditionally been the most common kind of performance dimensions used to appraise employees, because they universally relate to people doing all kinds of jobs. (How *well* they relate to actual job performance is the battle that rages over the use of traits.) Although trait-rating techniques have traditionally been accepted by management as being worthwhile indicators of performance, federal legislation and court rulings of the past 10 years have cast a dark shadow over their credibility. The integrity of trait-rating performance techniques and their ability to reflect actual performance have been questioned. There has been a minimal amount of success in validating a causal relationship between traits and performance. The many different ways that people interpret traits and the potential for bias have caused doubt about the worth and value of all trait-rating techniques.

Even with these serious and critical problems, the use of traits for the measurement of performance is certainly not dead. Traits that have a solid foundation in job content or workplace activities will continue to be invaluable for measuring employee performance. The use of traits will follow a process that starts with job-content analysis and moves forward into an investigation of appropriate and relevant job and workplace behaviors.

In most cases, relevant worker traits can be described in behavioral terms and, thus, can be converted into identifiable job-related behaviors. For example:

Honesty (trait). Employee can be trusted and does not steal, lie, or in any manner attempt to deceive.

Honesty (job-related behavior). Employee, entrusted with valuable technical information, maintained confidentiality when a competitor offered valuable inducements to divulge such information.

Honesty (job-related behavior). Employee does not use company property and materials for personal use.

Job-related behaviors that are trait-based can be identified and described in a manner that leaves little opportunity for perception problems or misunderstanding. They are extremely valuable in telling both the ratee and the rater what is acceptable and what is not acceptable behavior. The underlying concern must be that *the trait is job- or workplace-related.*

Traits and Organizational Values

Some experts in organizational behavior state that traits are still widely used in performance appraisal instruments because they recognize important organizational values. By using these trait-related dimensions for the measurement of behavior, management is kept informed as to how well the employee's values and related behaviors match the values deemed important by the organization. There is little doubt that a proper blending of organizational and employee values is critical to the successful operation of any organization.

If traits are used to measure employee values, this segment of the appraisal process should be clearly separated from job-content-related measurement; and raters, ratees, and reviewers should be able to recognize and differentiate among the various qualities being measured. There is a discussion at the end of Chapter 4 on non-position content-related factors that influence organizational productivity.

WEIGHTING OF PERFORMANCE DIMENSIONS

A step that must follow the identification and description of performance dimensions involves their ordering or weighting. Seldom are all job requirements of equal importance or value to the organization. If this is true, then the dimensions used to measure employee performance are also of different value. If performance dimensions are not ordered or weighted, it means that all items have the same value or worth. When it comes to the weighting of performance dimensions, another concern is that, from one rating period to another, the relative worth of performance dimensions may vary. To ensure the integrity of the measurement system, it is critical that the rater and ratee have a common understanding of which performance-related dimensions are most critical or considered most important at that time.

Jobs are complex because they are multidimensional and these dimensions vary in value from time to time. Organizational life works within constraints set by the limits on resources. Two of the most limited resources in organizations are the time and energy that each employee has to offer to the organization. To make best use of these limited employee time and energy resources, each person must know not only how to perform his or her job, but where and when to set time and energy priorities.

After determining the performance dimensions of a job, a measurement process must be established that permits the identification of the specific level or degree of performance that has been demonstrated by the ratee and observed by the rater with regard to a particular dimension. Establishing a scale of values starts with the development of performance standards.

PERFORMANCE STANDARDS

What is a standard? The dictionary describes a standard as a means of determining what a thing should be: a criterion, a gauge, a yardstick. Standards play an important part in all aspects of life. Moral and religious standards are a part of life, as are standards of beauty, honor, behavior, and so forth. It would be impossible to evaluate the worth of anything without first having something else with which to compare it.

Standards are vital to the success of any communication program, and a performance appraisal system is certainly one of the most critical communication programs in an organization. As previously mentioned, no word-based language system yet devised has been able to overcome human interpretation and perception differences. To minimize confusion and promote rational and logical understanding of words and terms, standards of measurement relating to all kinds of human activity have been developed. These standards of measurement provide a useful method for identifying differences of behavior.

Without standards of behavior, the "world of work" would never have reached its present level. In fact, with the ever-expanding division of labor and the interconnected and interchangeable systems and parts, standards are absolutely critical to an advancement in organizational productivity and to the life-style improvement of all people. Job-related standards provide a base for identifying, first of all, whether change has occurred and, second, how much change did occur. These standards act as reference points for estimating the relative value of employee workplace activities.

From the very term *performance appraisal,* it becomes readily apparent that standards must be an integral part of the process. Performance appraisal standards provide both the rater and ratee with a basis for describing work-related progress in a manner that is mutually understandable. In the complex, highly interactive and interdependent world of today, performance standards provide a degree of uniformity in the nonuniform world of work.

A basic performance measurement problem facing almost all organizations is the difficulty in making jobs uniform, which, in turn, makes it difficult to set standards. Performance standards that mean the same thing to at least the rater and ratee assist in establishing an understanding of job demands, job requirements, and job behaviors.

In the current work scene, performance standards only become useful when they are commonly understood and voluntarily acknowledged and accepted. Performance standards provide a mandatory guideline for work behavior or a minimum acceptable level of employee behavior; they state *how well* an assignment should be performed. Performance standards facilitate the trade between employee-provided availability, capabilities, and performance and employer-provided rewards.

Appraisals of performance are made continually, for example, "the most efficient secretary I've ever seen," "a top-flight manager," "a lousy report." These statements imply standards. In making them, mental judgments are also made, but it is not clear to anyone else what criteria were used in making these measurements. Such appraisals may be close to or wide of the mark, but there is no way to tell because the standard being applied is not evident.

Therefore, setting standards to measure performance is nothing new or unusual; the difference occurs in striving to be as objective and accurate as possible, in measuring the right things, and in documenting criteria for appraisal. The objective is to seek performance standards that are valid and useful in proving that the appraisal is accurate. The "right things" that performance standards should measure are results—the degree of accomplishment of specific, well defined work activities—and not such things as the character traits of the employee or how busy the employee appeared to be.

Performance Standard Characteristics

A set of performance standards describes the results that should exist upon the satisfactory completion of a job. A specific performance standard should have the following characteristics:

1. It should enable the user to differentiate between acceptable and unacceptable results.
2. It should present some challenge to the employee.
3. It should be realistic: attainable by any qualified, competent, and fully trained employee who has the necessary authority and resources.
4. It should be a statement of the conditions that will exist and will assist in measuring a job responsibility when it is performed acceptably and expressed in terms of quantity, quality, time, cost, effect obtained, manner of performance, or method of doing.
5. It should relate to or express a time frame for accomplishment.

6. It must be observable: there must be a means of measuring the performance against the requirements of the standards.

Criteria used for differentiating or measuring results use these five terms: *how much, how well, by when, how* or *in what way,* and *at what cost.* These five basic measurement terms are further identified by the terms: *quantity of output, quality of output, timeliness of output, effectiveness in use of resources, effects of effort, manner of performance,* and *methods of performing assignments.* Effects of effort, manner of performance, and methods of performing assignments are particularly valuable as qualitative standards when quantitative standards are unavailable or impractical.

When developing performance standards, quantitative measures may be identified through such statements as:

No more than (quantity or quality measures)

No less than (quantity or quality measures)

Within (a time measure)

By (a time measure)

No later than (a time measure)

At a cost of (resources actually consumed)

Quality of output (amount) is a standard that specifies how many work units must be completed within a specific period of time.

Example:

Conducts X surveys per Y period.

Quality of output describes "how well" or "how thoroughly" the result must be accomplished. It refers to accuracy, precision, appearance (beauty or elegance), usefulness, or effectiveness. It may be expressed as an error rate, such as the number or percentage of errors allowable per unit of work, or as general results to be achieved, or as the manner of accomplishing specified results (if numerical rates are impractical or unavailable).

Examples:

Not more than X customer complaints received in Y period.

X percent of reports submitted are accepted without revision.

Assignments completed in a _____ manner in view of _____ conditions.

Timeliness of output answers questions such as "when?" "how soon?" and "within what period?" In instances where definite quantity standards cannot be established, it may be possible to set time limits. Also, when work tends to fluctuate or when there are seasonal trends in the workload, a time per unit requirement may be a practical means of measurement.

Examples:

Proposed changes submitted X days before established deadline.

Suggestions evaluated within X days after receipt.

Effectiveness in use of resources may be used when performance can be assessed in terms of the amount of money saved, earned, or expended in the accomplishment of the work being performed; or as the quantity and quality of resources expended in accomplishing an assignment.

Example:

Travel costs will not exceed X percent of previous year's expenses.

Effects of effort is a measurement that may be used when the standard can be best expressed in terms of the ultimate effect to be obtained. In writing a standard of this type, phrases beginning with "so that," "in order that," "in order to," "as shown by," or "such that," are often used. This method of measurement can be used when results are not easily quantifiable.

Examples:

Decisions on supply needs made with sufficient accuracy in order that no supply item remains in short supply more than X days.

Reports are written clearly and accurately so that X percent are accepted without question.

Manner of performance is a measurement that is often helpful in establishing standards of performance for jobs in which personal contacts are an important factor, or when the employee's personal attitude, mannerisms, and behavior have an effect on performance. Standards of this type answer the question "in what manner?" or "how?"

Examples:

Speaks politely.

Attends work regularly and at specified times.

Assists other employees in the work unit in accomplishing assignments.

Improves interpersonal relationships among all members of the work unit.

Speaks clearly and with sufficient volume to be understood by persons attending briefing.

Methods of performing assignments is a measurement used when there is a legislative mandate, policy, standard procedure, method, regulation, or rule for accomplishing a task and when the use of other than the prescribed procedure is unacceptable.

Example:

Forms completed in accordance with office SOP. Deviations do not exceed X percent upon post audit.

Performance standards may be structured to measure different dimensions of performance; they also may be established on five different bases of measurement. Standards may be developed on the basis of history, characteristics, comparison, the specific objective of the work to be performed (sometimes referred to as an engineered standard), or negotiation.

Historical standards are based on results achieved in the past and are frequently set as a percentage higher or lower than results achieved for a previous period of the same duration.

Examples:

Rejects will be X percent fewer than last year.

The number of suggestions submitted by subordinates will be X percent greater than last year.

Basic characteristics identify certain features that establish an acceptable level of performance.

Example:

It works as it should, or it looks as it should.

Comparative standards are based on the performance or goals of other people or organizations.

Examples:

The number of awards granted to employees will be within guidelines established by the department.

Turnover rate will not exceed the overall rate for the division.

Engineered standards are stated as absolute requirements without comparison. These standards are developed under the expectation that everything goes as planned and that required resources are always available. These standards normally have both amount and time dimensions.

Examples:

Seventy-five units will be produced in 60 minutes.

Progress reports will be submitted by X date of each month.

Two weeks' inventory of supplies will be maintained at all times.

Negotiated standards are those in which the involved parties reach a compromise, recognizing requirements and the availability of resources.

Example:

If X resources are available and work is performed under Y conditions, Z results will be achieved.

Standards may be expressed in positive, negative, or zero (absolute) terms.

Positive standards state exactly what is wanted. The examples of engineered standards that are given here are stated in positive terms. A positive standard may also establish a requirement for an increase in something, for example, "The completion rate for processing vouchers will be increased by X percent."

Negative standards spell out what is not wanted or establish the requirement for a reduction in something. The standard referring to turnover, which was provided as an example of a comparative standard, is stated in negative terms. Another example is, "The accident rate will be decreased by X percent compared to the rate for the previous year."

FIGURE 5–2.
Standard Checklist Form

Basic Measurements	Additional Measurement Information
	Sources:
Quantity of output (How much?)	Historical (Past)
Quality of output (How thorough? How well?)	Basic characteristics (Looks or works like it should)
Timeliness of output (By when?)	Comparative (How done by others?)
Effectiveness in the use of resources (Amount of money saved, earned, or expended)	Engineered (Absolute requirements)
Effects of effort (So that; in order that)	Negotiated (Reached through agreement)
	Specified Levels:
Manner of performance (Personal attitudes or mannerisms)	Positive (Exactly what is wanted)
Method of performing assignment (Practices, etc.)	Negative (What is not wanted or a reduction)
	Zero (Nothing is to occur)

Zero, or absolute, standards tell when nothing is to happen. For example, "There will be no complaints from any source about telephone courtesy," or "There will be no deviation from the procedures manual." Zero standards should only be used when there is no possible alternative, because they mandate nothing less than perfection and deprive the employee of the opportunity to exceed expectations. Figure 5–2 identifies measurement information to be used as a checklist for establishing standards.

Developing Performance Standards

Now that the purpose, characteristics, dimensions of measurement and kinds of standards have been explored, it is time to consider the development of performance standards.

Performance standards can be established for all jobs. While it is true that specific quantitative standards are more easily established for routine, repetitive, production-type jobs, written standards can also be established for scientific and technical, professional, supervisory, and managerial jobs. It is important to remember that the major concern is with measuring results: the results expected from a job have been identified, as have its major responsibilities and performance dimensions. A job responsibility will normally be measured by more than one performance dimension. Typically, each duty can be transformed into a performance dimension.

The first step in developing performance standards is to ask questions. Taking each job responsibility and the duties supporting it, questions such as "What are the indicators of success for this responsibility?" "How soon or by when?" and "At what cost?" should be asked. The answers to questions such as these will help in focusing on the measurable aspects of the responsibility and the specific performance dimensions by which it can be measured. They will also help to identify the level of accomplishment required.

Performance standards should be established for each performance dimension. The number of standards necessary depends on how many different measurements (e.g., quantity, quality, time, etc.) are required to adequately define performance expectations. It is possible that some performance dimensions might be adequately covered by one standard. However, in many cases, it will be necessary to establish more than one standard for each dimension to adequately define performance expectations.

As stated previously, the characteristics of standards should be realistic and attainable and should present a challenge to the employee. In other words, the standards should describe the *fully acceptable* level of performance. Acceptable does not mean mediocre or average; it means a level of performance that will fully satisfy the supervisor's expectations and allow for successful accomplishment of that portion of the goals of the work unit for which the job in question is responsible. If standards are set too low, productivity will suffer and employees will lack a challenge in their work. If standards are set too high, most employees will continually fall short, eventually quit trying, and appear unacceptable or weak in any accurate application of the standards.

In establishing the acceptable level of performance to be indicated by a standard, it is sometimes advantageous to use a range of performance. (For example, "Processes 25 to 30 claims per week," rather than "Processes 27 claims per week," or "Costs will be reduced by 3 to 5 percent," rather than "Costs will be reduced by 4 percent.") A range of acceptable accomplishment is important where fluctuations in workload cannot be strictly controlled or where factors beyond the control of the employee may influence the level of productivity.

Standards should also measure performance in as many ways (e.g., quantity, quality, time, cost, etc.) as are necessary and appropriate to describe acceptable accomplishment adequately. For example, "Performance will be acceptable when X number of vouchers (quantity) are processed per week (time) with no more than Y number returned because of errors in calculation (quality)."

It is important to establish standards so that the level of accomplishment required can be measured and documented. Words such as "rarely," "seldom," "accurately," "reasonable," and so forth may appear to describe a performance level, but they leave a lot to personal interpretation. How frequent is "rarely" or "seldom"? A supervisor may think that they mean not more than one or two times a year, while the subordinate may think that these words mean 10 to 15 times a year.

Also, the use of percentages can sometimes cause problems. An accuracy rate of 90 to 95 percent may sound very high, but the nature of the work and the volume being measured might cause the percentage to be unrealistically low. Whenever possible, it is better to use the actual numbers of units being measured.

When establishing standards, it is necessary to ask, "How am I going to measure this? How easy/difficult will it be to keep track of?" "Do I have a recordkeeping system that already provides this information, or will I have to establish a new one?" At first glance, "Typing will be 95 percent error-free" may appear to be a reasonable standard, but what does the figure refer to—the number of letters without errors or the number of errors per letter? In either case, the supervisor would have to spend an inordinate amount of time counting and recording with such a standard. A standard such as "Not more than X number of letters returned for correction of typographical errors during Y period" would provide a measurement of accuracy (quality) but would require much less effort to count and record.

Because of the unique qualities of a job, performance standards should be written for each job, or possibly position, but not for a class of jobs. For example, identical performance standards cannot be written for all clerk-typist jobs. One clerk-typist may work primarily with statistical reports and charts, while another may prepare correspondence on a day-to-day basis. Only when several positions are very similar or identical in responsibilities; duties; knowledge, skills, abilities (KSAs); and working conditions may a single set of standards be established that will be equally valid for all positions.

When developing standards for identical positions, caution should be exercised in using the average performance of the group as the level of acceptable performance. The present performance of the group may be above or below the appropriate level of acceptability. Remember, standards should be geared to the responsibilities and expected results for the position. The need for the involvement of the employee in the development of performance standards is critical. By participating in setting the standards for one's own position, an employee is more likely to feel that the standards are fair and will more readily accept a personal responsibility for meeting them. The supervisor may draft the standards and then present them to the incumbent for review and comment, or the supervisor may ask the incumbent to develop the initial draft and work from that. Another method is to have the supervisor and the incumbent sit down together and draft standards jointly. However it is done, mutual effort toward commonly agreed-upon and understood standards is vital.

Setting standards should be a continuing process. It is unreasonable to expect to achieve perfection, particularly when first starting to work with standards. They may have to be written and rewritten many times before both supervisor and incumbents are satisfied with them. In addition, standards must be rewritten whenever significant changes are made in the organizational plans and goals or work-unit functions that directly impact the responsibilities of an individual position. When first starting out, it is far better to accept a less-than-perfect standard, if the supervisor and incumbent understand it, than it is to keep plugging away until effort becomes boring. There will be time and opportunity in the future to make the standard more precise and workable. Of course, at the end of the appraisal period, during the formal appraisal interview, the supervisor and incumbent should jointly review the standards to see whether or not changes are necessary to make them current for the next appraisal period.

Just as realistic, measurable, communicated, and understood performance standards will result in benefits to the supervisor and the incumbent, so will they enhance organizational productivity that is directly related to mission accomplishment.

INDUSTRIAL-ENGINEERING-BASED PERFORMANCE STANDARDS

In the latter part of the nineteenth century and the early years of the twentieth century, F. W. Taylor and his colleagues, who investigated the world of work from an industrial engineering perspective, focused their attention on the quality and quantity of output resulting from a worker's efforts. They developed methods, techniques, and procedures for generating job-related data and information and for establishing performance standards that are both valid and useful for identifying job competency and performance effectiveness. The basic criteria that must be met when establishing engineered performance standards are:

1. Standards must be consistent; that is, a standard must recognize similar employee inputs by providing similar employee outputs. (Similar work effort and contributions by employees performing

similar assignments should result in comparable performance appraisal ratings.)

2. Standards must be fair. Those whose performance is measured against a standard should be willing to accept the standard as being just and reasonable.

Industrial engineers continue to study jobs to find ways to standardize, simplify, and specialize work procedures and to establish performance standards. Among the various methods found useful are time and motion studies, micromotion analysis, and work measurement. Each method not only provides engineers with a better understanding of the job and the ways in which to make it easier for a worker, but also increases the overall productivity of the worker and the work group. These methods require a careful, detailed analysis of work requirements and usually have as their major goals finding a best way to do the job, determining what should constitute a fair day's work, and setting performance standards that provide fair pay for work performed.

Each of these methods was developed primarily for industrial applications and involves jobs having observable and measurable manual labor inputs. Because of the costliness of these methods, they are normally used for jobs having routine and repetitive activities. They all provide work standards that come from an analysis of job content. They are not, however, free of subjectivity, and all require skill in the method being used. Both a strength and weakness of work measurement is that each job standard requires an individual analysis, which is time-consuming and thus costly.

Time and Motion Study

In this oldest and simplest of the three methods, an analyst makes a time study by closely watching a worker and using a stopwatch to time performance. Most studies include a detailed analysis of each work element. These studies relate each element to the normal time required for the entire work cycle.

A time and motion study provides data on the time required of a "normal" worker to perform a specific operation. A "normal" worker refers to a qualified, experienced employee performing at an average pace while working under the conditions that usually prevail at the work station.

Time-study analysts must have an understanding of the job and be able to develop a harmonious relationship with the employees being studied. They must also possess skill in rating workers (establishing the degree to which the employee being studied performs better or worse than a "normal" worker).

Micromotion Analysis

A more sophisticated approach than time and motion study is micromotion analysis, which requires photographing a worker performing a job. The camera operates at a constant speed, usually 1,000 frames per minute. By studying the film, the analyst can determine work patterns for each part of the body. By studying each movement and counting the number of frames necessary to document a complete cycle of work, a work-methods analyst is able to determine acceptable methods and set standards. Using this approach, Frank and Lillian Gilbreth [9] established basic elements or fundamental human manual motions that proved most valuable for analyzing physical work relationships.

Work Measurement

Following the work of the Gilbreths, time-study engineers devised methods for combining standard time value with each basic work element. By assigning time values to these fundamental motions, engineers are able to work in a laboratory, to synthesize the motions necessary to perform an assignment, and to set a time standard for the work under study. Some of the better known synthetic time systems are Methods-Time Measurement (MTM), Work Measurement, Basic Motion Time-Study (BMT), and Dimensional Motion Times (DMT).

LIMITS TO INDUSTRIAL ENGINEERED STANDARDS

Output-based performance standards continue to be extremely valuable, but a major barrier to their use has developed over the past 30 years. This barrier involves the movement away from the heavy emphasis on physical effort involving eyes, hands, body, and feet coordination and dexterity, as required in the typical manufacturing environment of the early to middle twentieth century, to an emphasis on thinking, focusing, and interpersonal contacts that are so much a part of the job requirements in the service-related environment of the last half of the twentieth century.

The output of a worker in the traditional manufacturing environment is more amenable to counting and to quality measurement than

---

[9] F. B. Gilbreth, *Motion Study* (Princeton, NJ: Van Nostrand, 1911).

is the output of a worker in a service-related environment. Many of the physical requirements in the service world are performed by machines. The workers who service the machines and other workers who design machines or design and manage processes that combine the machines and human effort perform more knowledge-specialized tasks than their predecessors did a generation or two in the past; that is, the high degree of specialization is based on knowledge rather than on physical skills and dexterity. This change in worker requirements directly influences the measurement of performance. It is still possible to measure output but it is neither necessary nor possible within cost restrictions to do so for each incumbent. The knowledge-based specialization requires the interaction of a number of individuals, and the quality of each person's performance is difficult (if not almost impossible, at times) to observe and measure. In analyzing the performance of an individual in a manufacturing environment, it is possible for the analyst to identify the fundamental motions required to perform a specific activity. The analyst can then measure the speed at which these motions are performed and actually check the quality of the resulting output. In many service jobs, the fundamental motions of the incumbent involve actions within the individual's brain and are completely hidden from the view of the analyst. Even the quality of the work is extremely difficult to observe at the conclusion of a particular activity. The measurement of the results of the performance of one person may require an extended period of time and the interaction of a number of people to provide a final output that is observable and measurable. This is the major reason for the shift in emphasis to activity and behavior in the latter part of the twentieth century in contrast to the measurement of specific output that dominated the first half of the twentieth century.

Although the amount and quality of output have become more difficult to observe and measure, this does not mean that output-based performance standards are not being used. Whenever appropriate and applicable, industrial engineering work-methods studies are still found to be extremely useful. Time studies involving the actual observation of a work situation or synthetic studies resulting in the reconstruction of a specific activity are still valuable for identifying desired levels of output.

FLEXIBLE STANDARDS

Many employees have little or no opportunity for making inputs into the design and setting of the standards that they must meet when performing their work assignments. The design of their jobs permits them few, if any, decisions on what they do, when they do it, how they do it, how much they produce, and the quality of their output.

Their job activities are a mandate, and the standards of performance for their jobs are predetermined. Job outputs are limited by the inputs from others, the available technology, the resources provided, and the outputs demanded by the next party in the process.

In these cases, the incumbent does what he or she is told. However, supervisors may find it advantageous to explain why the standards are what they are and how the employees' efforts influence the efforts and contributions of those who follow in the process. Figure 5-3, Job Flexibility, describes the three boundaries that limit employee performance.

More and more people are performing assignments in which they have some degree of autonomy in what they do and when they do it. This latitude in the performance of job assignments, in turn, influences the upper limits of the outputs to be produced. For all jobs, there is a lower or base limit as to what is an acceptable level of output, but for many jobs the incumbent establishes the upper limit. When an employee has the opportunity to vary the upper limits of the output, performance goals become a critical part of standard setting and the performance review and rating process.

Performance Goals

Performance goals identify and define desired, measurable output that exceeds established minimum acceptable levels of performance. Performance goals become an important part of the appraisal process when incumbents have opportunities to significantly improve the use of available resources by the decisions they make concerning what they do and how and when they do it. In these cases, individual knowledge and skills, efforts, and interests play a critical role in the results achieved. Performance goals are valuable when incumbents can work at several different levels of acceptable performance. Although performance goals are standards, rather than being arbitrarily established they are frequently set in a participative mode. In this process, the incumbent and supervisor interact in establishing and defining desired or expected outcomes. Although the participative process was described at some length in Chapter 3, a brief summary of the process will further clarify what happens.

To be meaningful and useful to the incumbent, supervisor, and organization, everyone involved in setting performance goals must know (a) the goals of the work unit, (b) the activities that must be performed in completing job assignments, (c) the minimum acceptable levels of performance, (d) the priorities, if any, in the performance of assignments and the concentration of effort, and (e) the resources

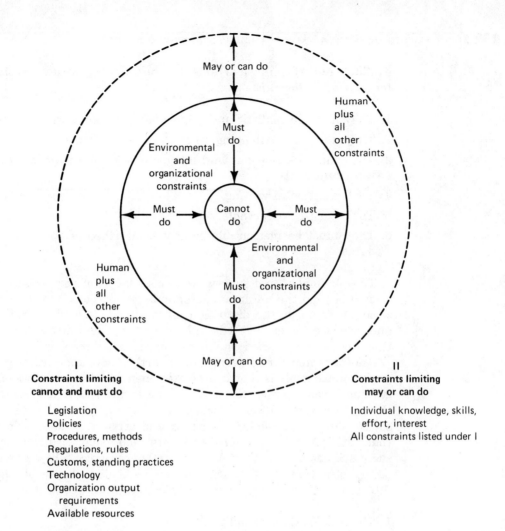

FIGURE 5–3. Job Flexibility.

I
**Constraints limiting
cannot and must do**

Legislation
Policies
Procedures, methods
Regulations, rules
Customs, standing practices
Technology
Organization output
   requirements
Available resources

II
**Constraints limiting
may or can do**

Individual knowledge, skills,
   effort, interest
All constraints listed under I

151

available in performing assignments. The following are desired characteristics of performance goals:

1. They must be realistic and achievable (attainable with effort).
2. They must be challenging, to stretch the performer.
3. They must be relevant and integrate with other incumbent and work-unit goals.
4. They must be in writing.
5. They must be observable.
6. They must be measurable against established performance standards.

The incumbent and supervisor discuss levels of performance that stretch beyond the minimum acceptable levels. To be more than just so much rhetoric, the discussion must include resource availability and priorities where effort is to be directed. The desired outcome of this process is to exceed established minimum standards.

Another important outcome of the participative approach to setting performance goals is that it promotes open and frank discussions regarding level of importance. When the incumbent is achieving less than a satisfactory level of performance, both incumbent and supervisor consider all possible reasons for and attempt to identify actions that both can take to improve the situation. They also can identify success areas and make sure both parties recognize why success has occurred so that these actions can be replicated (if possible) in the future. In this manner, the communication process identifies:

1. The actions that should be continued.
2. The actions that need improvement.
3. The actions that must be discontinued.

Setting Performance Goals. The position description and in particular its position definition section play a critical role in the setting of performance goals. The incumbent and supervisor review the existing position description. After making sure that it is current, complete, and accurate, they review all responsibilities and duties to identify any responsibility and duty or group of responsibilities and duties that are currently having the greatest impact on the successful accomplishment of the goals of the work unit or of the organization.

This review should enable both parties to identify where attention should be focused. Once again, this review should underline the importance of knowing the goals of the work unit and the responsibilities and duties of the position.

Performance goals may also be set in areas that relate to incumbent development. Emphasis in areas that improve or broaden the incumbent's knowledge base and skill levels should benefit both the incumbent and the organization.

A major reason for using performance goals is that they not only facilitate but also promote the use of the innovative talents of the incumbent. Problems are constantly arising that block the achievement of individual and work-unit goals. The performance-goal process brings problem solving to the bargaining table. The incumbent not only knows what the job requires, as set forth in the job definition, but is also permitted to identify results that can be achieved, given certain kinds of provided support (one very basic support may simply be "Stay off my back"). Through this kind of problem solving, the incumbent has made a significant input into overcoming unsatisfactory results or achieving improvement.

Setting performance standards is a time-consuming process, but it is a critical part of establishing a work relationship between the supervisor and subordinate that identifies what is to be done and then states the results expected. Through the use of performance standards, personnel practices benefit by improving:

USING PERFORMANCE STANDARDS

1. Selection of the job candidates.
2. Employee orientation.
3. Probationary reviews.
4. Recognition of training needs and the design of training programs.
5. Identification of the kind and extent of deserved recognition.
6. Identification of the kind and extent of disciplinary practices.
7. Recognition of job hazards and safe working procedures.

In addition, job-based planning benefits by improving:

1. Work simplification practices.
2. Work-unit planning.
3. Identification of budget requirements.
4. Recognition of changes in job requirements or assignments.
5. Cost consciousness.
6. The validity of performance ratings.

Chapter 6

Designing Performance Measurement Procedures and Instruments

No part of the performance appraisal system has demanded more attention than the design of measurement processes and rating instruments. To some people, performance appraisal is nothing more than an instrument, a sheet of paper—it may be simply a blank sheet of paper or it may be an extremely complex, preprinted form. To many involved in the appraisal of performance, the program is essentially the completion of the form and nothing more. The efforts of many professionals in the field tend to reinforce such a view. Research in the area of performance appraisal indicates an almost obsessive interest in the design of performance appraisal rating instruments. Many individuals responsible for the design and operation of a performance appraisal program frequently search for the "golden grail"—a universal rating process and instrument that will provide one basic document that leads to the valid rating of all employees in the organization.

It is time to examine the measurement procedures and instruments that have been recommended and are now being used and the options that are available to those who must develop a performance appraisal program for a specific organization with its own unique requirements. Researchers and designers have developed a wide variety of appraisal instruments, some of which go considerably beyond the conventional kind of instrument that consists of a set of simple rating scales on which to rate a number of dimensions or aspects of performance. The most sophisticated, from a psychological or psychometric perspective, is a newly-designed technique developed by Jeffrey S. Kane called Performance Distribution Assessment. Other sophisticated procedures are the forced-choice and mixed-standard rating scale instruments. The design of measurement processes also involves ranking employees in comparison with other employees or distributing employee ratings in some kind of distribution curve (e.g., normal or bell-shaped distributions).

155

In the past two decades, measurement that compares results that are achieved against performance goals has become widely used, and it is not uncommon for organizations to require some kind of a narrative or essay completed by supervisors or staff specialists that describes the employee's performance for a certain period of time. The narrative review may be part of a comprehensive form that includes checklists and recognition of goal accomplishment. However, with all of the work and effort expended in the design of performance appraisal instruments, improvement in the measurement process has in no way kept pace with organizational demands for accurate ratings. New instruments have led to the further hiding of the truth and game playing that, in turn, results in unsatisfactory or invalid performance ratings.

Depending on the particular desired outputs and uses of the performance appraisal program, one kind of instrument may be more appropriate than another. The instrument for recording the rater's views may range from a blank sheet of paper to forms that require the design efforts of skilled psychologists and psychometricians. The instrument design may use such performance dimensions as job-related responsibilities and duties, employee behaviors, traits, and desired results. Depending on design considerations and performance criteria, the scales used for measurement may have intervals identified by numbers, adjectives, or behaviors, or there may be no scale visible to the rater at all. These descriptive anchors may occur only at the terminal points of a scale, or they may assist in describing three, four, five, seven, even ten intervals. Some forms may only require that the most suitable interval response be checked or that a point be marked on an unbroken continuum, while others may use extended narratives. (The approach using a blank sheet of paper may require the rater to describe the performance of the ratee for a specific time period and to identify accomplishments and actions demonstrated in achieving them.) Instruments may permit, even require, ratees to respond to the report of the rater or simply to sign the form and acknowledge that an appraisal has occurred. The instrument may also require a review by higher levels of management. To many people, this is performance appraisal. To those who discuss validating performance appraisal, it is difficult to conceive that they view performance appraisal as anything more than an instrument, the inferences made, and the procedures relating directly to its completion.

To assist in determining the most appropriate measurement procedures and forms for an organization, it may be valuable to first develop answers to the following questions. Responses and an analysis of the procedures and available instrument options will provide a most useful insight into the direction that the organization should take at this phase of the process.

1. What uses will the organization make of the rating data and information? Chapter 7 discusses this topic in detail.

DESIGN ISSUES TO BE CONSIDERED

2. What does the organization wish to measure?

3. Which kind of instrument or combination of instruments best provides meaningful and useful distinctions among individual performances over specified periods of time?

4. What degree of psychometric precision is possible considering the procedures to be used and the dimensions to be measured?

5. What kind of measurement distributions does the organization require?

6. Which instruments are most appropriate for which groups of raters?

7. How will the reliability and validity of the instrument be determined, and how will related issues be resolved?

8. Should specific procedures and instruments be designed for specific occupations, work units, or levels or major groups of employees within the organization?

9. Is it possible to standardize rating scores when using different procedures and instruments?

10. Is it possible or worthwhile to use the global criterion—overall performance—to provide a standard measure of performance?

11. What adverse or undesired effect may occur because of the use of a specific rating procedure or instrument?

12. How much time and effort should be required on the part of the rater in completing the forms? How capable are the raters in performing rating assignments?

13. Should the performance appraisal system be developed in-house, or should outside consultants be used?

14. What kinds of check and balance programs could be implemented to ensure that raters are doing their jobs properly?

15. Are the costs incurred worth the benefits derived?

Before investigating the various kinds of procedures and instruments used to measure employee performance, it will be useful to review briefly the process of measurement. Measurement is the assignment of numbers or words to items or events to describe differences. To be useful, measurement information must be descriptive, unambiguous, and objective. In the processes discussed here, scales are used for measurement purposes. There are basically four different kinds of measurements or scales used to describe differences. They are listed

MEASURING PERFORMANCE

in order from least to most rigorous. Each succeeding scale includes all qualities of the preceding scale.

1. *Nominal scales* permit the classifying or sorting of differences through the use of specific numerals. Examples are a person's Social Security number, number on a football jersey, and identification of male = 1 or female = 2. Developing a nominal scale requires that (a) items or events be categorized and (b) the number of items or events within each category be counted and a specific number assigned to each item or event. Each identified item or event is a mutually exclusive subset. No arithmetic operation can be performed, but mode and median measures of central tendency can be used.

2. *Ordinal scales* sort differences among items or events on the basis of the relative amounts of some characteristic that they possess. This scale permits the ranking of each item or event with respect to some criterion. Although this scale provides a hierarchical ordering, it does *not* provide information on the absolute magnitude of items or events or on the magnitude of the differences between them. An example is an ordering of employees within a work unit by level of performance—first, second, third, and so on. Developing an ordinal scale requires (a) determining the criteria (i.e., what standards will be used to categorize and rank), (b) categorizing items or events, (c) counting the number of items or events in each category, and (d) ranking the items or events according to the criterion.

3. *Interval scales* provide information where differences between measurements have meaning. They involve the assignment of numbers to items or events in such a way that any given difference between the numbers reflects a constant amount of difference on the scaling criterion, regardless of the region of the scale in which the difference occurs. The point here is that the numbers actually used to anchor a scale do not have to differ by a constant amount as exemplified by the scale values of BARS/BES scale anchors. An interval scale has an arbitrary zero (the zero can be located anywhere on the scale). For example, in an interval scale, the scores of 10, 20, 30, 40, and 50 respectively identify items A, B, C, D, and E. They tell a reviewer that the difference between A and B (10 and 20) is the same as the difference between D and E (40 and 50). It does not, however, permit the reviewer to state that since D is 40 and B is 20 D has twice as much of the quality under discussion as B, because a base, or zero point, has not been established.

4. *Ratio scales* are the purest form of all scales. A ratio scale requires the use of an absolute or true zero or origin point, and all numbers on the scale can be used to form meaningful ratios. This means that the numbers can be used for multiplication and division purposes. For example, Individual "A" weighs 120 pounds and Individual "B" weighs 240 pounds, and it is correct to state that "A" weighs one-half as much as "B":

$$\frac{120}{240} = \frac{1}{2}.$$

This procedure is possible because there is a true zero or origin point—weightlessness—zero weight.

Barriers to Effective Use of Scales

A major problem with the proper use of any kind of a rating scale, or for that matter any rating instrument, concerns the amount of accurate information available to raters to precisely measure ratee on-the-job behaviors and accomplished results. This problem can further be described by these three issues:

1. Variations in demonstrated performance. Most workers over a given period of time will exhibit various levels of behavior relative to a general characteristic or job requirement.
2. Extraneous influences on demonstrated performance. The behaviors and more importantly the results achieved by many workers are strongly influenced by factors over which they may have little or no control.
3. Excessive demands on the know-how of raters. The level of rater discrimination is established not only by what is observable, but, also by what it is that the observer is actually seeing. Is the observer able to see and understand all of the forces that influence the behaviors and the results that are obtained? Is the level of discrimination accurate enough to make the inferential leap from the observations to a specific interval on a rating scale that provides a precise rating score?

If problems involving observation are not sufficient in themselves to block the selection of the most appropriate interval on a scale, the descriptions used for defining the intervals on a scale are seldom of sufficient precision to assist raters in making the proper selection.

Organizations use a wide variety of procedures and instruments to rate the performance of their employees. The process may be one that does not require the rater to complete any kind of a rating instrument. The rater may simply be requested to rank subordinate employees or participate in a round-table discussion with peer supervisors to rank-order all subordinates. In this case, supervisors may use their mental images to determine and support a specific ranking. The only measurement "instrument" that is used may be the writing of names of the ratees on a sheet of paper in order of overall successful job performance, contribution, or some other specified criterion.

One set of procedures that must be developed in conjunction with the design of measurement instruments concerns the specific rating score to be given to each employee. Will the employee be rated relative to a performance criterion and to a series of performance criteria—performance dimensions that reflect the multidimensionality of work and performance? In addition, will the employee be given some kind of ranking relative to other employees? If an organization requires a rater to rank subordinates, the following techniques will be helpful to those doing the ranking.

Simple or Straight Ranking

The simplest, least costly, and possibly one of the more accurate appraisal techniques (especially in small groups in which the rater intimately knows each member) is the simple or straight ranking technique, which provides an ordinal scoring—first, second, third, and so on. This technique requires the rater (normally the immediate supervisor) to rank from best to poorest all members of a work unit or workers performing the same job. The strength of ranking lies in the fact that the human ability to discriminate improves when comparing (ranking) one item with another. Its basic weakness is that many ranking techniques use a minimum number of performance dimensions, thus oversimplifying an extremely complex phenomenon—employee job performance. It is possible to convert rank or ordinal scores to interval scores through various statistical procedures.

Simple or straight ranking normally appraises employees relative to one factor, such as overall performance or effectiveness. This appraisal method gives very good results when raters are familiar with the members of their work units, have intimate knowledge of the job and employee inputs and outputs, and are able to suppress biases related to personality differences and to focus on work behavior. The straight ranking method can provide a high degree of interrater reliability (different raters giving the same results). A major problem, however, is that rankings are difficult to justify to those ranked, especially those who fall in the bottom half of the rated group. This type of ranking results in a zero-sum game, meaning that somebody wins and somebody loses. Since a basic intent of the entire process is to improve the performance of the organization, a zero-sum game is neither desirable nor valid. The goal is to allow everyone to be a winner. This is possible when performance appraisal leads to improved productivity. In this situation, most members gain increased rewards, including satisfactory recognition of performance. The negative aspects of a zero-sum game can be somewhat modified by permitting ties to occur. Allowing a rater to rank two or more ratees equally—granting ties—is called *unforced ranking*. Conversely, when ties are not allowed, it is a *forced ranking*.

Research indicates that practically *all* employees consider their own performance to be average or above average.[1] Thus, from an employee's point of view, a below average ranking is unacceptable and, in most cases, is considered unjustified. Ranking can stimulate intragroup hostility, resulting in lowered productivity and more worker dissatisfaction. Ranking is weak when comparing the members of one group to those of another. A relatively low-ranked employee in a high-performing unit may be superior to a highly ranked employee in an average or moderately performing work unit. Within the same unit, there may be a considerable difference between the workers ranked fourth over fifth, whereas workers ranked seventh, eighth, and ninth may be essentially equal performers.

Forced-Distribution Ranking

A slight variation of the straight-ranking method is forced distribution. This method requires the rater to allocate a certain percentage of work-group members to certain categories, such as superior, above average, average, below average, and unacceptable performance. The distribution of employees to be placed in each category usually approximates the bell-shaped curve or normal distribution. Five percent fall in each of the top and bottom categories, 15 percent in each of the next two, and 60 percent in the middle category (see Figure 6–1). Both the number of categories and the percentage of employees to be allocated to each can vary according to the design considerations of a specific organization.

---

[1] Herbert H. Meyer, "Self-Appraisal of Job Performance," *Personnel Psychology,* Summer 1980, pp. 291–295.

FIGURE 6–1.
Distribution of Employees with Forced-Ranking Method

Categories of Performance	Percentage of Employees to Be Allocated
Superior	5
Above Average	15
Average	60
Below Average	15
Unacceptable	5
	100 percent

It is certainly possible to observe and measure the performance of a group of employees in a particular work unit and then assign one-third to the top group, one-third to the middle, and one-third to the bottom. A problem arises, however, when merging incumbents in various work units into one overall ranking for the larger unit. Obtaining accurate relative standings in the merged ranking is extremely difficult. The merger of rankings of different work units by different raters may not accurately reflect relative standings between members of the different groups. If, for example, the bottom third of one work unit are performing acceptably and are, in fact, more productive than the middle third of another work unit, a merger based on the distribution of each work unit may be incorrect and unacceptable. In addition, when doing this kind of merged ranking, each rater must defend his or her rankings. This leads to either extreme cases of politicking or the exhibition of defensiveness and hostility that, in turn, make it extremely difficult to perform the merger with any degree of accuracy. These personal-bias, subjective issues, in fact, corrupt all kinds of rankings.

Paired-Comparison Procedures

A number of paired-comparison procedures are available for ranking employees. They include the deck-of-cards, stub selection, paired-comparison ranking table, card-stacking, and alternation ranking procedures.

The Deck-of-Cards Procedure. One of the simplest yet most effective of the paired-comparison procedures used for ranking a group of items is the deck-of-cards procedure. In this procedure, the rater:

1. Places each name or item to be compared on a separate card and into a pile.

2. Chooses two cards from the pile, compares them, and selects the best.

3. Holds the best in his or her hand and discards the loser into a new pile.

4. Selects another card from the first pile, compares it with card in hand, chooses the best, and discards the loser in the new pile.

5. Continues with this step, until the original pile has been depleted.

6. Places the card in his or her hand in a second new pile. This is the top selection.

7. Repeats all steps, using the first new pile as the replacement for the original pile for the eventual second choice.

8. Continues the process until all remaining names have been placed in the pile with his or her first choice. This gives the ranking for the group.

An additional step that may be included in this process to exclude rating bias is to perform the entire process a second time. Beginning in Step 2, the rater identifies the lowest or least important item and then builds to the highest by always returning to the pile that item rated higher. This reversal process should provide the same order of rank. Any discrepancy becomes an area for further investigation.

The Stub Selection Procedure. The stub selection procedure attempts to overcome two basic weaknesses of other paired-comparison procedures: (a) the inability of the human brain to store and compare a large variety of items (in fact, it is difficult for most brains to compare more than five items at one time), and (b) the "halo effect" (i.e., once an item is judged to be superior to a number of items, it begins to carry an inborn superiority over items that follow.) In the stub selection procedure, the name or item on each stub represents the name or item to be compared. In this case, the name or item circled represents a specific choice. The rater:

1. Cuts out the stubs.

2. Circles the selected item or name on each stub (the circled item is considered a vote).

3. Makes a pile for each circled item.

4. Counts the stubs in each pile upon completion of all comparisons.

The pile with the largest number of stubs is the highest ranking item, the next largest number is second, and so on. The lowest ranking item is the one that received the fewest votes.

The Paired-Comparison Ranking Table. An adaptation of the stub selection procedure is to develop a matrix in which all the items to be compared are listed in both the rows and the columns of a table known as a paired-comparison ranking table. In the boxes formed by the intersection of the rows and columns, the appraiser places an "X" where the item in the row is more important or valuable (or some other characteristic) than the item in the column. The item receiving the highest score (i.e., number of "X"s) is the most important or valuable or possesses some characteristic considered to be of more worth than the item in the column. Figure 6–2 gives an example of a paired-comparison ranking table when different jobs are being compared.

The Card-Stacking Procedure. In the card-stacking procedure, the rater receives a deck of cards. Each card contains the name of one employee who is an immediate subordinate.

1. The rater is asked to make three stacks. Stack 1 contains the cards of all employees who are above-average performers. Stack 2 contains the cards of all employees who are average or acceptable performers. Stack 3 contains the cards of all employees who are marginal, below average, or unacceptable performers.

2. The rater counts the number of cards in each stack to see whether there are 30 percent in the above average stack and 30 percent in the below average stack. If Stack 1 contains more than 30 percent, the rater must identify the least-effective performer(s) of this stack and place them in Stack 2 until Stack 1 contains only 30 percent. Then Stack 3 must be checked for the 30 percent quota and the same process performed. If Stack 3 contains more than 30 percent, the excess is placed in Stack 2. If Stack 3 (or Stack 1) contains less than 30 percent, then the rater takes the best performers of Stack 2 and places them in Stack 1 or takes the poorest performers of Stack 2 and places them in Stack 3. Upon completion of Step 2, 30 percent of the employees will be in the above-average stack, 40 percent in the average stack, and 30 percent in the below-average stack.

3. The final step is to review Stacks 1 and 3 and place one-third of each stack (the best performers of the above-average group and the poorest performers of the below-average group) into separate stacks. There are now five stacks, containing the superior 10 percent, the above-average 20 percent, the average 40 percent, the below-average 20 percent, and the least effective or poorest 10 percent. Each stack of employees can be rated using the paired-comparison, deck-of-cards procedure to give a final ranking of all employees.

FIGURE 6-2.

Paired-comparison Ranking Table

Rows \ Columns	Mes-senger	Data Proc. Mgr.	Data Entry Opr.	Exec. Sec.	Com-puter Opr.	Sys. Anal.	Con-trol Clk.	Pro-gram-mer	File Clk.	Asst. Dir.	Total
Messenger	—										0
Data Processing Manager	X	—	X	X	X	X	X	X	X	X	9
Data Entry Operator	X		—						X		2
Executive Secretary	X		X	—	X		X	X	X		6
Computer Operator	X		X		—		X		X		4
Systems Analyst	X		X	X	X	—	X	X	X		7
Control Clerk	X		X				—		X		3
Programmer	X		X		X		X	—	X		5
File Clerk	X								—		1
Assistant Director	X		X	X	X	X	X	X	X	—	8

Paired comparison is unwieldy when one is comparing large numbers of items, as shown by the following formula. This formula determines the number of comparisons to be made for a given number of comparison items:

$$\frac{N(N-1)}{2}, \text{ where } N = \text{the number of comparison items}$$

For example:

$$\text{Comparing 7 factors, } \frac{7(7-1)}{2} = 21 \text{ comparisons}$$

$$\text{Comparing 15 jobs, } \frac{15(15-1)}{2} = 105 \text{ comparisons}$$

Note: In this example, the approximate doubling of the number of factors to be compared increases the number of comparisons by a multiple of five.

The Alternation Ranking Procedure. Another available paired-comparison technique is alternation ranking. In alternation ranking, the rater has a list of all employees to be ranked. The first selection is the employee whom the rater considers to be the best performer. The name of this employee is placed on the first line of a sheet of paper that has numbered lines, one for each employee to be ranked. The rater then strikes the ranked employee from the list. The second selection is the employee considered to be the lowest rated performer; this employee's name is placed at the bottom of the list and is also crossed out of the original list. The third employee ranked is the highest re-

FIGURE 6–3.
Alternation Ranking List

	Order of Selection
1 Highest rated employee	first
2 Next highest rated employee	third
3 Next highest rated employee	fifth
.	
. etc.	etc.
.	
18 Next lowest rated employee	sixth
19 Next lowest rated employee	fourth
20 Lowest rated employee	second

maining in the original list; fourth is the lowest rated remaining employee, whose name is placed on the rank-ordered list and stricken from the original list. This process continues until all unit members are ranked.

An alternation ranking list with 20 employees to be ranked is shown in Figure 6–3.

Just as with any paired-comparison technique, if the rating is to be accurate, the rater must know the factors or characteristics to be rated and the people being rated.

Over the years, a wide variety of instruments have been designed to assist raters in documenting and rating employee workplace performance. With the passage of the Civil Rights Act of 1964 and the identification of performance appraisal as a test by the Equal Employment Opportunity Commission (EEOC), considerable attention was focused on the potentially adverse impact on protected groups by performance appraisal programs. By the mid 1970s, the commonly used traits that were a part of so many performance appraisal plans were under considerable attack by the federal courts and the EEOC. Therefore, more attention has been given to the development of appraisal systems that focus on aspects of job performance other than universal traits. For example, performance measurement and rating instruments may now include (a) a narrative descriptive review (it is possible, however, that the statements used in a narrative review can reflect or describe specific traits); (b) a checklist of performance dimensions that include job-related responsibilities and duties, demonstrated behaviors, and job-related traits; (c) performance dimensions and rating scales; and (d) goal setting/results achieved.

Designers of performance appraisal instruments attempt to minimize rater errors by limiting vagueness or ambiguity with regard to specific performance dimensions through the use of understandable and recognizable descriptions. Well written descriptions of performance dimensions will assist raters in correlating observed behaviors and results with appropriate ratings. However, good rater judgment will always be required.

PERFORMANCE MEASUREMENT AND RATING INSTRUMENTS

Narrative Descriptive Review Procedures

Over the years, the constant search for new and better ways to appraise performance has led to the development of a number of performance appraisal methods using narrative descriptive reviews. These include the essay, critical incident, and field review methods. Each of these methods requires the rater to provide a written description of the employee's performance. As mentioned earlier, any instrument, method, or process dependent on rater-provided written information becomes suspect because of an unwillingness to put anything into writing, the time required, and the variability in writing skills.

If a specific rating score is to be an output of any of the narrative methods, it may be necessary to establish a set of standards that converts sets of actions or behaviors to a specific score. Establishing these narrative standards is quite difficult and may be of limited value. However, some kind of a measurement system must be established to match a narrative description of an employee's performance to a specific rating score. Because of the difficulty involved in developing useful and valid standards, these methods are frequently avoided.

The Essay Method. In the essay method, the rater must describe the employee within a number of broad categories, such as (a) the rater's overall impression of the employee's performance, (b) the promotability of the employee, (c) the jobs that the employee is now able or qualified to perform, (d) the strengths and weaknesses of the employee, and (e) the training and development assistance required by the employee. Although this method may be used independently, it is most frequently found in combination with others. It is extremely useful in filling information gaps about the employee that often occur in the more highly structured checklist method.

The strength of the essay method depends on the writing skills and analytical ability of the rater. However, many raters have writing difficulties; they become confused about what to say, how much they should state, and the depth of the narrative. The essay method can consume much time because the rater must collect the information necessary to develop the essay and then must write it. The essay method also depends on the strength of recall by the rater.

A problem arising with this method is that raters may be rated on the quality of the appraisals that they give. The quality standards for the appraisal may be unduly influenced by appearance and grammar rather than content. Thus, a "high quality" appraisal may provide little useful information about the performance of the ratee.

The Critical Incident Technique (CIT). The critical incident technique (described in Chapter 5) requires the rater to maintain a log, containing observations of what the supervisor considers to be successful and unsuccessful work behavior, on each employee. This method demands continuous and relatively close observation. Many employees consider this type of constant surveillance a threat that is damaging to workplace relationships. The time elapsing between the observed behavior and its description has a definite impact on the accuracy of the description of what occurred. Here again, recall ability strongly influences the accuracy and validity of the review.

An example of a positive critical incident is:

4/18 Employee demonstrated a broad range of job knowledge in uncovering the cause of a quality problem with product "A" that Quality Assurance had been working with for over a month.

An example of a negative critical incident is:

7/28 Employee responded impulsively and with little tact when employee "Z" refused to work overtime in order to complete a prior assignment.

Like the essay method, the critical incident technique is time-consuming, costly, and requires that the rater have good analytical and verbal skills and the ability to provide straightforward, honest, accurate written descriptions. A rater who is an extremely competent writer and analyst may provide an impression to those reviewing the description that can unfairly bias the review either in favor of or against the ratee. This is not to imply that competent writing skills are undesirable, but simply that good writers have an advantage using these methods.

Supervisors involved in identifying and describing critical incidents often find the maintenance of a log to be excessively burdensome. Moreover, when supervisors are not given any structure for developing critical incidents, their observations may reflect their own idiosyncrasies. This, in turn, allows free rein to the supervisor's biases.

Although the critical incident technique was designed to overcome subjectivity, it may have little effect in reducing rater bias. Raters hesitate to describe an event that they consider to be detrimental to a particular individual or that possibly casts a doubt on their own managerial skills or makes them look bad. They may also tend to be inconsistent; for example, they may attack one individual by blowing a situation completely out of proportion and then protect another individual by deciding that the demonstrated workplace behavior is not worth the time and effort it takes to describe it. This kind of rater behavior can negatively influence the value of any kind of rating instrument or procedure.

Workers frequently develop anxiety and hostility when they know that their supervisor is keeping a log on them. To protect themselves, they may hide their actions and keep information from their supervisor that, if known, could lead to a poor performance rating. On the other hand, knowing that the supervisor is keeping a log could lead to performance improvement.

The critical incident technique is valuable in that it focuses on actual job behavior, not on impressions of ambiguous traits. Although the incidents do not lend themselves to quantification, they can be very useful when the rater counsels the employee or provides feedback on performance. The most valuable contribution of this method to the performance appraisal process is the likelihood of increased defensibility of appraisal ratings because of documentation of critical behaviors.

The adverse impact of a rater's documenting ratee behavior may be somewhat reduced by formalizing the process and requesting that all employees document the behaviors that they feel are worthy of future recognition. This process can be reinforced by giving all employees a form (see Figure 10–3 on page 327) that permits them to maintain files on their own demonstrated behaviors. It is unlikely that there will be any poor or unacceptable behaviors in a ratee's files, but, at least, recordkeeping is a two-way process, and the maintenance of a "black book" is formally open to *all* employees—raters and ratees alike.

The Field Review Method. In the field review method, the rater, normally a representative of the personnel department, a staff member of the specific work unit, or an outside consultant, interviews the employee's immediate supervisor and others who have observed or have knowledge of the employee's work. Based on their responses to a series of questions, the rater rates the employee. This method does not use standardized forms or rating factors, but, typically, a rater will follow some preconceived plan to collect and document the rating information. Following the completion of the documentation process, the rater provides a simple "outstanding," "satisfactory," or "unsatisfactory" rating.

Raters making field reviews normally receive training on how to conduct the interview and have developed their writing skills. Being independent of the work scene, they normally have less bias for or against the ratee than does the immediate supervisor. Even when a supervisor or others supply biased information, the rater may be able to pinpoint areas requiring training and development assistance. Requiring the use of an additional person in the process increases the cost of the appraisal, but it may focus greater attention on the process by both the immediate supervisor and those conducting the interviews.

The Checklist

Two major kinds of checklists used for rating performance that differ by the kinds of data they provide are classified under the general headings of preferential choice/proximity and preferential choice/dominance.

The Simple Checklist. This method, which is an example of the preferential choice/proximity kind, uses a list of job requirements, behaviors, or traits. These lists may include from 15 to 50 different items. The rater reviews the lists and checks those indicators that best identify the performance of the employee being rated. When making a selection using this kind of checklist, the rater makes a preferential choice that most closely describes a demonstrated workplace activity of the ratee. Some typical checklist items in the forms of behaviors are:

1. Maintains systematic and orderly records.
2. Instructs new employees in a manner that encourages learning.
3. Provides clear and detailed instructions to subordinates.
4. Uses company property only for business-related use.

The Weighted Checklist. The weighted checklist method adds a degree of sophistication by assigning a weight to each item, thus permitting the development of possibly a more accurate rating score. Normally, experts trained in testing and evaluation procedures review the items and, by using various psychological and statistical procedures and considering job analysis data, weight the items and assign a numerical value to each.

"Sophisticated" Checklist. Instruments using "sophisticated" checklists have been designed by psychologists and psychometricians to minimize rater fudging of scores. These "sophisticated" checklists are those classified as preferential choice/dominance. Two major examples are the forced-choice checklist and the mixed standard scale. When making a selection using a sophisticated checklist, the rater makes a preferential choice of a dominant, demonstrated workplace activity of a ratee. These checklists include lists of acceptable and unacceptable traits or behaviors that require the rater to make selections that best describe a ratee from among a list of what appears to be comparable items that actually have different psychologically-based weights. Rater responses are scored, based on the predetermined value for each item selected.

The *forced-choice checklist* involves combining checklist items into groups containing between two and five statements. There may be as many as 50 groups from which the rater makes selections. The design of the groups is usually such that each item appears to have equal desirability or to be of equivalent value. However, the items differ in that they distinguish between the more and the less successful performer.

The ability to discriminate rests on the fact that employees demonstrate a wide variety of behaviors in performing job assignments. Some behaviors are acceptable; others are unacceptable. Some acceptable behaviors relate directly to high-quality performance, whereas other acceptable behaviors have little or no impact on the quality of performance. On the other hand, some unacceptable behaviors relate directly to poor performance, whereas other unacceptable behaviors that may be distasteful to some raters have little or no influence on job performance.

In using the forced-choice checklist, the rater selects the one item that best identifies the workplace behavior of the ratee. In cases where the group includes from three to five characteristics, the rater may be asked to select the item that best describes the performance of the ratee and also the item that is least descriptive.

A simple forced-choice selection may require a rater to choose between the words *energetic* and *trustworthy*. Since both words refer to socially acceptable characteristics, it is considered difficult, if not impossible, for the rater to make a selection that has an intent other than to provide the most accurate description of the ratee. A more complex forced-choice selection requires a rater to select from a list of statements those most descriptive and least descriptive of the employee's behavior. For example, a list may be set up as shown in Figure 6–4.

Upon completion of a forced-choice checklist, the items selected as most and least descriptive (when requested) are grouped together. From these final groupings, "index of discrimination" and "index of desirability" scores are developed; these scores purport to identify the degree of successful job performance. (*Discrimination* refers to the ability of the rating technique to differentiate the effective from the ineffective employee; *desirability* refers to the degree to which the quality is valued.)

The major goal of the checklist technique is to minimize bias. In theory, the rater acts as a recorder of observed behavior, not as a judge. In this manner, he or she will not demonstrate typical patterns of rater bias. In reality, however, individual perceptions of actual behavior are still an unresolved issue.

FIGURE 6–4.
Forced-Choice Checklist

Most Descriptive	Least Descriptive	Item
☐	☐	Reviews work of subordinates and provides assistance as needed.
☐	☐	Follows up on all delegated assignments to ensure conformance with operating procedures.
☐	☐	Requests employee opinions and uses them when conditions permit.
☐	☐	Meets deadlines on work assignments.
☐	☐	Praises those whose workplace behavior has earned recognition.

The development of a weighted checklist and, to a far greater degree, a forced-choice checklist requires the effort of skilled professionals. Such checklists are extremely costly to design. Raters are also very leery of using any system in which they do not know the final determinations of their efforts and the effect that their ratings will have on the future of their subordinates (whether for pay adjustments or future career opportunities). The evidence available at this time does not indicate that the forced-choice method provides more accurate measurements of employee performance. This method also provides little opportunity for identifying areas of employee improvement or for assisting through employee counseling.

One relatively simple way for a rater to neutralize a psychologically derived appraisal technique is first to consider which employee qualities or behaviors contribute the most to output quality. Using this standard, the rater analyzes each item in the checklist and identifies those that correspond to high levels of performance. The rater then selects those items on the list that provide the kind of rating desired. For this reason, research on various kinds of checklists and rating scales indicates that the simple instruments provide ratings that are as accurate as the more complex instruments.

The *mixed standard scale* is a unique kind of preferential choice/dominance method in that it involves the use of a single stimulus in selecting one of three points on a rating scale to rate a dominant activity. Similar to the forced-choice, the mixed standard scale includes a list of possible employee behaviors, but instead of asking a rater to identify which behaviors are most descriptive and least descriptive of the ratee, the rater must now rate each listed behavior relative to a three-point rating scale. (Rating scales are described in detail immediately following this section.) The mixed standard scale was designed to minimize halo effect and leniency errors. This scale consists of three statements that describe good, average, and poor performance relative to each identified dimension (trait or behavior). The design of the measurement instrument requires that the statements be grouped together in random order. Friedrich Blanz and Edwin E. Ghiselli developed an instrument using 18 traits.[2] The Blanz and Ghiselli example has a list of 54 statements (18 traits × 3 statements for each trait). A rater then treats each statement independently of all the other statements and rates the employee relative to the statement. A "+" indicates that the ratee performs better than the description; a "O" means that the ratee fits the statement; and a "−" indicates that the ratee performs more poorly than the statement.

The relatively large number of statements—in the example, 54—and their random order minimize the chance that the rater will identify the designed order-of-merit of each set of descriptors. This in turn reduces the opportunity for the rater to rate the statements with regard to their designed order rather than honestly relating the statement to the ratee's demonstrated workplace behavior. This type of scale permits a 1- to 7-point score for each dimension or trait being rated (see Figure 6–5).

The following example provides three statements that describe a good, an average, and a poor level of performance relative to the performance dimension, "Ensures Effective Crew Training," as described in Figure 6–7.

I. *Good performance statement:* Looks for more efficient training methods and uses them.

II. *Average performance statement:* Has crew fully trained for normal job functions and an adequate back-up for all jobs.

III. *Poor performance statement:* Ignores training procedures and does not have trained back-up on key jobs.

[2] Friedrich Blanz and Edwin E. Ghiselli, "The Mixed Standard Scale: A New Rating System," *Personnel Psychology,* Summer 1972, pp. 185–199.

FIGURE 6–5.
Scoring Process for a Mixed Standard Scale

*I**	*II**	*III**	*Point*
+	+	+	7
0	+	+	6
−	+	+	5
−	0	+	4
−	−	+	3
−	−	0	2
−	−	−	1

* Roman numerals represent three statements used to identify levels of performance relative to a specific performance dimension.

The mixed standard scale requires a detailed job analysis to identify the basic or primary activities of each job. Supervisors of those intimately familiar with the job are then asked to recall critical incidents that provide examples of good and poor job behaviors. Behaviors further identified as critical job behaviors are then related to the previously identified job activities. The behaviors are again scored on a scale, e.g., 1 to 7, or 1 to 9, with 1 representing a very poor performance behavior and the highest value representing a very good behavior. From this list, the three statements for each activity or dimension are identified.

This approach for collecting scale development information is similar to the critical incident technique described in Chapter 5 and to the method used for collecting behavior information for developing behavioral anchored rating scales described later in this chapter.

Performance Dimensions

The first step in developing measurement instruments using performance dimensions and rating scales (often called graphic rating scales) is the identification of the requisite performance dimensions that adequately cover the activities of the job(s) under review.

Recognizing the multidimensionality of work, it is easy to understand the need for identifying and describing performance dimensions that permit a review and rating of total performance. To minimize problems of deficiency, contamination, and distortion, it is critical that (a) there are sufficient performance dimensions to cover all job requirements or behaviors essential to job success, (b) all dimensions that are irrelevant to successful performance be excluded, (c) dimensions are weighted to reflect the value of each dimension with regard to overall successful job performance, and (d) dimensions are properly defined. In developing a list of performance dimensions for inclusion with rating scales, the instrument designer must always be ready and able to answer these two questions: What do I want to measure? and Is this the best way I have available for describing this item?

A listing of performance dimensions must also consider their ordering and arrangement. Thought must be given not only to the influence that the dimensions have on each other but, also to how the actual order of the items may bias rater perception and, possibly, the rating itself. The same concern applies in developing checklists. The three major kinds of performance dimensions that appear as the items to be rated are responsibilities and duties, job-related behaviors, and traits. A brief review of these performance dimensions follows.

The *job responsibilities and duties* listed on the job description can be used as basic appraisal criteria. Using these job-based activities requires a separate appraisal form for each job. The appraisal form may only list the responsibilities or it may include both responsibilities and duties as the performance dimensions for identifying how well the jobholder has performed. Responsibility and duty appraisal forms may also include space for the rater to indicate the relative importance of each requirement. Chapter 4 discusses in detail how to identify and describe job responsibilities and duties.

Government intrusion into the area of personnel practices in the 1960s and 1970s intensified interest in the development of appraisal instruments that have a firm foundation in both job content and demonstrated *job behaviors*. Chapter 5 describes how the critical incident technique (CIT) can be used to identify job behaviors. Later in this chapter, there is a further discussion of this technique as it is used to establish behavioral anchored rating scales (BARS).

Although *traits* were under fire throughout the 1970s, it is not yet time to eliminate them completely as performance dimensions. As discussed in Chapters 4 and 5, traits can still be most useful, but they must be workplace effective or job content-related and described in such a manner that they minimize the opportunity for subjective rater bias. Duty statements or descriptions of behaviors that have actually been demonstrated by the employee while performing the job can reflect traits.

To better understand why traits continue to appear in performance appraisal instruments or to be reflected within performance dimension statements, it is necessary to consider organizational values. For example, such performance dimensions as cooperation, dependability, and integrity identify traits that may be qualities highly valued by the organization. These qualities cross all jobs at all levels within an organization. When such qualities have a universal appeal or accurately reflect organizational values, senior management will frequently require rating information on these dimensions. The issue to be resolved is proper and understandable descriptions of these qualities, as discussed in Chapter 4.

Rating Scale Design and Development

After identifying the criteria (performance dimensions) to be used to rate employee performance, the time arrives to develop useful and valid rating scales. The ideal or most useful rating scale is one that allows ratio scoring, although an interval scoring scale would normally be acceptable. Many rating instruments appear to be of an interval scale design and actually use the scales as if they were interval scales, but the appearance is deceiving, and their use may not be proper.

Interval-Ordinal Problem. In the coming pages, there are descriptions of various kinds of scales that look like interval scales. Each specific interval of the scale is identified by a different number or adjective, adjective phrase, or behavioral statement, which, in turn, also have assigned numbers. In most cases, however, these scales are truly ordinal in design. For example, a specific dimension—quality of work—has five interval points on the scale. The interval points may be described by "1," "2," "3," "4," and "5," or such words as "unacceptable," "needs improvement," "acceptable," "above average," and "superior," which are then numbered 1 to 5. If the scale were truly an interval scale, then the difference between the rating score of "4" and "5" would be the same as the difference between a rating score of "2" and "3."

In most cases, scale differences cannot be truly quantified in this manner. From the overall perspective of scale design, however, most designers and users completely ignore this problem and use scales that are actually ordinal in design as if they were interval scales. In review, if a scale is truly interval, the differences between adjacent intervals must be identical in value. If they are identical scores, they may be validly added or subtracted. A ratio scale permits such mathematical operations, but it may not always be possible to develop such a scale. When the rating instrument uses an ordinal scale, the adding of scores given for the different performance dimensions on a rating instrument do not provide a sum score that reflects a true difference in performance. However, ordinal rating scales are treated as if they were interval or even ratio scales, and numerical values derived from the summing of these scales are considered acceptable.

Discussions about the appropriate use of ordinal scales frequently fall back on a statement made by a recognized expert in measurement.

In 1946, S. S. Stevens of Harvard University stated, "Any particular scale, sensory or physical, may be objected to on the grounds of bias, low precision, restricted generality, and other factors, but the objector should remember that these are relative and practical matters and that no scale used by mortals is perfectly free of their taint." [3]

As stressed from the early pages of this book, performance appraisal must be orderly, procedural, and reasonable. Above all, it must be systematic. Performance appraisal must provide data and information that are practical. To be practical, the data and information must be period-oriented, must have a carry-over effect, and must be cumulative.

There are very definite limits to describing and, above all, rating human performance. The process of translating objective demonstrated behaviors—actions—into specific rating scores involves establishing a linkage (at some point) with the subjective value system of one or more individuals designated to represent the interests of the organization. Performance appraisal will never completely escape these subjective influences.

In developing scales that can capture the true intensity or feelings of a rater, ordinal rating scales will most often be the best available measurement device.

Although, strictly speaking, ordinal rating data do not lend themselves to addition or subtraction, measurement experts seem to agree that the adding or subtracting of data from ordinal rating scales is not improper. However, adding two or more ordinal scales becomes tenuous if the performance dimensions are unweighted. The argument in favor of using ordinal data for performance rating purposes takes this course:

1. Performance appraisal is an inevitable organizational action.
2. Organizations must do the best they can with the tools they have.
3. Rating scores must be meaningful. (This is a far more critical issue than whether or not it is appropriate to add ordinal scale values.)
4. Scale intervals must reflect the intensity or true feelings of the rater.
5. Rating scores can be interpreted and translated for useful organizational purposes. (Score interpretation may be the most important issue of instrument design and use.)

---

[3] S. S. Stevens, "On the Theory of Scales of Measurement," *Science,* Vol. 130, No. 27, 1946, p. 180.

In using ordinal data, the following concerns must also be recognized. Since ordinal scales do not provide the kind of data necessary to establish a normal or parametric distribution, nonparametric statistical procedures may be required to analyze the data. This means that parametric measures such as standard deviation, Pearson's correlation, and means may not be appropriate, while medians, percentiles, and quartiles would be appropriate. However, many measurement experts state that nonparametric distributions can be viewed as being parametric in nature. This means that statistical procedures used for describing a parametric distribution can, for all practical purposes, also be used in describing nonparametric distributions. Significant amounts of distortion are always a major concern in using ordinal scales. This means that the comparison of ranking or ratings among work units (employees in different groups rated by different supervisors) must be done with extreme care. Because there are few practical options available to organizations in the area of measurement and scale design, *care* must be demonstrated through these kinds of performance appraisal actions:

1. Complete and current descriptions of job content (job definition as described in Chapter 4).
2. Accurate identification and description of performance dimensions and performance standards (see Chapter 5).
3. Development of scales that permit the most accurate reflection of actual behaviors.
4. High probability that a higher-rated person is truly a better performer.

Through these kinds of actions, all involved in the measurement process can recognize and come to an agreement on the procedures to be used that will eventually lead to the assignment of a number that indicates a specific level of performance. This kind of an orderly process minimizes opportunities for manipulating numbers and permits all involved in the rating to have some voice in the processes that lead to the rating.

Other Problems in Designing Rating Scales. In addition to the interval-ordinal problem, other issues have caused considerable concern to those involved in designing rating instruments that accurately reflect the performance demonstrated by those being rated. A major problem any rater faces when using a measurement instrument consisting of performance dimensions and adjacent rating scales is that the ratee may have demonstrated behavior that relates to more than one interval on the rating scale. In fact, it is not unusual for an employee to perform in a manner that relates to a number of scale intervals. A rater, from available observations, must select an interval (score) that best describes the overall performance of the ratee relative to the specific performance dimension for that period. It is here that the rater's observation opportunities, observation skills, and biases come together to form one specific selection. This final rating decision is a judgment made from available information. Opportunities for subjective judgments for or against the ratee are widely prevalent.

An additional problem concerns the description of each interval in the rating scale, whether it be interval or ordinal. Often, descriptive information is not sufficient to permit a rater to discriminate among the ratees according to their observed and demonstrated performances. This problem is often identified as a failure of the raters to use the full extent of the measurement scale made available. The problem, however, may be that with the intervals and their descriptions and the opportunities available for rating, the instrument was used as validly as possible by the rater.

It is not difficult to either identify or rate the performance of the superior and unacceptable employee. It is difficult to assess differences among the 70 to 90 percent that frequently comprise the undifferentiated middle. The well designed instrument is one that facilitates a difference in rating scores that is as broad as the different levels of observable performance. The failure to provide rating scores that discriminate among the middle 80 percent or so frequently forces higher levels of management to require that their subordinate managers rank-order all subordinates against the universal criterion—overall performance.

Still another problem that has defied solution with respect to rating instrument and scale design has been the ease with which a rater can give a fake or false rating. If a rater consciously wishes to fake a rating or give an unfair rating decision, no rating instrument yet designed is capable of stopping such undesirable behavior. It is unlikely that any rating instrument will be able to solve this problem. Scaling techniques, such as BARS or the psychologically designed forced-choice and mixed standard scale, however, will minimize subconscious efforts to fake a rating, as will a requirement that each rating be documented or supported by comments describing direct observations of performance.

The desired strengths of practically all rating scale techniques are that they (a) be relatively easy to administer, (b) translate directly to quantitative terms, (c) permit standardization, thus allowing for comparability across various organizational lines (departments, functions, occupations, jobs),[4] and (d) relate to various kinds of qualities or performance dimensions.

Number of Rating Scales. George Miller's work on the processing of information and the magical number 7 plus or minus 2 also applies to scale design.[5] Miller recognized that there are severe limits to the capacity of the short-term memory. He concluded that the short-term memory is used primarily for identifying lists of unconnected events. (In the world of the rater, these unconnected events would be the level of demonstrated behaviors of ratees.) Short-term memory not only uses few items for measurement but also operates on a "push-down" principle for retrieving information stored in the human brain (Last-In, First-Out is an example of the "push-down" principle).

Miller theorized that most people can work concurrently with five to nine different items of information when making decisions. The more different items with which an individual works concurrently and the more input information required for analysis and discrimination purposes, the greater is the likelihood of making errors. When rating the level of performance relative to one variable—for example, quantity of work—it is possible to misidentify or inconsistently rate the overall level of demonstrated performance.

Over the years, Miller and other researchers have noted that individual short-term perceptual and memory abilities normally permit discrimination of about seven levels. Most people can work with at least five levels. Using less than five may unduly restrict an individual's ability to discriminate, and the results will not be as consistent as they should be. Using more than nine levels may result in an individual making discriminations that are too fine.

From his own research and that of others, Miller concluded that individuals possess finite, rather small capacities for making unidimensional judgments. An underlying reason for this characteristic is that human survival depends on the ability to adapt to ever-changing environmental conditions. Such adaptability requires a small amount of information about a lot of things. Raters acquire relatively small amounts of information about a significant number of different perfor-

---

[4] Some experts involved in the design and the psychometric qualities of performance appraisal rating instruments strongly feel that most appraisal instruments that use rating scales cannot validly produce standardized scores. If their concerns are correct, this means that it is not appropriate to use rating scores to compare levels of performance of employees in different jobs or work settings.

[5] George A. Miller, "The Magical Number Seven Plus or Minus Two: Some Limits On Our Capacity For Processing Information," *The Psychological Review,* March, 1956, pp. 81–97.

mance dimensions, which restricts their ability to precisely identify levels of performance.

A useful number of intervals on a scale to measure a specific dimension of performance can follow the directives emanating from Miller's research. Rating instruments must provide sufficient measurement criteria and useful measurement scales to model reality—the actual demonstrated behavior of the employee.

Performance measurement depends primarily on observation. Most appraisal observations rely on transient information, which is developed in real time (the here and now) and involves short but specific spans of attention and uses short-term memory.

Short-term memory involves concept identification. In concept identification, an individual learns to identify specific dimensions through learning and to select the most appropriate level of performance of that dimension when facing a specific stimulus. The appraiser is normally involved in complex situations with a short time to make observations. To be effective under such conditions, he or she must learn to classify stimuli. Most individuals can learn to respond almost perfectly to a reasonable number of previously learned and classified stimuli.

To achieve an acceptable degree of precision or provide an adequate distribution of scores, rating scales must have an adequate number of intervals. When there are few intervals (fewer than five), there is a good chance that the scale omits valid measures of performance. When the scale contains too many intervals (normally, more than nine), the descriptors are repetitious and make it very difficult for a rater to distinguish between interval points.

Weber's law of "just perceptible differences" is also valuable for understanding how many intervals to use on a rating scale. Weber's law resulted from investigations conducted in the early nineteenth century by Ernst H. Weber (1795–1878).[6] It states, "The increase of a stimulus necessary to produce an increase of sensation in any sense is not an absolute quantity but depends on the proportion which the increase bears to the immediate preceding stimulus." Thus, the small perceptible difference in two objects is not absolutely the same but remains relatively the same; that is, it remains the same fraction (percentage) of the preceding stimulus. For example, if we can distinguish between 16 and 17 ounces, we should be able to distinguish between 32 and 34 ounces, but not necessarily between 32 and 33.

Later in the nineteenth century, Gustav Fechner continued to work in this area and laid the groundwork for an area of study now called *psychophysics*. Psychophysics investigates the relationships between the magnitude of physical qualities and the magnitude of the corre-

---

[6] Encyclopaedia Britannica: Micropaedia Vol. X. 15th edition (Chicago, IL: Encyclopaedia Britannica, Inc., 1974), p. 593.

sponding subjective considerations. Current investigations now focus on complex situations in which there is no simple relationship between the stimulus as physically measured and the observer's judgment. This area of study may be extremely useful for the design and development of performance appraisal instruments.

In the 1940s, Edward N. Hay conducted a series of studies based on Weber's law. He noted that a 15 percent or approximately one-seventh difference in the importance of one factor as compared with the preceding factor was discernible by trained raters at least 75 percent of the time.[7] This 15 percent difference provides a valuable criterion for a variety of uses when just observable magnitudes of difference are a basic input. In review, it appears that there must be at least a 15 percent difference between any two objects or factors in the compensation-reward area before they have a workable recognition or discrimination value. Although Hay's work may be more appropriate for understanding the ability of judges to weight performance dimensions than it is for determining the number of intervals for scale design, the work of Hay and Miller may help in clarifying why raters have so many problems discriminating among the majority of employees who form the large undifferentiated middle in the area of performance.

To fully understand the importance of the works of Weber, Fechner, and Hay, the more recent efforts of Nobel prize winner Herbert A. Simon may help in tying these intellectual processes together. In his study of master chess players, Simon noted that a master could remember somewhere around 50,000 patterns, while a good chess player could remember only 2,000 patterns.[8] In any case, the number of patterns remembered is buried in the deep recesses of long-term memory, which far exceeds the short-term capacity of the brain. Therefore, performance appraisal instrument designers should provide conceptual patterns (e.g., descriptions of performance dimensions, location of performance dimensions on a performance appraisal instrument, different kinds of instruments, etc.) that are sufficiently consistent and relevant to various kinds of demonstrated behaviors so that they can be stored successfully in the long-term memory and then be recalled and properly matched with the few significant pieces of data picked up and stored in the short-term memory.

Odd or Even Numbers of Intervals. With rating scales, the issue of *odd* and *even* numbers of interval points also arises. When an odd number is used, raters are inclined to use the average or central tendency value. This is not necessarily unacceptable because most employ-

[7] Edward N. Hay, "The Application of Weber's Law to Job Evaluation Estimates," *Journal of Applied Psychology,* 34 (1950), 102–104.

[8] Herbert A. Simon, "Information Processing Models of Cognition," *Annual Review of Psychology,* Vol. 30 (Palo Alto, Calif.: Annual Reviews, 1979), p. 383.

FIGURE 6–6.
Obtaining An Average Score With Even Number Intervals

Performance Dimensions	Rating Scale
P.D. #1	1 ②　3　4
P.D. #2	1　2 ③ 4
P.D. #3	1 ② 3　4
P.D. #4	1　2　3 ④
P.D. #5	1 ② 3　4
Subtotal	6　3　4

$$\frac{\text{Total}}{5 \text{ (number of P.D.s)}} = \frac{13}{5} = 2.6 \text{ (average value} = 2.5)$$

ees do behave in an average manner, but all too often the rater uses a mid-value for rating a quality in order to escape making a decision. An even number of interval scales does not permit the rater to use an average value; rather, it forces a decision that differentiates among the large group in the middle—slightly above or slightly below average.

Even when using an even number of interval scales, a rater can provide an average rating by randomly selecting scores for the available performance dimensions that will result in the final score being average or in the middle of the potential rating distribution. For example, a performance appraisal instrument has five performance dimensions each with a four-interval rating scale. The average score is 2.5. The rater could provide a score close to 2.5 by selecting a rating for each performance dimension in the manner shown in Figure 6–6.

Rating Scale Descriptions. Rating scales use numbers, words, or phrases as labels to identify the degree or level of quality demonstrated. Each point on a rating scale must be meaningfully different. Although identification points on a scale can vary from two to more than fifteen, a scale of values that is applicable to most performance appraisal instruments ranges from five to nine. A warning to those using scales with numerical, even adjectival, interval descriptors: They provide an illusion of precision. It is not always easy to measure performance with the degree of precision that appears to be provided by the rating scale.

The typical appraisal instrument that uses a rating scale lists or describes a particular performance-related quality (e.g., job behavior, job duty, employee trait) and then provides some type of scale for the rater to identify the degree to which the employee has demonstrated that quality. For example, one of the qualities selected for appraising performance may be the trait "effort."

EFFORT: Considers accuracy, neatness, and attention to detail; is industrious.

The next step is to develop a scale that measures the degree of the quality that best characterizes the ratee. The scale may be an unbroken continuum with terminal anchors, such as those shown in Figure 6–7, or it may have discrete intervals such as those shown in Figure 6–8.

FIGURE 6–7.
Terminal Anchors

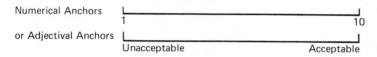

FIGURE 6–8.
Discrete Intervals

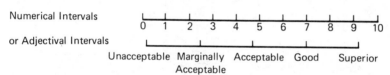

Effort	Unacceptable 0–1	Meets Minimal Requirements 2–3	Acceptable 4–6	Fully Proficient 7–8	Superior 9–10

In each case, the rater receives instructions to place a check along the line at the point or within the interval that most accurately identifies the degree of the quality or trait as demonstrated by the employee. A point score can be identified by the location of the check on the continuum. An interval scale provides the rater with more specific reference points when rating.

Another approach to scaling may be to provide a discrete or multiple-step rating scale in which the rater ranks the quality according to its importance in the performance of the job and checks the box that most adequately describes the characteristics of the ratee. For example, see Figure 6–9.

In (1), the rater rates the quality according to its importance in the performance of the job. In (2), the rater indicates the appropriate degree of the trait that the ratee exhibits.

FIGURE 6–9.
Multiple-Step Rating Scale

Effort	*Not Important*	*Marginal*	*Average*	*Very Important*
	(1) ☐	☐	☐	☐
(Considers accuracy, neatness, and attention to detail; is industrious.)	Provides less than acceptable effort.	Maintains minimum acceptable standards of effort.	Provides reasonable effort.	Consistently provides superior effort.
	(2) ☐☐	☐☐☐	☐☐☐	☐☐

FIGURE 6–10.
Simple Checklist

Effort: Performs assignments accurately, neatly, and with attention to detail; is industrious.

Check appropriate description:

Exceeds all work-related requirements _____

Meets all work-related requirements _____

Fails to meet work-related requirements _____

The checklist may also take the form shown in Figure 6–10.

The accuracy of the ratings increases when the performance dimension and rating scale identify work activities that are completely controlled by the ratee, that are relatively easy to observe, and when they adequately describe behaviors that facilitate recall. To be useful, rating scales must assist in minimizing rater prejudices and promote even-handed treatment. A problem that always exists with any kind of numbering system is that quantification may provide a sophistication that has no valid base. This points to the importance of developing anchors for the rating scales that have been derived from job analysis data. Two commonly used terms for identifying checklists that use numbers, adjectives, or nouns are graphic rating scales and summated rating scales. The term *graphic rating scale* refers to the written or pictorial design of the dimension to be rated and its adjoining scale, and the term *summated rating scale* stems from the requirements of the method to develop a final composite score by adding the values of the rating selection made by the rater for each performance dimension.

Normally, the scales on an instrument are considered to be interval or ratio in design. Even when they are not, it is possible to convert raw ordinal data into interval or ratio scores through some kind of a standardizing procedure or technique such as the use of percentages. When using different performance dimensions to rate different employees or groups of employees, some organizations establish summated scores by converting raws scores into Z scores thus making it possible to compare performance among employees. However, the psychometric problems related to the validity of comparing performance-related standard scores or even normalized Z scores becomes a critical issue. Once again, some experts involved in the design of performance appraisal instruments feel that it is absolutely incorrect to use standardized scores for comparing employee levels of performance.

In addition to using numbers for anchoring scales, two widely-used kinds of graphic rating scales are those that have (a) single words or short adjective phrases—simple adjective rating scales, and (b) lengthy phrases or sentences that describe a behavior.

Simple Adjective Rating Scale. A simple adjective rating scale is one that measures a quality by descriptors such as *unsatisfactory, marginal, satisfactory, commendable,* and *superior.* These descriptors may be defined as follows:

UNSATISFACTORY: Performance clearly fails to meet minimum requirements. (Other descriptors that may be used are *unacceptable, poor.*)

MARGINAL: Performance occasionally fails to meet minimum requirements. (Other descriptors that may be used are *needs assistance, below average, borderline, minimally acceptable.*)

SATISFACTORY: Performance meets minimum requirements. (Other descriptors that may be used are *average, proficient, acceptable, fully successful, competent.*)

COMMENDABLE: Performance consistently exceeds minimum requirements. (Other descriptors that may be used are *good, fully proficient, above average, highly successful.*)

SUPERIOR: All aspects of performance clearly and specifically exceed stated job requirements. (Other descriptors that may be used are *superlative, outstanding, excellent, exceptional, distinguished.*)

Behavioral Anchored Rating Scales. Behavioral anchored rating scales (BARS) are descriptions of various degrees of behavior with regard to a specific performance dimension. The behaviors act as descriptors for a set of intervals from most negative to most positive. These interval descriptions are essential if job-related behaviors are to be a basic part of performance appraisal. They identify in behavioral terms a complete range of behaviors relative to a performance dimension of a single job or group of jobs. Because of the number of behaviors that must be identified and the work involved in determining the levels of performance as related to a particular behavior, BARS are both difficult and expensive to develop.

Chapter 5 discusses in detail how job-related behaviors are identified and described. Once this has been accomplished, subject-matter experts or employees who are extremely knowledgeable about the behaviors required in the performance of a job order the identified behaviors from those that lead to superior job performance to those that would result in unsatisfactory or unacceptable performance. The behavior considered most negative or unsatisfactory and the behavior considered most positive or extremely acceptable become the behavioral anchor terminals for the performance dimension. An example of behavioral anchors is:

MOST POSITIVE: Solves problems affecting job performance no matter how complicated or time-consuming the resolution may be.
MOST NEGATIVE: Fails to identify the critical issue when attempting to resolve workplace problems.

A "middle-out" approach is also valuable for setting behavioral anchors. This approach starts by identifying and defining standard behavior. The scales are incrementally defined in moving away from standard behavior. This allows for an open-ended setting of the most and least desirable behaviors. The critical incident technique (CIT) is, again, most valuable for identifying and defining these anchor points.

BARS, which come directly from demonstrated workplace behavior, are the easiest of all performance appraisal techniques to substantiate and justify. The potential for acquiring content and criterion validity (see the discussion on validity in Chapter 11) is extremely strong. By using BARS, instrument designers avoid the use of vague, universal descriptors, such as *always, excellent,* and *average.* They also minimize the use of vague concepts or terms.

When the BARS that relates to a particular dimension is analyzed, there are at least two methods for identifying employee behavior. First, the rater selects the behavior statement that best identifies the employee behavior. Second, the rater identifies a minimum threshold (i.e., no behavior listed below it describes the employee's behavior) and a maximum threshold (i.e., no behavior listed above it describes the employee's behavior). A combination of the two methods is possible.

Figure 6–11 describes a behavioral anchored rating scale for a particular performance dimension—training.

	JOB DIMENSION: Ensures effective crew training.
Totally un- acceptable (incompetent)	Ignores agreed upon training procedures. Doesn't have sufficiently trained back-up on key jobs. When crew member calls in sick or is pulled off job, foreman has no immediate replacement—has to train someone to fill in. Doesn't check knowledge level of trainee before starting the training. New people assigned to crew stand around waiting for instructions. Has no written plans or schedule for crew training and upgrading. Doesn't follow up on newly trained operations and check job knowledge. Foreman tells someone on crew "Here is new man, show him the ropes," does not set training guidelines to follow up.
Needs improvement	Tells person how to do job, shows them when done wrong, but doesn't explain why or check whether person understands what he is doing and reason for method. Replacements filling in for vacations/sickness cause drop in production/quality. Expects understanding by "telling." No follow-up on training—does it once. Does not have all jobs covered with back-up people. Spends little time with crew in operating area — "expects but doesn't inspect" correct control. Does some training but no skills inventory taken for department upgrading. Has key position covered but not others.
Satisfactory or adequate	Has crew fully trained for normal job functions and adequate back-up for all jobs. Uses slack periods for training if people are spare. When crew member calls in sick or is pulled off job, foreman is able to cover job with trained person in crew. Foreman delegates training of new person to crew member who is a good coach, knows job well, and rechecks new or reassigned crews. Foreman uses Job Instruction Training (JIT) approach to structure skills training. Instructor who is crew member uses JIT approach in training new operator.
Commendable	Foreman encourages crew members to take outside courses related to industry. Has clear objectives for crew training and keeps abreast of changes in the operation that will require operator retraining. Cross-trains crew where feasible to increase overall effectiveness of crews.
Outstanding	Foreman promotes and organizes upgrading program for crew (e.g., grading course). Foreman determines training needs for each person on crew and sets up plan and schedule to complete this training by specified date. Understands various training techniques (e.g., learning curves) and uses them. Looks for more efficient training methods and upgrading programs. Influences others in achieving a high level of crew training and assists with training in other departments.

FIGURE 6–11. Behavioral Anchored Rating Scale for a Particular Performance Dimension. (Courtesy D. H. Lawson, Crown Zellerbach Canada Ltd.)

Other Behavior-Based Instrument Designs

Following the introduction of the term BARS to the vocabulary of those involved in the measurement and rating of performance, three additional acronyms have appeared to whet the inquisitive nature of these professionals. They are BES, BOS, and PDA.

Behavioral Expectation Scale (BES). For all practical purposes, BES is synonymous with BARS. The original development of BARS required job experts to identify the performance dimensions that best describe total performance for a job. Then, these or other job experts, using the critical incident technique, describe incidents of job performance that they consider to be examples of effective and ineffective behaviors relative to previously identified specific performance dimensions. An effective behavior is defined as one that a competent incumbent would be expected to demonstrate, while an ineffective behavior is one that, if demonstrated a certain number of times and under certain conditions, would cause an observer to doubt the competence of the incumbent. These behaviors are then related to a specific quality, characteristic, or dimension of performance, and through various statistical procedures they form a vertical scale, with each behavior given a specific score. The examples of behavior attached to a specific dimension are then edited into the form of an expectation of a specific behavior, thus providing the basis for the title Behavioral Expectation Scale (BES).[9]

Behavioral Observation Scale (BOS). This method was developed in the late 1970s by Gary P. Latham and associates.[10] Like BARS and BES, BOS uses the critical incident technique to identify a series of behaviors that describe the entire job, ranging from unacceptable to superior.

After developing an inventory of behaviors for a specific job, those behavioral items in which almost all incumbents receive the same rating are eliminated. The theory here is that, although a behavioral item may describe a highly critical effective or ineffective performance, it occurs so frequently or infrequently that it fails to assist in differentiating the good from the poor job incumbent. (An example provided by Latham of a behavioral item that was excluded is "has smell of

---

[9] Patricia Cain Smith and L. M. Kendall, "Retranslation of Expectations: An Approach to the Construction of Unambiguous Anchors for Rating Scales," *Journal of Applied Psychology,* April 1963, pp. 151–152.

[10] Gary P. Latham and Kenneth N. Wexley, "Behavioral Observation Scales," *Personnel Psychology,* Summer 1977, pp. 255–268.

FIGURE 6–12.
BOS Scoring

Rating Score	Percentage of Time Observed
1	0–64
2	65–74
3	75–84
4	85–94
5	95–100

liquor on his/her breath.[11] When a review of foremen was conducted, 90 percent received a "never" rating, while 1 percent received a "sometimes" score.) This behavioral item thus fails to differentiate performance among incumbents. The major difference between BARS and BOS is that, instead of identifying those behaviors exhibited by the ratee during a specific rating period, the rater indicates how often the ratee was actually observed engaging in the specific behaviors identified in the BOS.

Using the performance dimension, "Ensures Effective Crew Training," as described in Figure 6-7, a modified BOS may take the following form, (The term *BOS criterion* may be used interchangeably with the term *performance dimension,* and the behaviors listed within the criterion are called *behavioral items.*)

Influences others in achieving a high level of crew training.
Almost Never 1 2 3 4 5 *Almost Always*

Uses slack period for training, if people are spare.
Almost Never 1 2 3 4 5 *Almost Always*

Follows up on training to determine effectiveness of learning.
Almost Never 1 2 3 4 5 *Almost Always*

Develops written crew training plans and schedules.
Almost Never 1 2 3 4 5 *Almost Always*

Using the BOS scoring table (Figure 6–12), a rater would select a rating score of a number from 1 to 5 relative to the percentage of time the ratee is observed engaging in the specific behavior.

To appraise performance for the total job, all relevant BOS behavioral items for a job are identified and described, and a rater scores each item relative to its observed frequency of occurrence. The summed

---

[11] Gary P. Latham and Kenneth N. Wexley, *Increasing Productivity Through Performance Appraisal* (Reading, MA: Addison-Wesley, 1981), pp. 59–60.

rating score then provides an overall performance rating score for the ratee. Depending on the number of behavioral items included within a specific job, the score varies to achieve a specific rating. For example, a job that may be described through 32 items would use the following score to gain a specific overall rating:

Very poor	*Unsatisfactory*	*Satisfactory*	*Excellent*	*Superior*
32–102	103–118	119–134	135–150	151–160

A job with 118 behavioral items would have the following score:

Very poor	*Unsatisfactory*	*Satisfactory*	*Excellent*	*Superior*
118–378	379–437	438–496	497–555	556–590

The maximum rating score range for each performance rating interval is established by multiplying the total number of behavioral items (32 and 118 as presented in the two examples) times the maximum points (5 in the example) times the maximum frequency that a behavioral item can be observed in order to be given a specific rating. For example, the maximum score for the category "very poor" can be calculated by multiplying the number of behavioral items (32) times the maximum score (5) times the maximum frequency that the item can be observed and receive the rating (64 percent). Thus $32 \times 5 \times .64 = 102$. The minimum score for the "very poor" category is simply the lowest possible score an incumbent can receive (1×32 (number of items) $= 32$), and the minimum score for each higher category is 1^{+} the maximum of the previous category score.

A critical weakness of the BOS method that has been identified by H. John Bernardin and Jeffrey S. Kane is the distinct possibility that a given frequency interval (e.g., 75 to 84 percent) may indicate a much higher level of satisfactory performance for one behavior than it does for another.[12] The possibility of assigning an incorrect rating by using a fixed standard scale to observe frequencies of behaviors may be an extremely serious weakness of BOS.

Performance Distribution Assessment (PDA). Jeffrey S. Kane has proposed this new technique, contending that it will offer some unique advantages over all previous methods.[13] These advantages include its

---

[12] H. John Bernardin and Jeffrey S. Kane, "A Second Look At Behavioral Observation Scales," *Personnel Psychology,* Winter 1980, p. 810.

[13] Jeffrey S. Kane, "Improving the Measurement Basis of Performance Appraisals." Paper presented at the symposium entitled, "New Directions in Improving Performance Appraisal Effectiveness," 1981 meeting of the American Psychological Association, Los Angeles, CA, August 28, 1981.

amenability to (a) having its content tailored to each individual ratee's position while yielding scores on a ratio scale that allow direct comparisons between all positions, jobs, or even organizations; (b) excluding from consideration in the scoring the extent to which each performer's output record fell short of perfection as a result of extraneous factors beyond his or her control; (c) permitting the performance of each job function to be scored for its consistency and the extent of its avoidance of the negative outcome range and the average outcome level; and (d) minimizing the possibility of rater bias by reducing the nature of the data elicited from the rater to the most elementary, nonevaluative level.

The development of a PDA system for each job requires, first, that the job be separated into its component functions and that the functions be hierarchically ordered from the broadest ones to the narrowest. The component functions at one of these hierarchical levels are then designated as performance dimensions. Either these are entered directly into the PDA assessment process if they are measurable or, if they are not, then their constituent components at the first lower level at which they are found to be measurable are used.

Each of the resulting job functions on which performance is to be assessed is then subject to the following process. At the beginning of the appraisal period, the rater and ratee get together to define what constitutes the following four levels of outcomes that could occur as the result of any *single* instance of performing the function:

1. Most effective outcome (the best that anyone could possibly produce).
2. Least effective outcome (the least that would be allowed to occur without immediately removing the performer from further responsibility for the function).
3. Neutral outcome (the one falling halfway between number 1 and number 2).
4. Intermediate outcome (the one falling halfway between number 1 and number 3).

Three other outcome levels exist by interpolation between the listed four—those between 1 and 4, between 4 and 3, and between 3 and 2. (See Figure 6–13.) For each level except "most acceptable," the rater and ratee then try to agree on the number of times (expressed as a percent) the single function will occur during the forthcoming period and the possibility of achieving a more effective outcome than that which is occurring now. The final step at the outset of the period

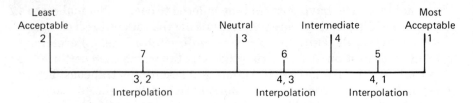

FIGURE 6–13. Levels of Outcome Scale.

requires the rater to make a rating of the loss that would be caused by producing the least effective outcome, using a special scale.

At the end of the appraisal period, the rater and ratee meet again to ensure the accuracy of their outcome level descriptions and surpassing percentage estimates in light of what was actually experienced during the period. The rater then proceeds to report the actual percentage of performance opportunities on which the ratee produced outcomes at each of the seven effectiveness levels. These percentages must add up to 100 percent. From this point onward a computerized scoring process takes over that expresses, in terms of a percentage, the extent to which the performance distribution reported for the ratee covered the range between zero and the value of the best distribution possible to achieve. The resulting scores (which may refer to the value of the average outcome level, the standard deviation, the negative range incidence, or any combination) represent the extent to which the ratee achieved all that was possible to achieve on each job function—a generic performance construed on which universal comparisons may be made.

Goal Setting

An approach for measuring performance that has become increasingly popular over the past two decades is the setting of goals. Management by objectives (MBO) was discussed at some length in Chapter 3, in which the contributions of Peter Drucker in this area were recognized. The concepts underlying MBO also provide the foundation for many similar programs that operate under such titles as management by objectives and self-control, management by results, work planning and review, and numerous other offshoots. The one critical element they all have in common is that employees work to achieve a preset goal. The programs differ according to (a) who is involved and how the goal is set; (b) the precision with which the goal is described; and (c) the procedures used to measure goal-achievement performance.

If goal setting is to be a successful method for measuring performance, the ratee must have some autonomy or personal control over the actual activities performed in the accomplishment of the goal and their timing and sequencing. The desired performance goal becomes a standard that will be used to measure the results achieved or behaviors demonstrated. If the ratee has minimal control over job activities, then it may be far better to set specific standards relative to job activities (responsibilities and duties or demonstrated behaviors) rather than to take the time for goal setting. When workers operate in a lockstep or highly prescriptive environment, goal setting may frequently be nothing more than a sham.

Weaknesses in goal setting relate to the difficulty of establishing goals in certain jobs. Possibly even more critical are the following issues:

1. Employees become overly enthusiastic when first involved in the setting of goals, which may lead to goals that become unachievable and result in the death of the program. Or, the opposite may occur—goals are set that are easily reached and may also be so nonspecific as to be meaningless.

2. Goals fail to measure dimensions of performance that should be measured.

3. Both raters and ratees involved in a goal-setting program require a certain amount of education to be successful participants.

4. Normally, an employee works toward the attainment of more than one goal. In this case, a different level of goal achievement for each goal is a probable occurrence. The same issue then arises that causes consternation, no matter what measurement method is used, and that is: How much weight or importance should be given to each goal and each level of goal achievement relative to overall job performance?

5. Providing a score that describes a level of performance that either fails to reach or exceeds an established or desired level is open to individual interpretation. In many cases, there is no limit to "outstanding" performance, and providing a score for outstanding performance can vary significantly among raters. Conversely, performance below an acceptable level can also draw a wide difference of rating scores.

6. It is extremely difficult to compare the goal success of one individual to that achieved by another. Situational factors that assist or hinder goal achievement block the development of a normalized or composite rating score from goal setting that can be used for comparing the performance of employees.

Goal-Setting Process

Measurement of goal achievement may take an approach identified by Peter Drucker as the *manager's letter,* in which an employee writes on a blank sheet of paper the goals and activities to be achieved and implemented during the coming performance period. At the end of the period, the employee takes another blank sheet of paper, identifies and describes goal-directed progress and results achieved, and then identifies possible new goals and activities for the next performance period. Sometimes, forms are prepared that require the employee to identify major job responsibility areas, goals, actions to be taken, and, finally, results achieved. (See Figure 6–14.)

In establishing goals with a subordinate, the manager should keep in mind that goals must be stated in a form that facilitates their use in measurement of results at a future time. The idea is to establish goals that measure both the effect of the behavior of the subordinate and the results achieved.

Three basic tools that are valuable in a goal-setting program are the job description, goal-setting and performance appraisal work papers and forms, and the interview. The interview is the principal means of developing an agreement between the manager and subordinate on expected results, and the completed forms confirm in writing what has been agreed upon between them.

The agreed-upon goals may be written on a form that is then used during the review period for self-guidance and self-feedback. Frequently, these goals have no influence on day-to-day activities. Many managers and subordinates act as if they were etched on copper and buried in a cornerstone to be disinterred a year later when senior management calls for a performance appraisal report.

To the extent practicable, expected results should be established in concrete terms—where possible, in quantifiable terms such as volume of output, profits, time limits, or cost limits. Where such perfectly objective measures are not practicable (i.e., nonquantifiable results or results that are not easily established or measured as part of the normal management planning and control process), qualitative measures should be set and communicated.

CHOOSING THE BEST PERFORMANCE APPRAISAL APPROACH

The combinations possible from the various methods and techniques available for appraising performance are almost limitless. The pressure is on the designers and implementers to analyze their situations, identify the requirements they wish to satisfy, and select those procedures and instruments that will meet both organizational and employee demands. Somewhere within the array of performance measure-

FIGURE 6–14
Goal-Setting Work Paper

Responsibilities	Performance Goals to be Achieved	Methods or Approaches	Actual Accomplishments
(What major activities must be accomplished in performing your job?)	(What are your specific goals? To the extent practicable, goals should be stated in concrete terms.)	(How are you going to achieve your goal? What is the specific plan of activity that will yield the results you seek?)	
1.			
2.			
3.			
4.			
5.			
6.			
7.			
8.			

ment instruments and tools lie one or more devices that will adequately and effectively perform the appraisal assignment. Unlocking the mysteries of performance appraisal requires knowledge of (a) the measurement tools that are available, (b) the people to be measured, (c) the ability of the instrument to provide ratings that are accurate and that discriminate among various levels of performance, (d) the intended uses of rating data and information, and (e) how conflicts among these potentially conflicting uses may be minimized.

Among these different approaches for measuring and rating employee performance is one that should satisfy the particular needs of any organization. If an organization wishes to use an identical instrument for measuring the performance of all employees, it must recognize that it is probably measuring employee behavior relative to organizational values rather than measuring employee performance relative to the requirements of the incumbent's job.

Organizations must look for the simplest tool possible to serve a particular purpose. If raters are going to cheat, fudge, or cover their rears, they can accomplish this mission no matter how sophisticated or complex the instrument. What must be recognized here is that any plan, program, or instrument designed by man can be destroyed or neutralized by man. If the purpose, intent, or even perceived purpose or intent of performance appraisal is to place the subordinate unfairly in a position of jeopardy, the subordinate will do everything possible to neutralize the influence of the process. It is absolutely essential that the great majority of all employees in the organization, from the CEO to the most recently hired file clerk, recognize and understand why their performance is being appraised and accept it as a rational and necessary process for managing the organization.

Chapter 7

Uses of Appraisal Data
and Information

For many years, employees with performance appraisal responsibilities have recognized that one of the major barriers to successful operation is the difficulty of resolving conflict among the uses of the performance appraisal output. Traditionally, the number one reason for implementing a performance appraisal program has been to assist in making compensation decisions. The concept of paying for performance is universal (and even sacred to a wide variety of social and political groups). The barrier that restricts successful implementation of such a goal is the difficulty in measuring performance. With ever-increasing specialization, more sophisticated machinery, and the dependence on many individuals, groups, and processes to achieve results, the valid measurement of performance also becomes exceedingly complex. There are *no* simple solutions to complex problems!

People become members of organizations and remain with them for a wide variety of reasons. Organizations, however, retain employees principally because of the contributions the employees currently make and have the potential for making. The linkage between attracting competent performers and retaining them relates directly to the reward system of the organization. Organizational rewards can be defined very broadly as anything the organization offers its members that elicits their performance in a manner that supports the achievement of organizational goals. Among the most significant rewards employers offer to employees are:

1. Money to purchase goods and services required not only for current and future survival but also for the luxuries modern life has to offer.

2. The opportunity to use innate and learned skills and talents in a productive manner that the individual and his or her managers and co-workers recognize as valuable.

199

3. Opportunities to interact with other people in a favorable working environment.

4. Opportunities to learn, grow, and make full use of their potential.

5. A sense of permanence and stability through the continuing existence of the organization and the job.

6. The opportunity to perform work assignments within an environment that not only protects but promotes physiological, emotional, and psychological health.

In one way or another, data and information outputs of a performance appraisal program can critically influence these coveted employer-provided reward opportunities. To gain a better understanding of the relationship between performance appraisal output and reward opportunities, the remainder of this chapter will focus specifically on the links between performance appraisal and

1. Compensation administration

2. Training and development

3. Employee movement

4. Validation of selection criteria and training activities

5. Planning

There are many appraisal experts who advocate only a single use for such a program. In such cases, the simple use most often recommended is to improve communications between supervisor and subordinate, so that the subordinate will know exactly what the supervisor wants the employee to *do* and the results expected. The feedback process is designed to remove ambiguities and permit objective ratings that minimize rater errors resulting from whatever reason.

This book takes the position that such a use does not require a formal appraisal program but, rather, a healthy, invigorating organizational environment which, in turn, requires good management processes. Such Camelots exist infrequently and may actually have existed only at the time of King Arthur. Organizational life is far from perfect and noble, and formal performance appraisals are required. Once a formal appraisal program is implemented, it must be used for all possible purposes. Even when organizations espouse and loudly advertise that the results will *only* be used for "this" or "that" purpose, employees will *not* believe such proclamations. Their fear of the future, concern for survival, and lack of trust in top management will sooner or later (probably sooner) cause them to recognize the opportunities organizations have for the adverse use of performance appraisal data and information.

Since many organizations formally measure and rate workplace performance and since most organizations believe that pay-for-performance is sacrosanct, it is only logical to believe that these two realities must eventually link together. This view is, in fact, conspicuous in some excellent research conducted in the early 1960s at General Electric (GE). The results of the research were described in the classic *Harvard Business Review* (January–February 1965) article titled, "Split Roles in Performance Appraisal," by Herbert H. Meyer, Emanuel Kay, and John R. F. French, Jr. In this article, the researchers described how pay drives appraisal ratings, and, when this occurs, the usefulness of appraisal ratings for any other purpose is severely limited. What is meant by "pay drives the appraisal rating" is that the pay decisions as related to the appraisal rating become the overriding concern of supervisors. The supervisors first decide what rating is required to achieve a specific pay decision and the subordinate then receives a rating sufficient to acquire a specific pay adjustment. The rating, however, may have little in common with the demonstrated employee behavior or the results of the individual's work efforts. Thus, the pay decision actually drives the rating instead of the rating decision driving the pay determination. This means that accurate and extensive appraisal-related information that can be useful for all other organizational purposes is not forthcoming or is critically flawed.

Carrying this consideration one step further, it is important to recognize that training and movement decisions (lateral transfer, promotion, demotion, and termination) are also critical pay-related decisions. The only difference is that they may just be a trifle more long-term in orientation than a merit pay decision or some other pay adjustment decision that uses performance appraisal rating information as an important determinant as to the *when* and *how much* of the adjustment.

Experts aware of this critical problem have frequently stated that either (a) performance appraisal ratings should not be used for compensation purposes, or (b) the appraisal process should be split into a review session for training and development purposes and, at another date—possibly three to six months later, a session for rating the employee for compensation purposes. This may sound good in theory or on paper and may even overcome the pay-driving-rating problem temporarily, but if this is the extent of the change in the appraisal process, it will soon lose its effectiveness for all of the previously identified supervisor/subordinate-related reasons. What has to be recognized here is that once an organization implements a formal appraisal program, the impact on compensation (both in the short and long term) is firmly entrenched in the brains of all employees. Does this mean that formal performance appraisal information can be used only for making compensation-related decisions and that the accuracy of ratings must always be in doubt? The answer is no.

What it does mean, however, is that a very realistic and rational analysis must be implemented regarding all parts of a formal performance appraisal system. The uses—actual or potential—made of performance appraisal measurement data and information must be clearly identified.

Another conflict among uses occurs because of the emotional and psychological problems that arise when individual self-esteem suffers because of negative feedback on performance. Employees want and need to have their performance appraised. Most employees want to know how they are doing on their jobs. They want someone to identify constructively and in a nonthreatening manner where and what kinds of changes or improvements they can make in their behavior to ensure that they will be more valuable contributors to organizational productivity. Certainly, it can be argued that this crucial assignment can be performed without a formal performance appraisal program; but, without a formal plan, will it be implemented uniformly and fairly by all managers? Most likely not. If performed informally, what wide-scale uses can the organization make of the results of the program? Few, if any.

Supervisors prefer for obvious reasons (e.g., self-protection) that rating information be a one-way process. It must be kept secret, and it must not be provided to the ratee. At the same time, however, if the rating information is to be useful, ratees must receive immediate feedback on (a) how their supervisor (rater) perceived their performance, (b) their demonstrated strengths and weaknesses, and (c) what the organization is willing to do and what each person must do to strengthen his or her performance. For one use (pay) and for one group (raters), secrecy of performance information is sought, while for other uses (training and development) and for other groups (ratees), free and open flow of appraisal information is essential. If rewards are to influence employee behavior in a manner desired by management, organizations must provide sufficient communication to inform employees about what rewards are available, what they have done, and what they must do to receive the rewards.

COMPENSATION ADMINISTRATION

To obtain desired levels of performance, organizations must establish a relationship between demonstrated employee behaviors and employer-provided rewards that have a high degree of both consistency and certainty.

Workplace *certainty* develops when both the supervisor and incumbent (a) fully understand job requirements, (b) have a similar perception of the outputs of the job and the priorities related to specific outputs, (c) are satisfied that standards of performance are well defined, (d) are confident that criteria used for measuring performance are accurate, and (e) know that specific levels of performance will result in particular kinds and amounts of rewards. *Consistency* develops when employees recognize that an accurate measurement of performance is necessary and possible and that employees performing similarly will receive similar reward treatment.

When an organization does not link its rewards to employee performance, it minimizes the importance of one of its most valuable assets— human resources. If survival and growth are basic objectives of most organizations, is it not consistent and imperative to recognize how rewards influence employee behavior and to make every effort possible to communicate to employees that rewards depend on their provided contributions?

Contrary to some popular conceptions, among all of the forms of rewards that an organization provides in exchange for the services of its members, the compensation system with its many components has the greatest opportunity to influence employee behavior. To determine which components of the compensation system have the most influence on specific patterns of behavior, the modern enterprise must first critically analyze the types of behavior that it wishes its members to exhibit. It then must design and manage a compensation system that stimulates this acceptable workplace behavior. This section describes those compensation components that are contingent on workplace behavior or the results of work efforts that can, in some manner, be identified, observed, and measured and then specified in the appraisal of performance.

Base Pay

Many organizations develop pay structures with pay grades and then assign a job to a specific pay grade according to its worth. Normally, a pay grade has a minimum and maximum rate of pay. The difference between the minimum and maximum is called the range. Sometimes, the grade is divided into a number of steps with specific rates of pay. At other times, all that is identified are the first quartile (25th percentile), midpoint (50th percentile), and third quartile (75th percentile) of the pay grade.

Advancement through a pay grade may relate strictly to seniority (time on the job), to merit (performance appraisal rating), or to a combination of seniority and merit. Where there are six to ten steps within a pay grade, the incumbent's pay may increase automatically within a predetermined time period. The automatic (seniority) increases may only go to the midpoint of the pay grade, and further increases may depend on merit.

Even when increases are based primarily on seniority, the employee may receive some type of a simple appraisal rating, such as "performs acceptably" or "needs improvement." An "acceptable" rating grants the employee an advance to the next step. A "needs improvement" rating freezes the employee in the current step and can be used as a warning that termination is possible.

In recent years, the *merit guidechart* has come into favor. This procedure ties performance appraisal ratings to increases in pay. It also permits cost-of-living or market adjustments to be incorporated into pay increases with the percentage of the increase being determined by the incumbent's position in the pay grade (those lower in the pay grade receive larger percentage increases than those that are higher, although both may receive identical performance ratings). Figure 7–1 is a merit guidechart. A review of the guidechart reveals that employees in lower levels of the pay grade receive larger percentage pay increases for comparable levels of performance. The reasoning is that employees at the higher levels still receive more absolute dollars and, also, that there is a definite limit to the amount of increase granted to an employee at the upper level of a pay grade. An "X" indicates a pay grade adjustment, which may be either an increase in the top and bottom (or top only) limits of the pay grade or an across-the-board adjustment of the pay structure that is prompted, in most cases, by inflationary pressure and the desire of management to assist employees to maintain the current purchasing power of their pay. When the guidechart is used, there is nothing automatic about any pay increase. Employees who perform in a less than acceptable manner and who are currently receiving pay in the upper levels of the pay grade actually receive a pay cut in *real* income (real income relates to the purchasing power of the income).

Tying performance appraisal ratings to adjustments in pay emphasizes the importance of having valid and reliable appraisal instruments and raters who rate and measure performance accurately. This also underlines a very real and important issue regarding performance appraisal: After an appraisal rating is performed, what is done with it?

There are those who feel that it is unwise and counterproductive to tie performance appraisal reviews directly to merit increases. If the organization states implicitly or explicitly that it is paying for performance, there is no way to minimize the relationship between a performance rating and pay adjustments. In fact, when an organization tries to impart such a view, employees simply look upon it as

FIGURE 7-1
Merit Guidechart

Current Position Within Pay Grade		Performance Appraisal Rating				
Quartile	Percentile	Superior	Good	Acceptable	Needs Improvement	Unacceptable
Fourth Quartile	75 to 100	X + 3	X + 2	X	0	0
Third Quartile	50 to 75	X + 4	X + 3	X + 1	$\frac{1}{2}$X	0
Second Quartile	25 to 50	X + 5	X + 4	X + 2	$\frac{1}{3}$X	0
First Quartile	1 to 25	X + 6	X + 5	X + 3	X	0

another devious maneuver by management. It is entirely possible to have more than one review session. The first performance review session focuses on behaviors that should be continued, those requiring some changes, and, possibly, those that should be eliminated; its purpose is for employee development. A second meeting that focuses primarily on pay review may be held four to twelve weeks later. This type of formal procedure *may* minimize the concern about pay adjustments at the first meeting, which should be developmental in orientation. However, pay adjustments may be an unspoken issue that clouds the developmental meeting.

To assist in linking pay adjustments to performance, it may be useful to develop a final global performance or rating score for each employee. A process that provides valid global rating scores is one in which employees in different jobs or different work units who perform at the same level receive the same score. When organizations use measuring instruments that include some kind of point scoring, it is possible through certain statistical procedures (standardizing) to develop a common global scoring process. Some measurement instruments and processes do not relate easily or directly to a score, for example, BARS and MBO. In a BARS, if the descriptors represent equal or nearly equal intervals, the behaviorally described performance appraisal can provide a point score.

Ranking and prioritizing goals and then relating results achieved to preset goals can provide a basis for the allocation of a certain number of points. For example, 100 points may be given if all goals are achieved. The problem that arises immediately is how this scoring system recognizes goal achievement greater than preset goals. Another critical issue that arises is how the point score will reflect either barriers or aids that influenced goal achievement over which the incumbent had absolutely no control. This is not an easy assignment, and it is one of the weaknesses of tying MBO to compensation practices.

Some rules-of-thumb frequently used for relating pay to performance are:

1. Top performers should receive 50 percent more than mediocre performers.
2. Merit increases should range between 0 and 20 percent.
3. Of all merit increases granted, 90 percent typically fall between 6 and 8 percent.

Direct Output (Individual)

Frequently, the amount of pay for employees whose work can be separated from others and measured accurately is tied directly to their identified output. Two widely used output payment systems are (a) piece rates for production workers in a manufacturing setting and clerical workers who are processing large numbers of forms with similar kinds of data and (b) commissions for sales personnel. In these systems, a definite rate of pay must be set for a specific output, and limiting factors that modify output-based earnings must be identified.

In many cases, all that the rater has to do is identify the actual output. However, some piece-rate and commission plans may be modified by such factors as quality of output, resource usage, wastes incurred, machine utilization, and product mix (especially in sales, where commission rates may vary according to the amount of different products or product lines sold). These variables that may change piece-rate or commission earnings point out the fact that, even in one of the simplest relationships between performance and rewards, factors arise that can quickly complicate the relationship.

Direct Output (Group)

Most of the discussion concerning piecework plans normally involves individual effort, but piecework programs can be just as effective for stimulating the performance of groups.

There are two basic approaches for developing group piecework plans. The first is identical to that used for setting individual piecework standards: Work standards are set for each member of the group, and a count of the output of each member is maintained. The difference between this group approach and that related to individual piecework arises in the method of payment. The group approach may use one of the following payment methods: (a) all members receive the pay earned by the highest producer, (b) all members receive the pay earned by the lowest producer, or (c) all members receive payment equal to the average pay earned by the group.

The second and far less common approach is to set a standard based on the final output of the group. This approach does not relieve management of the responsibility of performing a detailed analysis of the work performed by each member. Work flow and work processing information is still necessary for establishing the initial balancing of work tasks among the members. Once production is under way, the group may vary any management-developed work-balancing system to meet its own demands. This approach is more useful when all members work together to complete a single product. The first approach is applicable when members are performing similar or identical assignments.

The beauty of the group approach is not only the simplification of measuring output but also the support that the individual members provide each other. A well knit, properly managed work group assists in training new and less experienced members. It sometimes rotates jobs in order to make the most effective use of its human resources. The members aid each other in overcoming both on- and off-the-job problems that affect group performance. The piecework plan provides a goal that assists in coordinating and directing group efforts for the benefit of the organization, the group, and its individual members.

In most well functioning work groups, the total earnings (base pay plus any earned incentives) are split equally among the members. It is possible that the group itself may wish to grant a larger percentage to the more senior or experienced members, but this is the exceptional case and is strictly a group decision.

Short-Term Cash Bonuses

A short-term cash bonus may be defined as a payment within the current operating year to an employee, in addition to his or her regular earnings, for superior performance or an above-expected achievement. Eligibility for a bonus relates to the particular contribution for which the bonus is awarded. Bonuses are usually granted for results directly influenced by the skill and effort of the employee.

The amount of the bonus normally depends on (a) the significance of the contribution, (b) the base pay of the recipient, (c) the level of job in the organization, and (d) the kind of job. Some common types of bonuses are the (a) annual (profit or other economic indicator-related) bonus, (b) award for good performance, (c) award for an unusual or exceptional contribution, and (d) part of a contract between employee and employer. In all of these examples, performance appraisal ratings may have an impact on the size of the bonus and whether the employee receives or does not receive one. Frequently, bonuses are granted only to the top-performing 5 percent. Bonus size may range between 10 and 100 percent of base pay, with a normal range between 20 and 25 percent.

Annual Bonus. An annual bonus based on some type of economic indicator, such as profit, sales, market shares, or return on invested capital, is usually paid to executives and senior managers. In large organizations, top operating managers may be included. Usually, employees who work for companies that provide this type of bonus find that their base pay is less than that of those who work for non-bonus-paying companies. However, employees in bonus-paying companies find that their total base pay plus the bonus payments substantially exceed the payments received by employees in non-bonus-paying companies. Comparison of performance between bonus- and non-bonus-paying companies also indicates that, by most economic indicators, those that pay bonuses frequently outperform those that do not.

Annual bonuses that may include large numbers of employees (possibly the entire work force) are the *Christmas bonus* and the *Thirteenth Month bonus.* The Christmas bonus is usually made early in December and may equal the employee's pay for one week or one month. When merit influences base earnings or any additional performance-related payment, the amount of the Christmas bonus may, in turn, reflect the performance influences. The Thirteenth Month bonus is similar to the Christmas bonus, but it provides a thirteenth monthly payment to employees. This payment is normally made in December of each year. As with the Christmas bonus, performance rating and merit pay may have an impact on the size of the Thirteenth Month payment.

Award for Good Performance. Some kind of appraisal rating is vital to this process. Many organizations that have this kind of plan use degree of goal achievement for measuring performance.

Exceptional Contribution. This type of bonus has become more widely used in recent years. Many organizations establish special committees to determine whose performance warrants special consideration. A special type of bonus is the lump-sum or one-time cash bonus payment. These special awards may be made at an annual event, or they may be presented shortly after the occurrence or result of the behavior. A major reason for the popularity of the lump-sum bonus is that it recognizes a specific behavior or result and is not part of a permanent pay plan. Distinguished service bonuses are usually only paid to the top 1 percent of the organization. Organizations that have suggestion plans can use this type of bonus payment to recognize those who have made worthwhile or beneficial suggestions. The size of the bonus can be determined by the appraised value of the suggestion.

Executive Contract. There are times when top officials sign a performance contract with their employer. These executive contracts frequently have clauses that state that the executive will receive a certain bonus if the individual demonstrates a certain level of performance. The contract defines precisely the level of performance and the related cash bonus.

All of these performance-related cash bonus plans may, at times, include awards of stock or a combination of stock and cash. Stock-bonus plans are discussed in the following section. Long-term cash bonuses are similar in nature to short-term cash bonuses and are discussed in the section on deferred compensation.

Stock Acquisition Plans

Ownership of stock in the employer's business is thought to be mutually advantageous to employees and employers. For employees, stock ownership is a major means of developing an estate, generating additional revenue (through stock dividends and appreciation in the price of the stock), and sheltering income or delaying the payment of taxes on income. For the employer, the market price of the stock acquired by the employee is a tax-deductible business expense. Even more important, there is the view that an employee who owns stock in the business will take a more active interest in seeing that the business is successful in its many pursuits. Stock acquisition by employees instills in them the same interest and incentive for business success that the owners have.

There are four major types of stock acquisition plans: stock purchase plans, stock options, stock grants, and stock bonus plans. A lengthy discussion of each type of stock plan does not appear here, but particular types of stock acquisition plans that relate directly or have close ties to performance appraisal ratings are discussed.

Stock Purchase Plans. Stock purchase plans provide employees with a contract to buy stock in the business at the current market prices. The number of shares available for purchase, dates when purchases can be made, and methods available for purchase are specifically described in the stock purchase contract/agreement.

Stock purchase plans may be either qualified or nonqualified. A qualified plan is one that receives special tax treatment (normally for both employer and employee) because the plan design and administration meet very specific government regulations. Qualified stock purchase plans frequently include all employees, whereas nonqualified plans are usually management purchase plans.

A stock purchase plan that frequently has specific performance requirements is the *earn-out stock purchase plan*. In this type of plan, the employee receives a loan to purchase the stock; if the employee then meets certain performance requirements, he or she does not have to repay the loan (other requirements besides performance may be included within the earn-out stock purchase plan).

Stock Option Plan. Stock option plans permit designated employees to purchase set amounts of stock at a specific price within a prescribed time period. Normally, stock options are restricted to a select group of executives and senior managers. The concept underlying the issuance of stock options is that those who receive stock options have a direct and strong influence on the performance of the business and that the market value of the stock is an indicator or measure of their success in performing their jobs. (This is not necessarily true, because many factors that have an impact on the market price of stock are beyond the control of any one or all of the senior management group of a business.) Because of the impact that senior management decisions have on the market price of shares of stock, some stock option plans have unique features tied to the market price.

Stock Grant Plans. Stock grant plans assist employees in acquiring stock in the business by granting them stock at no cost. Stock grants are frequently types of deferred stock bonus plans.

Stock grants take two basic forms: stock appreciation grants and full-value grants. Stock appreciation grants entitle the recipient to receive payment that equals the appreciated value of a share of stock (or number of shares or units of stock granted) over a designated time period. A full-value stock grant entitles the recipient to receive the total value of the worth of a share (or number of shares or units of stock) over a predetermined period of time. Total value includes the base value of the stock at the time of the initial grant, dividends, and the appreciation of the stock value during the period when the grant is in force.

Examples of stock grant plans that include performance criteria in the plan design are restricted stock performance plan, performance share plan, and performance unit plan.

A *restricted stock performance plan* is a special type of restricted stock plan. A restricted stock plan is one in which the business awards a prescribed amount of stock to its key managers for continued high-quality service. In a restricted stock performance plan, certain performance criteria are set forth, and these criteria must be achieved before the recipient receives the stock grant. This type of plan usually requires executives and senior managers to set key performance goals. These select employees only receive the stock when the business achieves these goals. A restricted stock performance plan may also set a minimum performance goal that must be achieved before any reward grant is made.

A *performance share plan* (*PSP*) is a stock grant plan that stipulates the achievement of certain predetermined performance goals before the recipient may have rights to the stock. Because most PSPs have earn-out periods ranging from three to ten years, they are often classified as deferred stock bonus plans.

Although performance measures can vary significantly from business to business and industry to industry, some typical measures are (a) earning per share growth rate, (b) return on invested capital (ROIC), (c) return on assets (ROA), or (d) a combination of financial measures, such as earnings per share and return on assets. A typical goal is a 10 percent growth in earnings per share over the next five years.

A *performance unit plan* (*PUP*) has characteristics of a performance share plan (PSP) and a phantom stock plan. (Phantom stock plans grant the recipient a number of artificial units. The actual dollar payout on these units is equivalent to the value of a share of stock in the business at some stipulated future date set at the time that the grant is made.) As in the PSP, the recipient must meet certain performance measures in order to acquire the grant units. The PUP awards are made at the time of the grant, but the units only take on cash value at the end of the stipulated time period and upon meeting prescribed performance measures. Depending on their design, PUP awards may be made in a combination of stock and cash, cash only, or stock only.

Stock Bonus Plans. In stock bonus plans, employers provide employees with shares of stock in the business. Stock bonus plans can also be either qualified or nonqualified. A stock bonus plan has characteristics similar to a profit-sharing plan except that the stock bonus distribution is not tied directly to profits and the distribution is in stock, not cash. The similarity is that stock distribution is frequently made to trusteed pension (retirement) plans. A stock bonus plan designed to receive certain tax benefits must satisfy specific Internal Revenue Service tax requirements.

One way in which performance appraisal ratings affect stock bonus contributions made to an employee is when total annual earnings are used as a measure for determining individual allocation. If a business has a merit program that varies earnings according to performance ratings, then any type of deferred income plan that uses annual earnings as a measure for determining the amount of deferred income to be earned is affected by performance.

Deferred Compensation Plans

Deferred compensation plans came about because of laws that tax current income. Deferred compensation plans permit employees to shelter income from immediate tax payments until some future date when the employee's projected tax payment will be less than at present. (In some cases, deferred compensation plans may permit an employee to avoid tax payment completely.) Deferred compensation usually takes the form of pension payments upon retirement, but they may be used to fund payments made to a spouse of an employee who dies, to employees who become disabled and are unable to work, or to employees who are terminated through no fault of their own.

Many deferred compensation plans are designed to meet the specific requirements of senior management personnel. These deferred plans are frequently unfunded. This means that the business makes a contractual obligation to make a payment(s) of a certain amount at a certain time, but the business does not put any money into a fund to guarantee this future payment. It is possible to fund these plans by purchasing insurance or other assets to meet future deferred compensation obligations. Here, constructive receipt becomes a critical issue. *Constructive receipt* is a term established by the Internal Revenue Service. It means that certain actions taken by an employer to ensure a stream of income for an employee at some future date also grant that employee certain opportunities to have current use of those funds and is, therefore, immediately taxable as earned income.

Common types of deferred compensation plans are those in which employers make contributions to various types of stock acquisition, long-term bonus, and pension plans. Employer contributions are made in such a way that recipient employees are not required to pay taxes on them until they actually receive the payments (earn the contributions). Deferred income payments can be made in a number of ways. What is of interest here is the relationship between performance appraisal and the amount of employer contributions. The major impact occurs when performance appraisal ratings or the achievement of a particular goal or business performance indicator determines the amount to be contributed. In many cases, the contributions are flat or predetermined amounts that have no direct relationship to individual performance. However, more plans are being designed with a percentage of the contribution being determined by a performance rating measurement.

Profit Sharing

Profit-sharing plans normally include all or a significant portion of the employees. These plans focus on improving the overall productivity of the business. Similar to any employer-provided reward, the reasons for implementing profit-sharing plans are to attract and retain competent employees and to establish an incentive for securing high levels of productivity by encouraging interest in the objectives of the business. Although many profit-sharing plans do not directly link appraisal rating to profit-sharing distribution, there is an implicit relationship in that improved performance by all employees leads to increased monetary rewards.

Profit-sharing plans may provide distribution in the form of cash, stock, or a combination of cash and stock. The distribution may be made in the short term or long term, or a plan may provide for both short- and long-term payments. The distribution of the profit-sharing fund among the employees is normally determined through the use of a formula. The formula may include variables such as annual earnings, years of employment, and performance appraisal ratings.

Short-term profit-sharing payments are normally made on an annual basis, although some plans provide for quarterly distribution. One of the most widely known short-term profit-sharing plans in the United States is that of the Lincoln Electric Company, where the appraisal ratings influence the amount of money that each employee receives from the distribution of the profit-sharing fund. The annual bonus frequently equals 100 percent of annual earnings.

Most deferred (long-term) plans make distributions to employee pension plans. A major design difference between a deferred profit-sharing plan and a pension plan is that a deferred profit-sharing plan may permit an employee to withdraw profit contributions after two years. When profit-sharing payments are deferred, the employee benefits by not having to pay income tax on the sheltered income and its earned interest or dividends, and the business is able to deduct any payments as a current business expense.

When profit-sharing plans are designed for individuals (the executives), the plans may be noncontractual. A noncontractual plan is one in which the size of the payment is determined by the appraisal of the employee's performance and the financial strength of the business. The more common contractual type of profit-sharing plan defines the payment according to some predetermined formula.

Pension Plans

Pension plans take a wide variety of forms, but they all serve the major purpose of securing a satisfactory quality of life for employees after their productive working years are over. Pension plans provide a stream of income to employees after retirement. In many cases, a spouse may continue to receive pension plan payments after the death of the employee.

Although the actual size of the pension payment may be a flat amount, it normally varies according to some formula that has as its major independent variables the years of service and the amount of earned income. Here again, when a business varies annual earnings according to a performance rating, the size of the pension payment may be significantly influenced by the employee's appraisal ratings.

The Check-and-Balance System

A seldom discussed but extremely valuable use of performance appraisal is to employ it as a check and balance on the job evaluation program. If the performance dimensions, standards, and goals of the appraisal system come directly from job content and jobs are evaluated relative to content requirements, performance appraisals and job evaluations should be used as a check and balance to ensure legitimacy and credibility.

Two major problems in job evaluation are inflation of job requirements and obsolete ratings. There is the tendency for incumbents and supervisors to inflate job content and requirements so that the job receives a higher rating than deserved, thus granting employees who perform the job a higher base pay. This also increases the stature of the supervisor in the eyes of the employee. The second major problem is a failure to evaluate the job relative to current job requirements. Responsibilities and duties are changed, deleted, or added, and knowledge and skill requirements change. There is often a failure to note these changes in the job descriptions or to have the job reevaluated.

When the kind and/or degree of performance appraisal measurement criteria appears to be inconsistent with job responsibilities, it is a sign that something is wrong. It may be that job responsibilities and duties have changed or that the responsibility and duty statements never truly reflected job requirements. In either case, it is a sign that the job may require reevaluation and that the pay or pay grade assigned to the job may be incorrect.

Equity in Compensation

Satisfying equity demands requires that there be differences in kind and quantity among compensation components offered to incumbents in various jobs. It also requires that the compensation be differentiated according to incumbent performance. The degree to which compensation influences employee behavior depends as much (if not more) on relative considerations as it does on the absolute value or cost of each provided compensation component.

When it comes to rewarding performance, equal and equitable treatment requires minimizing the distribution of rewards based on personality and maximizing the allocation of rewards based on well defined work standards and provided contributions. The entire subject of consistency of treatment and certainty of results is an implicit, if not explicit, part of everything that is discussed in this book.

Of the many and varied rewards that employers can offer to their employees, none may be more valuable than the compensation rewards. Even with apparently unending legislation and organized groups wielding ever-greater influence over compensation procedures, management still has considerable control over the compensation practices of the organization. To ensure as far as possible that the entire compensation package is a "carrot"—highly desired by all employees—compensation system designers and administrators must make every effort possible to tie pay, bonuses, and other compensation components to demonstrated employee performance. In some areas, the linkage is nonexistent or extremely thin; in other areas, the tie is direct and absolute. There is no doubt that many of the additions incorporated into employer-provided compensation since the end of World War II have a minimal relationship to employee behaviors that further the productivity of the organization. This does not mean that management must accept this as the inevitable and unending direction that compensation must take.

A compensation system that stresses pay-for-performance must have an equity base, and equity in compensation requires well identified and measured workplace performance.

In conclusion, changes in compensation rewards eventually depend on the ability of the organization to pay. In turn, the ability of an organization to pay depends on the productivity of its employees. The importance of performance appraisal increases significantly when appraisal ratings have an effect on: (a) the size and distribution of the actual payroll, (b) the number of employees receiving changes in pay, and (c) the percentage of change in pay as related to current pay.

The following guidelines assist in successfully implementing a pay-for-performance program:

1. Employees should understand how rates of pay are established for jobs.
2. Rules for gaining pay increases should be understood by all employees.
3. Performance measures should be known and accepted by all employees.
4. Compensation rewards should be perceived to be adequate for the effort expended.

TRAINING AND DEVELOPMENT

Performance appraisal can provide certain additional human resource information that is useful in determining both individual and group training and development needs. The words *training* and *development* have different meanings, but they do overlap, and this causes terminology confusion. The following frequently accepted definitions assist in differentiating between these two words. *Training* provides participants with the knowledge and skills necessary to perform current assignments. *Development,* however, relates to personal growth and long-term career advancement through a series of training opportunities and varied job assignments. In the final analysis, development is still a personal choice. Each individual must make a decision regarding the acceptance and use of training, coaching, and counseling that provide growth opportunities. Chapter 10 focuses specifically on performance appraisal training provided to all involved in the appraisal process, while Chapter 9 focuses on interviewing and the opportunities available for changing behaviors through counseling and coaching.

Training

To enable the organization to operate in its most efficient manner, management implements training programs. A major goal of any training program is to establish and maintain the highest standards of performance. The identification of training needs is a natural and logical part of the performance appraisal process.

The immediate supervisor who is responsible for the quality and quantity of the output of his or her subordinates is in the best position to identify training requirements. Successful performance of this responsibility requires that all employees receive sufficient training so that they can adequately perform their job assignments. For these reasons, the immediate supervisor must have the primary responsibility for assuring that his or her employees receive proper training.

Training provides knowledge and skills necessary to perform the responsibilities and duties of the current job. In many cases, it also provides the knowledge and skills that an employee may be required to possess in order to perform future assignments. A prerequisite for an employee receiving training in higher level jobs or in jobs in different occupational areas is that the person be considered promotable.

An output of the appraisal process should be information that identifies the kind and level of knowledge and skills currently possessed (demonstrated) by the employee. A useful training program compares demonstrated knowledge and skills with those deemed essential for successful job performance not only in the currently held job but also in those that the employee may hold in the future.

In the development of a training program from demonstrated knowledge and skills, it is important to make the determination of whether or not performance deficiencies result from knowledge and skill deficiencies which, in turn, result from lack of training or because of such factors as the employee's:

1. Lack of opportunity to demonstrate the knowledge or skill(s).
2. Lack of natural ability to possess or demonstrate the knowledge or skill or a specific level of the knowledge or skill.
3. Lack of desire or insufficient energy to demonstrate the knowledge or skill.

When one of these factors is the cause, additional training may be of minimal value, although other managerial actions may be necessary.

Responding to these three issues may require the collection and analysis of additional performance-related data. It is entirely possible that a performance appraisal instrument, in itself, will not provide this kind of information, but in viewing appraisal from the systems concept presented in this book, additional performance analysis may reveal essential criteria for distinguishing among these issues. For example, a review of job responsibilities and duties may quickly identify a lack of opportunity to demonstrate knowledge and skills; deficits in ability may be revealed by reviewing the output of others who have the same learning and performance opportunities as the incumbent; and lack of desire or insufficient energy may appear as wide variations in the results achieved during the rating period or in comparison with other rating periods. At times, it may be difficult to determine whether a deficiency is based on either a lack of knowledge, or a lack of ability, or a lack of desire. An analysis of the problem area may help identify whether the problem occurred because of a lack of knowledge or skill, an inability to apply the knowledge or skill, or a lack of desire to apply the knowledge or skill. The important thing to recognize is that the completion of an appraisal instrument in a process that leads to improved employee performance or the continuation of a highly desired level of performance is only one part of the appraisal system.

By relating job requirements to employee job knowledge and skill deficiencies, it becomes possible not only to identify training actions but also to set training goals and to appraise how well the goals have been accomplished. Figure 7–2 is a training needs work plan.

Training and performance appraisals have important implications for those employees identified in the appraisal process as "unacceptable" or "needing improvement." Training is a major avenue available for bringing employees who receive such ratings to acceptable levels of performance. When training is not successful in improving levels

FIGURE 7-2.
Training Needs Work Plan [1]

Major Responsibilities	Primary Duties	Level of Performance		Demonstrated Strengths/ Weaknesses (Identify possible causes of weaknesses and deficiencies)	Action or Training Planned to Overcome Deficiency	Date Implemented	Appraisal of Results
		Satis-factory	Needs Improve-ment				

[1] If this form is to be copied for actual use, it is recommended that the columns requiring considerable written information (more than checks, yes/no answers, or dates) be widened. The actual form could cover two 8½ × 11 inch sheets of paper.

of competency or when lack of training is not the reason for unacceptable performance, other management action may be necessary. The transfer to jobs in which employee knowledge, skills, and personal characteristics match job requirements is a possibility. The final or ultimate decision is termination; selecting this option usually occurs when all other approaches have failed. Linking training and development programs to performance appraisal makes it possible to measure the effectiveness of such programs.

Development

A frequently unrecognized strength of the American economy is the variety of skills and aptitudes required to fill an almost unlimited range of jobs. Many organizations have so many different levels of jobs that they can hire and promote employees with a wide range of knowledge, skills, aptitudes, and desires. Even when employers provide limited opportunities to the employees, the mobility opportunities for employees within the United States are almost limitless. It is a wise employer who capitalizes on mobility by providing opportunities for current employment and the chance to develop knowledge and skills that will lead to better career opportunities, even though the employer knows the employee might seek advancement with another organization. A key concept is that in the United States there is no such thing as a dead-end job, only dead-end employees; the decision for growth and advancement rests within the brain of each employee.

When employers assist employees to develop and expand capabilities, they not only help employees to improve current performance but also help them to recognize the talents that they do possess and how they can make better use of these talents. Employee development may appear to be of little benefit to an organization that has minimum opportunities for advancement and promotion. If both employer and employee recognize that the employee possibly is not making a lifetime commitment to the current job or current employer but is using current efforts as a stepping-stone to some highly desired future opportunity, discontent and frustration will be reduced and performance and job satisfaction increased. To develop this type of a working environment, the skills and efforts of each employee must be utilized to the fullest extent possible. When employee skills, energy, and desires outpace opportunities provided by the employer, the eternal furnace of hope can be stoked by relating aspirations to current performance.

Upward mobility is practically a password in American society. Even employees with limited career potential possess abilities that can be developed for other jobs within most organizations. If nothing else, many jobs can be upgraded as job responsibilities and duties change, and, through training and development activities, the current incumbent can successfully perform enlarged or enriched jobs.

Active commitment by management (from the executive ranks to first-line supervision) to the development of employees and the promotion of career interests and opportunities is essential to the successful operation of a human resources program. The performance appraisal is a valuable source of development and career growth information. The appraisal process identifies demonstrated behavior that enhances current work activities and, through the interviewing and counseling processes discussed in Chapter 9, furthers employee interests, aspirations, and expectations, and supports the employee's self-generated demands.

In many organizations, performance appraisal provides information and data that significantly influence management decisions about employee promotion, demotion, transfer, lay-offs, and termination. Once again, the critical nature of performance appraisal comes to the front and center. All of these movement considerations can, and frequently do, affect the future life of the involved employee and his or her family.

EMPLOYEE MOVEMENT

Selection for Promotion and Failure to Promote

To many employees, a promotion is a most sought-after organizationally provided reward. Promotion may simply mean an opportunity for increased take-home pay or it may have a complex meaning that includes recognition of past performance, achievement of certain personal short-term goals, and another step toward the attainment of a long-term goal.

Since the development of intelligence tests in the early part of the twentieth century, psychological testing has played an important role in the selection of applicants for jobs, for either entry or advancement and promotion. Although many of the standardized tests used by organizations for selection purposes came under fire in the late 1960s and 1970s for being biased against certain groups, the importance of tests has never been doubted. The issue at hand is to design tests that are both valid and reliable (check validity and reliability in Chapter 11). Testing procedures since the passage of the Civil Rights Act have become more job-related, more comprehensive, and, in many ways, more sophisticated and complex.

Tests now provide selection information for management and information for employees to assist them in formulating their own career plans and training and development requirements. Possibly even more important, test-related information assists employees to obtain a better picture of their capabilities and fitness for particular kinds and levels of jobs. Developing a compatible match of employee skills, talents, and energy with job requirements is one of the most important assignments facing employers in the 1980s.

Some time after initial employment, the majority of employees begin to review their jobs and others available in their organization for future opportunities. From both a monetary point of view and the chance to learn and perform different job activities, promotion becomes an important consideration. From entry into an organization, performance appraisal plays an important role in the continuing growth and advancement of the employee. In the probationary period, the results of appraisal frequently determine who is to be retained and who is to be terminated. After completion of the probationary period, appraisals identify performance strengths and weaknesses. Management and employees identify where training is required for improving current job performance, for expanding current skills, and for developing new ones that are demanded in jobs that the employee may be seeking.

Management must always recognize that for each person who receives some kind of personal satisfaction because of a promotion decision, there are probably many more individuals who are dissatisfied because they did not receive a promotion. Management must be able to document why and how they arrive at a particular promotion decision. This does not mean that those who did not receive the promotion will be "happy" with the results, but at least the decision can be documented in a logical and rational manner.

A major determinant of promotability is performance in the current job, but this does not always provide a sufficient or complete picture of an employee's capabilities for performing a higher-level job or a job with similar degrees of responsibility in areas requiring different knowledge and skills.

Performance appraisal measures and identifies past performance, which is often an excellent indicator of future performance. However, it is not infallible. The possibility always exists that an individual is a step away from reaching a level of incompetency (the "Peter Principle").[1] For this and similar reasons, organizations are combining

---

[1] The "Peter Principle," as described by Laurence J. Peter and Raymond Hull in *The Peter Principle* (New York: William Morrow, 1969), states that in an organizational hierarchy every employee tends to rise to his level of incompetency and that this is the explanation for the universal phenomenon of occupational incompetence.

performance appraisal with other techniques, such as assessment centers, in order to identify employee potential.

In addition to actual job performance, other variables that limit potential for promotion are breadth of knowledge, personal qualities, different kinds of company experience, and overall comparison with others.

For these reasons, the integration of assessment center activities with the more traditional approaches to performance appraisal provides critically needed insights into human qualities that the traditional approaches alone do not reveal. Performance appraisal is no simple checklist of behavioral qualities, nor is it a grouping of performance dimensions. It is a system consisting of many components that, when properly joined together, provide the kind of valid and reliable information needed to make employee-related decisions.

Although it may not be possible for a supervisor to observe and measure all of the human qualities that influence promotion decisions, some behavioral dimensions are readily observable and can be measured by most supervisors. Among the approximately 25 assessment dimensions used by American Telephone and Telegraph Company in its assessment center program, eight have been identified as observable and measurable by supervisors and are frequently included in some form in its performance appraisal programs. The eight dimensions and subcategories are: [2]

1. *Oral communication*
   Ability to present ideas and information concisely and effectively in an oral presentation to a group.

   a. Organizes logically: presents ideas and information in a rational, logical sequence.

   b. Uses appropriate terms: uses words and phrases that are appropriate to the situation and the listener.

   c. Speaks clearly and concisely: presents ideas and information in simple style, without excessive explanation or irrelevant information.

   d. Acts confidently: appears generally calm, confident; gives smooth presentation.

   e. Obtains audience attention: audience typically appears attentive, interested, and positive.
   Note: Emphasis is on the manner in which ideas and information are presented.

---

[2] Although the assessment dimensions are qualitative rather than quantitative in nature, they have been selected because they are clearly visible to supervisors and the information gained in over 20 years of research has made validation possible.

2. *Written communication*

   Ability to express ideas and information concisely and effectively in writing.

   a. Organizes logically: presents ideas and information in a rational, logical sequence.

   b. Uses appropriate terms: uses words and phrases that are appropriate to the situation and the intended readers.

   c. Writes clearly and concisely: presents ideas and information in simple style, without excessive explanation or irrelevant information.

   d. Uses appropriate grammar and style: uses acceptable grammar, spelling and punctuation, and appropriate business format and terminology.

      Note: Emphasis is on the manner in which ideas and information are presented.

3. *Flexibility*

   Ability to change or vary one's approach or strategy for the purpose of accomplishing a task.

   a. Suits style to setting: varies manner of speaking or writing to suit different times, places or audiences.

   b. Suits approach to situation needs: varies actions or behavior to suit different task or problem.

   c. Tries alternatives: changes approach for dealing with a given situation when initial attempts to handle it are not fully effective.

      Note: Consider only actual changes initiated by the individual, not merely verbal expressions of a change of mind.

4. *Performance stability* (resistance to stress, tolerance of uncertainty)

   Ability to maintain a consistent level of performance under conditions of stress, uncertainty, or lack of structure.

   a. Maintains performance under increased pressure: continues to perform at the usual level when faced with increases in work pressure.

   b. Maintains performance under increased uncertainty: continues to perform at the usual level when given less structure or fewer guidelines for performance than are usually available.

      Note: Consider only the ability to continue to perform at the usual level, not ability to show signs of stress or uncertainty.

5. *Decision making* (decisiveness, quality of decision)

   Ability to make timely and effective decisions on the basis of available information.

a. Uses available information: bases decisions on rational analysis of all information available at the time.

b. Anticipates future: takes into account future needs or events that are predictable.

c. Recognizes interactions: takes into account, when appropriate, the effect on other business operations.

d. Considers situation and alternatives: bases decisions on the characteristics of the existing situation and examination of alternatives, not simply on tradition.
Note: Consider the quality of decisions only in the light of the information available at the time that they are made.

6. *Leadership*
Ability to influence others to perform a task effectively.

a. Shows active involvement: initiates ideas, asks appropriate questions, makes suggestions, and gives instructions or orders as appropriate without prodding.

b. Obtains positive response: group typically responds as desired to ideas, suggestions, or instructions.

c. Moves toward goal: leadership attempts are a significant factor in success of group in accomplishing goal.
Note: Consider the effectiveness of leadership attempts, not the style of leadership.

7. *Organization and planning*
Ability to schedule resources and personnel and to develop systematic and effective means for accomplishing a task.

a. Sets priorities: identifies correctly critical tasks and ensures that they receive adequate time and resources.

b. Anticipates needs, avoids schedule conflicts: specifies activities and schedules resources in time to meet needs; sees that personnel and materials are available when needed.

c. Delegates appropriately: sees that tasks are assigned by workload and capability.

d. Follows up: makes appropriate checks to ensure that work is correct and on time; knows the status of people, materials, and plans.

e. Gets work done: work is typically accomplished satisfactorily and on time.

8. *Inner work standards*
Extent to which an individual demonstrates a desire to perform at or near the limits of capability most of the time, even when a lesser effort would be acceptable.

a. Does best possible job: performs as well as capabilities permit most of the time.

b. Satisfies own criteria: typically works to satisfy own criteria for a good job, even when this means doing more than is required. *Note:* Consider the performance exhibited in comparison with the individual's capabilities, not in comparison with the performance or capabilities of others.

It is possible to measure the demonstrated appraisee traits (qualities) relative to the eight behavioral dimensions. Figure 7–3 is a Behavior Dimension Appraisal Form developed by the author using the Bell system dimensions, subdimension categories, and a Bell system five-interval rating scale.

By having the immediate supervisor appraise certain observable behavioral traits that have already been validated through assessment center efforts, it is possible to link the scores that assessees receive in the assessment centers with scores on the same qualities from demonstrated behavior in real-world situations. Combining assessment center information with management-generated appraisal information is possibly one of the most powerful employee measurements available for management decision purposes. It is also possible and highly recommended that the appraisal process require the supervisor and subordinate to be aware of such strengths and weaknesses and to develop constructive procedures and programs that strengthen these and other identified traits—skill areas—that will influence future growth and promotion opportunities.

The supervisor should arrive at the rating decision by using his or her collective experience in determining what constitutes average behavior for those employees who are at the same level as the appraisee. No rating should be assigned to any of the dimensions if there is no documentation for support; this should be a rare occurrence.

If behavior over the appraisal period has shown a clear and consistent change, the behavior shown at the end of the period is the best indicator of what rating should be assigned.

A potential problem with the use of a form such as Figure 7–3 is that the rating system does not provide a universal frame of reference or benchmark but relies significantly on each supervisor's perception of what constitutes average behavior. Many researchers would contend that differences in supervisory perceptions will significantly vary the ratings for a similar kind of demonstrated behavior. One approach for overcoming this possible weakness is the development of a series of statements that describe behaviors from "unacceptable" to "extremely effective" for each profile statement within these eight behavioral performance dimensions. This profile of behaviors would provide

Behavioral Performance Dimensions		Ratings					
	N.A. N.O.	1	2	3	4	5
1. Oral Communication Emphasis is on the manner in which ideas and information are presented						
(a) Organizes logically						
(b) Uses appropriate terms						
(c) Speaks clearly and concisely						
(d) Acts confident						
(e) Obtains audience attention						
2. Written Communication Emphasis is on the manner in which ideas and information are presented						
(a) Organizes logically						
(b) Uses appropriate terms						
(c) Writes clearly and concisely						
(d) Uses appropriate grammer and style						
3. Flexibility Consider only actual change initiated by the individual, not merely verbal expressions of a change in mind						
(a) Suits style to setting						
(b) Suits approach to situation needs						
(c) Tries alternatives						
4. Performance Stability Consider only the ability to continue to perform at the usual level, not ability to show signs of stress or uncertainty						
(a) Maintains performance under increased pressure						
(b) Maintains performance under increased uncertainty						
5. Decision Making Consider the quality of decisions only in light of information available at the time they are made						
(a) Uses available information						
(b) Anticipates future						
(c) Recognizes interactions						
(d) Considers situation and alternatives						
6. Leadership Consider the effectiveness of leadership attempts, not the style of leadership						
(a) Shows active involvement						
(b) Obtains positive reponse						
(c) Moves toward goal						
7. Organization and Planning						
(a) Sets priorities						
(b) Anticipates needs, avoids scheduling conflicts						
(c) Delegates appropriately						
(d) Follows up						
(e) Gets work done						
8. Inner Work Standards Consider the performance exhibited in comparison with the individual's capabilities, not in comparison with the performance or capabilities of others						
(a) Does best possible job						
(b) Satisfies own criteria						

N.A. — Not applicable
N.O. — Not observable
1 — Very little effective behavior shown compared with average behavior of persons at the ratee's level
2 — Some effective behavior, but less than most persons at the ratee's level
3 — About the same as the average person at the ratee's level
4 — More effective behavior than most persons at the ratee's level
5 — A great deal of effective behavior, more than all but a few at the ratee's level

FIGURE 7–3. Behavior Dimensions Appraisal Form.

commonly understood and accepted benchmarks to describe various levels of performance. Developing these kinds of standards requires an effort similar to that used for establishing BARS, as described in Chapters 5 and 6. Here again, the battle of cost versus increased accuracy comes into play. Universal benchmarks would certainly be a valuable addition, but their ability to increase the accuracy of ratings has yet to be proved.

A major theme of this book is that, above all, the total environment has the greatest influence on the accuracy of ratings. Next, well trained, properly supported supervisors can accurately discriminate in the ratings they offer with the limited kind of information provided in Figure 7–3. This book emphasizes the development of well defined responsibilities and duties as the primary support for any kind of performance measurement and rating process.

The dimensions and their respective profiles of behaviors in Figure 7–3 describe qualities that are highly prized by many organizations. The value of this kind of rating instrument is that it formally recognizes and informs ratees of those qualities or behaviors that the organization wishes to see demonstrated. Although the opportunity for unfair treatment (ratings) is certainly as possible with this instrument as it is with almost any performance measurement instrument, the employee's right to "grieve" or request review is critical in minimizing felt bias.

Demotion, Lay-Offs (Reduction-in-Force—RIFs), Termination

Few individuals and fewer organizations like to be in a position in which they have to make demotion, lay-off, and termination decisions. These decisions can cause untold anxieties to the decision-makers and frustration, hostility, and stress among those on the receiving end. The two most frequently used criteria for making these decisions are seniority and performance. Because of the many problems related to the accuracy of performance ratings, there is considerable resistance to the use of performance ratings for these kinds of movement decisions.

On the other hand, organizations frequently want to use their appraisal ratings as a major input to these kinds of decisions. If an organization is going to have and maintain an effective and efficient work force, it wants to retain its best performers and remove its poorest or least effective members. Performance ratings should identify those whose workplace behavior has been unacceptable or those who are relatively the poorest performers. When using performance ratings for demotion, lay-off, and termination decisions, organizations must make certain that the ratings and the documentation that supports these ratings are capable of withstanding the close scrutiny of a judge and jury.

A number of federal and state laws now protect employees from unfair treatment. In particular, Title VII of the Civil Rights Act and the Age Discrimination in Employment Act have been used effectively against employers who make specific movement decisions without proper support. The laws, court rulings, and the concepts of validity and reliability provide the content of Chapter 11, which focuses specifically on due process and employee rights at the workplace.

Organizations must be particularly sensitive to problems that arise when they use the results of a new or relatively new performance appraisal program for making movement decisions, especially in the area described in this section. There must be some kind of historical record of performance ratings, organization behaviors, and ratee behaviors. This means employees must be notified of deficiencies, organizations must demonstrate an ability and willingness to provide support to overcome deficiencies, and ratees must be given the opportunity to behave in a manner that demonstrates an ability or desire to overcome identified deficiencies.

In an ongoing organization where employees are not new hires and where an existing performance appraisal program is either drastically modified or a new one has been installed, sufficient time must be allowed for all parties to make full and proper use of rating information. When an organization is involved in reduction-in-force or demotion and termination, it would appear that a historical record of rating data and associated behaviors of all involved parties for at least two to three years would be a minimal requirement (and possibly as much as five years would be highly desirable). For these kinds of uses, an organization cannot implement a performance appraisal program and expect to make fair and valid judgments in a relatively short period of time, that is, less than two to three years. When faced with these kinds of problems and when good historical performance data are unavailable, organizations must rely on seniority. This may not be a desirable option, but it may be the only one available when performance appraisal deficiencies occur and have not been corrected.

Transfer

Another movement decision influenced by performance ratings is the lateral transfer. Again, for numerous personal reasons, many employees seek the chance to perform in the same job at another location or, possibly, in an entirely different kind of job. This kind of movement not only adds variety to workplace responsibilities but provides an employee with the opportunity to use and develop different sets of knowledge and skills. The transfer may also open the door for promotion in a different career ladder when the present one is blocked.

Here again, organizations normally use performance rating information to assist in making transfer decisions. Although transfer opportunities have always been considered important by employees, the importance of such opportunities may increase significantly in the coming decades as the large number of "baby-boom" workers compete for fewer and fewer promotion opportunities.

Human Resource Planning

Human resource planning focuses particularly on long-term human resource requirements and forecasts demands for human resource skills. In human resource planning, organizations identify replacements or backups for managerial, professional, and other key jobs. Human resource planning also identifies the knowledge and skills required for each of these jobs, those individuals who are fully qualified, and those who have the potential for acquiring the necessary knowledge and skills.

Accurate identification of the knowledge, skills, and responsibilities needed in the performance of each job—from the most senior to lower-level jobs that vary according to organizational demands—is a first step in human resource planning. The processes developed throughout this book fit neatly into any human resource planning operation. Valid and reliable selection and assessment of potential procedures require accurate and precise identification of job knowledge, skills, and responsibilities. Information from these sources provides those responsible for human resource planning with lists of knowledge, skills, and personal characteristics required to perform the jobs of the organization successfully.

Performance appraisals and other kinds of available information assist human resource planners to compare available knowledge and skills to those that will be required at some future date. The identification of organizational weaknesses in the area of current employee knowledge, skills, and personal characteristics signals a "red flag" to those responsible for training and development.

Human resource planning not only identifies those who are available and qualified to perform higher-level jobs but, also, assists in the development of career planning programs for employees. The part that counseling plays in the appraisal process is discussed in Chapter

9. Career development requires inputs from both human resource planning and performance appraisal. In addition, successful implementation of human resource planning and performance appraisal calls for two-way communication that provides vital and useful information to both programs.

One of the major responsibilities of personnel involved in the staffing area is the design and development of tests for use in making selection decisions. The underlying requirement of a selection test is that it is successful in its assignment of the testee to the appropriate job, that is, the job for which the individual is qualified. The purpose of a selection test is to identify or predict those individuals who will successfully perform the assignments of the jobs for which they are applying. The reliability and validity of a test is substantiated by the appraisal ratings received by employees in the performance of their jobs.

VALIDATION OF SELECTION CRITERIA AND TRAINING ACTIVITIES

In the same manner, organizations can also measure the effectiveness of their training programs. Performance appraisal can identify how well employees perform specific activities. This kind of observation and measurement may further identify knowledge and skills, strengths, and deficiencies. Training programs can be (a) designed to overcome knowledge and skill weaknesses or (b) measured to determine how well participants were able to transfer learning from the training program to actual job-related behaviors.

Performance appraisal is one major tool available to management that can link the almost dream-like desires of long-range (strategic) planning to the tough, no-nonsense world of the here-and-now plans and day-to-day operations. No matter how much knowledge, skill, realism, and integrity those involved in the design and development of the strategic plans have, it is seldom (if ever) possible to predict or identify the various conditions that will arise in the implementation of the plans that might support or block their achievement.

PLANNING

Once the reality of "doing" contaminates the strategic plans, modification begins to occur. In an ongoing organization, it becomes difficult if not impossible to distinguish between these two parts of a continuous interactive system. The mixing of the two parts can, however, easily result in misunderstandings, friction, and that eternal bug-a-boo—personal threats.

Any gaps or communication failures in the top-down planning process can easily lead to individuals performing job assignments that fail to support the achievement of organizational objectives. Opportunities for misunderstanding and incorrect assumptions are substantial in the evolution of the planning process, from the highest levels of the organization to the performance of work assignments by each employee. Nothing should be left to chance. All requirements and desired results should be communicated precisely and explicitly in terms that the jobholder understands. All organizations are interdependent systems that must fit together. The top-down planning activities provide the framework for fitting the many parts together. The failure to provide the specific guidelines necessary for all parts (and jobholders) to meet system requirements does grant higher levels of management a tool of flexibility. By not being constrained by specific and well communicated top-down goals, it is easier to change the "game plan" on subordinates. At the same time, however, the lack of specific and understood guidelines permits lower-level employees to play games and take courses of action that limit any threat to themselves while minimizing their contributions to the achievement of work-unit and organizational goals.

Performance Appraisal and Long-Term Planning

Two major barriers that block the inclusion of longer-term planning into the performance appraisal system are:

1. Longer-term planning has not been done or has been done so poorly that it cannot be communicated to lower-level managers or to non-management employees.
2. This kind of information is considered extremely sensitive to the survival and growth of the organization.

Top managers may feel that dissemination of this kind of information throughout the organization will probably lead to its eventual disclosure to competitors—those competing not only for financial, technical, material, and human resource inputs, but also for clients who use its outputs. When this kind of strategic information is in the hands of competitors, the survival and growth of the organization may be in peril.

It is possible that some aspects of organizational objectives and strategy must be held confidential. Since organizational objectives and strategies have an impact on the design and accomplishment of work-unit goals, it is extremely difficult to see how lower-level managers, even operative employees, may be excluded from understanding the great majority of issues and concepts found within the objectives and strategy of the organization, if a work environment that promotes trust is to be implemented.

The final decision about communicating this kind of information within the organization must be a choice between these alternatives:

1. If our competitors know what we intend to do, they can preempt our movement and capture our market.

2. If all of our employees know what we are doing and the importance of their roles in the successful accomplishment of our objectives and are willing to assume an active and forthright commitment to these objectives, we can provide a quality, quantity, and timeliness of output that our competitors cannot match.

There is almost no middle ground in this top-level decision. It is one of either (a) communicating top-level information to employees that enables them to make job-related decisions that support the accomplishment of the organization's mission and objectives, or (b) managing in a very authoritarian manner that requires only those directives necessary to keep all employees on the same wavelength.

Contemporary organizations must operate in an extremely complex environment, which causes a high degree of uncertainty. In order for top managers to make the best decisions for their organizations within this uncertain environment, they must have huge amounts of information. The generation of information for top management's processing requires increased employee involvement in the communication processes at all levels. In order for employees at these lower levels to provide the amount and quality of information required, they must be capable of performing their job assignments, willing to accept job responsibilities, and granted the opportunity to provide critical performance-related information.

A Trusting Work Environment

For over 30 years, those involved in the human aspects of organizational life have been screaming about the need for trust—for managers to trust managers, for managers to trust nonmanagement employees, and for employees at all levels to trust top management. The establishment of a trusting environment has its foundation in the communication system of the organization. It assists in explaining how a performance appraisal system fits into the operation of an effective and efficient organization. If employees at all levels are to integrate their job assignments and personal goals into the achievement of the overall longer-term mission and objectives of the organization, they must know exactly what the mission and objectives are.

Performance appraisal as a component of organizational planning is the process that directly ties together the planning, doing, results achieved, and results desired. If links are missing in the process, the chance of failure in the achievement of an organization's mission and objectives increases significantly. This situation may arise because of the failure of those at the top to receive communications on the real issues as they occur because those at succeedingly lower levels in the organization refuse to identify and discuss the threats and areas of potential failure they face in performing their job assignments. Goal accomplishment at lower levels in the organization becomes a game when truth related to goal accomplishment is perceived as a threat. For many, truth is only a good idea when it is not threatening. If, at the beginning of the planning process, top officials of the organization are unwilling or unable to communicate openly and truthfully with subordinates, then how can subordinates be expected to accurately recognize what is expected of them and be willing to communicate potentially critical information when the result could be the "loss of the head" of the upward communicator?

In recent years, a few progressive organizations have been willing to reject old customs that place the stamp of "top secret" on certain kinds of organizational information. Very little research, however, has been completed on the benefits and costs resulting from the elimination of the "for top management only" restriction on such information. In the area of compensation information, research does indicate that when organizations provide employees with what had previously been restricted information no ill effects or unsatisfactory, emotionally-charged scenes have been noted. An example is providing range information for pay grades and assigning jobs to pay grades. Frequently, those who want to maintain the confidentiality of information state that lower levels of employees are truly not interested. An opposite, and possibly more accurate, view is one that recognizes that employees accept the information, use it for their own personal decision making, and then drop the issue. The result is that most workers receiving information that was previously considered confidential feel that it is about time management provided them with that information.

Performance Appraisal Inputs and Outputs

Because performance appraisal ratings can influence so many operations of the organization, they should be tied directly to the strategic planning process, if at all possible. This linkage permits an orderly and systematic analysis of the appraisal activities.

By integrating performance appraisal into the strategic planning functions, those responsible for the design and the administration of the performance appraisal system are able to describe clearly and precisely why a formal performance appraisal program exists and the broad organizational factors that limit or guide its operation.

Top management sends a message throughout the organization that there is a critical need for performance appraisal when they use and depend on the information it supplies for making strategic planning decisions. Their involvement and insistence on accurate and identifiable measurement information is possibly the single most important demand that keeps the appraisal process functioning as designed. Commitment to the use of appraisal information rather than simple lip service that states that "we support our performance appraisal program" is necessary to maintain the continuation of this sensitive operation, because the seeds of self-destruction are extremely powerful.

Through the joining of performance appraisal and long-term planning, employees at all levels can more clearly visualize and understand the relationship between performance appraisal actions and the mission, philosophy, policies, and objectives of the organization. If performance appraisal is to have any chance for success, it must overcome a wide variety of intellectual, psychological, and emotional barriers. It is critical that the activities implemented to minimize the negative influence of these employee concerns have their roots planted firmly in the basic foundation of the organization.

It is far easier to see the relationship between performance appraisal and the shorter-term tactical plans of the organization. Almost all performance appraisal programs operate on a here-and-now basis. In most cases, supervisors rate the performance of their immediate subordinates relative to demonstrated workplace behaviors. When measuring a subordinate's performance, a supervisor normally reviews how well a person performed in completing required job assignments and the contributions the employee made toward the achievement of work-unit goals. In most cases, both supervisor and subordinate attention focuses on day-to-day activities. Performance appraisal reviews current operations. As soon after the appraisal activity as possible, feedback on demonstrated behavior should be provided so that employee behavior can be directed toward the most efficient use of organizational resources (including the employee's own time and effort) to achieve short-term goals.

Concurrent with the recognition that performance appraisal is an integral part of both the long- and shorter-term planning functions of the organization, the opportunity to make good use of performance measurement and rating information for other vital organizational programs arises. Figure 7–4 describes the role of performance appraisal in connecting planning and other major uses of performance appraisal information output.

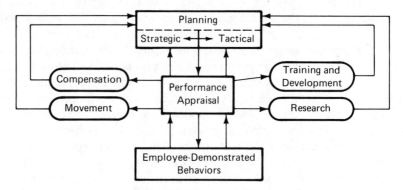

FIGURE 7–4. Performance Appraisal Information Flow.

Integrating Performance Appraisal and Planning

The integration and coordination of planning and performance appraisal is not an easy assignment under the best of conditions. What are the barriers that arise when those responsible for performance appraisal have minimal to absolutely no influence on organizational planning activities? Some common ones are (a) the difficulty planners have in fitting the measurement of employee workplace behavior to the long-range plans of the organization, and (b) the failure of the organization to have a formalized planning process that even closely resembles the strategic and tactical planning programs as described in both this chapter and Chapter 3.

As mentioned earlier, if performance appraisal is to have any opportunity for long-term success and, in most cases, short-term success, in light of the many and varied complex issues related to employee performance, it must be inextricably tied to the planning, doing, and control functions of the organization. Not only is the effectiveness of a performance appraisal program directly dependent on its links to organizational planning and control, but it just possibly may be that planning and control failures occur because of the inability of policy-makers and planners to recognize the importance of the performance appraisal program and to be active recipients of valid performance appraisal information. Linking performance appraisal to the entire planning-doing-control functions of an organization permits it to be the part of the operating system of an organization that detects problems that may occur anywhere, anytime in the organization and provides the kinds of inputs that can lead to the reduction of uncertainty and the changes in basic assumptions and policies that are so critical to the survival of the organization.

Planning Homework. Once the idea is accepted that performance appraisal programs must have a foundation firmly established in the planning function of the organization, the search must begin for all available long-range or strategic planning information. If an organization does not have a mission statement, a few pertinent questions directed at key officials will assist in developing one that will be helpful in designing a framework for a long-range planning program. The next step is to create a philosophy statement. To elicit senior management support and involvement, it may be wise to show how a philosophy statement that identifies the values and concepts of the leaders of the organization can be most useful in defining acceptable employee patterns of behavior.

The establishment of a performance appraisal policy statement must consider (a) who is to be involved, (b) the roles they play, (c) when prescribed activities will be performed, (d) the kinds of instruments to be designed and used, (e) the kinds of rating scores that are wanted, and (f) how the rating information will be used. Further information in this area will develop as strategic planning evolves into the tactical plans.

The next step is the establishment of organizational objectives. Here again, this component of the strategic planning function of the organization may never have been placed into writing. The effort and research exerted in collecting the information for this long-range planning component may not only assist in the development of the processes and mechanics necessary for a successful appraisal program, but may open the eyes of top management as to the kinds of support that they must provide in order for the performance appraisal mission to be successfully accomplished.

After completing this rough approximation of the long-range planning program, it is time to tackle the shorter-term tactical planning processes. A start in soliciting the support of all supervisors who will eventually have performance appraisal responsibilities is to ask them to respond to two requests for information:

1. Please describe as precisely as possible the goals your work unit must accomplish to enable the organization to achieve its objectives and goals.

2. Please describe the major or basic activities performed by your work unit (the function statement of the work unit).

Once this information has been obtained, an organization-goal activity chart can be developed. If the organization already has job descriptions, these should become a part of the goal activity chart by including the appropriate job descriptions under each function statement. If job descriptions are not available, the appropriate function statements should include a listing of job titles with the number of incumbents. This provides a first cut at what should be occurring and the kinds of work being performed in each work unit. It provides a solid base for identifying the various kinds of activities and results the performance appraisal program will have to measure and the most suitable processes and instruments to use in rating employee performance.

Developing an outline of the planning process that includes a description of the organizational mission, philosophy, objectives, and policy as well as individual work-unit goals, function statements, and job descriptions, if available, enables those involved in designing a performance appraisal program to describe the operations of the appraisal program under consideration or to defend one that is being reviewed by top officials of the organization.

This kind of thought and action process assists in identifying weaknesses and failures in current appraisal programs (where they now exist) and the actions the organization must take to design, implement, and administer a performance measurement and rating program that satisfies most of the demands of managers and employees.

At first glance, it may appear that the development of a planning-based performance appraisal program is unacceptably complex and costly. The first point to recognize is that a performance appraisal system involves or includes parts of many other operating systems of an organization. If organizations had to design, develop, and implement all of the parts of such a system as recommended in this book, few, if any, would even attempt such an undertaking. Most organizations, however, already have in operation and are using most parts of a performance appraisal system. It is not necessary to design and implement a whole new program. What *is* necessary, however, is to improve and expand some existing programs that are missing critical components (normally fewer than anticipated) and then to link all components into a comprehensive, continuous, and coordinated information collection, summarization, review, and output system.

ANALYZING PROCEDURES AND INSTRUMENTS FOR USE IN PERFORMANCE APPRAISAL PROGRAMS

To further assist in developing a performance appraisal program, the following guide chart can be used for examining procedures and instruments for acquiring and documenting performance data and information. Figure 7–5 is a matrix with potential uses of appraisal data and information listed on the rows and the major kinds of procedures and instruments currently being used in rating employee performance heading the columns. Criteria used for measuring the worth or useful-

Potential Uses	Ranking*	Narrative*	Checklist*	Performance Dimension Rating Scale*	Results Based*
1. Organization planning					
2. Work-unit planning					
3. Employee job planning					
4. Employee career planning					
5. Base pay adjustment					
6. Incentive awards					
7. Movement decisions (promotion, demotion, lay-off, termination)					
8. Training					
9. Development					
10. Validation of selection and other human resource instruments					

*Each procedure or instrument can be further subdivided into more specific kinds within the general class. This would further improve analytical process.

FIGURE 7-5. Matrix for Analyzing Value/Usefulness of Rating Instruments and Procedures.

How Well and How Completely Does the Information Provided by the Instrument or Procedure Describe the:	Rating Scale		
	Not Very Well	Moderately Well	Very Well
1. Work done by the employee?			
2. On-the-job problems faced by the employee?			
3. Resources made available to the employee?			
4. Effective use of available and provided resources?			
5. Resources desired or required to successfully complete job assignments?			
6. Specific contributions the employee made leading to the successful accomplishment of the mission and objectives of the organization?			
7. Knowledge and skills of the employee demonstrated in current work assignments?			
8. Knowledge and skills of the employee useful in other job assignments?			
9. Specific levels of performance to enable the organization to fairly allocate available rewards?			
10. Specific levels of performance that permit valid comparisons with similarly situated employees?			

Three additional dimensions that may be useful in measuring the worth or desirability of a particular rating instrument or procedure are:
1. Design cost
2. Ease and cost of installation
3. Ease and cost of operation (including completion by raters, reviewers, and total administration)

FIGURE 7–6. Criteria for Measuring Worth/Usefulness of Various Kinds of Rating Instruments and Procedures.

ness of each technique are listed in Figure 7–6. The various procedures or instruments being considered for use or being used by an organization can be evaluated with the matrix, the measurement criteria, and its simple rating scale. A score of 1 to 3 can be used to measure the effectiveness of each procedure, technique, or instrument. (Here again, the ordinal-interval problem arises, but for this use, the scale can be considered as interval and the scores added for each criterion.)

This kind of analysis may identify the need to use various procedures and instruments in some combination to acquire all of the necessary performance information. After doing this analysis, it may be useful to review these approaches from the perspective of (a) initial design cost, (b) ease and cost of installation, and (c) ease and cost of operation (including completion by raters, reviewers, and total administration). By performing this kind of analysis, it may be possible to identify not only information gaps, but also areas in which conflict may arise. This kind of planning can help minimize costly problems and blunders when operations are under way.

Chapter 8

Administration of the
Performance Appraisal Program

Forty or more years of suffering with ineffective performance appraisal programs may truly not be the result of a lack of understanding and failure of instrument and process designs. The failures may relate to an inability of organizations to collect, store, retrieve, analyze, and disseminate the wide variety and large volume of data required of an effective appraisal program. Multidimensions of performance, differences in performance dimensions for different jobs, performance dimensions and standards that may vary with changing situations or existing conditions, and variations in ratings among raters and by work groups all combine to make performance appraisal a most complex operation.

The information-gathering, analysis, and dissemination problems are now ready for solution. Computer hardware and software are now or will shortly be available at reasonable costs to all organizations interested in operating a formal performance appraisal program.

In many cases, those responsible for the operation of performance appraisal programs have had neither sufficient human resources nor the technical resources to process the data inputs and outputs of an appraisal program to meet the wide variety of informational demands. It just may be that, for the first time, organizations now have available the capabilities to properly operate an appraisal system through the computer-based information system (CBIS). The CBIS not only provides almost unlimited amounts of data and information to administrators but also permits each involved employee access to rating information that he or she has a right to know. The CBIS can tie everyone into the appraisal system. Properly designed and correctly used, it will minimize opportunities to evade rating and review responsibilities,

243

reduce unfair and undeserved treatment, and keep everyone in an up-to-date, real-time mode.

With the advent of the use of a CBIS in the total operation of performance appraisal, those responsible for its administration will no longer be involved in a "Mission Impossible." Whoever is finally delegated the authority to design the measurement and rating instruments and processes and to establish standing operating procedures will have the technology available to substantially increase the likelihood of success. Those having administrative responsibilities may find the following checklist helpful in determining the actions they should be taking.

1. How can performance be measured?
2. What kind of performance criteria should be identified and defined?
3. What measurement instruments will best facilitate the accurate and prompt rating of employees?
4. Who will be involved in the measurement and rating process?
5. How well do those involved know what is expected of them?
6. What do those involved think that they are doing?
7. What are those involved actually doing? What procedures and technologies will be used to monitor and audit the program?
8. Are rating outputs of value to those wishing to use them?

Recognizing that subjectivity will always play a major role in the appraisal of performance and, at the same time, that performance ratings can significantly influence the life of the ratee, administrators of performance appraisal programs must do their best to design and operate a program that provides current and accurate performance information.

Following the development of the measurement instrument and the establishment of operating procedures, the role of performance appraisal administrators is one of processing data and information. This requirement is no easy assignment, and it may be a major reason for past failures of performance appraisal programs.

This chapter discusses the administrative opportunities provided through a properly functioning CBIS. It discusses (a) the kinds of data to be entered into a computer-based performance appraisal data and information system, (b) how the data will be processed, (c) how these inputs and outputs are used, (d) who has access to specific parts of the system, (e) how access is made, and (f) some of the kinds of outputs that will keep the system honest and, above all, useful and valuable.

The electronic marvel introduced to the world of work in the last half of the twentieth century is now ready to assist those who have performance appraisal responsibilities. The computer and its numerous accessories permit the collection and storage of vast amounts of data that, in turn, can be rapidly analyzed, summarized, and transmitted to those seeking or wanting to use the processed data. For performance appraisal purposes, CAPA provides the following services:

1. Dissemination of specific and useful data to those having both the need and right to know.

2. Analysis of supervisors' ratings that provide a first indication of (a) common rating errors such as "halo effect," leniency or strictness, and central tendency; and (b) bias for or against certain groups of employees that can be identified through such characteristics as sex, race, national origin, handicaps, veteran status, and age.

3. Monitoring of the system to ensure the rating of an employee at the assigned time and the submission of all required data and information.

4. Identification of changes in an employee's performance rating over an extended period of time.

5. Exception information that becomes a "flag" item (pinpointing problems so that corrective actions can be taken).

6. Comparison of rating behaviors (distribution of ratings) among raters.

7. Distribution of ratings across a rating scale relating to each performance dimension.

8. Variations in ratings relative to a specific performance dimension.

9. Identification of action taken as a result of performance appraisal outputs.

Location of CAPA

In organizations where large computers are currently providing vast amounts of data and information from a wide variety of sources, it is quite likely that CAPA will be nothing more than an additional subsystem. Many small and medium size organizations, however, should consider the purchase and use of a minicomputer dedicated

---

[1] Charles F. Myers, management consultant, provided invaluable assistance in developing the concepts and plans related to CAPA.

to and operated by the individual(s) responsible for the administration of the performance appraisal plan.

Distributing Processing Approach. Organizations with large mainframes (central computers) that either have an existing operation of an organization-wide communication network that links all input and output data sources to the mainframe or are moving toward such an operation may find it advantageous to involve all computer-related personnel with administrative responsibilities in the flow of performance appraisal inputs and outputs.

The CBIS-CAPA program, whether mainframe centered or using a dedicated minicomputer, will connect all data entry and facsimile devices of the organization. On a command initiated through the tapping of a few keys, the network will permit the almost instant flow of appropriate data to the proper point. In a few organizations, terminals are now available to almost all of their employees. By the end of the decade of the '80s, most employees in the great majority of organizations will have ready access to terminals, making it quick and easy to obtain computer-stored and -processed data and information.

Dedicated Minicomputer. The organization that decides to link its performance appraisal program to a minicomputer will recognize a number of immediate costs. The first expense is the purchase of the hardware—probably between $75,000 and $150,000. Immediately following are the costs related to the development or purchase of necessary software that directs the operation of CAPA. An additional cost is the monthly maintenance fee. Next is the hiring and training of personnel to operate this kind of CAPA system. The major work areas include CAPA manager, data base administrator, analyst-programmer, computer operator, and data processing clerk. After acquisition of the computer and necessary software, it is possible that one individual could be trained to perform all five CAPA responsibilities.

The costs described here for a CAPA-dedicated minicomputer could be spread over practically all personnel-related activities. In reality, this would make the CAPA system but one part of a computerized total human resources system. Providing this kind of service reduces the impact of what may first appear to be a relatively large expenditure.

CAPA Components

To acquire a better understanding of the operation of a CAPA system, knowledge of the following components of CAPA is essential:

1. Data base.
2. File sets.
3. Data base glossary.
4. Data element dictionary.
5. CAPA reports.

A data base management system (DBMS) ties together these five components to ensure the successful operation of CAPA. Recognizing the sensitivity of CAPA outputs to practically everything that occurs in an organization, it is vital that these outputs be accurate and reliable. The same sensitivity issues also make it mandatory that confidentiality be maintained and that privileged information be transmitted only to those who have the right to know. The outputs must also be transmitted in a form that permits those using the data to scan the outputs and quickly understand and accurately interpret the data provided.

Data Base. The first step in developing a data base is to identify all of the data elements required to produce complete and acceptable reports to all end users of CAPA. These end users may include the following:

Performance appraisal administrators—Those responsible for the design and operation of the performance appraisal program.

Top management and its auditors—Those responsible for effective operation of the organization and their "eyes and ears" (auditors), who assist them in knowing how well the organization is operating relative to established procedures and guidelines.

Division and department heads and their monitors—Those responsible for the specific operation of divisions and departments and the group (monitors) who provide constant review information on the operation of the performance appraisal program within their areas of authority.

Ratees—Those whose performance has been appraised. This kind of information lets them know how they are doing and permits them to self-develop practices that will lead to improved performance.

Raters—Those who rate performance. This kind of information provides these individuals with comprehensive insights as to their rating behaviors and permits comparison with others in similar positions, allowing self-diagnosis and internally generated changes.

Reviewers—Those who have responsibility for reviewing rater ratings. This kind of information permits rapid and complete reviews of rating behaviors of supervisors and the comparison of these behaviors with others. It also directs attention to problem areas.

Users—Those involved in making decisions in such critical areas as (a) planning (programming and budgeting—resource allocation) in both the long and short term; (b) compensation (pay practices for base pay adjustments and decisions concerning a wide variety of performance-related incentives); (c) training and development (current job-related practices and future growth opportunities); (d) movement (promotion, lateral transfer, demotion, lay-off, and termination), and (e) selection (identifying those critical knowledge, skills, and abilities that lead to successful job performance).

Data elements may include such items as employee:

1. Name
2. Organization number
3. Social Security number
4. Birth date
5. Marital status
6. Number of dependents
7. Education
8. Sex
9. Race
10. National origin
11. Handicap
12. Veteran status
13. Initial hire date
14. Rehire date
15. Date appointed to current job
16. Employment status
17. Union membership
18. Current job
19. Occupation
20. Current supervisor
21. Current job number
22. Current performance review date

23. Current pay
24. Pay period
25. Job pay grade
26. Pay grade
27. Pay grade maximum
28. Pay grade minimum
29. Date of last pay adjustment
30. Amount of last pay adjustment
31. Kind of last pay adjustment
32. Date of last bonus
33. Amount of last bonus
34. Kind of last bonus
35. Sequential review number
36. Global performance review
37. Rating of performance dimension one
38. Rating of performance dimension two
39. Rating of performance dimension three
40. Rating of performance dimension four
41. Rating of performance dimension five
42. Rating of performance dimension six
43. Rating of performance dimension seven
44. Rating of performance dimension eight
45. Rating of performance dimension nine
46. Rating of performance dimension ten
47. Date of review
48. Job at review date
49. Department
50. Current shift
51. Termination date
52. Reason for termination
53. Job title

Each data item must be identified by a unique element name. The element name may be abbreviated, or it may be an acronym. It is always written in upper case letters. For example, current pay is CURRPAY; date of birth is BIRTHDAY. The number of characters in the element name may be constrained by the equipment. A common limit is eight characters.

Organizations that already have an existing data base—say, for example, one being used for payroll administration—may find that there is considerable overlap between the existing data base and one required for CAPA. Normally, it is unnecessary to repeat what is already available. What may be required is simply to merge data elements not previously identified into the existing data base.

File Sets. In identifying the needed data elements, the user will undoubtedly note that the elements will fall into sets of logical, natural groupings. These groupings are referred to as file sets. In the example of CAPA discussed in this book, all of the data elements can be grouped into four file sets:

1. The employee file. This file contains all of the "constant" data elements related to each employee (e.g., name, Social Security number, etc.).
2. The job file. This file contains all of the constant information related to all jobs (e.g., job title, pay period, etc.).
3. The pay grade file. This file contains information related to the organization's pay grades (e.g., maximum and minimum).
4. The performance review file. This file contains information related to all employee reviews. This file will grow larger year by year as historical review information is added.

File sets can be one of two types—a master file set or a detail file set. Each master file set consists of a set of data elements, with one of the data elements identified as the unique file key. Upon entering all of the data associated with the unique file key, a logical record is established. Entering all logical records establishes a file. In the employee file, for example, the employee number is the unique file key. All of the information associated with a particular employee number (e.g., employee name) forms a logical record for that one employee. All the records for all the employees forms the employee file, which is a master file set.

The job file is another master file set with the job number being the file key. The pay grade file is also a master file set. Here, the pay grade is the file key.

The other file type—the detail file—can have more than one file key per record. It can also have more than one record with the same file key. The performance review file is a detail file set because file keys must be duplicated. For example, if employee 1468 had more than one performance review, the number 1468 will appear as often as the employee had a review (see the Performance Review File in Figure 8–1 on page 252).

In order for the computer to identify a specific data element in a particular file, each data element must have a unique element name (e.g., in the employee file employee number is EMPLOYEE, while in the performance review file employee number is REVEMP).

Once the user has established file sets, the DBMS can be used to link the file sets through the file keys. For example, if a report were desired that showed all employee names and their job titles, then CURRJOB in the employee file could be linked to JOB in the job file. This would allow NAME and JOBTITL to be printed on a report.

The user may wonder why the job title should not be in the employee master file. An example will clarify this. Suppose that job number 601 is a clerk-typist and that 75 people hold this job. Now suppose that the personnel department wants to change the job title to secretary. If the job title were in the employee master file, it would have to be changed in each of the 75 records where it appears. By putting it in the job file, however, only one change is required.

Depending on the user's particular situation, it may be necessary to add data elements and possibly organize them into slightly different file arrangements than are shown in the examples that follow. These examples represent the author's feelings on what would constitute a fairly typical CAPA system.

These four file sets provide an appropriate schema for the data base. A schema is simply a statement of the elements of data in the data base and their logical relationships. Figure 8–1 shows how the three master files and the detail file link together.

Data Base Glossary. To ensure a full understanding of all data elements, a glossary must be developed that lists alphabetically all data elements, their abbreviated titles, and a complete definition that precisely describes them. Examples of glossary descriptions of some items previously listed within the data base section are:

EMPLOYMENT STATUS—EMPSTAT: Organizational status of the employee, i.e., permanent full-time, permanent part-time, temporary full-time, temporary part-time.

KIND OF LAST PAY ADJUSTMENT—KINLASPAYADJ: Identifies reason for pay adjustment, i.e., seniority (tenure); cost of living adjustment; market adjustment; pay structure adjustment; merit increase; special recognition award (may include further description of specific kind or name of award).

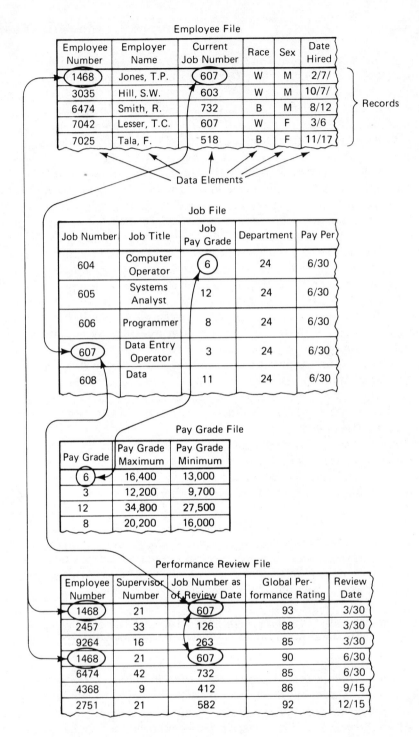

FIGURE 8–1. Linking CAPA Master and Detail Files.

252

Data Element Dictionary. This reference book identifies and completely describes each data element on a separate page. The dictionary is a resource that allows DBMS users to understand the exact meaning of the data element. The dictionary is especially valuable when different departments or sections of an organization develop their own data base or make inputs into a common base and in cases where it is

Example:

EMPLOYEEFILE: The employee file includes the following:

Item	Element Name (Field)
Employee number	EMPLOYEE (File key)
Employee name	NAME
Social Security number	SSNUMBER
Sex	SEX
Race	RACE
Marital status	MARITAL
Number of dependents	NODEP
Date of birth	BIRTHDAY
Current job number	CURRJOB
Normal review date	REVDATE
Current job supervisor	CURRSUPV
National origin	NATION
Veteran status	VETERAN
Date appointed to current job	JOBAPTDATE
Rehire date	REHIRDATE
Education	EDUC
Employment status	EMPLSTAT
Date of last pay adjustment	DATLASPAYADJ
Amount of last pay adjustment	AMTLASPAYADJ
Kind of last pay adjustment	KINLASPAYADJ
Date of last bonus	DATLASBON
Amount of last bonus	AMTLASBON
Kind of last bonus	KINLASBON
Union membership	UNIONMEM
Handicap status	HANDICAP
Date hired	HIREDATE
Current rate of pay	CURRPAY
Current shift	CURRSHIF
Termination date	TERMDATE
Reason for termination	REASTERM

Example:

JOBFILE: The job file defines attributes of the job and includes the following elements:

Item	Element Name (Field)
Job number	JOB (File key)
Job title	JOBTITL
Job pay grade	JOBPAGR
Overtime status	OVERTIMEX
Department	DEPARTMENT
Occupation	OCCUPATION
Pay period	PAYPERIOD
Number of performance dimensions used	NOPERDIM

Example:

PAYGRADEFILE: The pay grade file includes the following elements:

Item	Element Name (Field)
Pay grade	PAYGRADE (File key)
Pay grade maximum	PAYGMAX
Pay grade minimum	PAYGMIN

Example:

PERREVFILE: The performance review file is a detail file that contains employee performance ratings. It includes the following elements:

Item	Element Name (Field)
Sequential performance review number	REVNO (File key)
Employee number	REVEMP (File key)
Supervisor number	REVSUP (File key)
Global performance rating	REVRTG
Review date	REVDT
Job number as of review date	REVJOB (File key)
Rating of performance dimension one	PERDIM1
Rating of performance dimension two	PERDIM2
Rating of performance dimension three	PERDIM3
Rating of performance dimension four	PERDIM4
Rating of performance dimension five	PERDIM5
Rating of performance dimension six	PERDIM6
Rating of performance dimension seven	PERDIM7

Item	Element Name (Field)
Rating of performance dimension eight	PERDIM8
Rating of performance dimension nine	PERDIM9
Rating of performance dimension ten	PERDIM10
Organizational contribution performance rating	ORGPERRAT
Organizational support dimension one	ORGSUPDIM1
Organizational support dimension two	ORGSUPDIM2
Organizational support dimension three	ORGSUPDIM3
Organizational support dimension four	ORGSUPDIM4
Organizational support dimension five	ORGSUPDIM5
Organizational support dimension six	ORGSUPDIM6
Organizational support dimension seven	ORGSUPDIM7
Organizational support dimension eight	ORGSUPDIM8
Organizational support dimension nine	ORGSUPDIM9
Organizational support dimension ten	ORGSUPDIM10
Organizational support dimension eleven	ORGSUPDIM11
Organizational support dimension twelve	ORGSUPDIM12
Organizational support dimension thirteen	ORGSUPDIM13
Organizational support dimension fourteen	ORGSUPDIM14
Organizational support dimension fifteen	ORGSUPDIM15

This file expands with each additional rating as it provides a lengthening historical base of employee performance data.

quite possible that two or more different words or terms have the identical meaning. The dictionary permits the data base element to be consistent and have compatibility in meaning. Figure 8–2 is an example of a page from a data element dictionary. (The right-hand column would not be part of a page in a data element dictionary. It is shown here for teaching purposes.)

CAPA Reports. The reason for the existence of CAPA is to provide performance rating information on time, as needed, and in a suitable form so that those involved in the process can make decisions that lead to improved organizational effectiveness. Because of the critical nature and variety of sensitive information that must be made available to many different users for various purposes, performance appraisal measurement and rating data must be packaged to meet specific user requirements and, at the same time, maintain confidentiality.

The actual development of reports requires a thorough knowledge of the capabilities of the particular hardware (computer) being used in the CAPA system. The following examples of possible CAPA reports for specific users may require modification, depending not only on user demands but also on computer capabilities. The programs written

Characteristics and Attributes	Description	Meaning of Dictionary Item (This column does not appear in dictionary)
Name of element	Employment status	Unique, meaningful, precise term
Data element abbreviation	EMPSTAT	Shortened form for processing convenience and efficiency
Definition	Indicates organizational employment status of the person	Explains meaning of the data element
Classification and coding	1. Permanent full-time 2. Permanent part-time 3. Temporary full-time 4. Temporary part-time	
Uses	For personal profile	
Derivation rules (if any)	Personnel Form 324	Described how data are derived; identify abbreviation, rules or guidelines
Units (if any)	None	Specific units of measurement
Format	Numeric	Defines how data element is stated
Justification	NA	Right or left justification
Width of field	One digit	Width required
Validity rules	Required ☒ Optional ☐	Specify whether this field is required (i.e., must be entered in all cases) or optional (i.e., may not be required in every case)
	Range: 1-4	Lists acceptable values which may be inputted. In this case, the user must input a 1, 2, 3, or 4. No other value is permitted. The field may not be left blank.
Person processing form	C. Myers	
Date issued	2/21/82	
Comments		

FIGURE 8–2. Page from a Data Element Dictionary.

to produce the following reports must be applicable to the specific computer of the organization.

The CAPA system described in this chapter requires the use of a computer with a data base management system (DBMS). A software program written for one manufacturer's computer will most likely not work on another manufacturer's computer. Although there are currently no "canned" CAPA packages available, a competent programmer can write the necessary software.

When writing a CAPA program, it is important for the programmer to select a language to enter and retrieve data (write reports) that are easy to learn, English-like, and "friendly" to or compatible with the user. This kind of language enables a clerk with minimal or no special program writing skills to write a specific report in just a few minutes. The data base described in this chapter allows for quick and easy development of special reports that a manager may request. A special report may be a list of handicapped employees, who are also veterans, who act as peacemakers among individuals and groups. The special report feature may be as useful as the CAPA report.

Through the use of DBMS, reports can easily be written that involve the selection and sorting of any data element. Most reports will normally access one of the four previously described files, and that data base file acts as a master file. Through the use of the file key, data in the master file can be linked to any of the other three files.

An example of a report that would use three files is a list of all employee names, their job titles, and their last global performance ratings. The report would link the current job number (CURRJOB) in the EMPLOYEEFILE, which is the master file in this case, to the job number (JOB) in the JOBFILE, to the employee number (REVEMP) in the PERREVFILE (performance review file). Then NAME, JOBTITL, and REVRTG would be printed.

One final warning on the acceptance of a specific language for report writing: Not all DBMS report writing languages permit the user to access four files at one time. Some languages permit the use of only one file at a time. To make full use of a CAPA system, the organization must select a language that permits the linking of all files. A special benefit of DBMS is the ease with which other data elements may be added to the data base.

Although the development of CAPA reports is the final section of this chapter, it may be the first project to be considered when establishing a CAPA system. Even before the development of a data base, the designers and operators of the performance appraisal system may wish to identify the kind of rating information that must be offered to each user in the CAPA universe. An initial analysis may reveal such interest areas as:

Ratee Reports:

1. What is the most recent rating received?
2. How does the most recent rating compare with past ratings?
3. How do the ratee's ratings compare with other, similarly located employees (similar job, similar organizational setting, similar tenure in organization or on the job)?
4. What performance dimensions or criteria appear to have low or relatively low ratings? (Identify key areas where improvement is necessary.)
5. What strengths of the ratee are being identified?

Rater Reports:

1. What ratings were given all ratees this past rating period?
2. How do the ratings given this past period compare with ratings given in the past?
3. How does the distribution of global ratings of this rater compare with other, similarly situated raters (division or department, level in the organization, kind of work supervised)?
4. What is the distribution of ratings given by the rater for each performance dimension?
5. How does the rater's distribution of ratings with regard to specific performance dimensions compare with such distributions given by other raters?

Reviewer Reports:

1. What are the ratings given by subordinate raters this past rating period?
2. What is the distribution of ratings given by each subordinate rater?
3. What are the distributions of ratings given by each subordinate rater relative to the following ratee characteristics—age, sex, race, national origin, handicap status, veteran status, pay grade/pay level?
4. What is the relationship between the performance rating given a subordinate and the distribution of the ratings given by that subordinate?
5. What is the relationship between subordinate performance ratings and the ratings these subordinates gave their subordinate ratees?

6. How do subordinate ratings with regard to some organizational, division, or department norms compare to such ratee characteristics as age, sex, race, national origin, handicap status, veteran status, pay grade/pay level?

7. What is the comparison between subordinate global performance ratings and an organizational, division, or department global performance rating/norm?

Top Management Reports:

1. What is the distribution of global performance ratings by division, department, and work unit?

2. What is the distribution of global performance ratings in comparison with overall performance ratings of the specific division, department, and work unit?

3. What divisions, departments, and work units appear to be given unusually high or unusually low performance ratings?

4. Are the performance appraisal auditors' reports identifying such critical issues as

   a. Failure to comply with existing practices or procedures.

   b. Existing unacceptable or potentially weak components within the performance appraisal system.

   c. Areas where dishonest or less than accurate appraisal information appears to be given?

Division/Department Head Reports:

1. What is the distribution of ratings within each work unit of the division or department?

2. What comparisons are there between work-unit performance ratings and the ratings given by work-unit managers?

3. What is the relationship between rater ratings in the division/department and ratings given throughout the organization?

4. What deficiencies in the operation of the appraisal system are being identified by the division/department monitoring system? Deficiencies may include:

   a. Failure to complete ratings and submit them on time.

   b. Failure to establish a workplace environment in which honest appraisals can be performed.

   c. Failure to properly rate employees.

   d. Failure to give ratees useful feedback on observed and demonstrated performance.

   e. Possible occurrence of common rating errors, i.e., halo, central tendency, strictness, leniency, same as me, different from me.

   f. Failure to properly use rating instruments or to make full use of rating scales.

   g. Possible occurrence of bias in ratings because of ratee characteristics.

Organizational Reports:
Compensation:

1. What kind of performance rating data and information are required to make in-grade step adjustments based on performance?
2. What kind of performance rating information is required to make bonus and other kinds of special awards decisions?

Employee Movement:

1. What kinds of performance rating information are required for promotion purposes?
2. What kinds of performance rating information are required for lateral transfer into other jobs or other work units?
3. What kinds of performance rating information are required when making demotion, lay-off, or termination decisions?

Training and Development:

1. What areas of knowledge and skill deficiencies are being identified through the performance appraisal?
2. In what kinds of jobs or in which divisions, departments, or work units are specific knowledge and skill deficiencies being identified?
3. How widespread and how critical to improvement in organizational productivity are those knowledge and skill deficiencies?
4. Who provides performance feedback to ratees and what kind of feedback are they receiving?
5. What kinds of rater errors and rater biases are being identified?
6. Are rater errors and biases widespread throughout the organization, or are they most apparent among certain groups of raters?

Research:

1. What relationships exist between performance ratings and predicted success based on selection devices (instruments or test)?
2. What relationships exist between the training programs that have been provided and demonstrated performance?

Government Agency:

1. What information is required or may be required by government agencies responsible for the administration of employment-related legislation?
2. Is there sufficient documentation to support all personnel activity decisions that use performance-related inputs?
3. Is there a valid relationship between performance ratings and job content?

Administrator Reports:

1. Are performance appraisal rating reports submitted on time and are they completed as directed?
2. Do appraisal ratings indicate the possible existence of rater errors (halo, central tendency, etc.) or the existence of rater biases (age, sex, race, etc.)?
3. Are standing performance appraisal directives and procedures being carried out in a timely and acceptable manner?
4. Is there any indication of variances between distributions of ratings within work units and the performance of these work units?
5. Are raters making full or appropriate use of rating scales?
6. Are only specific performance dimensions useful in identifying performance differences among employees?

Rating Appeal Judge Reports:

1. What kinds of ratings has the appellant received in the past?
2. What kinds of ratings has the rater given to other employees?
3. Is there any indication of rater bias?
4. What is the rater's rating history?

Analyzing CAPA Report Requirements. From an analysis of the various CAPA reports, it is possible to identify the kinds of data output required and, more importantly, the form that performance appraisal instruments must take in order to provide the kinds of input data that will eventually be processed into various CAPA user reports. A review of the previously described user interest areas will assist in identifying the kinds and forms of data that the appraisal instrument should provide if an organization wishes to make use of a CAPA system.

The *ratee* interest area requires:

1. A global performance rating score.
2. A rating score for each performance dimension.
3. Conversion of performance dimension scores into a global rating score.
4. Performance dimension scales that permit the quantification of differences between scale intervals (items).
5. Permanent storage of past ratings with such identifiers as date of rating, supervisor who performed the rating, job of ratee at time of rating, etc.
6. Development of norms or standard ratings by supervisor; by supervisor by pay grade/job level; by job or by occupation; by similar jobs in department, division, or organization. These standards or norms should be available for global performance ratings and for the ratings of special performance dimensions.

These interest areas may also be part of the reports for other CAPA users, but they will not be restated in the analyses to follow. There will be, however, interest areas for specific CAPA users that should not be provided to other users.

The *rater* interest area requires:

1. Intervals used by raters for rating, using specific performance dimensions.
2. Performance dimension ratings that best identify differences or are able to discriminate between individual performances.
3. Rater rating behaviors that result in possible rating errors.
4. Rater biases identified through rating behaviors as related to ratee characteristics/qualities.
5. Rater knowledge and skill deficiencies that may require further training, coaching, and counseling.
6. Ranking order of all subordinates rated.

The *reviewer* interest area requires:

1. Potential rater knowledge and skill deficiencies and biases that may require future training, coaching, and counseling.
2. Ranking of all subordinates by job, pay grade/organizational level, and by specific performance dimensions.

The *organizational* interest area requires:
Compensation:

1. Distribution of global performance ratings by pay grade/level in the organization, location within the pay grade, job, seniority.
2. Distribution of performance dimension ratings by job by organization/work unit.

Training and Development:

1. Relation of knowledge and skill requirements to specific performance dimensions.
2. Identification of incumbents performing in a less than acceptable or competent manner from a global performance perspective and from the perspective of individual performance dimensions.
3. Recognition of training, coaching, counseling deficiencies identified by raters and reviewers.

The *administrator* interest area requires:

1. Compliance with performance appraisal standing orders and procedures.

Examples of CAPA Reports. After establishing a data base, it is possible to write programs that use the available data elements. These programs will provide desired reports to specific users. The program language for these CAPA user reports should be simple to use and English-like. Languages that meet these requirements are available to run on some DBMS. By having a system that permits entry to the computer through commonly-used and understood words and terms, clerks and managers in the personnel-performance appraisal unit can write their own programs in a matter of minutes. This quick and easy access to the computer to gain specific kinds of information in a short time span minimizes—in some cases eliminates—the personnel department's report-writing dependency on an EDP staff. Figure 8–3 is an example of a CAPA report.

Report	Instruction
1	SET REPORT DEVICE PRINTER
2	SET REPORT LIMIT 100
3	SET PAGE WIDTH 132
4	ACCESS EMPLOYEE
5	SET PAGE TITLE "LIST EMPLOYEES' SCHEDULED PERFORMANCE REVIEW DATES"
6	REPORT NAME EMPLOYEE SSNUMBER SEX RACE MARITAL NODEP REVDATE CURRPAY CURRSUPV
7	SORT ON NAME
8	GO

REPORT

LIST EMPLOYEES' SCHEDULED PERFORMANCE REVIEW DATE

Employee Name	Employee Number	S/S Number	Sex	Race	Marital Status	# of Dependents	Scheduled Review Date	Current Pay	Current Supervisor
ANDERSON, T.E.	10	166-98-4785	F	B	M	1	01/07	265	7
HEINRICH, L.W.	9	355-23-5234	M	W	S	1	04/06	260	7
JAMISON, P.R.	3	908-55-1234	F	B	M	3	09/10	280	4
NORRIS, W.M.	2	660-98-5489	M	B	M	1	06/12	220	4
RICHARDSON, C.G.	5	235-98-0122	F	W	S	1	01/08	250	4
SINGER, A.C.	8	256-01-8667	F	W	M	2	11/01	220	7
SMITH, E.J.	1	344-87-0948	F	W	S	0	03/15	280	4
VALDEZ, J.F.	7	654-00-9823	M	H	M	2	06/30	440	11
WILLIAMS, J.D.	6	262-98-4398	M	W	M	3	12/16	280	7
WITMAN, W.W.	11	434-23-0923	M	W	M	2	N/A	625	0
YOUNG, R.L.	4	156-34-0933	M	B	M	4	02/09	450	11

FIGURE 8-3. CAPA Report.

The entire purpose of the CAPA reports is to provide performance-related information that leads to improved organizational productivity. The specific reasons for the reports range from allowing ratee and rater to know how they are doing to permitting higher levels of management and staff specialists to critically examine performance-related behaviors at all levels throughout the organization. Using a CAPA reporting system, every aspect of performance appraisal must be carefully organized and controlled. All processes must be explicit and then communicated to all involved parties so that they understand their roles and the influence that this part of the program has on their work lives.

A CAPA report allows appropriate levels of management and staff officials to recognize whether or not rules and procedures are being followed. If procedures and rules are not followed, they should be modified, dropped, or enforced. Recognizing the sensitivity of the entire program, nothing should be permitted to occur that could undermine or destroy its credibility.

When employees at all levels know that (a) the organization is willing and able to provide the resources necessary to maintain and update the performance appraisal program, (b) areas needing improvement are being identified and necessary changes are being made, (c) all operations are being monitored, and (d) accurate, fair, and timely ratings are being developed and the rights of all employees are being protected, the likelihood of having an effective performance appraisal program increases.

CAPA not only permits these kinds of activities to occur, but also allows them to happen with minimal cost and disruption to the everyday practices of the organization.

Chapter 9

The Interview Process: Reviewing Performance

The skills required of a supervisor are many and varied, but the most difficult to master are those used in interpersonal relationships. Supervisors must talk, listen, gather and analyze information, and negotiate the availability and use of resources with others. One place where these interpersonal skills and activities come together is in the performance review session.

The goals of the performance review are (a) to change the behavior of employees whose performance is not meeting organizational requirements or their own personal goals; (b) to maintain behaviors of employees who are performing in an acceptable manner; and (c) to recognize superior performance behaviors so that they will be continued. Performance reviews, however, do not always meet desired goals. Failures frequently occur because of error and miscalculation in attempting to make adjustments between *what is* and *what is perceived*. Supervisors may feel certain that they have the facts and know *what is* and that the views of their subordinates are merely perceptions—that is, images or concepts developed from past experience. Attaining a common base for understanding requires concern for both perception and reality. Both are vital issues. A supervisor must realize that the subordinate's perception is reality to the subordinate.

In the performance review session, communication must flow in two directions. If the information flow is predominantly in one direction, neither the rater nor the ratee will benefit from this time-consuming but vital human resource activity. The performance review session should provide knowledge that assists in (a) better understanding employee feelings, attitudes, and situations; (b) determining courses of action that are most beneficial to the employee and the organization; and (c) relating rewards to demonstrated workplace behavior.

There must be recognition by subordinates that their concerns are critical to the process, that they influence the outcome of the review, and that the session is in their best interests. The review must be job performance-related. It must pertain to job requirements; how job activities are performed; when appropriate, behaviors demonstrated while working; changes that could be made; and future opportunities for the subordinate—the ratee.

From the moment of the first contact between the supervisor and subordinate, feelings, values, and various other emotional and intellectual considerations develop that enhance or block future productive relationships. Most supervisors sooner or later realize (and rightly so) that there are some interpersonal issues and situational demands over which they have little or no control that influence their relationships with their subordinates. However, this in no way minimizes the requirement for a supervisor to be a skilled diagnostician in order to understand, explain, and even predict employee behavior. In fact, the existence of factors beyond the supervisor's direct control makes it all the more important that he or she use the proper skills and preparation to maximize the opportunity afforded by the performance interview to influence the subordinate's behavior in a positive manner.

This chapter discusses the benefits to be derived from a successfully conducted performance review. It identifies behaviors that commonly arise to obstruct open, two-way communication, which is essential for conducting a successful interview, and presents skills that the supervisor may use to prevent or overcome these behaviors. Suggestions are made for preparing for and conducting the performance review so that maximum mutual benefits for both the rater and the ratee will be attained.

WHY REVIEW PERFORMANCE? Mutual benefits for the employee and the organization to be gained from a well conceived and conducted performance review include (a) improving workplace performance through the identification and solution of problems; (b) fostering the on-going growth and development of competent employees in their present job assignments by meeting identified training needs and providing an environment conducive to trust; and (c) providing valuable information for the employee and the organization for career planning purposes.

Improving Workplace Performance

A major purpose of the performance review is to assist in the identification and definition of problems that affect workplace performance and to bring about a positive change in the ratee's behavior. Successful problem solving depends on the quality and quantity of available information about the problem. Everything discussed in this chapter involves extracting, gathering, summarizing, and analyzing performance-related information. A brief review of the possible results of a performance review session may assist in providing an appreciation of the importance that employees attach to the process.

Claim on present assignment. An unsatisfactory performance rating may lead to the loss of the present job or even to complete termination of employment. A satisfactory or better rating, on the other hand, may lead to a desired pay increase or performance bonus.

Promotion to a higher-level job. For some employees, the most valuable reward that an organization can bestow is promotion to a higher-level job. Increase in status, esteem of self and others, recognition, and additional compensation are only some of the valued rewards that accompany most promotions. Performance in the current assignment is one, if not the most important, determinant for advancement.

Opportunity for desired job improvement. Requests for a more desirable work site, better equipment, more acceptable co-workers, etc., may rest on the performance rating.

Transfer to new job. A chance to develop new job skills, to obtain additional job knowledge, and to work in a different environment all may depend on the appraisal.

Selection for education and training program. Opportunities to gain additional knowledge and acquire new skills may not only be useful within the current organization but also as a stepping-stone to more lucrative opportunities in other organizations.

From an analysis of these five critical employee interest areas, it becomes rather easy to recognize the possible relationship between fear and performance appraisal. When employees feel that they have minimal influence over the appraisal process and that their final appraisal rating may depend on the whims and unfair or biased perceptions of the raters, fear quickly arises. This kind of situation promotes uncertainty, especially uncertainty about future workplace opportunities. With uncertainty, emotional and psychological concerns dominate the process, and anxiety and tension begin to develop and, if of sufficient strength and duration, transfer into alienation, hostility, and unhealthy competition. As long as one individual is responsible for appraising the performance of another, some degree of stress will exist. The amount of stress varies according to individual qualities, environmental conditions, and the relationship between the rater and the ratee. When physical conditions such as increased pulse, pains in the back of the neck, butterflies in the stomach, or perspiration-soaked palms frequently accompany performance reviews, it may be time to analyze what is happening during the appraisal process.

Growth and Development

For many employees, as important as pay adjustments that relate to performance are and as critical as promotions may be, the most vital outputs of a well designed, properly administered performance appraisal system are the opportunities for training and development. In the final years of the twentieth century, the employer of the well educated, capable employee must recognize the employee's need for growth and development opportunities. For many employees, the major opportunity for growth and development occurs at the work site.

Employee growth is a continuous process and is primarily an individual responsibility and opportunity. However, organizations facilitate or hamper growth opportunities through the environment that they establish at the workplace. The amount and quality of teaching, counseling, and coaching information and feedback that they provide to their employees further facilitate growth and development. A well-designed, formalized performance appraisal process requires supervisor and subordinate participation in the flow of job knowledge and job-related information. The employee has the opportunity to make decisions concerning the kind and degree of growth that he or she personally desires. Growth and development in this process are not a once-a-year occurrence or a particular event occurring at some specified time. Growth and development are continuous processes that end only when the individual makes that determination.

Growth and development have been magic words related to human resource utilization for the past 30 years or more. Over these three decades, mystical concepts such as sensitivity training, T-groups, encounter therapy, transactional analysis, organizational behavior (OB), and organizational development (OD) have received widespread acclaim as processes available for overcoming employee apathy and even employee hostility. The golden carrots dangled in front of managers who implement these enlightened endeavors include decreased absenteeism and turnover, improved quality and quantity of output, reductions in costs, and increases in profit. Although many of these organizational elixirs have proven to be of some value, the time has arrived to return to basics and to be willing to do the detailed, trench-digging work necessary to build and defend a trusting workplace environment.

It all starts with the job, but this is only the start because a job without a jobholder is as valuable as a set of false teeth for someone who has never had a tooth pulled. The productive, profitable organization requires the services of cooperative employees who actively want to assist their employers to achieve their missions, their objectives.

This is where and when employee growth and development emerge. Fear, frustration, and concern for survival do not facilitate growth and development. Communicating information concerning what the job is and how to perform it within an environment that must relate to ever-increasing rates of change shines a light into the tunnel of job uncertainty. Involvement in developing performance dimensions and performance standards assists employees to understand and recognize their obligations and contributions. It is this type of interchange that permits the supervisor and subordinate to identify job-related goals that encourage a spirit of self-reliance and, possibly even more important, a spirit of responsibility for self.

As the supervisor and the responsible, involved subordinate work together to achieve work-unit goals, shortcomings will be recognized and addressed more readily. The removal of fear and uncertainty allows the employee's desire for success, both in current job assignments and in future opportunities, to prompt the identification of individual deficiencies. These shortcomings may be identified by either the supervisor or the subordinate as they work together to improve workplace performance.

Even the most motivated, industrious employees will not attain the maximum desired performance unless, first, this "desired performance" is clearly defined in terms of the detailed job activities and specific, required job knowledge; and second, the employee has the knowledge and attains a high degree of competency in the performance of these activities. A lack of specific job-related knowledge and skills is a first cue for training requirements. The training may come on the job, from a co-worker, from a specialist in the identified area, or from the supervisor. The training may be a formal program held by the organization or some other organization that provides such services or may include invaluable coaching and counseling sessions involving only the subordinate and supervisor. Other types of training may involve various specialists who address specific needs.

Development needs may go beyond immediate job-related demands. Recognizing the potential available within the specific individual, the supervisor and other personnel specialists may recommend any of a wide variety of learning opportunities that enhance employee growth and assist the employee to achieve what he or she is capable and desirous of attaining.

Career Planning

A basic purpose for the performance review session is to assist employees to utilize their own resources. It is important to recognize that performance reviews are not only the consequences of employee behavior, but also the stimuli—they cause and form behavior.

A valuable role that the performance review plays is the providing of information to ratees, permitting them to gain a more realistic view of themselves. Most people tend to overestimate some skills that they possess and to underestimate others. They often do not recognize how certain characteristics that they possess limit future opportunities and how other characteristics, if capitalized upon, can lead to career advancement.

Performance appraisal information links current performance with and reinforces career development goals. Some aspects of appraisal review information that assist ratees to develop their career plans are:

1. Rater identifies ratee's strengths and weaknesses.
2. Rater provides ratee with specific training and development recommendations.
3. Rater and ratee discuss career plans of the ratee.
4. Rater and ratee discuss potential and realistic opportunities for advancement.
5. Rater and ratee design training and development plans for future career growth.

To many employees, two very important pieces of information that they want from their employers are "Where do I go from here?" and "How do I get there?" The various activities discussed in this interchange of information assist employees to develop their career plans.

Part of any career development program includes a discussion of training for promotion opportunities. Necessary knowledge and skills can be acquired from current on-the-job experience, self-development activities, outside courses, and transfers to other assignments. The types of training activities not only will depend on development needs, but will also be determined by the assessed promotability of the employee, his or her career aspirations, and the opportunities that are realistically available in the organization. Certainly, the kind of work an employee desires and the promotions he or she aspires to should be explored when preparing personal career development plans. Also, the supervisor should record an assessment of the employee's promotability, both in terms of qualifications for present and future positions and a designation of the positions, if any, for which the employee might be qualified.

Whether or not assessed promotability should be discussed with an employee is debatable. Should one who is considered promotable be so informed? Should the employee be told of the positions to which promotion is possible? If the employee is considered unpromotable, should the situation be explored? The answers to these questions depend primarily on the policies of the organization. Many organizations refuse to discuss promotion potential with employees. Other organizations let employees know where they stand by informing them of their promotability and even go so far as to spell out the promotion positions under consideration.

There is considerable variation in the role that the supervisor plays in organizations that have career development programs. When an organization delegates authority for appraising employee performance to the supervisor, it has automatically involved that supervisor in the determination of the career progress of the employee. Other than lack of competence, there is no logical reason to eliminate the supervisor from further involvement in the subordinate's career development.

TIMING OF REVIEWS

Ideally, performance review should be a continuous process consisting of informal reviews, coaching and counseling as frequently as possible, and the formal, scheduled review. Formal performance reviews are scheduled most often on an annual basis. However, some organizations now schedule semiannual, quarterly, or bimonthly reviews because many supervisors do not properly document performance and do not informally provide feedback (especially negative feedback) to subordinates. These additional performance reviews are usually conducted in preparation for the formal annual review.

In addition to the degeneration of performance-related information over time as described in Chapter 2 in the section on Timing of Appraisals, another major reason for reviewing performance more than once a year is to reduce the possibility of unexpected information. Few if any people like to be unpleasantly surprised, especially if the surprise can, in some way, cause damage or harm. Survival or its workplace counterpart, job security, is of primary concern to most employees. Anything or any action that may have a damaging effect on job continuity in the immediate present or at some future time is going to be resisted with as much effort as possible.

Any time that a supervisor judges a subordinate's performance to be in any way deficient, it is only fair that the matter be discussed with the subordinate so that improvement can be made through increased effort or by providing needed coaching and training. It is this on-going process that makes performance appraisal developmental and positive rather than punitive and negative.

Another reason for formalizing more frequent performance reviews—three, four, even six times a year—is to assist in clarifying job assignments, reset work activity priorities, further define and fine-tune performance standards, and identify and allocate available resources. These sessions allow for more frequent rating and development interchange between the rater and the ratee. These kinds of information exchanges assist in reducing perceptual differences and misunderstandings and minimize the possibility of unpleasant surprises.

The bimonthly or quarterly appraisal process also permits an averaging of a number of rating reports, thus de-emphasizing the importance of any one appraisal or any one set of activities. The once-a-year appraisal, on the other hand, may overemphasize recent activities and thus distort their actual value.

It may also be desirable to have two *annual* reviews—the annual performance rating review, which provides pay adjustment information, and an annual training and development session, which (a) analyzes how activities were performed, (b) identifies and describes strengths and weaknesses, (c) discusses opportunities for improvement, and (d) outlines future job improvement and career development plans. Research conducted at General Electric in the early 1960s identified the conflict between rating and development.[1] One of the recommendations of this research was to split appraisal interviews into two parts—one that centered on salary administration and one that centered on employee development.

Normally, when annual and final review time arrives, the employee mainly wants to know, "What rating am I receiving, and what influence will this rating have on in-job pay increases, desired lateral transfers, or promotions with pay increases?" This emotionally charged interest area precludes any worthwhile discussion of growth and development opportunities. Thus, a final growth and development session is often held four to eight weeks later when the ratee is likely to be more receptive to coaching and counseling inputs.

Some experts believe, however, that the training and development session should precede any discussion regarding pay. They feel that pay or other compensation-related discussions that precede training and development sessions jeopardize any opportunity for effective coaching and counseling.

---

[1] Herbert H. Meyer, Emanuel Kay, and John R. P. French, Jr., "Split Roles in Performance Appraisal," *Harvard Business Review,* January–February 1965, pp. 123–129.

An annual formal performance review schedule could take the form presented in Figure 9–1. (Numbers are substituted for months so that the schedule can fit a formal performance review schedule of an organization, which may range from one relating to anniversary date reviews to one linked to common review dates for specific work units or the entire organization.)

It is possible to separate performance appraisal interviews into two kinds of information exchange sessions. In one session, the rater acts as a judge by providing and substantiating performance ratings. The major topics to be discussed during a rating session are (a) job assignments and requirements; (b) observable efforts, results recognized, and standards used to measure results; (c) efficient use of available resources; (d) contributions to improved work-unit and organizational effectiveness; and (e) the rating of performance.

THE SPLIT ROLES OF PERFORMANCE REVIEW

The other kind of review centers on ratee growth and development. The focus here is on coaching and counseling. In other words, the role of the rater changes from one that centers on a "tell and sell" mode to one that focuses on problem solving.[2] The major reason for a problem-solving interview is to assist the employee to recognize his or her current strengths and weaknesses, the performance requirements of the current job, the job(s) desired at some future date, and the actions he or she can take to achieve desired personal and organizational goals.

The reason for dividing the appraisal interview process into at least two distinct sessions is that it is difficult, if not impossible, for a person to act as a judge and, within a period of minutes, change roles to coach and counselor. The conditions that result from playing the role of the judge are so pervasive that they effectively block the transfer to a role of helper and supporter. What must be said in the rating session has such a wide variety of critical influences on the ratee that it is extremely difficult for that person to hear any messages that do not directly relate to the rating received. A rating session

---

[2] One of the most respected authors on interviewing skills identifies three kinds of appraisal interviews as (1) tell and sell: the rater reviews the ratee's performance, identifies what is right and wrong, describes corrective actions for the ratee to take, and tries to convince the ratee to accept the recommendations; (2) tell and listen: the same as tell and sell, but the rater listens to the ratee's reasons for his or her demonstrated behavior and view of the correctness of the rating decision; (3) problem solving: the ratee identifies performance problems, establishes his or her own rating, and describes actions to take that will lead to improved performance. Norman R. F. Maier, *Psychology in Industrial Organizations,* 4th ed. (Boston: Houghton Mifflin, 1973), pp. 558–559.

Month	Performance Review Activities
1	
2	1) Annual performance growth and development review[1] 2) First bimonthly work progress review
3	First quarterly work progress review
4	Second bimonthly work progress review
5	
6	1) Second quarterly work progress review[2] 2) Third bimonthly work progress review[3]
7	
8	Fourth bimonthly work progress review
9	Third quarterly work progress review
10	Fifth bimonthly work progress review[2]
11	
12	Annual performance rating review[3]

[1] This review actually occurs in the second month of the coming year, or during the fourteenth month.

[2] If the organization wishes to have an organizational values review, this session could focus on non-job-content-related behavior that influences the successful operation of the work unit and the larger organization

[3] This session would include a summary of past reviews for the year. It could include an analysis of employee strengths and weaknesses and the setting of one or two work-related personal development goals.

FIGURE 9–1. Performance Review Schedule.

may become laden with emotion and can quickly degenerate into one in which hostility and defensiveness dominate. For coaching and counseling to have an impact, there must be receptiveness and openness of communication.

Initiating and carrying out a successful interview session requires both coaching and counseling skills. In the past, raters were frequently required only to gather and assess information about job performance and to provide a rating. Today, however, coaching and counseling skills that aim at facilitating the achievement of change and the redirection of job behavior so that it is beneficial to both the individual and the organization are an essential part of the rater's job.

INTERVIEWING SKILLS AND BEHAVIORS

To be successful as a coach, the rater must be able to recognize the kinds of barriers that are blocking ratee performance. At this time, the rater-coach must be able to identify whether the problem occurs because (a) the ratee lacks knowledge or skill; (b) the ratee does not know when, why, or where to use the knowledge or skill; or, possibly, (c) the ratee is just not interested in doing an acceptable job. Of course, a rater must always be able to recognize whether the problems are beyond the control of the ratee. Through this kind of analysis, coaching can focus on a self-correcting approach or the kinds of assistance that will be most useful.

Three major methods are available for use in face-to-face encounter sessions in which there will be both a gathering and dissemination of information, an appraisal of past workplace behaviors, and recommendations for the direction of future behavior. These methods are the directive, nondirective, and combination reviews.

Directive Approach

The directive approach follows a specific format in which answers to particular questions are sought. The rater may either develop the questions, or they may be in a standardized form, in which case he or she must ask the questions exactly as they are worded and in the exact order of their appearance. To ensure the uniformity of information obtained which, in turn, leads to comparability in analysis, questions must not be added or deleted by the rater. The checklist assists in recalling and recording information. The range of questions can be very wide, and the checklist can cover the topics relevant to a specific issue. For example:

"Do you like your job?" Yes_____ No_____

"Can you identify one thing that you find enjoyable in doing your job?"

This kind of approach is the easiest and fastest to administer and ensures the collection of specific kinds of information. However, it may fail to collect the kinds of information that are truly needed and is very weak in identifying and further clarifying personal issues. It does not grant the flexibility necessary for analyzing workplace problems and developing solutions to unacceptable workplace behaviors. Also, the rigid formality of the process tends to "turn off" the ratee and fails to evoke a sense of mutual concern or participation.

Nondirective Approach

This approach follows no rigid format but requires more question-asking and listening skills on the rater's part. The rater must depend on his or her own skills because the interview session is extremely flexible. He or she must have the knowledge or skill to ask appropriate questions as demanded by the situation without conscious deliberation. This approach frequently makes use of very broad, general, or open-ended questions, such as: "How do you feel about your work?".

The major advantage of the nondirective approach is that it draws the ratee into the process. It permits the employee to come to grips with real issues and to discuss feelings or problems that are disturbing or adversely affecting his or her performance. The rater can focus questions on specific areas when in-depth information is needed. Through the nondirective approach, ratee motives, attitudes, feelings, and emotions can be uncovered and recognized, making it possible to minimize the impact of these behavior-influencing factors. This kind of approach requires a significant amount of time. It may lead to the discussion of issues for which the rater may be unprepared or may not wish to discuss. Unless tightly controlled, this kind of interview may degenerate into discussions that have little or no relationship to workplace performance. Bringing the ratee back into the mainstream of the conversation requires considerable interviewing skills. Still other interviewing skills, including patience, timing, correct use of words and statements, and so on, are required in facing threatening or unfavorable pieces of information.

Combination Approach

Because of the weaknesses of the approaches described above, it is better for the rater, in most cases, to combine the two, using the strengths of each to the best advantage. Identifying topical areas and developing a list of relevant general questions focuses the review session on the subject at hand—employee past, current, and future performance. Here, the rater has considerable freedom to formulate additional questions and to reword or reorder suggested questions. This approach permits the rater to provide as much or as little structure as the situation requires. For ratees who feel most comfortable in a structured environment, the rater provides a significant amount of order and direction. For those who enjoy involvement opportunities and the freedom to express their views, the rater can provide more flexibility. The combination approach provides sufficient structure and order to cover the subject but enough flexibility to allow the rater to follow the natural flow of events as they arise during the interview. The problems that arise with this approach are similar to those just described in the nondirective approach but are less pronounced.

Since a complete review of performance requires face-to-face interaction between the rater and ratee, it is advantageous to have an understanding of intra- and interpersonal dynamics to effectively conduct these personal interview sessions. This is because any of a number of human behavior barriers are likely to surface and a general prior knowledge will better equip the rater to work with them effectively. Some of the more common behaviors are listed in Figure 9–2.

Because of these and other personal issues, almost anything may happen at any moment during a performance review. The session may be extremely dull, with the ratee's responses being merely an occasional nod of the head or an appropriate "yes" or "no." On the other hand, the ratee may take a major exception to the rater's analysis of his or her performance, with the result being a bitter and hostile confrontation. Although the rater can definitely influence the interview process, it is often difficult to predict the way an interview session will go.

Questioning Skills

To be successful in interviewing, the rater must have knowledge and skills both in asking the right question at the appropriate time and in being a constructive listener. This section will focus on types of questions to ask, when to ask them, when to listen, and how to stimulate ratee responses.

Penetrating Questions. The successful combination approach to interviewing requires that the rater ask the right questions at the proper time. The right questions provide structure for the interview. Questions that may increase the accuracy, scope, and relevance of information fall into three major categories: responsibilities and duties, job environment, and job stress.

Barrier	Behavior
Personal differences	Rater younger than ratee; rater and ratee of different race, sex, national origin, cultural background; ratee has more seniority in the organization or more experience in a particular functional area. These conditions can cause discomfort, restricting open communication.
Game playing	One or both parties refuse to discuss or face real issues, such as the failure to meet a specific performance standard or exhibited behaviors that had a debilitating impact on the performance of the work unit. Trick questions and devious responses are symptomatic.
Language or semantics	One party does not speak or communicate in words and terms understandable to the other party. Rater should be careful not to use words or terms unknown to the ratee. The inflection and tone of voice of the rater can adversely influence the interview.
Lack of respect	Ratee feels rater is incompetent. The quickest way to gain the respect of the ratee is to be recognized as competent, if not expert, in supervisory responsibilities. Rater may also feel that the ratee is incompetent, which leads to the establishment of a self-fulfilling prophecy: that is, the ratee recognizes the rater's feelings and acts in a manner that reinforces those feelings. For example, "You think I'm incompetent; I will be incompetent."
Unsatisfactory past experiences	Rater has, in the past, failed to recognize the ratee's contributions or suggestions or has not given an accurate rating (at least from the ratee's perspective), and anything said can only hurt the ratee.
Non-job-related issues	Rater or ratee is experiencing poor physical or emotional health or is facing significant pressures not related to the workplace, causing an inability to concentrate on or identify job-related issues.
Changes in behavior	Rater displays an unsatisfactory recent change in behavior, which causes the ratee to be uncomfortable or even to perform differently as he or she tries to predict the behavior desired by the rater.

FIGURE 9–2. Common Human Behavior Barriers to Effective Interviewing.

The following questions focus, in one way or another, on job performance, performance requirements, and possible barriers to acceptable performance. Remember, the rater should ask only one question at a time; phrase the question in simple, understandable words; keep the question as brief as possible (a general rule is that any question over two sentences is too long); be specific; keep the question in a positive vein; and use care in asking questions that permit a "yes" or "no" response. Throughout the interview, the rater should be sure to follow up on any leads provided by the ratee. A "why" question may be useful in further investigating a specific point.

Some questions that may be of value are:

Job Responsibility- and Duty-Related:

What responsibilities and duties are you currently performing that are not included in your job description?

What responsibilities and duties are you *not* currently performing that you feel that you should be performing?

Which of your responsibilities and duties do you feel should be performed by someone else?

Which responsibilities and duties do you feel are most critical for successful job performance?

These questions provide a nonthreatening, job-focused opening to the interview. Both the rater and ratee should bring to the session a copy of the ratee's current job description. (Each employee should have a formal job description to bring to the interview; there should be one in the employee's personnel file that the rater can use for this part of the interview.) From answers to the above questions, job responsibilities and duties can be updated, and, above all, the rater and ratee can be on the "same wavelength" and can reach a common understanding of what the job is and is not.

Job Environment-Related:

Can you identify conditions in the work environment that are causing you problems?

Will this particular suggestion work in your particular situation? Why not?

Responses to these kinds of questions permit the rater and ratee to identify ways of overcoming causes of particular problems and to identify and begin developing possible actions. This kind of investigation can assist in identifying required resources, available resources, and those that can be shared. Opening the interview to situational demands permits the rater to recognize the ratee's perspective and to clarify vague or obscure points. The "What do you think?" approach is useful in appealing to the ratee's self-interest.

Job Stress-Related:

What do you like about your job?

What do you find most enjoyable in what you do?

What job activities do you find most difficult to perform?

What in your job is working against you?

What do you find most demanding about your job?

What do you dislike about your job?

What do you consider good about your job?

Who provides you with the most support in doing your job?

Where do you obtain job-related support?

What problems do you have in working cooperatively with other members of your work group?

What troubles have you encountered in obtaining the cooperation of others in working toward group goals?

Do your peers, subordinates, or supervisors cause you any undue, unnecessary stress?

Is your job causing you any emotional or health-related problems?

In reality, these may be the most critical and revealing questions to be asked. Some of these questions will be useful in any performance review session. Evaluating the responses to these kinds of questions requires knowledge of the ratee, the job, and current workplace situations, as well as considerable skill in developing and presenting useful and acceptable counter-responses. Developing potential answers to these kinds of questions and preparing appropriate responses is a critical part of the rater's homework.

Additional Information-Gathering Approaches

To acquire the full and specific information desired, the rater may find that additional techniques, such as open-ended questions, projective questions, reflective questions, and follow-up questions, will be useful. These approaches should be combined to the extent necessary to obtain a meaningful, two-way flow of communication between the rater and the ratee.

The questions that the rater asks determine, to a large extent, the responses that he or she will receive. Some of the previously listed questions can be answered with a simple yes or no. To elicit a more in-depth response, the rater may ask for more elaboration:

> Q: Is your job causing you any emotional or health-related problems?
>
> A: Yes.
>
> Q: Would you please tell me what is causing these problems?

The open-ended question (one that does not require a specific response but permits the respondee to develop his or her own answer) will usually provide better and more useful information. Open-ended questions require answers that are more time-consuming than questions that may be answered with a yes or no or with answer "b" rather than "a" or "c."

Projective Questions. There may be times during an interview when there is a need for information of a very sensitive nature. When this situation arises and the rater feels that a direct open-ended question is inappropriate, he or she may phrase the question relative to some hypothetical situation; this is called the projective method of questioning. In this case, instead of requiring the ratee to describe how he or she personally feels about an issue, the rater develops a hypothetical situation and the employee responds according to his or her true feelings. For example, "If you were responsible for meeting this delivery date on Product XYZ and two of your key subordinates were having interpersonal problems and were not supporting each other, what would you do?" In this case, the type of responsibility or product would not be within the job domain of the ratee.

Projective questions are difficult to phrase, and the answers are often even more difficult to interpret. Although this type of question can be a very worthwhile addition to the rater's interviewing techniques, he or she must have considerable knowledge and skill in order to use it properly.

Reflective Questions. To clarify an issue or to make certain the full importance of the issue is recognized, it is often helpful to restate what the ratee just mentioned. The rater can say, "I just heard you say. . . . Is this what you mean?" Or, "This is what I just heard you say. . . . Did I correctly understand what you said?" Or, "It's interesting that you feel that. . . ." This kind of questioning helps to minimize misunderstandings.

Follow-up Questions. When a ratee demonstrates a bias and there is an indication that the information being received may not reflect an accurate or honest assessment of the situation, further questioning in this area may be in order. It may not be appropriate to continue the discussion on the subject at that time, but the rater may want to file a mental note and return to the subject when the time is right. In determining consistency of information, the rater should constantly be alert not to ask questions that cause ratees to give the responses that they think the rater is seeking.

The rater must also recognize that only so many points can be discussed or analyzed at one time. There is always a tomorrow, and it is quite possible that a delay in probing into certain areas will avoid overloading the current interview and, thus, increase its value.

Constructive Listening

To be an effective interviewer, it is important to be both a willing and a skilled listener. It is not easy to get a subordinate with a problem to "open up" and describe areas of conflict. Bitter experiences have taught many people to believe that the best defense is to say nothing. The ability to encourage subordinates to talk requires (a) an active interest in them as unique individuals and in their problems, (b) a feeling on the part of the subordinate that the rater really wants to be of assistance, and (c) an understanding of the situation that enables the rater to ask the right questions at the right time.

When one person is talking, it is difficult to hear what the other person is saying. The amount of time that the rater should spend talking is a matter of current debate. There are those who believe that a rule of thumb for interviewing should be that the rater should talk for no more than one-third of the total interview. Others take the opposite view and state that the rater should spend about two-thirds of the time talking.

Those who propose the two-thirds–one-third *ratee* speaking ratio contend that the major purpose of the interview is to grant the ratee the time to discuss his or her job and job-related problems. It is impossible to hear what the ratee has to say when the rater does most of the talking.

The supporters of the two-thirds–one-third *rater* speaking ratio take the approach that the major benefit that the ratee gains from the interview is to know what the rater expects and how he or she views the ratee's past performance. The ratee also expects to learn from the rater future events and available job-related opportunities. The rater is expected to be the major source of official job-related information.

As in most cases of this type, the best approach to how much time should be spent talking and how much time should be spent listening is "It all depends on the situation." There is no one right way. There may be times when the rater spends two-thirds of the interview talking and other times when two-thirds of the session is spent listening. Both may be correct. The most important thing to learn here is that careful preparation for the session will assist the rater to recognize what is appropriate and best serves situational demands. However, if the rater errs relative to talking or listening, the error will probably be in talking too much.

The following is a list of guidelines to constructive listening:

1. When an employee has something on his or her mind, the listener should allow that person to talk it out. The listener should not respond with sharp answers or identify the apparent unreasonableness of the statement.

2. The listener should minimize, even set aside, the use of any clever retorts to an employee's problem. This is the opportunity for the ratee to express attitudes, feelings, and concerns about the job.

3. The listener should restrain the natural impulse to be curious and should avoid asking questions that show a bias. The employee may later regret answering such questions.

4. If feelings or emotions become the center of discussion, they should not be abruptly dismissed. Discouraging the expression of emotional issues can inhibit an employee's ability to work with and relate to critical problem areas. The employee should be allowed to vent frustrations.

5. Violent and deep-seated negative expressions require understanding rather than judgment. If possible, the employee should be permitted to develop his or her own solution to the problem.

6. Although it may be difficult to be silent, the listener should speak as seldom as possible. A series of "eloquent and encouraging grunts" may be all the sound that is needed. A few seconds of silence may frequently be appropriate. The expectant pause is one of the ways by which to indicate a sympathetic willingness to hear more—along with acceptance of the fact that the employee does not have to say anything. A slight forward movement also indicates interest.

7. New ideas should not be introduced nor should the direction of a conversation be changed. It is perfectly acceptable to repeat what the speaker has already said. A slight rephrasing of the topic may assist the speaker to realize what he or she has been saying.

8. The listener should not moralize. The role of the listener is not to make the speaker over in his or her image. The listener should not only avoid saying, "You're wrong," but also refrain from saying, "The other person is wrong."

9. Acceptance does not require agreement. It is not necessary to say,

"I think you are absolutely right." Possibly the only thing to say that is worse is, "I think you are absolutely wrong."

10. Advice should not be given on personal matters. An old saying states, "A wise man does not need advice; a damn fool will not take it." Constructive listening leads the speaker into deciding which is the best approach.

11. A trap to be avoided at all costs is the tendency to daydream to escape from listening to a boring, often-heard, or even undesired dialogue. The listener should minimize distractions and concentrate on the issues at hand. Concentration can be improved by staying relaxed, sharing feelings, and reducing concern about self.

12. Eye contact should be encouraged throughout the interview. This can be accomplished by focusing on the speaker without staring. When the speaker demonstrates constant eye contact, the listener responds in a similar manner. The listener can further encourage the speaker by nodding the head to signify interest.

Supportive Relationships

The ratee must realize that he or she is both part of the problem and part of the solution. The interview should build rapport and trust. When ratees understand and appreciate that there is an opportunity for improving an unsatisfactory condition, there is a much greater chance that they will feel encouraged to elaborate on the problem area and, frequently, even to develop their own solutions.

The posture of both the rater and ratee in this process can be mutually supportive. Almost everyone wants to make friends, not enemies. A supportive supervisor-subordinate relationship involves listening, teaching, and guiding. Attention is focused on job requirements and employee efforts. Interpersonal skills interrelate with job knowledge and skills. Both the rater and ratee are better able to cope with each other from a supportive position than from one requiring defensiveness. The entire interview process emphasizes problem identification and problem solving. It is in this type of workplace atmosphere that trust develops. Within such an environment, there is a greater likelihood that each employee will accept a performance rating as an honest effort.

The supervisor in the modern organization seldom has the time, the necessary skills, or sufficient energy to be a director of subordinate action. Rather, the supervisor provides direction to the subordinate. At first glance, these two phrases—"director" and "provides direction"—appear to be similar if not identical, but that is far from the case. The "director" type supervisor takes the position of telling the subordinate the "how," "when," and "where" of doing the assignment;

in this relationship, the "why" is usually of importance only to the supervisor. On the other hand, the "provides direction" type supervisor assists subordinates to perform their assignments by providing the information, training, coaching, and counseling appropriate to the demands of the subordinate, the job, and the situation.

Performance appraisal is a formalized process designed and implemented by the organization to facilitate the "provides direction" role. The front-end costs of this process are extensive. But in the world of the 1980s, the cost considerations must include both the costs of doing it right the first time and the costs of review, repair, adjustment, and waste when "right the first time" occurs infrequently.

In the authoritarian, directive world, the burden is on the back of the director. The director must provide the how-tos, whens, wheres, whats, and constant review necessary to ensure acceptable performance. Can the managers of the modern organization carry this weight? Do they want to? Current events certainly cast doubts on their ability and desire to do so.

On the other hand, in the "provides direction" role, the supervisor furnishes subordinates with sufficient quality and quantity of information to allow them to make their own decisions and to control their own jobs. Training, coaching, counseling, and providing sufficient resources are the inputs made by this type of supervisor.

The well educated worker who has a relatively high level of aspirations and expectations cannot function in a productive manner in a job environment that requires conformity, blocks self-expression, and minimizes the need for employee intelligence and enthusiasm. When this occurs, the intelligence, enthusiasm, and energy are channeled into behaviors that lead to "no growth" conditions and to more devastating behaviors that sabotage or block opportunities for achieving the objectives and goals of the organization. When employees recognize their responsibilities and supervisors provide the support necessary to achieve identified and accepted goals, the burden shifts to the back of the employee. The employee is now in a position to improve his or her own workplace conditions. Fear of the unknown begins to dissolve as employees accept the challenge of performing a job under conditions of uncertainty, recognizing that support is available when risk situations arise.

Feedback and Supportive Relationships. By its very nature, feedback is a very personal situation. Here, the rater relates his or her view of the ratee's past performance. When providing feedback, the rater should focus on personal observations and verifiable results and minimize any use of hearsay or rumors. It is at this time that the rater has the opportunity to review what the ratee is doing and the standards used to measure level of performance. By focusing on the "what" of the job and the standards to be met, the discussion can be specific, and both parties can discuss perceptual differences.

Research indicates that timing is the most critical factor of a performance feedback session. Feedback is most effective when it closely follows the behavior to which it relates. Employees should not receive feedback solely on unacceptable or below-par performance. Feedback that recognizes above-standard performance is appreciated by most employees and sets the stage for better acceptance of any subsequent, constructive feedback. Most employees like to know that their supervisors are aware of what they are doing, and consider that their efforts are worthwhile and are making a valuable contribution to the achievement of group goals. Feedback on performance is the basic ingredient of the day-to-day coaching responsibilities of a supervisor.

Some well designed performance appraisal systems include frequent performance review sessions that relate to specific results and demonstrated and observed behaviors. Reviews are used to analyze performance goals and results that may lead to a redefinition of goals or redirection of work activities. These goal-oriented reviews may range in frequency from monthly to quarterly. They vary according to the kind of work performed and the job knowledge of the incumbent. Usually, this kind of program includes an annual review in which there is an analysis and a rating of performance for the year.

PRE-INTERVIEW HOMEWORK

The performance appraisal review is too important and serious to be left to chance. Raters should not enter a review session unprepared. They should know what they want to learn and the points they want to make. However, they should not go into an interview with preconceived conclusions (i.e., "Don't give me any facts; I've already made up my mind.") They should not expect to follow some well defined order of events; rather, they should be able to combine their plans with improvisation as it becomes necessary. The ratee should also be given the same consideration. Days or possibly a week or two prior to the scheduled performance review, the ratee should be notified of the time, date, and place of the scheduled review. The review session will be more informative and constructive when *both* parties have had ample time to do their homework.

The importance of self-review also becomes evident at this stage of the appraisal process. In situations where employees formally review their own performance, comparisons of self-ratings with ratings provided by the supervisor become a focal point for discussion of past performance. In fact, prior to the actual review session, the supervisor and subordinate may exchange their completed rating instruments and then use the subsequent analyses for starting the interview.

Many employees basically mistrust anything that involves a review or measurement of their performance; therefore, by expecting the least and the unexpected, they protect themselves from disappointment. Subordinates frequently are reluctant to discuss their workplace behavior. This does not mean that raters cannot obtain a complete picture of what has happened. The raters must acquire on a piecemeal basis what may appear to be information about a number of unrelated activities and join these data together like pieces of a jigsaw puzzle. They must realize that detailed or specific information on isolated issues is of far less value than information that pertains to the overall job behavior of the ratee. For this reason, the rater must be a good listener and be willing to maintain the two-way flow of conversation.

Although many raters are unwilling to spend much time in the appraisal process, their involvement is critical to the overall success of the program. The supervisor should realize that performance appraisal is not a program separate and apart from the supervisory process but, rather, is an integral part of that process. Performance appraisal, when successfully and enthusiastically applied, is, in fact, the most efficient and successful on-going means at the supervisor's disposal to obtain the desired ultimate goal—maximized workplace performance. The time the supervisor spends with his or her subordinates in reviewing performance can have both short- and long-term benefits that far exceed the cost of preparing and conducting a performance review.

In preparing for the review, the rater must gather all the information that has any meaningful bearing on the discussions. The appraisal information must be carefully analyzed, and the various events that transpired during the rating period must be identified. By instituting a systematic, orderly, and in-depth preparation for an interview, the rater becomes more prepared for the unexpected. The better the preparation, the greater the opportunity for effective flexibility. By knowing what information is wanted and what is already available, the rater can accept fragmented pieces of information, place them in a particular compartment, and collect additional information that will provide an overall picture of the employee's behavior.

One approach that may be extremely useful in developing a constructive review session is for the rater to review performance-related information and to develop an agenda for the meeting. This agenda should identify the major points to be discussed during the interview. The rater can provide the ratee with the agenda prior to the review session so that the ratee can review it and make additions or deletions regarding topics to be discussed. This provides an additional dimension for facilitating employee awareness of what to expect and how to prepare for the coming meeting more effectively. If there is an agenda and it has not been presented to the ratee prior to the session, it should be reviewed early in the meeting and the ratee should provide feedback on any points of interest or contention.

Knowing the Employee's Job

To be effective as a supervisor requires being effective as a rater of performance. To be effective as a rater of employee performance, the supervisor must be able to assess and understand:

1. Job requirements and work-unit goals.
2. The relationship between short- and long-term work-unit goals and organizational objectives.
3. Employee capabilities and energy levels.
4. Employee goals and demands.
5. On- and off-the-job conflicts that affect workplace behavior.
6. The influence of performance ratings on employee reward opportunities.

There is no sense in falling into the management trap that there is "one right way" to do anything. Among the many alternative processes available for appraising performance, none appears to provide more benefit than one that starts with a valid, accurate, and comprehensive description of job responsibilities and duties. The employee should have a vital role in developing these requirements or, after becoming fully acquainted with the job, in reviewing the responsibility and duty statements to ensure that they accurately describe the job as it is currently being performed and that they are listed in an acceptable ordering.

A performance rating review should specifically address job requirements and demonstrated workplace behavior. However, all involved parties are subject to their individual perceptions. Subjectivity and unfair biases can occur in any review. The best defense a rater can have against an unfair review is to be aware of inadequate or inconsistent emotions. Such awareness can minimize the possibility of their occurrence or of an unfair slanting of an employee's performance review.

As previously mentioned, the responsibilities and duties are what the organization identifies as the processes necessary to achieve job-required outputs that lead to the accomplishment of the goals of the unit and group, and, eventually, the mission of the total organization.

These responsibilities and duties facilitate the identification of the situational and human variables that individualize each job and, in turn, assist jobholders in meeting the dynamic requirements of their jobs.

Recognizing Reward Opportunities

Over the past 100 years, labor has been able to obtain an increasingly greater share of the total revenue of the business. The point has now been reached where there is little slack left in the revenue allocation process for increasing the amount available for compensating employees. In the past 20 years, private-sector businesses have increased labor's share of the revenue at the expense of dividends to shareholders, research and development, and capital investments. In the public sector, increased taxes on businesses and the public have been used to increase compensation payments to employees. A major result of these actions has been a rapid increase in costs without corresponding increases in productivity. This cycle has been a major contributor to the inflation that is being felt around the world.

In the 1980s, as businesses attempt to increase their margins of profit and improve their competitive advantage, they will continue to take the slack out of their organizational structures. Constant review of human resource requirements will result in relatively fewer promotion opportunities in the 1980s.

With a limited number of promotional opportunities and many intelligent, energetic, enthusiastic employees competing for them, organizations will be hard pressed to meet employee reward demands through promotions. Where does this leave the management that wishes to establish or maintain a workplace environment that rewards quality performance? A major opportunity for rewarding performance that leads to improved organizational productivity may take this route:

1. Ensuring that all employees know what is expected of them in performing their job assignments.
2. Adequately preparing employees to perform job assignments.
3. Providing employees with up-to-date and accurate job-related information.
4. Instilling in each employee the feeling of importance of his or her role in processing productivity-improvement information.
5. Permitting and facilitating employee involvement in setting work-related goals.

6. Supporting goal-achievement behavior.

7. Reviewing and sharing the results of workplace efforts in an interactive and supportive manner.

8. Providing rewards relative to the quality and quantity of job performance.

When taking this approach, the organization demonstrates through its actions that its employees are very important. The employees develop an awareness of the contributions that they can and are making—which enhances their self-images—and, through their job efforts, obtain the intrinsic rewards that come from doing a good job.

When an employee has the confidence to meet a job challenge, the opportunity for self-reliance and self-esteem increases dramatically. The performance appraisal system permits employees to improve their performance through expanded job knowledge and the recognition that the supervisor is there to provide support. The job itself becomes a challenge; meeting situational variables provides variety to the work and also learning opportunities. This is how growth and development can flourish even in organizations where there are very few promotional opportunities.

A critical determinant of success for any organization occurs when an employee decides to do or not to do something. The responsibility-based performance appraisal system assists in getting employees to act and in ensuring that in the process of acting they understand what they must do; recognize the impact of their actions; and appreciate collaborative efforts.

The entire work progress, results-oriented review process is one that leads to positive initiation and expenditure of efforts to secure a result that benefits all involved parties. This kind of process assists in establishing that sought-after condition—a trusting workplace environment. Figure 9–3 identifies major events that occur during supervisor-subordinate interchanges within the formal performance appraisal process that lead to a trusting workplace environment.

In preparing for a performance review, a rater must recognize that the opportunity is available for establishing a workplace environment that elicits employee motivation, which, in turn, benefits everyone.

The Physical Setting

The need for "doing homework" (gathering, analyzing, and summarizing information that identifies and characterizes demonstrated work-

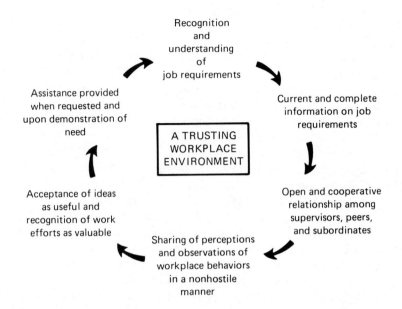

Recognition
and
understanding
of
job requirements

Assistance provided
when requested and
upon demonstration of
need

A TRUSTING
WORKPLACE
ENVIRONMENT

Current and complete
information on job
requirements

Acceptance of ideas
as useful and
recognition of work
efforts as valuable

Open and cooperative
relationship among
supervisors, peers,
and subordinates

Sharing of perceptions
and observations of
workplace behaviors
in a nonhostile
manner

FIGURE 9–3. Major Supervisor-Subordinate Interchange Events.

place behaviors) before the interview has already been mentioned. Preceding the actual meeting, the rater should arrange for a physical setting that will enhance interviewing success. If at all possible, a neutral meeting place should be sought. The basic requirement is a private room with comfortable chairs and, if possible, no desk or other barrier between rater and ratee. The rater and ratee must be able to discuss relevant issues in total confidentiality, preferably with *no* outside interruptions.

Since it is desirable that the ratee discuss personal feelings and points of view, he or she must feel secure that only the rater is hearing what is said or, at least, that confidentiality of information is well defined. There should be no distractions, such as the ringing of the telephone, interruptions by a secretary, or a jovial "What's new?" from a passing colleague. If available, coffee and ashtrays should be provided; if the ratee is a smoker, this is one time that smoking should be permitted.

Scheduling

The rater must allow sufficient time to conduct the review. It is not fair to either the rater or the ratee to terminate an unfinished review because of another commitment. Because of both the importance and sensitivity of the performance review, it is not appropriate to cancel a review or even to make a ratee wait because of other job requirements. Any of these things can happen, but good planning can keep cancellations or delays to a minimum.

However, it is always possible that a situation will arise that, in some way, can affect the rater's intellectual, emotional, or psychological outlook. An interruption may eliminate the opportunity to do some last-minute, critical preparation. Or, some condition may arise that could cause the rater to be distraught, angry, or have some other emotional feelings that could destroy the effectiveness of the interview. When such a situation occurs, the best answer may be to delay the interview for 30 minutes, an hour, a day, or more. The same conditions may also exist for a ratee and cause a delay. Although it is extremely desirable to maintain an interview schedule, the successful completion of an interview is more important than the maintenance of a schedule.

THE INTERVIEW A brief but thoughtful introduction may make the difference between a successful and an unsuccessful interview. The ratee frequently enters the session apprehensively. First and foremost, this thought may occur: "What am I going to be chewed out for today?"; then, "How are 'they' going to get me?"

The rater should put the ratee at ease as quickly as possible. A moment or two for some light discussion such as, "You're looking well today" or "Congratulations on the new baby" will break the ice. There should be a brief discussion about what is to be accomplished during the session. The agenda for the meeting should be shared with the ratee. If this has not been done in advance, the rater should invite the ratee to share in the responsibility for successful completion of the interview and explain how the ratee's views can influence the results of the meeting. A simple statement such as "I'd like to share my observations with you and would appreciate your offering any suggestions that might aid my perceptions" will underscore a desire for the ratee's participation.

Recognizing that the interview is, in itself, a stress-laden situation for many people, the rater must realize that it is not easy, and at times not possible, to learn all that he or she needs to know. An important point to remember during the interview is that *what one hears is not necessarily what one needs to know*. Whether acquired through learning or instinct, survival is fundamental, and what we say often has a way of coming back to haunt us or hurt us. Raters should remember that "foot in mouth disease" has a very special meaning to ratees. Consciously or subconsciously, ratees think, "I will tell them what they want to hear" or "what I *think* they want to hear"; "I will not say anything that could put me in a bad light"; "I must be careful about what I say about my work companions—after all, they belong to my church or my social organization. They go fishing or hunting with me. I will be working with them for the rest of my life. A slip of my tongue could place them in jeopardy, and their friendship is certainly more important to me than this organization and its operations"; "Even if I do speak my mind about what is wrong, the bosses will not do anything about it anyway—except possibly get me in trouble with my associates." These are just a few examples of the many thoughts that may go through a ratee's brain that block or prohibit the transfer of valid, meaningful, and timely information.

People seem to have an innate protective device that prohibits them from explicitly and precisely stating real and valid issues. Providing information about job-induced stress frequently has negative connotations, and many employees are not too anxious to discuss such issues. Throughout the interview, ratees will at times respond to questions with answers that they feel are socially acceptable or even with what they *think* the rater wants to hear but not with what the rater wants or needs to know. The rater may find it necessary to skillfully return to a point several times before it is understood and responded to in an acceptable manner.

By using activities performed and results achieved as major points of discussion, it is easier for both parties to identify areas requiring improvement. When a ratee has performed below acceptable levels, there is a good chance that this level of performance is recognized by the individual when he or she compares the results of a recently completed work effort with desired results. Discussions about negatives are seldom, if ever, enjoyed by either the rater or ratee. In an interview session, the opportunity for injecting surprises into the situation decreases and the opportunity for constructive criticism increases when attention and discussions focus on job requirements, observed behaviors, and identifiable results. When this occurs, opportunities for arbitrary confrontations decrease, and it becomes easier to focus on important facts or pertinent issues. The redirecting of behavior toward the accomplishment of meaningful and acceptable results is the major contact point between the rater and the ratee.

Providing a Rating

A particular stress-related situation occurs when the rater must provide a performance rating during the interview session. The previously mentioned General Electric study indicated that supervisors had a very difficult time providing negative feedback to employees during a performance review session. From these findings, General Electric researchers concluded that it is best to split the role of performance appraisal, conducting performance rating and reward identification in one session and providing feedback useful for motivation and development purposes in another session.

Other studies have indicated that by inflating the ratings, raters overcome the stress of providing information regarding appraisal ratings that are lower than the ratee expects. Again, the General Electric studies in the early 1960s indicated that the great majority, over 90 percent, of employees interviewed felt that they performed in an average or above-average manner.[3] Designing an appraisal system that permits or forces raters to give untrue ratings is a disservice to the ratee and to the organization. Improvements in performance will not be realized unless problems are identified and faced together. In fact, individual performance, as well as total organizational performance, will tend to deteriorate (that is, not even maintain the status quo) unless valid feedback and problem identification and correction occur.

If a rater must give a performance rating during the interview session, the timing of the rating can be most critical to the progress and effectiveness of the session. Providing an excellent or commendable rating causes no problems to most raters. The rating can be given early in the interview and then the rater can discuss future actions the ratee may want to take.

On the other hand, when less than satisfactory or even satisfactory ratings are to be given, it may be best to let the rating evolve throughout the interview process. In this case, areas requiring improvement should be analyzed one by one. Opportunity for self-examination should be encouraged. The discussion of each performance dimension should conclude with a brief review or a recap. The final rating can be given with a summary of the total interview.

When two or more performance reviews are conducted during the year, these progress reviews may also require that the rater provide a rating score for that period. *It is important here for the ratee to recognize that the rating score at this time is only an indicator of current performance and can change as performance changes.* A major reason for the review session and the rating is to center on what can be done to improve performance. In these interim review sessions,

---

[3] Meyer, et al., "Split Roles," p. 126.

both the rater and ratee have opportunities to see activities and results from the perspective of the other person and are able to modify future behaviors.

Conducting the Interview

During the interview, a flow of questions, responses, unsolicited statements, and probably many nonverbal communications (position of body, gestures, eye contact, facial expressions) contribute to the accomplishment of the goals of the meeting. In addition to identifying the information to be provided and requested, the rater can increase the probability of success by employing empathy, maintaining objectivity, minimizing secrecy, and utilizing keen observation and constructive criticism. These qualities, when demonstrated by a rater, will encourage the ratee to be comfortable and possibly more confident, increasing the usefulness of the interview.

Empathy. Empathy is the ability to understand why a person behaves in a certain manner, see something through the eyes of the other person, or replicate another person's thinking or feeling. It allows a rater to understand more fully why and how certain things transpire to cause unacceptable workplace behavior. This kind of understanding can then lead to better solutions of workplace problems. Although it is always possible that empathic views may be incorrect or deceptive—that is, misjudging reasons for behavior—it is better to be empathetic than overly critical.

Although empathy is essential in conducting an interview, there is truly no place for *sympathy*. If the time is right and the interviewee feels that he or she can pull it off, out comes the "sob story," the tale of woe. This is not the time to hide performance failure behind a situation that requires compassion. This does not mean that it is possible to eliminate the sad story. When it arises, the rater should listen courteously and, as soon as possible, redirect attention to the subject at hand—workplace behavior and what can be done in spite of certain unsatisfactory events.

Objectivity. A difficult but important perspective that the rater must maintain is one of objectivity. He or she must be as fair and impartial as possible. Facts must provide the basis for performance-related decisions. Personal feelings and prejudices must not cause the distortion of facts or their unjust use.

Maintaining a nonjudgmental attitude is not always easy. It is all too possible to be overpowered by the smooth and glib talker or the well groomed, physically attractive ratee. However, when tempted to make a less than acceptable judgment based primarily on the speech or appearance of the ratee, the rater should remember that the employee may be a "diamond in the rough" who is only giving a partial picture of the contributions that he or she has made during the appraisal period. (Of course, this employee could also be just a piece of cut glass.)

It is just as possible that the ratee can say something that the rater considers unreasonable, causing the rater to become hostile or angry. Now, the rater must keep "cool." When this situation arises, the rater must first decide whether or not the comment is pertinent to the goals of the interview. If it is not, the rater should move the conversation on to other matters despite any urge for an emotional response. If the content of the ratee's comment is germane to the interview, the rater may *restate* in more reasonable terms the words that caused the initial anger and *reflect* or encourage further explanation of the ratee's understanding of or feelings about the specific problem. The use of restatement or reflecting upon a particular statement made by the ratee is an extremely useful tool available to assist any interviewer.

Secrecy. "Grapevines" exist to fill gaps where information is missing. The strength and activity level of the grapevine in an organization is, to a significant degree, inversely related to the amount and accuracy of information shared by the organization with its employees. A strong grapevine often provides information that supports goals of the informal organization that are frequently incompatible with those of the formal organization. Information desired by employees *will* be supplied. It may be fabricated, erroneous, and more damaging than the actual facts, but the grapevine will fill in any information gaps. The organization must weigh the perceived dangers of sharing information against the predictable benefits. That is, secrecy fosters an "us against them" supervisor-subordinate perception, while shared information is essential to building a trusting relationship that leads to mutual acceptance of goals.

In any supervisor-subordinate relationship, there is the additional fear on the part of the supervisor that if certain information is provided, the subordinate either will make demands of the supervisor that are unreasonable or will require the supervisor to do things he or she is unwilling to do. Here again, decisions must be made as to the total impact of keeping information from the subordinate that the subordinate desires or feels is critical.

Keen Observation. Ratees constantly give both oral and nonverbal clues regarding their understanding and acceptance of a specific topic.

The rater must watch for these clues in order to determine when further clarification is required or when an issue is understood. The lighting of a cigarette, raising of an eyebrow, checking the time, or uttering a barely perceptible, "I'm not sure," may provide the rater with the clue to what his or her next step should be.

The rater's actions also affect the quality of the review. Are his or her eyes focusing on the ratee, on a sheet of paper, or out the window? The rater's questions, responses, tone of voice, and body movements also send a special message that may intimidate or inhibit the ratee and, in turn, affect his or her response.

The rater must be in charge of the interview. Through keen observation, he or she will be able to recognize what must be done in order to direct the session toward the desired goals.

Constructive Criticism. An attack of any kind on the personality of an individual (from his or her perspective) is almost certain to result in defensive behaviors. In reviewing performance, there is often the need to recommend, even insist upon, changes in behavior. Accomplishing this task without damaging a person's self-image is no easy assignment. The following hints may be helpful here:

1. Get the point across. State it directly and concisely without attempting to "soften the blow" with introductory or modifying comments. Mixing positives and negatives does not always work. The ratee may hear only the positives and fail to hear the negatives. As a result, he or she never receives the message that a change is necessary.

2. Don't argue. Establish the fact, use credible, real-time examples. Allow the ratee to discuss his or her view or side of the subject as completely as possible. Listen attentively and attempt to develop solutions to the problem from the ratee's comments. If the ratee refuses to accept facts or continues to disagree, remain calm and simply state, "This is what I saw, here is what I expect," and move on.

3. Establish a review schedule. Set and agree on a time when problem areas will be reviewed in order to identify the level of success in solving identified problems.

4. More is not better. Only so many negatives can be accepted by any person at any one time. Most people have a very low threshold for accepting the need for improvements or changes in behavior. Thus, the rater must list the negatives and only present the few that, when corrected, will result in the greatest contributions to improved workplace performance.

Closing and Summation

The interview is now coming to a close. The major goals have been accomplished. The rater and ratee have had their "day in court." However, it is still necessary to summarize what happened, what has been agreed to, what recommendations are to be made, the accuracy of the identified behaviors, and what should take place from now until the next interview. It may be advantageous to share an outline of these items with the ratee as an impetus for the agreed-upon actions to take place.

Following the completion of the interview, the rater must carefully analyze what was said and what transpired. The following steps provide hints for analyzing and summarizing the results of the interview:

1. Distinguish between the cause of behavior and the effect of behavior. For example, a cause is that a child is at home sick or that the spouse ran off with a salesperson; an effect is tardiness or a series of unexplained absences.

2. Identify factors leading to certain behaviors, such as peer pressures resulting in a reduced quantity of output.

3. Separate internal and external pressures. Examples of the respective pressures are, "Spouse thinks that I should be making more money" and "My pay is low compared with that of my co-workers."

4. Assess employee strengths and weaknesses. Examples are "Employee cooperates well with co-workers" and "Employee demonstrates little interest in guiding group efforts."

5. Indicate employee's potential for success and failure. Examples of the respective traits are "Employee appears to have unlimited energy and willingness to perform assignments" and "Employee has minimal skills in speaking before a group."

6. Identify the capability of the employee to tolerate or resolve stress-related issues. For example, a novel or unusual situation frequently results in the complete disruption of expected employee output.

7. Identify opportunities for supporting the employee and directing behavior so that it benefits both the employee and the organization. For example, the employee is seeking a marketing job; schedule the employee so that it is possible for him or her to complete a graduate-school program and also to attend an in-house marketing-oriented training course. In addition, the rater could ask:
   What additional job-related support from me would you like to have?

   What types of training would you like to receive?

What additional resources or support can the organization provide?

Do you desire or are you seeking a promotion? To what job? Where? When?

Are you prepared/ready for a promotion?

What promotion assistance do you need?

What do you want from your job?

Recording the Interview

If at all possible, the rater should record all pertinent information immediately following the session. The following questions may be useful as a checklist for identifying what should be recorded upon the completion of the interview.

1. Were job requirements reviewed?
2. Does the employee understand job requirements?
3. Were areas of job conflict discussed?
4. Were resource allocation issues resolved?
5. Were job goals and performance standards established?
6. Were goal attainment steps analyzed?
7. Was there a discussion of what the employee would like to accomplish from the job?

Recording Personal Reactions. At the conclusion of the interview, the rater should note personal reactions and impressions. This type of information may prove to be invaluable in preparing for future interviews or for analyzing what happened during this interview at some future date.

Personal feelings about the ratee should influence neither the rater's future performance reviews nor those conducted on the same individual by other raters. On the other hand, it may be extremely useful for future reviewers to know about the rater's feelings during the review and about behaviors that both parties exhibited (ease, pleasantness, hostility, anger, frustration). Noting and recording these behaviors that might block achievement of a future successful review may guide the rater or a subsequent rater in avoiding these undesirable behaviors. As much as humanly possible, the rater should keep the tone of the review on a positive, constructive base. Understanding one's potential weaknesses from a general consideration or as related to a specific ratee can only help the rater to improve the interpersonal dynamics exhibited during a performance review.

Interviewing Skills Checklist

When conducting an interview, the following points should be considered. These points form a mental checklist that can assist any interviewer in improving his or her chances of success.

1. *Focus on workplace problems, not personality.* A performance review is neither the time nor the place to discuss personality problems.
2. *Use facts, not opinions.* Performance decisions must be based on fact. Evidence must be available to document the claims made by the rater and ratee.
3. *Provide feedback in a nonthreatening manner.* An effective performance review requires two-way communication. To be effective, this information must flow in a constructive, open manner.
4. *Refuse to accept responsibility for the ratee's behavior.* Although situations can certainly influence behavior, each worker has the final responsibility for the direction of his or her actions.
5. *Establish rapport.* Support and goal achievement must be the dominant theme of a performance review.
6. *Keep to one point, one subject at a time.* Maintain order by minimizing, even eliminating, unnecessary, dysfunctional digressions.
7. *Provide useful information in understandable amounts at appropriate times.* Although he or she may be thirsty for information, don't drown the ratee.
8. *Don't try to manipulate the interview.* Although threatening situations may be present in a performance review, the rater must not use his or her position unfairly.
9. *Promote self-review, self-assessment.* The entire review process, starting even prior to the review session and continuing throughout, should be designed to promote ratee involvement and interaction that leads to constructive self-analysis.

THE PERFORMANCE REVIEW AND THE CONTEMPORARY WORLD OF WORK

Even in the most highly structured, routine, repetitive assignment, variation or change occurs. The kinds and degrees of change do not occur in any well defined sequence. The ability to adapt and perform acceptably in an environment in which change is the rule requires the willingness to accept risk. Accompanying risk is the chance of failure. With failure comes fear of the unknown.

In the workplace, the more information the employees have about the variables, factors, or forces that may cause change, the greater is the likelihood that they will successfully adjust to changing situations. When confronted with a novel situation, an employee who concludes that possible errors or mistakes will result in an unsatisfactory performance review may do nothing. In the modern organization, which, in many cases, is large and impersonal, and where individual desires, efforts, and reasoning go unnoticed or unrecognized, fear of making a mistake leads directly to doing nothing. This type of attitude stifles the courage to try something different, to implement an innovative approach. When employees demonstrate a "do nothing" behavior, they and the organization lose one of the great learning opportunities available—learning from past mistakes. When mistakes become part of the learning process and are not part of a punitive performance appraisal process, they reinforce the qualities that overcome job-related fear and minimize unhealthy stress.

The performance appraisal process facilitates the sharing of information and perceptions between supervisor and subordinate. The possibility of a supervisor–subordinate adversary relationship diminishes when these two individuals work together to solve workplace problems. When both parties better understand the different sets of issues facing the other party and also recognize mutual interdependencies, the opportunity for supportive interaction increases significantly and the probability of improving workplace performance increases.

Chapter 10

Performance Appraisal
Training Opportunities

A legitimate right of all employees involved in or touched by performance appraisal is to understand what the appraisal program is all
about. Would an organization place an employee on a job to operate
a new and sophisticated piece of equipment without providing the
employee with training on how to use that equipment? Would the
organization place the employee in the job with no concern for
the adverse impact on the use of organizational resources if the equipment is not used properly?

Just as training an employee as to how to properly perform the
job is critical, so is training as to how to participate in the performance
appraisal program. All employees have the right to know how and
why they perform their various roles in the appraisal processes. The
fulfillment of these rights is also necessary and beneficial from the
organization's perspective, because a critical factor leading to the ultimate success of an appraisal program concerns the degree to which
these rights to know "why" and "how" are attained.

Prior to starting an appraisal training program, those supporting
or responsible for it may have to face the following reasons for not
implementing such a program:

1. No funds are available for training.
2. Training makes excessive demands on employee time.
3. Skilled trainers and useful training tools are not available.

Obviously, if an appraisal training program is to become a fact, a
great many "public relations and selling" activities must be performed
to obtain top management support.

Only a naive individual would believe that if an organization provided sufficient appraisal information and training it would automati-

cally have raters who provide performance ratings that accurately reflect employee behaviors. On the other hand, if an organization provides accurate and timely performance-related information to all involved employees and actively supports the appraisal process through well designed and effective training programs, the chance for improved ratings is significantly enhanced. The skills developed and the information provided through the training program assist in the growth and development of all employees. It is through such a process that "unknowns" become "knowns" and hidden or secret information becomes available and understood.

When they are involved in risk-taking situations, a sufficient amount of valid and current information assists employees to direct their actions to where their chances for success are greatest. The greater the availability of this kind of data and information to employees at all levels, the greater the likelihood that decisions will be made that benefit the organization and the individual.

There are few who would argue that organizational life constantly becomes more complex. Hand in glove with complexity is change; with change comes the unknown; and with the unknown comes risk. Almost every job requires the incumbent to make operating decisions. Each employee must have some latitude or flexibility in making these operating decisions. The training program provides employees with skill and information on what is wanted, when it is wanted, how much is wanted, and, to a degree, how it is to be done. This program should also assist employees to recognize what they must do, what they cannot do, and how they can make the best use of their knowledge, skills, and efforts. Balancing these organizational desires with unidentified or unrecognized contingencies in a manner that leads to improved organizational productivity is the reason organizations implement formal performance appraisal programs.

This chapter will investigate and describe the various kinds of training and information that can be provided to those involved in performance appraisal. Like the appraisal process itself, the training must be tailored to fit specific requirements. However, all training programs should encompass such subjects as:

1. Why the organization conducts performance appraisal.
2. What uses the organization makes of performance observations, measurements, and ratings.
3. How to identify and rank job activities.
4. How to observe and record performance behaviors.
5. How to measure and rate performance.
6. How to minimize rating errors.

7. How to interact with others (communication and listening skills).

8. How to conduct an appraisal interview.

9. How to influence others positively.

10. How to share information so that it will be well received.

11. How to train, counsel, and coach.

12. How to negotiate for resources to perform the job in an acceptable manner.

13. How to acquire sufficient data and information to perform job assignments acceptably.

The overriding reason for an organization to provide performance appraisal training is to have those involved in the process recognize and accept the idea that it works for them. Within this kind of environment, employees will actively participate in the program because they want to. To create this kind of environment, employees must, first, understand *why* performance appraisal is beneficial both to the employees and the organization; second, know *how* to play their roles in the performance appraisal process; and, third, be granted sufficient information, resources, and authority to solve performance-related problems and make decisions that are in both their best interests and the interest of the organization.

TRAINING OPPORTUNITIES

Over the past quarter of a century, much research has been conducted on how to improve the learning process. Tried and true as well as innovative approaches to the transfer of information have been used. Understanding how people learn, like almost any process related to the human brain, has almost defied solution. Hundreds of concepts and theories exist, but no one method of instruction has been found to be consistently and universally superior to all others. For particular individuals and/or for particular uses in specific situations, one instructional method may prove to be more effective than another. There are, however, a few basic concepts that have fairly universal applicability and can significantly improve the transfer of knowledge. They include the following:

1. A person tends to learn more when there is an interest in the subject.

2. Interest in a subject increases when the learning material leads to self-improvement.

3. Adults (possibly people of all ages) learn more when they take an active role in the training.

4. A person tends to learn more when the instructor knows the subject, clearly communicates information that is accurate and relevant, and is able to establish a learning environment.

5. Most students retain more through their senses of seeing and hearing than they do through reading. However, learning programs that combine seeing, hearing, and reading (in that order of importance) will probably provide the most successful results.

6. Learning occurs faster when trainees have a chance to practice what they have learned and when they receive immediate feedback about their performance.

Early in this book, considerable attention centered on the human and technical barriers facing raters in the successful completion of their performance appraisal responsibilities. To overcome these barriers, rater training must focus particularly on the following areas:

1. Enhancing human interaction skills.

2. Conducting an effective interview.

3. Learning how to influence higher-level managers to recognize, appreciate, and take necessary actions to resolve workplace problems.

After acquiring these skills, raters must have access to (or must use these skills to obtain) necessary information to share with others so that they may influence subordinates, peers, and higher-level supervisors to assist them in accomplishing their assignments. A fundamental goal of the training program described in this chapter is to enhance the rater's skill in influencing others through gaining and sharing worthwhile and valuable information.

TRAINING TO IMPROVE APPRAISAL SKILLS

Prior to designing and developing a training program, those responsible for the training must determine whether or not there is a need for it. This pretraining activity first requires determining the effectiveness of the existing appraisal system (if there is one) in identifying and correcting weaknesses or deficiencies in the job performance of employees. The next step is to determine whether or not an appraisal training program can be developed that will rectify these identified weaknesses and deficiencies through improvements in the appraisal process.

The following list of common symptoms of inadequate performance appraisal systems may be helpful to the trainer as a partial checklist during the investigation of the existing appraisal system:

1. Employees throughout the organization do not know how or why the appraisal program operates.

2. Employees do not know what use the organization makes of appraisal measurement and rating information.

3. Employees are not sure what their supervisors expect of them.

4. Employees have a minimal or unclear understanding of the performance standards used to measure their performance.

5. Employees have a low expectation of any consequences (positive or punitive) if their performance exceeds or falls short of identified and recognized performance standards.

6. Raters frequently feel very insecure when they have to discuss employee performance formally.

7. Raters have minimal skills in providing constructive feedback relative to demonstrated unsatisfactory ratee behaviors.

8. Raters have poor skills when negotiating with their supervisors for resources necessary to successfully perform assignments.

Using this checklist should aid the trainer in determining areas of the appraisal process that deserve particular emphasis in the training program.

Following the identification of training needs, the trainer should develop program, session, and behavioral objectives; a course outline; and a lesson plan. *Program objectives* identify and describe the desired outcome of the entire program. They provide a broad guide for all of the training activities. The *session objectives* should identify and describe the kinds of knowledge to be transferred to the participants. These objectives act as guides for deciding which training methods are most appropriate and which standards should be set for measuring training effectiveness for each session. *Behavioral objectives* define the knowledge and skills the participants should possess at the end of each training session. Performance-appraisal-related training objectives will link the organizational reasons for having a performance appraisal program with the specific training activities to be implemented. As with any set of useful and worthwhile objectives, they should be written in clear and precise language so that anyone involved with the training can understand the full meaning of the objectives. Three possible objectives for a performance appraisal training program are (a) increased employee understanding and acceptance of the appraisal process; (b) expanded rater, reviewer, and administrator skills in the accurate rating of performance; and (c) improved organizational productivity through performance appraisal.

TITLE:

PRESENTER(S):

DATE(S) AND TIME(S):

LOCATION:

PARTICIPANTS:

PARTICIPANT PREPARATION:

METHODOLOGY:

TRAINING AIDS:

PROGRAM OBJECTIVE(S):

SESSION OBJECTIVE(S):

BEHAVIORAL OBJECTIVE(S):

LESSON OUTLINE:

FIGURE 10–1. Training Session Lesson Plan.

After writing the session objectives, the trainer's next step is to develop a *course outline*. The course outline identifies the major subject areas to be covered in each segment of the training program and then lists under each major subject area the specific topics to be discussed. The outline identifies specific teaching methods and training aids to be used for each subject.

The instructor then develops an even more specific description of what will be included in the training by preparing a *lesson plan* and relating the material to be presented with specific training techniques, training aids, and available and allotted time. The instructor now has the opportunity to modify training activities to make the best use of his or her specific skills and the training resources available to enhance learning opportunities. An example of a lesson plan outline is shown in Figure 10–1.

Training Techniques and Training Aids

For most organizations, fairly traditional training techniques will be suitable for performance appraisal training. These include: (1) lectures, (2) group interaction exercises, (3) role playing, and (4) individual and group decision-making exercises. Training aids that will be invaluable in communicating the training messages are audio-visual presentations (films and tapes), slides, overhead transparencies, case studies, programmed instruction, role-playing scripts, and a wide variety of reading materials (books, pamphlets, outlines, etc.).

An essential part of these kinds of training programs is that the training materials be current, simulate real-world situations, and be easily understood by the students. Although tapes and films are emphasized in the training sessions, cases may also be used. These would require student involvement, leading to increased interest and greater retention of what has been presented.

No matter what technique and aids or group of techniques and aids are used, some critical "homework" assignments should be completed by the trainer prior to the start of any performance appraisal training program.

In preparing for a training session, the trainer may find the checklist in Figure 10–2 useful.

A training program may range in length from a one- to two-hour orientation program on "Why XYZ Corporation Appraises Performance" to an extended three- or even five-day workshop. Or, it may be a series of workshops over an extended period of time that covers the critical training needs identified during the investigation of the existing appraisal system. This "series of workshops" method allows the trainees to practice and apply (and, hopefully, *master*) each step of the appraisal process when they are back on the job before learning

---

FIGURE 10–2. Checklist for Training.

	Yes	No
1. Knowledge of subject is adequate or sufficient.	☐	☐
2. Teaching methods have been identified.	☐	☐
3. Training aids have been selected.	☐	☐
4. Participant involvement opportunities have been developed.	☐	☐
5. Materials to be presented are current and valid.	☐	☐
6. Examples to be used are relevant and understandable.	☐	☐
7. Information is to be presented in proper sequence or order (i.e., outline of how the session is to be conducted).	☐	☐
8. Classroom environment is attractive and orderly.	☐	☐

the next step in the process. This method also allows the trainees to learn from each other (including some real-life examples of what *not* to do) as they share their on-the-job experiences at the next training session.

A performance appraisal training program may include the following kinds of training sessions:

1. Introduction to performance appraisal (for all employees involved in appraisal programs).
   How does appraisal benefit our company?
   How does appraisal help you do your job?
2. Rater responsibilities in appraising performance. (Sessions 2–7 are designed for those who have rating and rating review responsibilities.)
3. Influencing behavior positively.
4. Proper use of rating instruments.
5. Documenting workplace behavior.
6. Preparing for the performance review.
7. Conducting a performance review.

The following may be used as a guide to aid the trainer in developing these or other sessions. Included within each session is a discussion of the content or basic information to be communicated to the participants/trainees. In some cases, there is extensive discussion of the content material in other chapters and, in these cases, the specific chapters are referenced. The seven training sessions cover the following topics:

TRAINING SESSION #1

LESSON PLAN

Title: Introduction to Performance Appraisal.

Presenter(s): Names of trainers, consultants, other knowledgeable and skilled individuals.

Date(s) and Time(s): (As scheduled—approximately one to two hours in length.)

Location: (Specific address of physical site.)

Participants: All employees involved in performance appraisal rating.

Participant Preparation: Review employee performance appraisal manual.

Methodology: Lecture, question and answer sessions.

Training Aids: Audiovisual aids, printed handouts.

Program Objectives: Improve organizational productivity through the accurate and timely appraisal of performance.

Session Objectives: Gain acceptance of performance appraisal by providing information that will assist participants in understanding its operation and purpose.

Behavioral Objectives: Know organization policies and procedures regarding performance appraisal; describe individual's role in performance appraisal program; relate rater-ratee interactions in appraisal process; list uses of appraisal rating information; identify processes to ensure accurate ratings of performance.

Lesson Outline: (As developed.)

INFORMATION TO BE DISCUSSED

A logical start for any performance appraisal training program that may be offered to all employees is to explain why the organization has a performance appraisal system and the uses it intends to make of appraisal observations, measurements, and ratings. A brief manual should be developed and distributed to the trainees before the training session, to be read as a pre-course assignment. This manual should cover such topics as:

1. What is performance appraisal?
2. What uses are made of performance measurement and rating information?
3. What procedures does the organization have to ensure honest and accurate ratings?
4. What due process rights are granted to all employees whose performance is formally observed, measured, rated, and documented?
5. What instruments are being used?

These topics would then be reviewed, discussed, and emphasized during the training session.

This training session provides a bird's eye view of the entire appraisal process. The lecture method is appropriate for presenting this kind of information. In addition to the performance appraisal manual, other aids that would assist in getting desired messages across to the participants are overhead projector transparencies, slides, and some kind of audiovisual aids (tapes or films). Two important points the presenter should consider are organizing material in a logical order, permitting relationships to develop and flow naturally, and using organization-related examples, such as describing why the organization wishes to recognize merit, and the need for measurement, rating, and documentation to link performance to organizationally-provided rewards. The purpose of this training session is to provide sufficient introductory information so that employees will begin to understand the appraisal process. The trainer should "sell" the need for the appraisal program and begin to remove the fear of the unknown through the sharing of information.

A question and answer session at the end of the presentation provides participants with interaction opportunities. It is quite likely that some who have read the manual and followed the presentation have questions they want answered. Group size may be a determinant here. If this session is offered to a large number of employees, it may be useful for small groups of participants to meet later with their supervisor and possibly a person trained in the operation of the appraisal program for a question and answer session.

This kind of group meeting can also be useful for discussing personal problems that block effective ratee-rater interaction. Here, the opportunity arises to provide information on such critical issues as:

1. How the specific supervisor/rater will handle the interview and what the ratee should do to prepare for the interview.
2. Where information is provided that describes job requirements, performance standards, and work-unit goals.
3. What opportunities are available to modify job requirements relative to personal strengths and weaknesses.
4. The kind of support employees expect to receive from the organization and higher levels of management.

TRAINING SESSION #2

LESSON PLAN

Title: Rater Responsibilities in Appraising Performance.

Presenter(s): Names of trainers, consultants, other knowledgeable and skilled individuals.

Date(s) and Time(s): (As scheduled—approximately eight to sixteen hours in length.)

Location: (Specific address of physical site.)

Participants: All raters and reviewers.

Participant Preparation: Review handouts on "Commonly Made Rating Errors" and "The Need For Accurate and Current Job Descriptions."

Methodology: Lecture, role playing, case analysis, group interaction.

Training Aids: Audiovisual aids, role-playing scripts, cases, TV camera and replay equipment.

Program Objectives: Improve organizational productivity through accurate and timely appraisal of performance.

Session Objectives: Enhance rater awareness and understanding of his or her influence on the operation of an effective appraisal program.

Behavioral Objectives: Discuss importance of properly described job and well defined performance standards; identify rater errors and biases; explain how to eliminate or minimize making of rating errors.

Lesson Outline: (As developed.)

INFORMATION TO BE DISCUSSED

This session is extremely prescriptive in design and operation. All phases of this training session focus on and stress the critical role of the rater. One of the first steps a trainer must take in developing this training session is to examine what is occurring and identify organizational barriers currently existing that may block the accurate rating of employee performance. This investigation may include a review of (a) the design of the appraisal instrument, (b) the accuracy of descriptions of job requirements, and (c) the existence and quality of performance standards. Environmental constraints should be analyzed, including such possible disturbances as an attempt to unionize the organization, a possible forthcoming lay-off or reduction in force, or an unwillingness of top management to permit the flow of certain kinds of information throughout the organization. This familiarity with organizational constraints can be effectively used in organizing and presenting the material for this session.

An initial training activity would stress the relationship between job requirements and performance measurement. If the organization does not have job descriptions or if they are inadequate, it may be necessary to have a separate session on how to identify and describe job content requirements. A review of the section in Chapter 4 on job content would be helpful in preparing such a training session.

This session includes a section on rating errors and rating bias. Possibly the most important part of rater training takes place in this part of the session. (Rater errors are described in detail in Chapter 1.) Here, role playing and role modeling become invaluable techniques.

Case studies may also be a teaching aid in this phase of the program. These training techniques and aids grant the participant-rater a chance to learn through doing. The involvement exercises provide the opportunity to present valuable and immediate feedback in a non-threatening environment.

Rating errors such as *halo, central tendency,* and *leniency* may best be attacked through the use of a case in which participants have the opportunity to respond to written dialogue and discuss the results in a group session. Other rater errors such as *same as me, latest behavior, initial impression,* or *the contrast effect* may be best described through various kinds of role-playing exercises. Here, selected participants act out roles from a script and make identifiable errors. Other participants in the classroom acting as observers can identify the errors, discuss the *whys* and *hows* of such errors, and try to determine what can be done to reduce the likelihood of their occurrence.

Possibly the most powerful of all training aids is the use of some kind of tape or film. A film or audiovisual tape may be purchased or developed that portrays a rater making certain kinds of performance observations, measurements, and ratings. The participants review the film and discuss rating strengths and deficiencies and determine actions that can be taken to reinforce and support correct rating behavior.

Another important use of visual media is to videotape participants enacting certain performance appraisal roles (role playing with certain script guidelines). Following the completion of the role playing, the class critiques the entire performance. Those playing the various roles can defend or further explain certain behaviors. Following this kind of discussion, the videotape is replayed and the participants and observers have another chance to review the entire scenario. This review has a twin impact: It permits everyone to observe and identify what actually happened, and it gives the instructor and participants the opportunity to make useful comments.

The reason the tape is such a powerful learning tool is that the participants actually see *themselves* performing specific activities. Mannerisms—oral and nonverbal behaviors—become obvious. These kinds of observations make it difficult to deny behaviors and are a forceful influence for self-improvement.

In addition, participants learn which kinds of physical movements, even facial expressions, facilitate success. They also learn to eliminate actions and behaviors that may lead to failure.

Focusing on typical rating errors is an important phase of this training session. From the point of view expressed in this book, subjectivity is and always will be an inherent part of any workable performance appraisal program. This does not mean to imply that rating errors resulting in unfair or biased ratings are acceptable. In this training session common rating errors are identified and defined so that all raters are aware of the kinds of rating traps waiting to ensnare the unsuspecting. In addition to rating errors that occur when raters fail to recognize differences in performance relative to different performance dimensions and fail to properly use the rating scale are the errors that arise because of favorable or unfavorable predispositions toward other people that are wired into almost every individual. Possibly the best way to reduce such personality errors is to identify biases people have because of another's sex, race, religion, national origin, physical makeup, intellectual abilities, emotional maturity, and social graces and inform those making such errors that they are unacceptable and will not be tolerated.

Possible Session Activities

Scenario I:

Activity 1. The trainer describes rating errors and provides recognizable and valid examples of common rating errors.

Activity 2. The class divides into groups (four to seven members) and generates examples from past experiences. The members discuss why errors occurred and what can be done to minimize reoccurrences.

Activity 3. Each group presents identified rating errors. The entire class then develops solutions to eliminate or minimize occurrences of these problems. The class also discusses why the rating errors occur and the damage they do to the appraisal process.

Activity 4. The trainer summarizes materials presented and learning opportunities are discussed.

Scenario II:

Activity 1. The trainer describes rating errors and provides recognizable and valid examples of common rating errors.

Activity 2. The class observes a film/tape presentation in which a rater rates a subordinate. Rater activities are discussed and results identified.[1]

Activity 3. Each participant reviews the film and makes two kinds of rating decisions. First, the participants pretend to be

---

[1] An excellent description of activities involved in using films and tapes for improving rating skills is in Gary P. Latham and Kenneth N. Wexley, *Increasing Productivity Through Performance Appraisal* (Boston, MA: Addison-Wesley, 1981), pp. 107–118.

the rater and rate the subordinate as they think the rater would have rated that person. Then the participants rate the subordinate as *they* observe and perceive that individual's activities and results.

Activity 4. The participants are then requested to turn in their ratings to the trainer. The ratings are processed and the results presented to the class. A discussion follows as to the reasons for the differences in rating behaviors, the kinds of errors made, and actions that can be taken to reduce such errors.

Activity 5. The trainer summarizes what has been presented and emphasizes important concepts.

Scenario III:

Activity 1. The trainer describes rating errors and provides recognizable and valid examples of common rating errors.

Activity 2. Role-playing scripts are given to all participants. Some of the class enact the roles of raters and ratees; the remainder of the class act as observers.

Activity 3. The participants follow scripts and make their own additions. (This part of the exercise could be videotaped and replayed in a later activity.)

Activity 4. The class reviews the role-playing exercise and identifies rater errors.

Activity 5. The videotape is replayed to assist both observers and actors in reviewing actual rating behaviors. A discussion follows in which events and perceptions are more accurately identified. Further discussion centers on errors and what can be done to reduce them.

Activity 6. The trainer summarizes what occurred in the previous activities and emphasizes important concepts.

If the organization has problems with its job descriptions, it may wish to include this additional training activity within this session. Problems may be the lack of (a) accurate and precise job definition, (b) personnel available to identify and describe job activities and tasks, and (c) employees skilled in writing responsibility and duty statements. A training exercise that is designed to assist employees to identify and describe job content requirements and to write job responsibility and duty statements may take this form:

Activity 1. Each participant completes an activity and task questionnaire of his or her job.

Activity 2. Each participant develops a comprehensive task list and then defines each verb as to its meaning relative to job requirements.

Activity 3. Using the work completed on activities, tasks, and verb definitions, each participant develops a job definition—a list of job responsibility and duty statements.

A review of the discussion about identifying job content requirements in Chapter 4 would be helpful in developing this training exercise. This exercise requires approximately four hours to complete. (*Note:* If training time is limited, it is recommended that this section be omitted. It is more important that the allotted time be spent reviewing the more significant aspects of the actual performance appraisal process.)

TRAINING SESSION #3

LESSON PLAN

Title: Influencing Behavior Positively.

Presenter(s): Names of trainers, consultants, other knowledgeable and skilled individuals.

Date(s) and Time(s): (As scheduled—approximately four hours in length.)

Location: (Specific address of physical site.)

Participants: Raters and reviewers.

Participant Preparation: Review and identify personal problems when involved in coaching and counseling subordinates.

Methodology: Lecture, role playing, group exercise.

Training Aids: Cases and handouts on coaching behaviors.

Program Objectives: Improve organizational productivity through accurate and timely appraisal of performance.

Session Objectives: Recognize barriers to performance and opportunities available to overcome them.

Behavioral Objectives: Identify barriers related to employee knowledge and skill, interests, energy levels, efforts to be expended. Relate coaching-counseling behavior to specific barriers.

Lesson Outline: (As developed.)

INFORMATION TO BE DISCUSSED

If one is to be effective as both a supervisor and a rater, coaching and counseling skills are a basic requirement. To be an effective coach or counselor, the individual must first be able to identify the problems that currently block successful—or even super—performance. Problem identification relating to barriers blocking acceptable or even improved employee performance may take the following form. Are the barriers

1. Beyond the direct control of the ratee?
2. Due to lack of knowledge, skills?
3. Caused by an inability to use available knowledge and skill?
4. Resulting from physical problems, or are they more emotionally or psychologically oriented (just doesn't care to provide an acceptable level of performance)?

Once the rater has recognized and identified the probable cause of the unacceptable level of performance, decisions are made as to the kind of interaction that may be most appropriate in reducing the barriers and improving worker performance.

If the issue involves conditions outside the control of the employee, then the rater must be able to determine whether or not he or she can provide the assistance necessary to overcome the barriers. It may require the transfer of resources or some kind of reassignment of responsibilities or duties. It may be something beyond the control of rater and ratee, and adjustments may have to be made regarding performance standards or redefining expected output.

When the issue is lack of knowledge or skill, the problem is first to determine whether, through training, the employee could overcome the identified deficiency and then to identify how the training will be delivered, that is, on the job, in-house training programs, or programs provided by some external source.

If the problem is an inability to use available knowledge and skills, then actions must be taken to provide the direction necessary to show the employee how to use his or her knowledge and skill at the appropriate time when facing a specific situation.

When the problem concerns physical issues, a decision must be made regarding physical limitations and the current assignment. However, if the problem relates to a lack of concern or an "I don't give a darn" attitude, an entirely different course of action may be necessary.

The foundation of coaching-counseling is support. The problem is that support may be provided in many ways, and the kind of support given relates to personality issues and situational constraints. The most elementary kind of support is to review the problem in such a manner that the ratee identifies the issues and is able and willing to take the necessary action for overcoming barriers to acceptable performance.

When skill and knowledge deficiencies are barriers, the issues become more complex. What training can the rater provide directly, or what is readily available? What further actions are necessary to secure more difficult-to-acquire or more costly training opportunities?

The most difficult coaching-counseling problem facing most managers is some kind of ratee emotional or psychological problem that blocks the attainment of successful performance. Most raters do not have the depth of training to identify deep emotional or psychological issues, and it is here that decisions must be made to determine rater behavior. Should the rater behave in a collaborative manner, or does the situation require an extremely authoritarian approach? No matter what approach is taken, the rater must show an interest in working with the ratee and provide suggestions on ways the ratee can make improvements. The rater/coach must always convey the message to the ratee that their joint effort is a "two-way street" and that the ratee's interaction is essential.

If the situation has deteriorated to the point that past supportive action has resulted in no behavioral change, then the supervisor/rater may be left with no alternative other than to say, "Here is what I expect of you . . ." (in no uncertain terms) ". . . and this is what will happen if these expectations do not materialize. . . ." (again in straightforward and understandable terms).

No matter what the problem may be and no matter what various actions are taken by both parties, the rater/coach must be certain to follow up on actions taken. The rater must know what the ratee has done to correct any identified problem and, also, must let the ratee know that there is sincere interest and concern on the rater's part. In the follow-up stage, the rater/coach can identify levels of success, places where changes must be made, and places where reinforcement can be supplied to support continuation of change and desired behavior. Reinforcement can be supplied in many ways. It may be the nonverbal "pat on the back," the oral "Thanks a million, Jane. You are doing great," or a written memo that is placed in the employee's file after having gone to higher levels of management. Whatever the form, all employees want and appreciate recognition.

Possible Session Activities

Activity 1: The trainer discusses the underlying concepts involved in coaching employees. The trainer focuses on the establishment of supportive relationships, problems about individual differences, and the importance of identifying performance barriers.

Activity 2: The class is divided into groups, and each group is given a performance problem. The group discusses normally available approaches open to supervisors within their organization for solving problems. Group problems could be (a) some kind of environmental problem outside the control of the employees; (b) lack of knowledge and skills; (c) inability to apply knowledge and skills; or (d) an apparent "don't give a darn" attitude.

Activity 3: A class discussion is held about when to be extremely supportive and collaborative, when to be extremely authoritarian, and when to behave somewhere in between.

Activity 4: Using some kind of scripts, the class is divided into groups and prepares to act roles described in the script. The scripts may describe various results achieved or kinds of behavior demonstrated by employees under certain situations. The roles may involve the supervisor/rater/coach and the subordinate/ratee. Other group members act as observers. The observers are given forms to complete that require them to do some kind of analysis of the performance of the rater and ratee.

Activity 5: A wrap-up of the previous discussions and the role playing can focus on a discussion of such issues as:

The most acceptable supervisory response to different kinds of situations.

The ability of supervisors to predict subordinate behavior.

The kinds of responses a supervisor may make when a specific situation arises.

The training session can then be concluded by analyzing the responses to these issues and how a supervisor/rater conducts a coaching interview.

TRAINING SESSION #4

LESSON PLAN

Title: Proper Use of the Rating Instrument.

Presenter(s): Names of trainers, consultants, other knowledgeable and skilled individuals.

Date(s) and Time(s): (As scheduled—approximately 8 to 10 hours in length.)

Location: (Specific address of physical site.)

Participants: Rater and reviewers.

Participant Preparation: Review current rating instrument; identify problem areas, strengths and weaknesses.

Methodology: Lecture, individual presentation, group exercise.

Training Aids: Rating instrument.

Program Objectives: Improve organizational productivity through accurate and timely appraisal of performance.

Session Objectives: Understand performance measurement and rating instruments; recognize how to use performance instruments properly.

Behavioral Objectives: Describe design of rating instrument; explain how to make an accurate inferential leap from demonstrated employee behavior to the relevant interval on the rating scale; distinguish among ratings given by various raters.

Lesson Outline: (As developed.)

INFORMATION TO BE DISCUSSED

An effective way of linking training to the design of the rating instrument is to use a training session for (a) reviewing each rating factor-performance dimension, (b) analyzing the rating scales and the performance meaning of each identified interval, (c) describing rating distribution information that allows each rater to review his or her own rating behavior, and (d) discussing rating indexes or norms that will be provided to raters that will allow them to compare their rating behaviors with other raters.

If the appraisal instrument is to have any value, it must both allow and encourage raters to make meaningful distinctions in employee performance. Meaningful distinctions require the development of a well designed rating instrument and the availability of skilled raters who know how to use the rating instrument and can observe and accurately identify differences in levels of performance. Possibly most important, the rater must be willing and able to use appropriate rating intervals on the scales provided in the rating instrument.

This training session focuses on the effective use of a rating instrument and discusses the influence of rater rating behaviors and instrument scale design on obtaining a distribution of rating scores. If a rater rates everyone the same or if ratings of a particular performance dimension have little or no variability, the rating scores have minimal organizational value. The reason for measuring and rating employee performance is to identify differences. All employees do not perform at the same level of global (overall) performance, and various employees perform differently from others in specific performance dimensions. The degree of difference in ratings received by different ratees relative to specific performance criteria is called *discriminant validity*. (Validity is discussed in greater detail in Chapter 11.) Many performance appraisal programs fail to recognize meaningful distinctions in employee performance over a specified period of time.

Major topics to be covered in this session are:

1. Differences in performance are very likely.
2. Recognition of performance differences is essential.
3. Performance is measurable.
4. Ratings must closely correspond to demonstrated performance.

A training exercise that is extremely useful in helping raters improve their understanding of the design of the rating instrument is to involve them in the identification and description of a behavioral-anchored rating scale for a particular performance dimension.

Possible Session Activities

Activity 1: The trainer discusses the development of the rating instrument. The discussion includes a review of each item on the instrument, why it is included, and how to properly complete each item. The major focus of the discussion is on performance dimensions and rating scales.

Activity 2: The class divides into groups. Each group is given a specific performance dimension, and each group member is requested to identify, from past experience, examples of an employee behaving in a superior manner, an acceptable manner, and an unacceptable manner relative to the performance dimension. Each group then reviews all examples developed by the group members and establishes a rank ordering of identified examples from one that describes the most superior behavior to one that describes the most unacceptable behavior.

Activity 3: The class reconvenes, and the group examples of behavior are scrambled. Those who were not involved in the original development and ordering of the behaviors rank order the behaviors for each performance dimension.

Activity 4: The results of the group and class orderings are reviewed.

Activity 5: The trainer describes how behaviors that receive 70 to 80 percent agreement as to ordering may be kept as anchors for a behavioral-anchored rating scale. The trainer describes in greater detail how the process would evolve if valid and useful behavioral anchors are to be the end results of such a program. The trainer then summarizes the critical importance of, first, being able to observe workplace behaviors and, then, correctly categorizing these behaviors relative to some previously set scale of values. The discussion of the critical incident technique in Chapters 5 and 6 and behavioral-anchored rating scales in Chapter 6 provides useful background information. (*Note:* This kind of training exercise may be most valuable if it precedes the actual design of the rating instrument.)

TRAINING SESSION #5

LESSON PLAN

Title: Documenting Workplace Behavior.

Presenter(s): Names of trainers, consultants, other knowledgeable and skilled individuals.

Date(s) and Time(s): (As scheduled—approximately two to four hours in length.)

Location: (Specific address of physical site.)

Participants: Raters.

Participant Preparation: Review handout, "Need for Documenting Employee Behaviors."

Methodology: Lecture, role playing, group interaction.

Training Aids: Audiovisual aids, role-playing script, cases, handouts.

Program Objectives: Improve organizational productivity through accurate and timely appraisal of performance.

Session Objectives: Assist employees to recognize and describe actual workplace behaviors.

Behavioral Objectives: Document workplace behaviors as actually demonstrated; describe procedures that assist in storing and recalling demonstrated behaviors.

Lesson Outline: (As developed.)

INFORMATION TO BE DISCUSSED

Even the best trained and most observant individuals have limitations when recalling and processing observed behavior. The supervisor, in the normal daily chain of events, observes a wide variety of behaviors and various employees under a broad range of conditions. The observed behaviors in some manner modify those previously observed, and recollections of past behaviors will, in fact, vary the perception of actual behaviors.

To overcome human weaknesses in processing, storing, and recalling observed behavior, there must be continuous documentation of behavior as it occurs or as soon as possible after its occurrence. These human weaknesses also underscore the necessity for training supervisors to observe behavior and then provide feedback about what was observed. The success of the entire performance appraisal process eventually hinges on the supervisor's ability to accurately recall and disseminate job behavior information. The dissemination or feedback of job behavior information to ratees is the topic of discussion in Chapter 9.

Methods, procedures, and practices that tie appraisal to actual workplace behaviors are very important. It is essential that the identification of workplace behaviors be as accurate as possible. Passage of time "clouds" human memory, events become blurred, and other emotions blunt awareness of what actually happened. One of the best ways to keep past performance as fresh and accurate as possible is to document behavior as it occurs. Documentation must be job-related. Information related to traits and other individual characteristics is valuable and useful only when the traits or characteristics relate directly to work-required behavior or have an influence on future career opportunities.

Direct observations are better than those that emanate from second- or third-hand sources. This does not mean that it is improper to use hearsay information; it just means that it is not as good as what has been personally observed. (But even firsthand observation may be clouded by perceptual barriers, and what one thought one saw may not have been what actually happened.) There are times when it is impossible or impractical to obtain firsthand observations. These conditions may result when an employee is temporarily assigned to another supervisor or to a work unit operating in some remote location or is working independently and the client/consumer of the services or workplace results provides the behavioral information. This situation also occurs when an employee is assigned to a special task force or work group requiring actions that are not under the control of the immediate supervisor.

Figure 10–3 is a preprinted behavior identification form that could be supplied to all raters. This form assists the rater to identify relevant,

Employee's
Name _____

Employee's
Job
Title _____

Date of
Occurrence _____

Time of
Occurrence _____

A.
P.

Location of
Occurrence _____

Identify Observed Behavior (If reporting hearsay information, identify source and location of actual observer.)

Date Form
Completed _____

Time Form
Completed _____

A.
P.

Signature and
Title of Person
Completing Form _____

_____

Items to be considered in identifying behavior (may be used as a checklist)

What specifically occurred?
Is there sufficient detail to support future judgment?
Have you described results of behavior?
What circumstances influenced behavior?
      Was there an emergency situation?
      Did unusual or adverse conditions exist?
Behavior Being Documented:
      Insubordination
      Attendance
      Quantity of Work
      Quality of Work

      Theft
      Malicious Damage
      Interpersonal Relations
      Acceptance of Job-Enlarging
        Responsibilities

Other Factors Being Rated in the Current System:

Second-Party Observations:

      Remote Location
      Works Independently

      Temporarily Assigned to Others

FIGURE 10–3. Performance Documentation Form (Identification of Employee On-the-Job Behaviors).

specific information required for documenting employee performance. A rater who completes such a form as soon as possible after the occurrence of a specific activity will build a file that is helpful for guiding and supporting appraisal decisions. A review of the form identifies some of the critical elements that must be included in any performance documentation form:

Employee's name. No question as to who behaved in the identified manner.

Job title. Permits easy review of work-required responsibilities and duties. Useful also if employee was temporarily assigned to another job and this relates to work performed when on the assignment.

Date, time, location of occurrence. When and where behavior occurred.

Date, time, completion of form. Accuracy of recall rapidly declines as time increases between occurrence and description.

Observed behavior. Description of what occurred, circumstances affecting behavior, and results of behavior. (Each individual description of a workplace behavior may not appear to be sufficiently important to take the time required for documentation; however, over an extended period of time, a systematic identification of behaviors provides powerful support for actions that a supervisor must take in performing his or her responsibilities.) *Describe only; avoid interpretation.*

Many raters find it difficult to complete a formal document, such as described in Figure 10–3, shortly after the occurrence of a behavior that should be identified. It may be necessary for a rater to keep a notebook available for listing and briefly describing behaviors that should be described in greater detail at some more appropriate date. With the declining cost and increasing availability of all types of recording instruments and systems, these devices provide splendid support in this area. The purpose of the notebook or taped observation is to preserve as accurate a description of the behavior as possible. In this way, it is more likely that the behavior will be described in writing and that the description will conform to what actually happened. (The Critical Incident Technique, or CIT, discussed in Chapters 5 & 6 is a similar approach that is useful for documenting employee workplace behavior.)

A major reason for documentation is to minimize unfair and unjust appraisal of employee workplace behavior. Practically everyone is subject to biased thoughts and feelings. Written descriptions assist raters to maintain a true perspective of what the employee is doing while performing work requirements. The documentation must use "hard" information. "Hard" refers to information that can be documented; confirms something that happened; can be measured in quantitative terms or in actual results that describe qualitative measures; and can be identified by date, time, and location of occurrence. By providing some kind or degree of measurement to demonstrated behavior, it becomes much easier to assess the effectiveness of employee performance. Raters must be aware that documented employee behavior must be available and open to that employee's review. This information is critical, both to the operation of successful organizations and to the future security and progress of the employee. Documentation is not an opportunity for unsupported innuendos or rumors; it is an opportunity for stating facts.

The procedures described in Chapter 4 for writing responsibility and duty statements apply equally to the procedures to be used for describing employee workplace behavior. First, the most descriptive action verb should be selected, then an appropriate object must be used that best describes the action.

The more often raters use this writing style, the easier it will become, and the more skilled they will be in written communications. The entire writing process should result in the rater thinking in terms of the action verb plus objects and other necessary descriptions that further explain the how, when, why, even where of the action. This writing style, which is discussed in detail in Chapter 4, keeps rater attention focused on *what* the employee is doing, not on some nonrelated trait or characteristic that might distort the description of actual behavior.

A training session on the documentation of workplace behavior can make use of films, tapes, role playing, and cases. Students can actively participate in the process by documenting observed behaviors (films, tapes, role playing) or described behaviors (cases) using instruments or tools provided or recommended by the trainer. Once again, following the documentation session, the students and trainer can discuss results achieved and problems faced. This discussion naturally leads to suggestions or recommendations for overcoming the identified barriers. This training exercise could be linked with exercises previously described in Session 2.

TRAINING SESSION #6

LESSON PLAN

Title: Preparing for the Performance Review.

Presenter(s): Names of trainers, consultants, other knowledgeable and skilled individuals.

Date(s) and Time(s): (As scheduled—approximately two hours in length.)

Location: (Specific address of physical site.)

Participants: Raters.

Participant Preparation: Review performance review preparation checklist.

Methodology: Lecture, questions and answers, individual involvement.

Training Aids: Cases, performance rating instrument, performance appraisal policy and operating procedures manual.

Program Objectives: Improve organizational productivity through accurate and timely appraisal of performance.

Session Objectives: Understand what to do in preparing for a performance review; know how to make best use of time in getting ready for a review of performance.

Behavioral Objectives: List activities to be performed in preparing for a performance review; describe best physical layout for a performance review.

Lesson Outline: (As developed.)

INFORMATION TO BE DISCUSSED

Although raters are constantly preparing for performance reviews as they observe ratee performance and review the results of ratee efforts, there are certain activities a rater must do prior to making a formal rating. The way a rater prepares for the formal rating (both in determining what the rating(s) should be and in providing rating feedback to the ratee) consists of a series of very personal actions. Raters can be assisted in preparing for the performance appraisal by training them to use their time more effectively.

The first step in this training activity is to analyze what raters must do and then assist them to develop a plan of action that ensures the completion of all appraisal activities acceptably and on time. An appraisal schedule includes a listing of each activity to be completed and the time for completion. This effectively establishes a priority or hierarchy of activities. The activity schedule must include reports to be completed and where the data and information come from to complete each report. The schedule should clearly identify what the rater must be doing. This responsibility cannot be assigned to others. Critical decisions are being made, and the lives of many people are affected, to some degree, by appraisal decisions. An understanding of requirements and sufficient preparation will reduce fear of results.

The preparation training session may require the participant to complete various preappraisal forms with the appraisal data and infor-

Performance Dimension Summarized_____

Dates of Performance Documentation Forms_____

Briefly describe how workplace behaviors support identified dimensions, both positively and negatively:

FIGURE 10–4. Performance Dimension Attainment Summary Sheet.

mation available in the form of a case. This training package replicates the kind of "homework" a rater must perform prior to rating subordinates. The case may require the participant to review a file that includes a series of documents that identify employee behaviors and the results of workplace efforts. At this time, the participant must summarize behavior and results associated with specific performance dimensions. Figure 10–4 is useful for summarizing and analyzing behaviors with regard to specific performance dimensions.

Consolidating a series of behaviors occurring during the appraisal period provides a more accurate picture of what actually happened than does any single event or dependence on memory. Summarizing behaviors that describe a performance dimension makes it easier and permits a more accurate appraisal of employee behaviors relative to that quality. It may only be necessary to summarize behaviors relating to performance dimensions that have been previously identified by rater and ratee as critical components of job-related performance.

This training exercise focuses on the many discrete or specific judgments a rater makes that lead to a final rating score. As with the previous exercises, a major goal is to expand rater awareness of the many processes and interactions that influence the final rating.

Chapter 9 includes a discussion of the preparation of the physical site for conducting the performance review. The activities identified should be part of a checklist for all raters to use in preparing for the interview.

TRAINING SESSION #7

LESSON PLAN

Title: Conducting a Performance Review.

Presenter(s): Names of trainers, consultants, other knowledgeable and skilled individuals.

Date(s) and Time(s): (As scheduled—approximately eight to sixteen hours in length.)

Location: (Specific address of physical site.)

Participants: Raters.

Participant Preparation: Review handout, "How to Conduct an Interview."

Methodology: Lecture, role playing, group interaction.

Training Aids: Audiovisual aids, cases, role-playing script, slides, overhead transparencies, handouts, TV camera and replay equipment.

Program Objectives: Improve organizational productivity through accurate and timely appraisal of performance.

Session Objectives: Improve rater interviewing skills.

Behavioral Objectives: Contrast effective and ineffective rater interviewing skills; describe nonverbal actions that can influence a review session; list actions available to a rater that keep the review session on a desired path when using a nonstructured interview approach.

Lesson Outline: (As developed.)

INFORMATION TO BE DISCUSSED

Skills in interviewing are required in many managerial activities—not just in performance appraisal. The ability to conduct successfully an interview may be one of the most important determinants of managerial success. The various training techniques and training aids previously discussed in this chapter are applicable to an interview training program. Chapter 9 focuses on this topic and is useful in preparing for this training session.

A well designed interview training session combines materials that describe interviewing do's and don't's and "helpful hints" about what to do and how to react to varied situations and demands. Following a review of written materials, participants become involved in very realistic role-playing situations. Through actual involvement exercises, they learn through doing. Here, once again, the miracle of the instant replay audiovisual tape is a most powerful learning aid.

The concept underlying role modeling is to observe someone (including oneself) behaving in an acceptable or unacceptable manner, recognize these behaviors, and make a conscious effort to behave in an acceptable manner. Through role playing, participants have the opportunity to rehearse and practice what they have learned in varied situations. In the classroom environment, they receive feedback from both the instructors and other participants. In a properly developed classroom environment, feedback from demonstrated role-playing behaviors is constructive, not threatening. The instant replay of behaviors exhibited during the role playing permits each person to observe himself or herself in action and then to be better able to recognize what must be done to improve interviewing skills. It is impossible to overstate the importance of involving students in an interview, taping the interview, and, finally, analyzing the behaviors portrayed on the tape.

Films can also be used, and in these cases all participants have the opportunity to identify interviewing strengths and weaknesses and to develop role models for acceptable interviewing behaviors.

Major points that should be developed in any interviewing workshop may include the points provided in the Interviewing Skills Checklist found on page 302.

Interview training must emphasize the need to direct any criticism toward subordinate workplace behavior. All employees have self-images that they will protect at almost any cost. The more criticism they receive, the more defensive they become. The more defensive they are, the less willing they are to accept any hint of criticism. Personality criticisms imply the need for change. Most people are quite content to do things the same way they have in the past. Change requires effort and attention. Employees' psychological denial of their inadequate performance limits their need to implement constructive changes. To accept change, people must recognize its value to themselves. An ideal way to gain this kind of recognition is to involve the affected individuals in the change process.

During the appraisal interview, the supervisor must be able to clearly identify and describe what he or she can do for the interviewee, what the interviewee must do for himself or herself, and what they can do together.

The following five topics should be included in a session on improving rater interviewing skills:

1. How to establish a two-way communication environment.
2. How to keep the interview moving.
3. How and when to give a rating to the ratee.
4. How to work through a problem.
5. How to discuss the ratee's future opportunities.

Through a well designed and implemented training program, organizations can provide employees with the kind of support necessary to be contributors to an effective appraisal system. From the outset, it is important to recognize that those who preach training as another

MAKING EFFECTIVE USE OF TRAINING

panacea to appraisal problems may be selling a witch doctor's magic elixir to their clients. Unless the trained rater works within an environment where all parties involved in the appraisal process recognize the value of ratings and accept the integrity of its operation, the training may result in the rater's (or trained parties in whatever their role) becoming even more efficient in "beating the system" or subverting the entire process.

There is no doubt that well designed, properly taught training programs can significantly increase the accuracy and effectiveness of the appraisal process. Training, like the entire rating process, should include involvement opportunities. Participant interaction during training sessions helps to clarify problem areas and to minimize resistance to change. Through the training session, employees are able to identify and understand organizational requirements and, possibly most important, their own requirements. Pitfalls from the perspective of design, implementation, and administration are also recognized. Bringing these critical issues into the open is a major goal of performance appraisal training.

Chapter 11

Legislation, Court Rulings, and Due Process

During the 1970s, legislation and court rulings were the major stimuli for increased management interest in performance appraisal. The Equal Pay Act of 1963, the Civil Rights Act of 1964, the Age Discrimination in Employment Act of 1967, and the Vocational Rehabilitation Act of 1973 all have either explicit or implied sections that require employers to document employee performance before making various human-resource-related decisions. Increased government pressures in these areas required organizations to implement formal performance appraisal systems whether they wanted to or not.

The sad side of this story is that all too often this valuable management tool was being used almost totally to escape unacceptable government action. As government-based pressure begins to wane during the 1980s, organizations may take a different view of their performance appraisal programs. Instead of an escape mechanism, performance appraisal becomes a positive tool to improve organizational productivity.

An issue management now must face relates to the tradeoff between the benefits and costs associated with a well designed, properly managed appraisal system and one that meets minimum government requirements. Costs must include (a) the time that professionals, managers, and employees spend in the design, implementation, and operation of the system and (b) the higher costs due to reduced productivity. Poorly designed and managed appraisal systems, or even unfair, biased informal appraisal processes, can easily lead to employee anxiety, frustration, and hostility that, in turn, lower employee performance.

With the passage of the Civil Rights Act of 1964, the federal government began taking an active interest in employment/personnel practices that discriminate unfairly against any individual because of race, religion, sex, color, or national origin. The Equal Employment Opportunity Commission (EEOC), the federal agency responsible for administering and enforcing the Civil Rights Act of 1964, as amended, looks with extreme disfavor on any employer who measures job performance and uses the measurement data to make personnel decisions in such a manner that job-relatedness cannot be demonstrated. To be in compliance with the Act, to avoid costly lawsuits, and to demonstrate good personnel practices, employers are reviewing the various instruments that they use for test purposes to ensure their validity and reliability. (A test is any method, process, or procedure used in making employment decisions that sorts individuals on relative capability to perform important job functions; in other words, the purpose of a test is to predict an individual's performance in a given job by evaluating his or her capabilities with regard to significant aspects of the job.)

Court rulings and EEOC's interpretations and guidelines that relate to Section 703(h) of Title VII of the Civil Rights Act of 1964 have made organizations very cautious about implementing any personnel-related action that may be considered discriminatory. Section 703(h) states:

> It is *not* an unlawful practice for an employer to give and act upon the result of any professionally developed ability test provided that such test, its administration or action upon the results is not designed, intended or used to discriminate because of race, color, religion, sex, or national origin.

GOVERNMENT REGULATIONS, COURT RULINGS, AND PERFORMANCE APPRAISAL

Employees constantly exert pressure on supervisors to learn where they stand and on managers to provide an equitable relationship between pay and performance. As if these internal pressures were not enough for management to face, legislation and court rulings make the entire appraisal process more complex and difficult to manage.

Title VII of the Civil Rights Act of 1964 and EEOC guidelines state that:

1. Employers must take affirmative action not to discriminate because of race, color, religion, sex, or national origin when making employment decisions.

2. Employment decisions include those involved in the selection, training, transfer, retention, and promotion processes.

3. Any paper-and-pencil or performance measure used in making employment decisions is a test.

4. A test must be fairly administered and empirically validated. (A test is any selection device used to hire, promote, demote, terminate, provide merit increases, or permit entry to training programs.)

Most formal performance appraisal techniques rely on paper-and-pencil methods to identify employee work behavior. The information provided by these techniques assists management in making employment decisions. The EEOC and the courts recognize the impact that the appraisal process has on employment opportunities and the possibility of inherent bias in many parts of the process. The EEOC and the courts have played and will continue to play an important role in the development of the process of performance appraisal.

Uniform Guidelines On Employee Selection Procedures (1978)

To accomplish a coordinated approach to federal requirements regarding employee selection, the EEOC issued the *Uniform Guidelines on Employment Selection Procedures (1978)*. These guidelines have an impact on performance appraisal because appraisal continues to be viewed as a selection procedure. The guidelines provide detailed standards regarding minimum validation requirements, with particular emphasis on content, criterion, and construct validation efforts. To assure compliance with the *Uniform Guidelines,* those involved in selection procedures must either use selection procedures that have no adverse impact on protected classes or be able to validate the procedures.

Validation is easier said than done. If performance appraisal is truly a system, a validation process may require that all components of the system and the system as a whole be validated. At this time, validation of performance appraisal instruments has been slow and has achieved minimal success. Little effort has been directed toward validating performance appraisal systems. It is quite likely that it is impossible to validate a performance appraisal system, especially one such as that described in this book. However, it may be necessary and extremely useful to be able to demonstrate the relationship between each component of the performance appraisal system and acceptable job performance. In this way, all components of a performance appraisal system can be linked directly to the job and demonstrated employee workplace behaviors.

The 1978 *Uniform Guidelines* states that a selection procedure must not adversely impact any group protected by Title VII of The Civil Rights Act of 1964. The *Guidelines* further defines adverse impact as a selection rate for any Title VII group that is less than 80 percent of the rate for the group with the highest rate. This is known as the "rule of thumb" or four-fifths rule. When the overall selection process does not adversely impact protected groups, EEOC will normally not examine the individual components of the selection process for evidence of validity. The *Guidelines* calls this approach the "bottom line."

Age Discrimination in Employment Act of 1967 (*ADEA*)

In the past several years, this act and its 1978 amendment have possibly had more adverse impact on organizations relative to performance appraisal programs than any other government legislation. A declining economy and a need to develop a more productive work force from top to bottom have caused a major housecleaning in organizations that frequently has resulted in failure to promote, demotion, and termination of many older workers. Organizations have often been unable to justify these employment decisions. Court cases simply identify the tip of an iceberg that has caused severe organizational financial losses. A review of major ADEA- and Title VII-related court cases reveals that the defendant (the organization) frequently has emerged victorious. What the court cases do not identify is that a large number of expensive out-of-court settlements have been made by organizations. These cases do, however, emphasize the points courts look for and accept when they find organizational actions to be nondiscriminatory.

Before analyzing these court cases, a review of the ADEA will provide an additional insight into the major issues organizations face when conforming to existing legislation.

The objective of the ADEA is to provide employees between the ages of 40 and 70 with the same opportunities offered to all other employees to reach the same level of desired success. Major employment-related decisions involve hiring, failure to promote, demotion, layoff, discipline, forced early retirement, and termination.

The Equal Employment Opportunity Commission is responsible for enforcing ADEA, and its guidelines for employer compliance are as follows.

Bona Fide Occupational Qualification (BFOQ) Defense. In order to make use of the BFOQ defense, an employer must prove that (a) the age limit used is reasonably necessary to the essence of the business; and either that (b) all or substantially all individuals excluded are in fact disqualified; or that (c) some of the individuals so excluded possess a disqualifying trait that cannot be ascertained except by reference to age. The use of exceptions for reasonable factors other than age must be decided on the basis of all the particular facts and circumstances surrounding each individual situation. Employment criteria that are age-neutral on their face but that nevertheless have a disparate impact on members of the protected group must be justified as a business necessity. The employer has the burden of showing that what seems like discriminatory treatment actually resulted from a "reasonable factor other than age," such as business necessity.

The employer must enforce work rules consistently and uniformly. The rating of employee performance must be performed in the same consistent and uniform manner as all other work rules that are used as a basis for employment-related decisions. Employers must perform appraisals honestly and follow some logical or rational schedule.

Performance appraisal provides employers with performance information that demonstrates that the employee was measured in terms of definite, identifiable criteria based on quantity and quality of work.

In order to establish prima facie evidence of discrimination, the following requirements were established in *McDonnell Douglas Corporation* v. *Green* (identified later in this chapter).

1. Employee's membership in the protected group.
2. Unacceptable employment action taken.
3. Employee's replacement with a person outside the protected group.
4. Employee's ability to do the job.

Once a prima facie case of age discrimination is established, the defendant bears the burden of proof of "going forward" with any evidence to demonstrate reasonable factors other than age for the plaintiff's related action. Burden of proof in ADEA action remains with the individual bringing the action even though prima facie showing of age discrimination will require the employer to come forward with evidence demonstrating reasonable factors other than age for treatment of the individual. In an employment-related decision, the employer must show that the action was for good cause. In an ADEA case, actual discrimination must be found.

Landmark Court Cases

A review of some of the court rulings that have identified and defined the responsibilities that management must accept in designing and managing appraisal programs indicates the direction that organizations must take with performance appraisal. These court cases are listed in alphabetical order, not necessarily in order of importance.

Allen v. *City of Mobile*, 18 FEP Cases 217 (1978). Service (performance) ratings of black police officers were discriminatory. Special performance appraisal programs outlined by the court must be implemented.

Brito v. *Zia Company,* 5 FEP Cases 1207 (1973). Performance appraisal ratings resulted in the layoff of a disproportionate number of Spanish-surnamed employees. The court concluded that the practice was illegal because (a) the ratings were based on subjective supervisory observations, (b) the ratings were not administered and scored in a controlled and standardized fashion, and (c) some raters had little daily contact with the ratees.

Davis v. *Washington, D.C.,* 12 FEP Cases 1415 (1976). Direct relationship between scores on aptitude test and police officer's performance was sufficient to validate the tests.

Douglas v. *Hampton,* 10 FEP Cases 91 (1975). Content validity is to be employed only in those instances where criterion-related validity is proven to be infeasible.

Dowdell v. *Dun & Bradstreet, Inc.,* 14 EPD ¶7797 (U.S. Dist. Ct., Ala., 1977). An employee claiming discrimination in an employment decision lost the case when the business provided detailed, comprehensive information on the quality and quantity of work done by individuals involved in the promotion decision.

Flowers v. *Crouch-Walker Corporation,* 14 FEP Cases 1265 (1977). The employer had not expressed displeasure with an employee's performance prior to dismissal and the employee was subsequently replaced by a white employee. This resulted in a prima facie case of racial discrimination as the employee was qualified for the job and met normal job requirements.

Griggs v. *Duke Power Company,* 3 FEP Cases 175 (1972). In this landmark case, the central issue was that an educational restriction on an employment decision is useless unless it can be proven that there exists a bona fide occupational qualification (BFOQ) between the test and actual job performance. The burden of proof is on the employer to show nondiscrimination in any employment decision related to discrimination.

The decision in the *Griggs* case also states that "The Equal Employment Opportunity Commission having enforcement responsibility has issued guidelines interpreting Section 703(h) to permit only the use of job-related tests. The administrative interpretation of the Act by the enforcing agency is entitled to great deference."

James v. *Stockham Valves and Fittings Company,* 15 FEP Cases 827 (1977). A program for selecting individuals for an apprenticeship program was discriminatory, since selections were made by predominantly white supervisors without any formal written guidelines and a disproportionately low number of blacks were selected for the program.

McDonald v. *Santa Fe Trail Transportation Co., Inc.,* 12 FEP Cases 1577 (1976). Reverse discrimination is illegal. The Civil Rights Act covers all employees.

McDonnell Douglas Corporation v. *Green,* 5 FEP Cases 965 (1973). Simple proof is enough to prove nondiscrimination, but tests must be job-related.

Moody v. *Albemarle Paper Company,* 10 FEP Cases 1181 (1975). Supervisors must use criteria that are not vague and open to divergent interpretations in making employment decisions. Performance ratings that do not have a job-content base have a built-in bias, and such tests must be validated statistically. In this landmark case, the employer (defendant) attempted to validate its preemployment testing methods by using postemployment performance appraisal ratings as supportive criteria. The Supreme Court ruled that the performance ratings were inadequate because of their subjective, vague nature.

Rogers v. *International Paper Company,* 10 FEP Cases 404 (1975). The use of subjective considerations was considered when a court ruled that, in all fairness to applicants and employers alike, decisions about hiring and promotion in supervisory and managerial jobs cannot be made realistically using only objective standards.

Rowe v. *General Motors Corporation,* 4 FEP Cases 445 (1972). All-white supervisory recommendations were based on subjective and vague standards leading to a lack of promotions and transfers for black employees that, in turn, led to discriminatory practices. Of particular importance in this case are the five points the Court used as evidence of discriminatory practices that highlighted the inadequacy of the performance appraisal process:

1. The recommendation of the foreman was the most important factor in the promotion process.

2. Foremen received no written instructions pertaining to the qualifications necessary for promotion.

3. The standards that most influenced the ratings were vague and subjective.

4. Hourly employees were not notified of promotional opportunities.

5. The appraisal-promotion process contained no safeguards to protect against discriminatory practices.

Wade v. *Mississippi Cooperative Extension Service*, 12 FEP Cases 1041 (1976). Trait-rating systems can be subjective and biased and are usually not based on job content. There must be a BFOQ between the trait and the work performed. Data must be provided that show a relationship between appraisal instruments and job analysis and show that the appraisal instrument is a valid predictor of job performance.

Court Rulings on Major Employment Decisions

The following major cases have been used as guides to determine the legal actions to be taken by plaintiffs and defendants with regard to various employment decisions.

Hiring. Performance-appraisal-generated data and information validate criteria used for making selection and placement decisions.

Major court cases:

(D) [1]   *Hodgson* v. *Greyhound Lines, Inc.*, 7 FEP Cases 817 (1974).

(D)   *Brennan* v. *Greyhound Lines, Inc.*, 9 FEP Cases 58 (1975).

(D)   *Usery* v. *Tamiami Trail Tours, Inc.*, 12 FEP Cases 1233 (1976).

(P)   *Smallwood* v. *United Airlines*, 26 FEP Cases 1376 (1981).

(D)   *Murnane* v. *American Airlines*, 26 FEP Cases 1537 (1981).

In the three identified bus line cases, a policy of refusing to hire applicants between the ages of 40 and 65 for initial employment as intercity bus drivers is a BFOQ that is reasonably necessary to the normal operation of the business. The defendants presented statistical evidence indicating that there is a correlation between age and accident frequency. Although chronological age could not be isolated as a factor automatically indicating that an individual could not perform required assignments, evidence was provided that available tests are unable to distinguish those drivers over age 40 who could be accident-prone because of an impairment such as loss of stamina.

Defendants normally had a seniority system in which new hires had to work through a series of jobs before acquiring more senior status. Junior members either performed a series of jobs that qualified them for the most skilled, most responsible position or they had to perform assignments that were least preferred because of scheduling requirements and time away from home.

---

[1] The letters in parentheses—"D" for defendant and "P" for plaintiff—indicate in whose favor the court ruled.

In the *Smallwood* case, the appeals court judges ruled that medical examinations are so effective in predicting the possibility of strokes and heart attacks that the airline hadn't any basis for presuming that "all people over 35 would be unable to perform safely and efficiently the duties of a flight officer." In September 1982, United Airlines settled its age discrimination case by agreeing to pay 114 pilots and engineers a total of $18 million.

In the *Murnane* case, however, the essence of safe transportation again was the basic issue. A court of appeals found the airline's policy of not hiring persons over the age of 40 for the position of flight officer is a BFOQ. The airline showed that it takes from 10 to 15 years for an individual to progress to captain. They also showed that older captains who had served in that position for the longest possible period of time would be the safest captains. There is a mandatory retirement age of 60 for flight personnel.

In 1983, however, Northwest Airlines settled a number of lawsuits by agreeing to reinstate 37 pilots who were forced to retire at age 60 as flight engineers. The pilots would be retrained for other jobs, would retain full seniority and benefits, and would receive a cash payment.

Promotion. Information on the actual performance of an employee is a preliminary concern that is critical but not sufficient in itself to the courts. Rather, the potential of the employee relative to other employees for the desired advancement is the significant concern. Courts place great significance on the fact that, irrespective of age, the employee's performance to date in comparison with others, was not deserving of promotion and *also* that the employer can substantiate these claims through past performance appraisals.

Major court cases:

(D)   *Braswell* v. *Kobelinski*, 428 F. Supp 324 (D.D.C. 1976).

(D)   *Zell* v. *United States*, 20 FEP Cases 929 (1979).

(D)   *Johnson* v. *Adams*, 20 FEP Cases 1534 (1979).

In these cases, the defendants provided evidence of valid and documented performance appraisal criteria. The plaintiffs were rated not only against identified criteria, but also relative to peers who were equally skilled professionals working within highly competitive work environments. The plaintiffs failed to show that the criteria used for rating performance were age-biased or that the individuals with whom they were competing received credit because of age differences. In the *Braswell* case, the defendant used such criteria as ability, knowledge, experience, and maturity required of an incumbent in the sought-for promotion against similar criteria possessed by the plaintiff.

Demotion. Performance appraisal information must be able to support a claim that the employee's performance is *the* determinative factor for such action.

A major court case is:

(P) *Spagnuolo* v. *Whirlpool Corp.*, 25 FEP Cases 376 (1981).

In this case, an appeals court ruled that although age was not the only factor, if it hadn't been for the plaintiff's age, the demotion would not have occurred. The defendant had held the plaintiff in high esteem, and the demotion action was a willful violation of the ADEA. The defendant's performance appraisal program failed to survive close scrutiny by the court.

Layoffs and Forced Early Retirement. An employee's performance must be compared with similarly situated employees as in promotion-related cases. Independent management decisions or economic maladies also are given significant weight by courts. The employer must be able to justify the need for any layoff, for instance, economic factors such as lagging sales, growing inventory, or a depressed economy. The employer must be able to demonstrate why one employee was selected over another.

Major court cases:

(D) *Stringfellow* v. *Monsanto Co.*, 3 FEP Cases 22 (1970).

(D) *Gill* v. *Union Carbide Corp.*, 7 FEP Cases 571 (1973).

(D) *Usery* v. *General Electric Co.*, 13 FEP Cases 1641 (1976).

(D) *Reed* v. *Shell Oil Co.*, 14 FEP Cases 875 (1975); 18 FEP Cases 1059 (1978).

(D) *Mastie* v. *Great Lakes Steel Corp.*, 14 FEP Cases 952 (1976).

(P) *Mistretta* v. *Sandia Corp.*, 15 FEP Cases 1680 (1977); 24 FEP Cases 316 (1980).

(D) *Raggett* v. *Foote Mineral Co.*, 16 FEP Cases 1771 (1975).

(D) *Oshiver* v. *Court of Common Pleas*, 20 FEP Cases 1328 (1979).

In the majority of these cases, the defendants were able to defend their actions to the satisfaction of the courts. Although different techniques and procedures were used, common threads throughout these cases were (a) an honest attempt was made to identify the best performers and, in turn, keep these employees on the active work roles; (b) appraisal procedures used performance-relevant criteria, immediate supervisors were used to rate subordinates, and performance-related behaviors and ratings were documented; and (c) there was no intention to discriminate because of age.

In the *Mistretta* case, appraisal decisions were not based on definite, identifiable criteria that were supported by some kind of record. The defendant's claim that performance declined with age led to a finding that the defendant's appraisal policy was age-biased.

Discharge. The employer must show that an employee failed to perform in an adequate or acceptable manner. Appraisal measurement and rating must recognize minimal acceptable levels rather than relative levels of performance.

Major court cases:

(P)   *Schulz* v. *Hickok Manufacturing Co.*, 5 FEP Cases 1010 (1973).

(D)   *Magruder* v. *Selling Area Marketing, Inc.*, 15 FEP Cases 1506 (1977).

(P)   *Buchholz* v. *Symons Mfg. Co., Div. Symons Corp.*, 16 FEP Cases 1084 (1978).

(D)   *Havelick* v. *Julius Wile & Sons*, 17 FEP Cases 32 (1978).

(D)   *Cova* v. *Coca-Cola Bottling Co. of St. Louis*, 17 FEP Cases 448 (1978).

(P)   *Scofield* v. *Bolts and Bolts Retail Stores, Inc.*, 21 FEP Cases 1478 (1979).

(D)   *Sutton* v. *Atlantic Richfield*, 20 FEP Cases 1292 (1978); 25 FEP Cases 1619 (1981).

In cases found for the plaintiffs, the preponderance of evidence showed that age was an important factor in the termination decision. The defendants failed to explain to the plaintiffs the reasons for their discharge or to document observed or demonstrated behaviors through formal appraisals of performance.

When the courts decided for the defendants, various kinds of both oral and written evidence were supplied that supported claims that the plaintiff exhibited unsatisfactory work behavior. The right of employers to discharge employees for good cause at any time, as long as there is no discrimination, has been recognized by the courts.

Although EEOC guidelines and court rulings leave much to be desired, they do provide a significant amount of useful information regarding actions to be taken by performance appraisal designers and administrators. Duane E. Thompson, Charles R. Klasson, and Gary L. Lubben have made the following 11 recommendations to assist in complying with EEOC guidelines and court rulings:

1. The overall appraisal process should be formalized, standardized, and, as much as possible, objective in nature.
2. The performance appraisal system should be as job-related as possible.
3. A thorough, formal job analysis for all employment positions being rated should be completed.
4. Subjective supervisory ratings should be considered as only one component of the overall evaluation process.
5. Evaluators should be adequately trained in the use of appraisal techniques.
6. Evaluators should have substantial daily contact with the employee being evaluated.
7. If the appraisal involves various measures of performance, the proportion that each measure carries, with respect to the overall assessment, should be fixed.
8. Whenever possible, the appraisal should be conducted independently by more than one evaluator.
9. The administration and scoring of the performance appraisal should be standardized and controlled.
10. Opportunities for promotion or transfer should be posted and the information made available to all interested individuals.
11. An employee-initiated promotion/transfer procedure should be established that does not require the immediate supervisor's recommendations.[2]

Three additional recommendations may also be useful to designers and administrators of performance appraisal systems:

1. Criteria used for appraising performance must not unfairly depress the scores of minority groups.
2. Appraisal forms and instructions to evaluators are an essential part of the process and require validation.
3. Criteria such as regularity of attendance, tenure, and training time are usually not considered part of actual work proficiency. Because they are frequently used as performance appraisal criteria, they require validation evidence.

---

[2] Duane E. Thompson, Charles R. Klasson, and Gary L. Lubben, "Performance Appraisal and the Law: Policy and Research Implications of Court Cases," pp. 5–6. A paper presented at the 39th Annual Meeting of the Academy of Management, Atlanta, Georgia, August 9, 1979.

For performance predictors to be acceptable to the EEOC and the federal courts, they must be valid and reliable.

Validity

The most useful way to describe validity is that it is the degree of accuracy of an inference made about a direct relationship between a particular outcome of a testing device and the demonstrated performance of the individual being tested. From this definition, validity can be viewed as a continuum where various degrees of validity can range from a terminal anchor at one end that identifies the inference as having no relationship to reality to a terminal anchor at the other end that identifies the inference as predicting reality with 100 percent accuracy. It is unlikely, however, that any testing device, including performance appraisal instruments, will ever be 100 percent valid.

In other words, a performance appraisal system cannot be stamped "validated" like a parking ticket.[3] Validation can only be established when there is a correct relationship between an inference and a demonstrated result.

The three principal kinds of validity are content, criterion-related, and construct.

Content Validity. Content validity provides a measure of the relationship between items on a test instrument (remember, a performance appraisal form is a test instrument) and the actual properties the test instrument is designed to measure. It shows through documentation of job data and methodology that the content of a testing procedure is representative of all important skills, job behaviors, or outputs required in the performance of a job. This is a pragmatic or logic-based validity which, in the case of performance appraisal, requires an easily identifiable relationship between appraisal form items and job-related activities, situations, and outputs.

Face validity is a form of content validity. It is the observed similarity between the content of the predictor of performance and actual job content; that is, on the surface, the items or content of the predictor *appear* to be job-related. Face validity *per se* is not recognized as an acceptable kind of validity in the *Uniform Guidelines*, but it is important in the sense that if a test does not even *appear* to be job-related, then the possibility may be increased that its validity is questionable

---

[3] The validation of the parking ticket example comes from Virginia R. Boehm, "An Assessment Center Practitioner's Guide to the Division 14 Principles," *Journal of Assessment Center Technology*, Vol. 4, No. 3, 1981.

or doubtful. It could be said that face validity is a necessary but insufficient aspect of content validity; that is, if a test is content-valid, then, on the surface, it should *appear* to be job-related. But appearance alone is not sufficient to demonstrate content validity. However, lack of face validity is, in itself, an insufficient reason to destroy a claim of content validity. For example, in the forced-choice method, discriminatory items may not appear to have face validity, but the method itself may be content valid.

Criterion-Related Validity. Criterion-related validity measures how well a test predicts an outcome. It is a statistical statement based on *empirical* data that describe the direct relationship between scores on a predictor (a selection procedure—resumé, completed application form, letters of reference, results of an interview, test results) and scores on a criterion measure (a performance appraisal instrument—performance dimension(s) on the instrument). For example, measures of job success as identified by various factors on a selection instrument must be relevant and critical to the job and must relate either positively or negatively to employee job performance (criterion) or some set of performance subfactors (criteria) that may be identified in a performance appraisal instrument. (It must be recognized that the performance appraisal instrument can also be used as a predictor. For example, when using performance appraisal ratings for making promotion decisions, the performance appraisal instrument is used as a predictor.) The inference is that individuals receiving high scores on the predictor actually perform better than those receiving low scores. There are two kinds of criterion-related validity.

Concurrent validity is an "existing status" statistical correlation between predictors of performance (selection items) and actual job performance or present indicators of job performance (rating from an appraisal form). In this type of validity, predictor scores and criterion measures are obtained at the same time, which means that current employees can be involved in a concurrent validity study. For example, suppose a test for police sergeant has been developed, and the employer wants to determine the validity of the test. In a concurrent validation study, the test would be administered to a group of sergeants, and then, soon after, performance appraisal scores on this same group of sergeants would be obtained. If those sergeants who received high test scores also received high performance appraisal ratings and those who received low test scores likewise obtained low performance appraisal ratings, the result would be a high positive correlation between the two sets of scores. The inference could therefore be made that the test appears to predict the performance of sergeants fairly well, that is, it is valid.

Predictive validity is a "future status" statistical correlation between predictor factors and subsequent criteria indicators of performance. Scores on the predictor are obtained at one time, and, at a later date, criterion measures are obtained. For example, a rater rates a subordinate as promotable; the employee receives a promotion and does well on the job. This may be an indicator that the appraisal instrument has predictive validity. In this case, performance appraisal has been used as a selection device. In the example given earlier concerning the police sergeant test, the study could have involved predictive validity; in this case, the test would have been administered to the sergeants at one time, and then, at a later date, the performance appraisal ratings would be obtained and the correlation between the two sets of scores determined. In this example, the past performance appraisal ratings also could have been used as the predictors of future success, and their validity would be determined by their correlation with the future appraisal ratings on the new job.

The basic requirements for the assessment of both concurrent and predictive validity are:

1. The job is static.
2. There is a large influx of applicants with similar characteristics.
3. There is a large number of candidates seeking the jobs.
4. Motivational determinants for all taking the test are the same.
5. Scores on the test are not related to experience.

These requirements constitute restrictions on the applicability of these two kinds of validity because they are not always satisfied in each situation where a validity assessment is needed.

Construct Validity. A construct is a theoretical idea developed to explain and to organize some aspect of existing knowledge. Construct validity is the degree to which scores obtained through a test may be interpreted as measuring a hypothesized trait or property (the construct—motivation, intelligence, leadership.) To demonstrate construct validity, the construct must, first of all, be well defined and understood, and the important components of job behavior must relate to the construct. The issue involved in measuring a psychological quality in performance appraisal is the ability to obtain an objective measure of the degree to which an individual possesses the quality. The appraisal instrument designer must clearly identify and describe what constitutes the psychological quality of the construct. For example, cooperation is a trait or construct on the form, and the assumption is made that employees rated high on cooperation actually are more cooperative than employees rated low. If it can be shown that this relationship is true, then it can be said that the measure has construct validity. The problem is how to get an objective measurement of cooperation. This would require extensive research on cooperation, including its meaning, its relationship to other constructs, and, possibly most important, the relationship between cooperation and the work done by employees. Accomplishing this kind of assignment that includes all kinds of jobs at all levels in an organization is quite difficult and costly.

Convergent and Discriminant Validity. Two kinds of validity that are complementary forms of evidence for construct validity are convergent and discriminant validity. *Convergent validity* is the extent to which multiple raters agree on their measurement of the same dimension or the extent that different rating instruments provide the same rating for a specific performance dimension. The correlation between the same dimension as rated by different raters or different instruments should be significantly different from zero. That is, the ratings converge.

In *discriminant validity,* (a) the correlation between the same dimension as rated by different raters should be higher than the correlation between different dimensions rated by the same rater, and (b) the correlation between the same dimensions as rated by different raters should be higher than the correlation between different dimensions rated by different raters.

Validation Establishment Procedures

Designing and implementing a performance appraisal procedure or system that has any chance of being "validated" must have its roots firmly planted in the content of the job. Chapters 2, 3, and 4 provide detailed information on activities an organization can perform to assist it in developing a job-content base to the appraisal process. A recommended job-analysis process requires

1. Identifying all tasks required in the performance of job assignments.
2. Identifying major activities that can be used as general or umbrella statements for describing critical or significant job activities. These statements, in turn, become the responsibilities of the job.
3. Relating relevant tasks to specific responsibilities to minimize vagueness and ambiguity and enhance understanding and agreement with regard to each responsibility. These task statements now become job duties.
4. Editing all responsibility and duty statements to gain precision and clarity of description.

5. Establishing the priority of all responsibility statements as to their criticality or importance in the successful completion of the job.

6. Establishing the priority of all duty statements within each responsibility as to their importance or criticality in the successful completion of a responsibility.

7. Translating all responsibilities and duties into performance dimensions.

8. Developing performance standards for all performance dimensions or those dimensions identified as critical for successful job performance during the coming performance appraisal rating period.

9. Rating performance on behaviors that are demonstrated and results that are achieved.

This process for defining job content and establishing performance dimensions and performance standards is applicable to all jobs. It may not always be possible to identify specific results in quantitative terms at a particular point in time, but it is possible to determine whether or not certain actions were taken, when they were taken, and even the frequency and duration of the activity. This may be all that is possible to observe and measure. Those skilled in job and organizational requirements can then make inferences from the occurrence of these activities to the quality of job performance.

This approach in no way negates the value of the results that are achieved, but the complex, interdependent nature of many jobs and the time lag that frequently exists between the activity that is performed and the results that are achieved in this process are all that a rater of performance has to work with. There must be well documented understanding and agreement that these rated activities have been identified and understood by all included parties and that they cover all important aspects of the job.

Reliability

Reliability is a measure of the consistency or stability of a test or other measure over time or with its use by different raters. Reliability is also defined by measurement experts as

$$\frac{\text{true variance}}{\text{true variance} + \text{error variance}}$$

A reliable test is one that provides similar or comparable results regardless of when it is used or who uses it. Since performance appraisal is considered a "test" by federal agencies responsible for enforcing legislation that relates to the personnel actions of organizations, the reliability of performance appraisal instruments is of serious concern. In almost all cases where people are involved in making ratings, error is involved. Rater error is a distinct problem in performance appraisal. A review of the primary ways of estimating reliability and relating these reliability measurement opportunities to performance appraisal indicates the problems with establishing the reliability of performance appraisal instruments, let alone going any further into the performance appraisal process.

Three commonly used methods for estimating reliability of tests in general are the test-retest method, the subdivided test or split-half method, and the parallel test method.

Test-Retest Method. The test-retest method requires administering the same test at two different points in time. This method is the easiest to use of the three. It requires the rater, ratee, ratee performance, and instrument to be stable over time. When this method is used for measuring the reliability of a performance appraisal instrument, stability problems quickly arise. Few things are constant in the world of work; people change, and situations change. As a result, work-related behaviors change. These kinds of changes make it impossible to determine how well the appraisal instrument estimates true variance in performance.

Subdivided Test or Split-Half Method. The subdivided test method requires that a test be split into two equal parts. The test can be administered as one test. The comparable test items are split into equivalent halves for scoring purposes. If the test is reliable, each half will give the same or comparable ratings. The division can be by odd-even numbers, and the actual test items can be randomly placed or placed by any other method. It is only necessary that each part represent all types of test questions asked in the original instrument. The problem in performance appraisal is that measurement instruments seldom have items that measure the same qualities. This method of estimating reliability requires two sets of items that are able to measure the same qualities or characteristics. Performance appraisal instruments seldom, if ever, include two complete sets of items that measure the same quality. For this reason, this method is of no practical value for use in performance appraisal.

Parallel Test Method. The parallel test method uses two completely comparable or equivalent test instruments. The items included in each instrument do not have to be identical, but they must cover the same qualities and have a measuring scheme that permits a meaningful comparison of the qualities. The parallel instruments may be administered consecutively or after a lapse of a period of time. If the measurements are reliable, they will provide the same results. The major problem with this method is the development of two instruments that are truly equivalent.

In following the requirements for this measurement of reliability in performance appraisal, two separate instruments must be designed that have different performance dimension and measurement scales but that measure the same qualities. This is an extremely unlikely condition and, for all practical purposes, eliminates the use of the parallel test method for measuring reliability.

Tests must also meet intrarater and interrater reliability standards:

Intrarater Reliability. Intrarater reliability means that the same rater using the same instrument at different times produces the same results. The performance-appraisal-related issues involved in this kind of reliability measurement concern the fact that the performance-related conditions may have changed and that the rater is truly not measuring comparable behavior. This, in turn, makes it very difficult to arrive at comparable results.

Interrater Reliability. Interrater reliability means that different raters produce the same results using the same instrument over a similar period of time. In the world where performance appraisals are made, it is unlikely that any two raters will have the same opportunity to acquire and use the same information about any one person's performance. Although there is much talk about multiple raters, in the great majority of cases, there is only one rater for a set of ratees, thus negating any opportunity to gain interrater reliability. (Even in the case of multiple raters, they may not be observing the same behaviors and rating comparable performance dimensions.)

Internal Consistency. Another issue to be considered in determining the reliability of a test instrument is internal consistency.[4] A high degree of reliability (i.e., a coefficient that is equal to or greater than .70; 1.0 is a perfect coefficient) tends to indicate that the items on the instrument are (a) accurately measuring the qualities or characteristics being rated, and (b) resulting in similar response patterns by different raters. Internal consistency can be estimated through statisti-

---

[4] Internal consistency refers to any of several statistical techniques for estimating the degree to which a test measures whatever is being measured (i.e., its *content reliability*).

cal procedures that provide correlation coefficients such as the Kuder-Richards formula (KR-20) or the Alpha correlation. Some measurement experts feel that internal consistency is the only measure of reliability that is truly applicable to performance appraisal. In this area, as in most other areas of validity and reliability, there appears to be considerable variation as to which procedures are appropriate or most applicable.

DEVELOPING VALID AND RELIABLE IMPLEMENTATION PROCEDURES

Gathering sufficient and accurate information that completely describes job requirements and then processing this information into responsibilities and duties, knowledge and skills, performance dimensions and standards, and objectives and goals is neither easy nor inexpensive. Once professionals have developed the approaches, techniques, methods, and procedures for appraising performance and have identified who will be involved, the design of the instruments to be used, and the timing of the appraisal(s), successful operation lies primarily in the hands of the raters. There is no reason not to believe that the primary rater in the future will be the same person who today is responsible for appraising—the immediate supervisor.

A major reason for an organization to expend the effort and incur the cost necessary for developing a valid and reliable appraisal process is to support the rater. Very few people like to "play God" with other people, and making judgments on individual behaviors that have an impact on current and future pay, retention, transfer, demotion, and promotion is a large responsibility. If organizations want their supervisors to make decisions or assist in making decisions in the critical, human resource areas, they must support these individuals in every way possible.

In the final analysis, if appraisal processes are to be valid and reliable, the immediate supervisors must be willing and capable of implementing their areas of responsibility in a valid and reliable manner. Validity and reliability from the point of view of the rater mean that this person must know how to (a) collect sufficient and accurate job-content and performance data, (b) process identifiable and observable behavior information, and (c) communicate this information in a nonthreatening manner that keeps levels of anxiety, hostility, and fear to a minimum.

DUE PROCESS

For 30 years following the end of World War II, many workers in the United States viewed their jobs as an inalienable right. Not only did they have a right to their jobs, but they believed they owned them, i.e., a person's job was his or her own property, and were entitled to whatever rewards they were already receiving as well as any additional ones they could influence their employers to provide. In the early 1980s, the meaning of entitlement began to return to its original definition—a property right that must be earned. Up until this time, survival generated through job security had been taken for granted. In the 1970s and in the early 1980s, however, some very unsettling events occurred in the United States and in the rest of the world. Employers and employees alike recognized that resources had become truly limited. Not only that, there was world-wide competition for these resources. It came as a shock that the desired and expected "good life" may only be available to those who work for it, and that there is no such thing as a free lunch.

Do two recessions, rapid and devastating inflation, and work to survive mean an end to a claim for due process and a worker's bill of rights? No one can accurately predict the future, but if history can teach us anything, due process and the concept of job ownership are both very much alive and kicking.

What is due process? It is a legal concept that relates to the carrying out of certain legal proceedings for the purpose of ensuring individual rights in accordance with established rules and procedures. Citizens of the United States are guaranteed the right to due process under the Fifth and Fourteenth Amendments to the Constitution. Since employment at will is still very much alive, employees are not guaranteed due process rights as far as the employee-employer exchange process is concerned unless they are stated and described in specific pieces of legislation or within a contractual obligation.

Although the employer continues to own the job, these ownership rights have been eroded over the past 50 years by an ever-lengthening number of legislative actions and contractual obligations. A review of legislation enacted over the past 45 years assists in clarifying why workers have considered the job to be a property right.

The National Labor Relations Act, enacted in 1935, provides the right of employees to bargain collectively with their employers. The Fair-Labor Standards Act of 1938 and its amendments establish minimum pay, overtime pay for hours worked in excess of 40, and equal pay for equal work. The Age Discrimination in Employment Act of 1967 and its 1978 amendment protect persons between the ages of 40 and 70 from discrimination on the basis of age in any terms or conditions of employment. Title VII of the Civil Rights Act of 1964 and its amendments require employers to act in a nondiscriminatory manner when making personnel-related decisions. The Employee Retirement Income Security Act of 1974 protects employees against unwise administration and capricious use of retirement plans. The Occupational Safety and Health Act of 1970 is designed to promote the

safety and health of employees at the work site. The Vocational Rehabilitation Act of 1973 requires most government contractors and subcontractors to make reasonable accommodations to persons having
physical or mental handicaps. The Vietnam Era Veterans Readjust-
ment Act of 1974 requires government contractors and subcontractors
to employ and promote qualified disabled veterans and Vietnam Era
veterans.

These and other acts are establishing a body of due process in human
resource jurisprudence that provides protection to employees in all
kinds of work situations. However, unless specifically stated through
legislation, employers are not required to provide individual rights
to employees on the job. Nevertheless, good management practices
necessitate additional considerations.

Although employees do not have full *legal* ownership of their jobs,
it is in management's favor to recognize that a contract is being established when it provides a wide array of rewards in exchange for employee-provided availabilities, capabilities, and performance. To ensure that both parties understand the stipulations of the contract,
instruments must be developed that identify certain obligations.

Recognizing the historical trend toward increasing due process
rights, employers may be wise to develop and implement programs
that provide due process opportunities to their employees. Demands
on the part of both the employer and employee for improved understanding of what job requirements are and what they are not are
increasing daily.

When a job applicant is hired and becomes a member of the organization, a first step in providing due process to this incumbent occurs
by clearly identifying and describing job requirements. Many organizations have a probationary period of employment. During this period,
the employment contract can be terminated with minimum explanation of the cause or minimal use of due process. Even in the probationary period, however, more organizations are taking the time and effort
to establish and implement a well defined process to observe and measure the on-the-job performance of the probationary employees.

Training employees about what the company expects and in areas
that improve job knowledge and skills is a second step. Permitting
and assisting employees to set job performance standards is another
step in expanding due process at the workplace. Active and valid participation in performance appraisal reviews continues due process.
Providing rewards that relate to observed and demonstrated workplace
behavior ensures continuation of due process to a logical workplace
conclusion.

Possibly the most important documents that management can prepare and use are those that identify job content and job requirements

and those that identify and analyze job performance. The job description, in essence, becomes a deed and title to the job. It actually provides *substantive due process*. The responsibilities and duties identified in the job description describe the assignments that must be performed for acceptable accomplishment of the job—they establish conditions or reasons for the existence of the job. The performance appraisal system and its accompanying instruments provide *procedural due process* that identifies and communicates the desired and actual results. They describe acceptable ways of performing the job. Performance dimensions and performance standards recognize contingencies that develop because of environmental influences and the variations in contributions arising because of the unique qualities of each incumbent. To ensure continuing possession of their jobs, employees must accept responsibility for satisfactory performance of these workplace obligations. In turn, they have every right to due process in protecting ownership rights to their jobs. A well designed, properly managed performance appraisal system provides a course of quasi-legal proceedings that is performed regularly in accordance with well established rules and principles—a system of due process.

Because of the often-mentioned human problems related to performance appraisal, a due process operation will require organizations to include the following review procedure:

1. Review of the rater's ratings by higher levels of management.
2. Monitoring of the rater's rating behaviors by those responsible for the day-to-day operation of the organization in the appraisal system.
3. Auditing of the entire appraisal system to ensure its operation as intended and designed.
4. Appeals so that the employee who has a grievance regarding a rating may have the opportunity for review of complaints by higher levels of management or by those having authority to hold a hearing.

Ensuring Due Process in the Organization

In Chapter 2 there is a discussion of the auditing, monitoring, and appeals processes in an organization. These three components provide a high level of quality control to performance appraisal.

The auditors act as the eyes, ears, even noses of top management. They provide top management with information on how well the appraisal system is operating. They identify deficiencies that may otherwise go unrecognized. Like all kinds of organizational auditing, it is a watchdog activity that reviews what is required by regulations, procedures, and rules as compared to what is actually happening. Auditors' reports assist top management in enforcing its procedures and rules, changing those that are either unenforceable or in need of modification and removing those of no value.

Monitors, on the other hand, work with each unit in the organization to ensure operation of programs as planned. Monitoring is a continuing operation that involves all levels in the organization. It identifies any discrepancies between what is supposed to occur and what actually does occur. Monitoring information should feed into the auditing system.

The third leg of this check-and-balance system is the appeals process. By granting each employee the right to appeal an appraisal rating, the organization informs all employees that there are rules and procedures to follow that will be enforced in a fair and impartial manner.

A performance appraisal program with auditing, monitoring, and appeals components informs everyone that their actions are being reviewed. It forces all programs and processes to be explicit, clearly communicated, and understood. It permits everyone to know where he or she stands with regard to performance-related criteria and organizational reward opportunities.

Auditing Report Information. Auditors' reports go directly to top management and provide this level with such information as:

1. Purpose of the audit.
2. Units audited.
3. Performance appraisal components.
   a. Job content base.
   b. Use of workable performance standards.
4. Ratings given.
5. Distribution of ratings by demographic characteristics.
6. Rating errors and other problems with existing instrument(s) and processes.
7. Value for specific organizational uses.

Monitoring Report Information. Instead of sampling specific units in an organization, monitoring activities cover all parts of a work unit. The assignment here, also, is to identify problem areas and make recommendations for improving the program.

The following kinds of information come from a monitor's report:

1. Which individuals/units are not implementing programs as designed?

2. Are job activities and performance standards accurately stated in understandable terms?
3. Is there sufficient information available to support or justify ratings?
4. Are problems with the appraisal program being uncovered and described?
5. Do employee ratings reflect the performance level of the organization?
6. Do the rating processes and instruments contribute to the overall performance of the unit?

Appeals Process. The essence of due process rests with the right to appeal. As mentioned earlier in this chapter, employees have minimal on-the-job guaranteed rights. Frequently, the immediate supervisor plays the role of arresting officer, jury, and judge. This may not be the best situation for all involved parties. The appeals process lets everyone know that:

1. There is a body of rules that must be followed.
2. Each person has the right to voice his or her side.
3. Decisions will be made on the basis of fact, and the burden of proof rests with all parties.
4. Every effort will be made to treat everyone the same.

This kind of a check-and-balance system facilitates the movement of critical performance-related information throughout the organization. Problems that require resolution are identified. Attention focuses on what is right, what is wrong, and what can be done to improve things. A theme of this book is that performance appraisal is an extremely complex and sensitive problem. It has a direct impact on the life of the employee and the life of the organization. If performance appraisal is worth having, it is worth enforcing. Enforcement, however, requires a high level of professionalism and a commitment at all levels to its implementation. Without enforcement appraisal will quickly die or disintegrate.

SUMMARY

In 1978, David W. Ewing identified seven guidelines organizations should follow that will result in all employees being treated in an equal and equitable manner.[5] These guidelines, which have been para-

[5] David W. Ewing, *Freedom Inside the Organization: Bringing Civil Liberties to the Workplace* (New York: McGraw-Hill, 1978), p. 156.

phrased here, can be most helpful to those responsible for designing and operating a performance appraisal program that provides due process rights to all members of the organization. In essence, they state that the appraisal program must:

1. Follow set procedures—prohibit arbitrary actions.
2. Be visible and known—both potential violators of rights and victims of abuse must know it.
3. Be predictable—engender confidence that certain employee behaviors will lead to specific actions by the organization.
4. Be institutionalized—be a relatively permanent part of the organization.
5. Be perceived as equitable—a majority of employees accept the actions as fair.
6. Be easy to use—neither complexity in administration nor potential ill effect prohibit their use.
7. Be applicable to all employees—all employees from lowest to highest can expect to receive similar treatment.

Properly implemented in both the letter and the spirit, due process may be the most important action organizations can take to improve productivity.

References and Resources

Over the past 30 years, thousands of articles have been published that, in some way, relate to and describe some aspect of performance appraisal. These articles have appeared in the most prestigious professional journals, in respected business magazines, and in almost any kind of magazine that relates to some lifestyle activity. Over the past decade, a dozen or more books have been written that focus specifically on the subject of performance appraisal. In addition, the information explosion on performance appraisal has led to the production of dozens of video cassettes, films, slides, filmstrips, and audio cassettes. For all practical purposes, it would be impossible for any one individual to have the time to spend the effort to digest this mountain of available information.

In addition to my experiences as a manager, consultant, and teacher and in just plain living, my ideas and views on performance appraisal have certainly been shaped by the hundreds, if not thousands, of articles I have read on this subject in particular and management in general. Many of the audio and visual presentations on the subject have been most interesting and the books of other authors most helpful. It would take more pages than are found in this book to list and briefly describe the articles, books, and audiovisual aids that have led to my views and concepts. However, I would like to present some of those that I have found to be most useful.

The eleven chapters of this book have been grouped for the purpose of developing a bibliography into four major areas. They are:

Chapters 1 to 3: The Conceptual Base

Chapters 4 to 6: Instrument Design

Chapters 7 to 8: Uses and Administration

Chapters 9 to 11: Supporting the Process

Following this portion of the bibliography is a list of some of the books and audiovisual aids that may be of interest to those involved in this area.

THE CONCEPTUAL BASE

Chapter 1: Human Barriers to Effective Appraisal of Performance

Chapter 2: Individuals and Groups Involved in Performance Appraisal

Chapter 3: The Linking-Pin for Planning

Bassett, Glen A., and Meyer, Herbert H. "Performance Appraisal Based on Self-Review." *Personnel Psychology,* Winter 1968, pp. 421–30. A discussion of research conducted at General Electric, where comparisons were made on the effectiveness of appraisals in which: (a) the supervisor completed an appraisal form before the interview; (b) subordinates only completed the appraisal form; and (c) during the review session, the supervisor and subordinate came to agreement on each subordinate rating. In this study, the self-prepared form resulted in (a) superior upward flow of information, (b) self-raters required to do systematic thinking about jobs and their performance, and (c) clarification of differences of opinions and perceptions.

Benford, Robert J. "Found: The Key to Excellent Performance." *Personnel,* May–June 1981, pp. 68–77. Supervisors who communicate the relationship between organizational goals and employee needs have work groups that enjoy high levels of productivity and satisfaction.

Bolt, James F., and Rummler, Geary A. "The Dark Side of Management: How to Close the Gap in Human Performance." *Management Review,* January 1982, pp. 38–44. There is a significant level of untapped human energy in the modern work force. The great majority of workers operate significantly below their capacity. To improve human performance, a chain with these major links must be formed: (a) task clarity; (b) feedback; (c) consequence; (d) individual; and (e) resources.

Brouner, Paul J. "The Power to See Ourselves." *Harvard Business Review,* Nov.–Dec. 1964, pp. 156–65. If employees are to fulfill their potential, a vital part of any development program is permitting employees to develop a useful and workable self-concept. This requires self-examination, self-expectation, self-direction, and broadened perceptions.

Conant, James C. "The Performance Appraisal: A Critique and an Alternative." *Business Horizons,* June 1973, pp. 73–78. A discussion of the negatives resulting from performance appraisal. The author recommends the use of management by objectives to overcome the inadequacies inherent in most performance appraisal methods.

Cunningham, Mary. "Productivity: Does Business Need Values?" *Across the Board,* December 1981, pp. 7–11. The modern corporation must have a recognized and acceptable system of values if it is to have a loyal, cooperative work force. Employees are seeking a sense of meaning from their life and from their work.

Dayal, Ishwar. "Some Issues in Performance Appraisal." *Personnel Administration,* Jan.–Feb. 1969, pp. 27–30. A review of barriers to effective performance appraisal and some suggestions for improving the performance appraisal process.

Fritz, Roger J. "Self-Appraisal for Results." *The Personnel Administrator,* August 1977, pp. 26–29. Involving the employee in performing a self-appraisal is a positive step in developing an effective appraisal system. Reasons for and rewards to be gained from self-appraisal are discussed.

Horovitz, Bruce. "When Should An Executive Lie?" *Industry Week,* November 16, 1981, pp. 80–87. Telling the truth is not always possible or appropriate in organizational life, but the giving and receiving of straightforward, honest information is critical to the successful operation of organizations.

Kellogg, Marion S. "The Ethics of Employee Appraisal," *Personnel,* July–Aug. 1965, pp. 33–39. Whether deliberate or not, all too often managers violate ethical principles when making appraisals. This article develops a checklist for appraisers to follow to keep the appraisals honest.

Kelly, Philip R. "Reappraisal of Appraisals." *Harvard Business Review,* May–June 1958, pp. 59–68. An examination of the historical evaluation of formal management appraisals, including a questioning and even challenging of some of the assumptions and concepts underlying performance appraisal.

Kipnis, D. "Some Determinants of Supervisory Esteem." *Personnel Psychology,* Vol. 13, 1960, pp. 377–91. The rating process in appraising performance is influenced by: (a) physical proximity of rater and ratee, (b) degree of job stress, (c) organizational climate, and (d) superior–subordinate dependence.

Kirby, Peter G. "Performance Improvement the Adult Way." *Personnel,* November–December 1980, pp. 35–42. Performance improvement systems should incorporate these eight basic principles of adult learning: self-diagnosis, climate, resources, use of experience, problem orientation, pacing, feedback, and evaluation.

Koontz, Harold. "Making Managerial Appraisal Effective." *California Management Review,* Winter 1972, pp. 46–55. Developing a meaningful appraisal process requires setting the proper business objectives and measuring results against these objectives. The author discusses problems that arise when appraising against objectives.

Landy, Frank J.; Barnes, Janet L.; and Murphy, Kevin R. "Correlates of Perceived Fairness and Accuracy of Performance Evaluation." *Journal of Applied Psychology,* December 1978, pp. 751–54. Frequency of evaluation, identification of goals to eliminate weaknesses, and supervisory knowledge of a subordinate's level of performance and job duties are significantly related to perceptions of fairness and accuracy of performance evaluation.

Latham, Gary P.; Cummings, Larry L.; and Mitchell, Terrence R. "Behavioral Strategies to Improve Productivity." *Organizational Dynamics,* Winter 1981, pp. 5–23. The three stages of the process that lead to improved employee productivity are: identifying poor performance, deciding what causes poor performance, and coping with the cause(s). Steps for coping with poor performance include defining performance behaviorally, training managers to minimize rating error, setting specific goals, and ensuring that employees enjoy positive consequences from their hard work and their achievement of goals.

Lazer, Robert I. "Performance Appraisal: What Does the Future Hold?" *Personnel Administrator,* July 1980, pp. 69–73. A challenge facing organizations that wish to grow is to implement a workable and useful formal performance appraisal program. A major reason for current failure is too many uses and conflicting objectives. The system must be job-related and standardized. It must be a total system functioning with objectives.

LeBoeuf, M. Michael, and Villere, Maurice F. "TAMBO—Applying TA to MBO." *Atlanta Economic Review,* March–April, 1975, pp. 29–35. An improvement in communication in goal-setting sessions is possible when the concepts of transactional analysis are placed into the MBO goal-setting process.

Levinson, Harry. "Management by Whose Objectives?" *Harvard Business Review,* July–Aug. 1970, pp. 125–34. Making management by objectives more valuable to organizations is possible by analyzing group action and personal goals prior to or in conjunction with organizational goals.

Lewis, Robert W. "Measuring, Reporting, and Appraising Results of Operations with Reference to Goals, Plans, and Budgets in a Case Study of Management Planning and Control of General Electric." New York: *Controllership Foundation, Inc.,* 1955, pp. 29–41. A classic study of the key results areas used for directing and measuring the efforts of management personnel at General Electric. The eight key results areas are: profitability, market position, productivity, product leadership, personal development, employee attitudes, public responsibility, and balance between short-range and long-range goals.

"Managers Rate Performance Appraisal Programs." *Industry Week,* 30 May 1974, pp. 52, 56, 58. An in-depth discussion and comparison of the results of surveys on performance appraisal conducted by the Bureau of National Affairs in 1964 and 1974. It appears that more organizations are using performance appraisals, but discontent with the results is also growing.

Marcus, Edward E. "What Do You Mean, 'Evaluation'?" *Personnel Journal,* May 1971, pp. 354–58, 411. Performance appraisal includes weighting measuring, testing, averaging, persuasion and negotiation, mechanical feedback, and autopsy. These procedures may be employed upon completion, at timed intervals, at critical junctures, by exception, by random sampling, and continuously.

Mayfield, Harold. "In Defense of Performance Appraisal." *Harvard Business Review,* March–April 1960, pp. 81–87. A useful discussion of differences in perceptions between supervisors and subordinates, and why and how the performance appraisal interview is a valuable tool for overcoming perception problems.

McGregor, Douglas. "An Uneasy Look at Performance Appraisal." *Harvard Business Review,* May–June 1957, pp. 89–94. A classic in the literature of performance appraisal in which the author discusses one of the most distasteful and disliked activities facing managers—the appraisal of subordinate performance. Placing the major responsibility on subordinates for establishing short-term targets and appraising progress is a potential approach for overcoming the undesirable features of performance appraisal.

McGuire, Peter J. "Why Performance Appraisal Fails." *Personnel Journal,* September 1980, pp. 744–46, 762. A major reason for appraisal failure is the unresolved conflict of appraisal information that is valued and useful to the ratee and that is valued and useful to higher-level reviewers. The ratee–reviewer need conflicts described in this article may only be the tip of the iceberg of performance appraisal problems.

McLaughlin, David J. "Reinforcing Corporate Strategy Through Executive Compensation." *Management Review,* October 1981, pp. 8–15. This article stresses the role compensation plays in focusing the chief executive officer's attention on corporate strategic planning. Implicit in this article is the concept of paying for performance. It takes little imagination to move just one brief step backward to realize that to measure performance requires a valid and useful performance measurement and rating program that ties directly to the long-term plans of the organization.

Meyer, Herbert H., "Self-Appraisal of Job Performance." *Personnel Psychology,* Summer 1980, pp. 291–95. There is a definite "self-delusion" when it comes to employees rating their own performance. Self-esteem and self-protection are just two of many variables that influence a rating decision.

Miner, John B. "Management Appraisal: A Capsule Review and Current References." *Business Horizons,* October 1968, pp. 83–96. An excellent review of the performance appraisal process. The author describes the various components of the appraisal process and identifies research to support his concepts and views regarding acceptable approaches available to management.

Moravec, Milan. "How Performance Appraisal Can Tie Communication to Productivity." *Personnel Administrator,* January 1981, pp. 51–54. To achieve the kind of communications necessary to improve productivity, a performance planning system must include these critical components: (a) new or reassigned employee informed of performance standards; (b) employee completes worksheet 10 to 15 days before appraisal, describing areas of proficiency, job accomplishments, performance difficulties, suggestions for improvement; (c) appraisal reviewed by higher levels of management; and (d) development plans and goals for employee identified in the completion of the rating instrument.

Moskal, Brian S. "Employee Ratings: Objective or Objectionable?" *Industry Week,* February 8, 1982, pp. 47–51. Widespread disenchantment with performance appraisal practices relate to such issues as: (a) employees had no idea of their standing in their company; (b) accomplishments go unrecognized; and (c) employees feel the organization does not have adequate information for making sound decisions about compensation, promotion, training, and development. Employees' feelings that their organizations' appraisal systems are unfair is one of, if not the major, human resource problem areas.

Nalbandian, John. "Performance Appraisal: If Only People Were Not Involved." *Public Management Forum,* May/June 1981, pp. 392–96. It is thought that objective performance appraisal programs will work if (a) employee contributions can be expressed in an objective "performance contract," (b) it is based on results and job-related behaviors, and (c) modern appraisal techniques are used. However, without trust, acceptance of appraisal by raters, sensitivity by higher levels of management of the influence of appraisals, and useful training programs, technically sound appraisal systems will not work as desired and designed.

O'Reilly, A. P. "Skill Requirements: Supervisor–Subordinate Conflict." *Personnel Psychology,* Spring 1973, pp. 75–80. A review of various research studies indicates that there are marked discrepancies between perceptions held by supervisors and subordinates as to what the subordinate understands the job to be and the levels of skill/knowledge needed to perform the job satisfactorily.

Patz, Alan H. "Performance Appraisal: Useful But Still Resisted." *Harvard Business Review,* May–June 1975, pp. 74–80. A discussion of the major barriers that continue to hinder effective performance appraisal. The author develops a four-point strategy that emphasizes manageability and directions. His four points are to keep it simple, separate, contained, and participative.

Perry, Lee T., and Barney, Jay B. "Performance Lies Are Hazardous to Organizational Health." *Organizational Dynamics,* Winter 1981, pp. 68–80. Lies designed to deceive others in an organization about individual or group performance may arise from either individual or situational causes. Group coalitions can result in control of the information top management receives about performance.

Roadman, Harry E. "An Industrial Use of Peer Ratings." *Journal of Applied Psychology,* August 1964, pp. 211–14. A discussion of the results of peer ratings of 13 behavioral qualities and subsequent promotions of the individuals involved in the peer assessment. Four of the 13 qualities appear to be significant indicators of future potential.

Taggart, William, and Robey, Daniel. "Minds and Managers: On the Dual Nature of Human Information Processing and Management." *Academy of Management Review,* April 1981, pp. 187–95. Over the years, researchers studying the operation of the human brain and human personality have identified different approaches to human information processing. Differences in individual decision styles must be recognized and be integrated into the design of a performance appraisal program.

Thompson, Paul H., and Dalton, Gene W. "Performance Appraisal: Managers Beware." *Harvard Business Review,* Jan.–Feb. 1970, pp. 149–57. Using a goal-oriented approach for appraising performance assists in overcoming widespread discouragement, cynicism, and alienation found to accompany appraisal of performance and feedback in technology-based companies. This article includes a penetrating critique of peer appraisal.

White, B. Frank, and Barnes, Louis B. "Power Networks in the Appraisal Process." *Harvard Business Review,* May–June 1971, pp. 101–9. Do superiors have the right to control subordinates, and, more importantly, will subordinates accept the control? Performance appraisal leads to a de-emphasis of control, and that control should be exercised on a mutual basis between superior and subordinate.

Winstanley, N. B. "How Accurate Are Performance Appraisals?" *Personnel Administration,* August 1980, pp. 55–58. Performance appraisal is an extremely complex process, and much of the work being done today has little to no impact on improving the accuracy and validity of the rating process.

Yankelovich, Daniel. "Lying Well Is the Best Revenge." *Psychology Today,* August 1982, pp. 5–6, 71. Lying is no longer socially unacceptable. Individuals at high levels have been caught telling lies. Substantial numbers of people accept deceit as a legitimate way to protect oneself against the intrusion of government or the organization. Flouting rules to gain rewards is tolerated when the victim is the large, impersonal organization.

Chapter 4: Establishing a Job Content Foundation

Chapter 5: Performance Dimensions, Performance Standards, and Performance Goals

Chapter 6: Designing Performance Measurement Procedures and Instruments

INSTRUMENT DESIGN

Barton, Richard F. "An MCDM Approach for Resolving Goal Conflict in MBO." *Academy of Management Review,* April 1981, pp. 231–41. Recent work in multiple-criteria decision making (MCDM) can help in the formulation of goal-conflict decisions in MBO contexts. An MCDM framework is useful in resolving conflict among simultaneous goals and reveals value conflicts between managers and subordinates. A simplified MCDM framework involves the listing of tentative alternatives, the identification of tentative dominant alternatives, and a value-generating procedure for resolving conflict.

Bernardin, H. John, and Smith, Patricia Cain. "A Clarification of Some Issues Regarding the Development and Use of Behaviorally Anchored Rating Scales (BARS)." *Journal of Applied Psychology,* August 1981, pp. 458–63. Many different methodologies have been used for developing BARS. Some of these methodologies have resulted in the haphazard development of BARS. A proper procedure for developing BARS is the one proposed by Smith and Kendall in 1963.

Blanz, Friedrich, and Ghiselli, Edwin E. "The Mixed Standard Scale: A New Rating System." *Personnel Psychology,* Summer, 1972, pp. 185–99. The authors present a method for minimizing rating errors such as halo error and leniency and provide a useful index for measuring the reliability of rating. This study uses 18 traits and three statements to measure each trait. The 18 traits are further reduced to four general trait factors.

Borman, Walter C. "The Rating of Individuals in Organizations: An Alternate Approach." *Organizational Behavior and Human Performance,* August 1974, pp. 105–24. A problem arising when using a multi-rater analysis of employee performance is that raters holding jobs at different levels observe different behaviors and have difficulty reaching agreement on various performance dimensions. The author develops a hybrid matrix for analyzing performance ratings.

Campbell, John P.; Dunnette, Marvin D.; Avery, Richard D.; and Hellervik, Lowell V. "The Development and Evaluation of Behaviorally Based Rating Scales." *Journal of Applied Psychology,* February 1973, pp. 15–22. A discussion of a procedure used for identifying and weighting workplace behaviors and translating those behaviors into behaviorally anchored rating scales.

Cohen, Barry M. "A New Look at Performance Appraisal: The Specimen Check-List." *Human Resource Management,* Spring 1972, pp. 18–22. A brief review of the strengths and weaknesses of four principal methods of performance appraisal: ranking, rating, essay, and checklist. The author focuses on the development and use of behavior-oriented checklists that identify and measure employee behavior, yet also relate to job behaviors ranging from highly effective to highly ineffective.

Cornelius, Edwin T. III; Hakel, Milton D.; and Sackett, Paul R. "A Methodological Approach to Job Classification for Performance Appraisal Purposes." *Personnel Psychology,* Summer 1979, pp. 283–97. Using worker-oriented job inventories and Tucker's Three-Mode Factor Analysis, it is possible to identify task information useful for developing appraisal instruments for specific kinds of jobs.

Cozan, Lee W. "Forced Choice: Better Than Other Rating Methods?" *Personnel,* May–June 1959, pp. 80–83. Research indicates that the forced-choice techniques do not provide consistently more valid ratings than do graphic or peer rating techniques. They do, however, appear to ensure greater objectivity in rating.

Delamontagne, Robert P., and Weitzal, James B. "Performance Alignment: The Fine Art of the Perfect Fit." *Personnel Journal,* February 1980, pp. 115–17, 131. To improve organizational performance, the following descriptive information must be obtained: (a) of the person, (b) of the position, and (c) of the relative "fit" between the person and the position. Performance appraisal assists in establishing a proper fit.

Durant, Peter. "Surviving the Budget Wars, How Performance Standards Can Trim Federal Spendings." *Management,* Spring 1981, pp. 18–20. Performance standards can provide action plans for achieving spending reductions. Standards must be living documents. Performance appraisal based on viable standards is a key tool in obtaining efficient operations.

Flanagan, John C. "A New Approach to Evaluating Personnel." *Personnel,* July 1949, pp. 35–42. A classic article that advocates the use of critical job requirements for appraising employee performance. By using these requirements, it is possible to observe and measure performance and behaviors that relate directly to the work required of the employee.

Fogli, Lawrence L.; Hulin, Charles L.; and Blood, Milton R. "Development of First-Level Behavioral Job Criteria." *Journal of Applied Psychology,* February 1971, pp. 3–8. A discussion of the methods used for identifying job criteria and developing performance dimensions with behaviorally anchored rating scales. The researchers defined the dimensions and the staff members of a grocery chain then allocated behavioral examples to the dimensions.

Haynes, Marion G. "Developing an Appraisal Program." *Personnel Journal,* January 1978, pp. 14–19; and February 1978, pp. 66–67. These articles stress the need for using objective criteria in measuring performance. Appraisals based on objective standards are more versatile and allow for more open discussion of performance.

Hoffman, Randall. "MJS: Management by Job Standards." *Personnel Journal,* August 1979, pp. 536–40, 555. Both the organization and employees benefit by establishing criteria that inform each employee what is expected of him or her. Establishing a base for identifying satisfactory levels of performance is critical to successful operations. This article describes standards and how they were established for a bank.

Holley, William H.; Feild, Hubert S.; and Barnett, Nora J. "Analyzing Performance Appraisal Systems: An Empirical Study." *Personnel Journal,* September 1976, pp. 457–63. This study identifies the types of performance criteria—traits, behaviors, results—and their frequency of use in manufacturing, nonmanufacturing, and government organizations. The authors identify three types of rating techniques used by respondents: numerical scale rating, essay evaluations, and a combination of the two.

Jacobs, Rick; Katry, Ditsa; and Zedeck, Sheldon. "Expectations of Behaviorally Anchored Rating Scales." *Personnel Psychology,* Autumn 1980 pp. 595–639. An in-depth analysis of the development and utilization of BARS and the comparison of BARS to other methods indicates that BARS is no better nor worse than other methods when assessed on a quantitative basis, whereas it has greater potential when assessed on utilization and qualitative criteria.

Kane, Jeffrey S., and Lawler, Edward E. III. "Performance Appraisal Effectiveness: Its Assessment and Determinants." In Barry Straw (Ed.), *Research in Organizational Behavior* (Greenwich, CN: JAI Press, 1979), Vol. 1, pp. 425–78. This in-depth analysis of performance appraisal procedures results in (a) a meaning of effectiveness as applied to performance appraisal procedures, (b) identification and description of existing models of performance appraisal, (c) development of a programmatic model to guide future theory, and (d) selective review of existing research. From these efforts, the authors develop Behavioral Discrimination Scales (BDS) that they claim will significantly improve distributional measurement ratings.

Kavanagh, Michael J. "The Content Issue in Performance Appraisal: A Review." *Personnel Psychology,* Winter 1971, pp. 653–68. Job-oriented traits are still useful in rating job performance. Personality traits, however, should be relevant to job performance and should be described in sufficient detail so that raters are identifying the same qualities. To improve identification of relevant dimensions of job performance, more than one rater should provide rating information.

Kearney, William J. "Behaviorally Anchored Rating Scales—MBO's Missing Ingredient." *Personnel Journal,* January 1979, pp. 20–25. Performance is a product of motivation level, abilities, and role perception. The link between MBO and BARS occurs in the action planning stage of MBO. Here BARS provides critical behavior-related data that clarify role perceptions.

Keaveny, Timothy J., and McGann, Anthony F. "A Comparison of Behavioral Expectation Scales and Graphic Rating Scales." *Journal of Applied Psychology.* December 1975, pp. 695–703. In a comparison of ratings derived from behavioral expectation scales (BES) and graphic rating scales, the BES ratings resulted in less halo error but did not correct for leniency. Neither format was judged superior to the other; however, the BES format was found to possess greater discriminant validity.

Keeley, Michael. "A Contingency Framework for Performance Evaluation." *Academy of Management Review*, July 1978, pp. 428–38. The author identifies three fairly distinct classes of appraisal techniques: behavior-based procedures, objective-based procedures, and judgment-based procedures. He further states that behavior-based procedures are most suited to jobs that are highly mechanistic in structure; objective-based procedures relate to jobs more "organic" in structure; and judgment-based procedures relate to jobs highly organic in structure. Organic refers to less routine jobs or jobs having a high degree of change or uncertainty.

Kindall, Alva F., and Gatza, James. "Positive Program for Performance Appraisal." *Harvard Business Review*, Nov.–Dec. 1963, pp. 153–59, 162, 165, 166. Most managers recognize the shortcomings of traditional appraisal systems. Superiors judge subordinates in terms of their own personality traits. There is a significant difference in agreement over use of terms and scales used for rating. The result is that most managers receive high ratings and the system is useless in terms of differentiating among levels of performance.

Landy, Frank J., and Farr, James L. "Performance Rating." *Psychological Bulletin*, January, 1980, pp. 72–107. An extremely comprehensive review of academic-based research performed on the subject of performance ratings. The authors investigate the roles of raters and ratees, the context of the appraisal process, the design of the vehicle (instrument) used for measurement purposes, and rating processes. From their efforts, they suggest the possibility of a unified approach to understanding performance judgments.

Latham, Gary P.; Fay, Charles H.; and Saari, Lise M. "The Development of Behavioral Observation Scales for Appraising the Performance of Foremen." *Personnel Psychology*, Summer 1979, pp. 290–311. Using a method based on the critical incident technique, behavioral observation scales (BOS) provide explicit, job-content-based scales that identify behaviors required of an employee in the performance of a specific job.

Latham, Gary P., and Yukl, Gary A. "A Review of Research on the Application of Goal Setting in Organizations." *Academy of Management Review*, December 1975, pp. 824–45. A review of goal setting in organizations to determine whether goals that are heard, understood, appraised, and reacted to have an effect on performance. The results indicate that specific goals and the more difficult to achieve but accepted goals lead to improved performance. Individual traits, however, may moderate the effectiveness of goal setting.

Levinson, Harry. "Appraisal of *What* Performance?" *Harvard Business Review*, July–Aug. 1976, pp. 30–32, 34, 36, 40, 44, 46, 180. The importance of how results are achieved, as well as the actual results achieved, is the focus of this article. The author promotes the need to establish job descriptions that are behavior- as well as results-oriented.

Lochner, Allan H., and Teel, Kenneth S. "Performance Appraisal: A Survey of Current Practices." *Personnel Journal*, May 1977, pp. 245–54. In a survey conducted in California, the author found that three major types of techniques were used in appraisals: rating scales, essays, and MBO. Four seldom-used techniques were critical incident, behavioral statement checklists, forced-choice questionnaire, and ranking.

Massey, Don J. "Narrow the Gap Between Intended and Existing Results of Appraisal Systems." *Personnel Journal,* October 1975, pp. 522–24. A recommendation for the use of standards to measure demonstrated behavior (performance) and the use of a team approach for the actual rating. The standards proposed in this article are the rating group's standards.

McAfee, Bruce, and Green, Blake. "Selecting a Performance Appraisal Method." *The Personnel Administrator,* June 1977, pp. 61–64. The authors present a five-step approach for selecting a performance appraisal method. This article also presents a procedure for analyzing the strengths and weaknesses of an appraisal method relative to various criteria.

McConkie, Mark L. "A Clarification of the Goal Setting and Appraisal Processes in MBO." *Academy of Management Review,* Winter 1979, pp. 29–40. A review of the work of 39 authorities quoted in the field of MBO literature: what they consider the goal-setting process to include and how goals and objectives are defined, set, reviewed, and weighted.

McIntyre, Francis M. "Use of Coached Rating Appraisal Data in Development." In Banker, K. A., (Ed.), *Performance Appraisal Necessities.* Verities and Strategies Proceedings. (Palm Beach, Fla., 1974 Executive Study Conference), pp. 21–32. A discussion of a performance appraisal system developed by Chevrolet Sales Division of General Motors Co., detailing procedures used by appraisers for rating subordinates on nine primary factors: responsiveness to job demands, interpersonal relations–communications, relations to supervisor, practical judgment, marketing strategy, work problems, time utilization, development of subordinates, and job knowledge and skill.

Miller, George A. "The Magical Number Seven Plus or Minus Two: Some Limits on Our Capacity for Processing Information." *The Psychological Review,* March 1956, pp. 81–97. A review and analysis of research into the relationship between information input and the ability of the brain to process this information in the short term. An important piece of evidence uncovered by Miller is that the short-term memory has a finite and rather small capacity for making unidimensional judgments.

Miner, John B. "Bridging the Gulf in Organizational Performance." *Harvard Business Review,* July–Aug. 1968, pp. 102–10. An approach available for bridging the gulf between organizational performance and managerial motivation is to relate managerial behavior to company goals and clearly defined job requirements. The integration process requires an understanding of the value system of the company. Within the value system lies the key to accurately identifying performance standards, personal effectiveness, and compensation rewards.

Patton, Arch. "Does Performance Appraisal Work?" *Business Horizons,* February 1973, pp. 83–91. The first step in improving performance is to establish an expected standard of performance. The setting of standards must be followed with information that adds objectivity to the appraisal process and the individual will to apply the information.

Schwab, Donald P.; Heneman, Herbert G. III; and DeCotiis, Thomas A. "Behaviorally Anchored Rating Scales: A Review of the Literature." *Personnel Psychology,* Winter 1975, pp. 549–62. A brief discussion on how to develop BARS, followed by a discussion of research using BARS and the results of the research. The researchers investigated such areas as the impact of BARS on learning effects, dimension independence, and reliability. The research has, to date, not been encouraging.

Smith, Patricia Cain, and Kendall, L. M. "Retranslation of Expectations: An Approach to the Construction of Unambiguous Anchors for Rating Scales." *Journal of Applied Psychology,* April 1963, pp. 149–55. This classic article describes a procedure for constructing a rating scale anchored by examples of expected behaviors. Expectations, based on having observed similar behavior, were used to permit rating in a variety of situations without sacrifice of specificity.

Tosi, Henry L., and Carroll, Stephen. "Some Factors Affecting the Success of 'Management by Objective.' " *The Journal of Management Studies,* May 1970, pp. 209–23. A discussion of research that focuses on the consequences of MBO and various factors that influence the success of an MBO program.

Villareal, Morey J. "Improving Managerial Performance." *Personnel Journal,* February 1977, pp. 86–89, 96. The author describes a results-oriented performance appraisal system that focuses on well defined performance standards that are developed through negotiations between supervisor and subordinate.

Zedlewski, Edwin W. "Performance Measurement in Public Agencies: The Law Enforcement Evaluation." *Public Administration Review,* September/October 1979, pp. 488–93. After years of effort to improve the quality of law enforcement through the setting of standards and goals for measuring performance, the results have not been good. Resource availability, quality considerations, and interdependency of results to organizational policy limit the value of standards and goals. In attempting to define performance in a practical and meaningful way, it has been recognized that measures of "performance" are not report cards but rather diagnostic devices. Each manager must decide the appropriate level of performance along a spectrum. Essential to performance measurement is the ability to define performance and then to intelligently interpret data relevant to performance.

USES AND ADMINISTRATION

Chapter 7: Uses of Appraisal Data and Information

Chapter 8: Administration of the Performance Appraisal Program

Basnight, Thomas A. "Designing Master, or 'Ideal,' Pay-Performance Matrices." *Compensation Review,* Fourth Quarter 1980, pp. 44–50. Matrices that relate performance ratings to location in salary range can be used to effectively link salary increases to available and budgeted funds.

Deci, Edward L. "The Hidden Costs of Rewards." *Organizational Dynamics,* Fall 1976, pp. 61–72. When receipt of the reward—pay—is directly related to performance, there is great likelihood that the reward will be viewed as a control device and will limit the possibility of gaining intrinsic satisfaction from the work performed.

Hayden, Robert J. "Performance Appraisal: A Better Way." *Personnel Journal,* July 1973, pp. 606–13. Appraisal system design requires the use of various appraisal techniques if it is to satisfy the various demands placed on it by management. This article reviews the various parts of the performance appraisal system and recommends approaches relative to each part.

Kearney, William J. "Performance Appraisal: Which Way to Go?" *MSU Business Topics,* Winter 1977, pp. 58–64. A development of answers to such relevant performance appraisal issues as purpose, what is appraised, how performance is appraised, who the appraisers are, the timing of the appraisal, and the use of feedback in the process.

McMillan, John D., and Hoyt, W. Doyel. "Performance Appraisal: Match the Tool to the Task." *Personnel,* July–August 1980, pp. 12–26. Where salary administration is the primary use of appraisal, responsibility ratings would yield significantly more useful appraisals and also improve supervisory and employee attitudes toward the program itself.

Meyer, Herbert H. "The Annual Performance Review Discussion: Making It Constructive." *Personnel Journal,* October 1977, pp. 508–11. Deviating from his earlier stand, Meyer states that salary issues may be covered in the appraisal interview, but skill in providing feedback is critical for a successful review discussion.

——— "The Pay for Performance Dilemma." *Organizational Dynamics,* Winter 1975, pp. 39–49. Focusing on a potential area of conflict between intrinsic and extrinsic rewards and employee motivation, the author stresses the need to relate pay to performance.

Meyer, Herbert H.; Kay, Emanuel; and French, John R. P., Jr. "Split Roles in Performance Appraisal." *Harvard Business Review,* Jan.–Feb. 1965, pp. 123–29. A classic article that describes performance appraisal research and processes at General Electric. A discussion of G.E.'s Work Planning and Review (WP&R), which uses job responsibilities as the basis for setting goals and goal achievement as the basis for appraising performance. The appraisal interview was split into two sessions: one session focused on appraisal of performance and salary review; the second session focused on performance improvement plans.

Mobley, William H. "The Link Between MBO and Merit Compensation." *Personnel Journal,* June 1974, pp. 423–27. A discussion of the arguments for and against linking MBO to merit compensation, followed by a discussion of the need to tie MBO to compensation. This link between MBO and compensation then serves to enhance role clarity and feedback aspects of the MBO process.

Randle, C. Wilson. "How to Identify Promotable Executives." *Harvard Business Review,* May–June 1956, pp. 122–34. An early study that identifies and classifies behavior qualities promotable individuals possess. From an initial group of 30 qualities, eight qualities tend to distinguish promotable individuals from those who are nonpromotable.

Salton, Gary J. "VARIMAT: Variable Format Performance Appraisal." *The Personnel Administrator,* June 1977, pp. 53–58. The development of a flexible performance appraisal instrument through the use of the computer. This approach requires the development of a catalog of appraisal criteria applicable to jobs in an organization. The appraiser checks off those items to be used in the appraisal process and develops a tailor-made appraisal plan for each employee.

Shick, Melvin E. "The 'Refined' Performance Evaluation Monitoring System: Best of Both Worlds." *Personnel Journal,* January 1980, pp. 47–50. Computerization of the performance evaluation system can eliminate the inflation of ratings. A computerized program will permit the development of weighting factors unique to each rater.

Teel, Kenneth S. "Performance Appraisal: Current Trends, Persistent Progress." *Personnel Journal,* April 1980, pp. 296–301, 316. Four persistent problems facing most organizations are (a) arriving at an overall performance evaluation, (b) getting managers to follow a strict merit philosophy, (c) obtaining employee involvement in the appraisal process, and (d) reconciling developmental and administrative requirements. Trends that lead to optimism with performance appraisal are increased use of ratings and narrative descriptions on the same instrument, the increased tying of pay to performance, and more frequent revisions in the performance appraisal system.

Varney, Glenn H. "Performance Appraisal—Inside and Out." *Personnel Administrator,* Nov.–Dec. 1972, pp. 15–17. A survey conducted in 1972 found that formal appraisal of performance of exempt-salaried employees is widespread. The use of MBO-type appraisal plans appears to be common. Businesses use performance appraisal for pay decisions and for management development.

Winstanley, Nathan B. "Are Merit Increases Really Effective?" *Personnel Administration,* April 1982, pp. 37–41. "There is little evidence that merit pay has much, if any, effect on employee motivation and performance," states Winstanley. The ingredients for successful merit pay programs are missing in most organizations.

———. "Performance Appraisal: Another Pollution Problem?" *The Conference Board Record,* September 1972, pp. 59–63. The author recommends that if the objective of performance appraisal is pay information, then the performance criteria should be results-oriented. If, however, the intent is personal development, then the focus should be on skills and abilities.

———. "The Use of Performance Appraisal in Compensation Administration." *The Conference Board Record,* March 1975, pp. 42–46. If a business wishes to get out of the merit increase trap, there are these alternatives: (a) base increases strictly on company service, time in grade, internal and external economics; (b) rate employees relative to three categories: marginal, competent, exceptional; and (c) use merit pool to finance an award program for 5 percent of covered employees who receive 5 percent of annual salary for exceptional work.

SUPPORTING THE PROCESS

Chapter 9: The Interview Process: Reviewing Performance

Chapter 10: Performance Appraisal Training Opportunities

Chapter 11: Legislation, Court Rulings, and Due Process

Alpander, Gurenc G. "Training First-Line Supervisors to Criticize Constructively." *Personnel Journal,* March 1980, pp. 216–21. Supervisors must learn not to expect popularity as an umpire—their job is to be respected and get work done. An appraisal interview training program can be most useful in enhancing supervisors' willingness to conduct an interview that focuses on performance—negative as well as positive.

Altman, Steve. "Performance Monitoring Systems for Public Managers." *Public Administration Review*, Jan./Feb. 1979, pp. 31–35. A performance monitoring system provides a dynamic view of the organization's operation through a series of static snapshots. This kind of system is based on establishing measurable objectives, defining the operations or work processes necessary to achieve these objectives, and then monitoring the performance of the work processes and the attainment of these objectives. Performance monitoring systems consist of a data component, an analytical component, and an action component.

Basnight, Thomas A., and Wolkinson, Benjamin W. "Evaluating Management Performance: Is Your Appraisal System Legal?" *Employee Relations Law Journal*, Autumn 1977, pp. 240–54. An examination of the problems of subjective management appraisal systems under existing legislation and court decisions. Employers, to protect themselves, must develop appraisal programs that are applied uniformly without unfair bias, and operate within objective standards.

Beer, Michael. "Performance Appraisal: Dilemmas and Possibilities." *Organizational Dynamics*, Winter 1981, pp. 24–36. Problems that relate to the conflict between counseling and evaluation functions of performance appraisal may be reduced by minimizing avoidance by supervisors and defensiveness by subordinates. These barriers can be overcome by improving supervisor–subordinate relationships.

Bernardin, H. John, and Buckley, M. Ronald. "Strategies in Rater Training." *Academy of Management Review*, April 1981, pp. 205–12. There is no evidence to support the belief that rater training programs focusing on changes in rating distributions lead to increased accuracy or validity. However, rater training that (a) emphasizes diary-keeping procedures to increase observational skills, (b) focuses on the establishment of a common rater frame of reference to enhance agreement on what constitutes effective job performance, and (c) increases rater self-efficiency regarding negative appraisal situations can improve rater effectiveness.

Bernardin, H. John, and Pence, Earl C. "Effects of Rater Training: Creating New Response Sets and Decreasing Accuracy." *Journal of Applied Psychology*, February 1980, pp. 60–66. From experiments conducted in rater training, the researchers found that those who received the most extensive amount of training had the lower levels of halo error and leniency but they were also the least accurate raters.

Borman, Walter C. "Exploring Upper Limits of Reliability and Validity in Job Performance Rating." *Journal of Applied Psychology*, April 1978, pp. 135–44. Sixteen scripts were made of persons performing on two jobs. These scripts described performer's effectiveness on various dimensions of performance. Raters who were knowledgeable about the two jobs rated the taped performance. High levels of convergent and discriminant validity were obtained, but interrater agreement was far from perfect. The analysis identifies possible reasons for errors in rating.

Burke, Ronald J. "Why Performance Appraisal Systems Fail." *Personnel Administration*, May–June 1972, pp. 32–40. The author identifies and describes a number of problem areas related to accomplishing successful appraisal of performance. A major determinant appears to relate to the ability of the appraiser to provide feedback during an appraisal interview.

Calvin, C. O. "Everything You Always Wanted to Know About Appraisal Discrimination." *Personnel Journal,* October 1981, pp. 758–59. A discussion of the wide variety of human biases that lead to unfair appraisal discrimination.

Campbell, Donald T., and Fiske, Donald W. "Convergent and Discriminant Validation by the Multitrait-Multimethod Matrix." *Psychological Bulletin,* March 1959, pp. 81–103. This is a classic on the validation of performance appraisal. It focuses on the convergence of ratings between independent measures of the same trait and the discrimination between measures of different traits. The authors advocate a validation process utilizing a matrix of intercorrelations among tests representing at least two traits each measured by at least two methods.

Cook, Daniel D. "Whistle-Blowers: Friend or Foe?" *Industry Week,* October 5, 1981, pp. 51–56. Allow employees who have something to say about potentially bad or unacceptable organizational activities the opportunity to have their say within the confines of the organization. Unwanted publicity can hurt the organization and now one state (Michigan) has a law that protects employees who criticize their employer publicly.

Farson, Richard E. "Praise Reappraised." *Harvard Business Review,* Sept.–Oct. 1963, pp. 61–66. An interesting and valuable discussion regarding the pitfalls that may develop when involved in praising an employee. The author presents various alternatives available for establishing a relationship in which praise is accepted as positive and useful in creating a motivating workplace environment.

Fletcher, Clive, and Williams, Richard. "The Influence of Performance Feedback in Appraisal Interviews." *Journal of Occupational Psychology,* Spring 1976, pp. 75–83. A study of discussing individual strengths and weaknesses during appraisal interviews indicates that the most productive interviews contain a balanced review of individual strengths and weaknesses. This type of interview achieved the greatest positive effect overall.

French, John R. P., Jr.; Kay, Emanuel; and Meyer, Herbert H. "Participation and the Appraisal System." *Human Relations,* February 1966, pp. 3–20. The effect of participation in the performance appraisal process is modified by a wide variety of individual variables; but the influence of participation appears to be widespread and long-lasting, although the impact itself may not be as strong as frequently discussed.

Holley, William H., and Feild, Hubert S. "Performance Appraisal and the Law." *Labor Law Journal,* July 1975, pp. 423–30. A review of appraisal systems and problems that exist within the systems leading to unfair and illegal discriminatory practices. This article focuses on job content as the starting point for developing a valid appraisal effort.

_____ "Will Your Performance Appraisal System Hold Up In Court?" *Personnel,* Jan.–Feb. 1982, pp. 59–64. An analysis of 66 court cases involving alleged discrimination caused by the use of performance appraisal reveals that employers should (a) attempt to reduce an employee's ability to establish a *prima facie* case of discrimination by establishing affirmative action programs; (b) have the content of the performance appraisal system based on job analysis; (c) provide clearly written instructions and give necessary training to all raters; and (d) provide ratees with feedback from raters on rating received and ways of improving performance.

Kay, Emanuel; Meyer, Herbert H.; and French, John R. P., Jr. "Effects of Threat in a Performance Appraisal Interview." *Journal of Applied Psychology,* October 1965, pp. 311–17. Through an intensive study conducted at General Electric, the authors found that when subordinates perceived their supervisor's identification of areas needing improvement as a threat, the result was defensive behavior. The more threatening the recommendations to employee self-esteem, the less favorable the attitude of the employee to other appraisals and to the company.

Kaye, Beverly L., and Krantz, Shelley. "Preparing Employees: The Missing Link in Performance Appraisal Training." *Personnel,* May–June 1982, pp. 23–29. Training employees for their role in the performance appraisal process will help them assume more control over and responsibility for their own performance. Seven helpful suggestions that should be considered when designing a training program that will help employees are: anticipate the appraisal interview, clarify the supervisor's performance expectations, know personal strengths and weaknesses, recognize the negative "shoulds," be able to accept help, probe for information, and avoid overly defensive behavior.

Klasson, Charles R.; Thompson, Duane E.; and Luben, Gary L. "How Defensible Is Your Performance Appraisal System?" *Personnel Administrator,* December 1980, pp. 77–82. The authors provide four characteristics that a defensible performance appraisal system should have and four processes a defensible appraisal system should include.

Latham, Gary P.; Wexley, Kenneth N.; and Pursell, Elliott D. "Training Managers to Minimize Rating Errors in the Observation of Behavior." *Journal of Applied Psychology,* October 1975, pp. 550–55. Managers receiving workshop training that made extensive use of videotapes were directed toward the elimination of rating errors that occur in performance appraisal such as contrast effect, halo effect, similarity, and first impression. Six months later, when observing hypothetical candidates on a videotape, these managers committed none of these errors.

Lawshe, C. H. "A Quantitative Approach to Content Validity." *Personnel Psychology,* Winter 1975, pp. 563–75. A thorough discussion of content validity that will assist those involved in validating performance appraisal in understanding this crucial topic. The article includes a discussion on how to identify, describe, and weight job information for establishing content validity.

Lazer, Robert I. "The 'Discrimination' Danger in Performance Appraisal." *The Conference Board Record,* March 1976, pp. 60–64. An analysis of major court cases identifies significant points those responsible for the design and administration of performance appraisal should consider.

Meyer, Herbert E. "The Science of Telling Executives How They're Doing." *Fortune,* January 1974, pp. 102–6, 110–12. An interesting review of how many top businesses appraise the performance of their managers. The message here is to stress the opportunities available through effective appraisal of performance and to minimize stress and develop candid and open exchange of performance information.

Smith, Michael. "Documenting Employee Performance." *Supervisory Management,* September 1979, pp. 30–37. Yes, documentation requires time and effort, but the factual base for decisions, ratings, and discussions that it provides makes it all worthwhile. The ABCs of documentation are provided. A = Accurate; B = Behavioral; C = Consistent.

Wallace, Les. "Nonevaluative Approaches to Performance Appraisal." *Supervisory Management,* March 1978, pp. 2–9. Examples of statements that are descriptive, problem-oriented, empathic, and equality-oriented. These approaches to interviewing are designed to reduce ratee defensiveness. They emphasize analysis rather than appraisal.

Wexley, Kenneth N.; Singh, J. P.; and Yukl, Gary A. "Subordinate Personality as a Moderator of the Effects of Participation in Three Types of Appraisal Interviews." *Journal of Applied Psychology,* August 1973, pp. 54–59. An investigation into problem-solving, tell–listen, and tell–sell types of appraisal interviews indicates that satisfaction and motivation increase for individuals with different personality variables related to the need for authoritarianism and the need for independence when involved in a problem-solving (participation) type appraisal interview.

BOOKS   Baird, Lloyd; Beatty, Richard; and Schneier, Craig Eric. *The Performance Appraisal Sourcebook.* Amherst, MA: Human Resource Development Press, 1982. This book contains 26 source readings that provide background on such appraisal areas as The Legal Aspects of Performance Appraisal; Guidelines for Performance Interview; Documenting Employee Performance; and Performance Appraisal and Compensation.

Barrett, Richard S. *Performance Rating.* Chicago, IL: Science Research Associates, 1966. An outstanding technical book on the mechanics of developing appraisal procedures and reasons for their use. Includes a discussion of various rating procedures and forms that are useful in the appraisal process.

Beatty, Richard W., and Schneier, Craig Eric. *Personnel Administration: An Experiential/Skill-Building Approach,* 2nd ed. Reading, MA: Addison-Wesley, 1981. The book provides exercises that build familiarity with job analysis, testing, affirmative action, salary administration, and performance appraisal.

Block, Judy R. *Performance Appraisal On the Job.* Englewood Cliffs, NJ: Spectrum Books-Prentice-Hall, 1982. A distillation of the most successful methods for conducting appraisals on the basis of formal, structured systems. Includes case histories and such vital points as choosing an appraiser, using an appraisal scale, conducting an appraisal interview, and coaching employees.

Bower, Sharon Anthony, and Gordon H. *Asserting Yourself: A Practical Guide for Positive Change.* Reading, MA: Addison-Wesley, 1976. Through the use of self-analysis questionnaires and worksheets, this book helps people carry out their own self-change program. It includes a step-by-step plan for handling interpersonal conflicts, and includes guides for improving self-esteem, coping with stress, being more assertive, and developing friendships.

Bray, Douglas W.; Campbell, Richard J.; and Grant, Donald L. *Formative Years in Business: A Long-Term AT&T Study of Managerial Lives.* New York: John Wiley & Sons, 1974. A classic product of three AT&T professionals that provides a vast amount of information to those involved in improving organizational productivity through a better understanding of the critical criterion, human resource utilization.

Carroll, Stephen J., Jr., and Schneier, Craig Eric. *Performance Appraisal and Review Systems: The Identification, Measurement, and Development of Performance in Organizations.* Glenview, IL: Scott, Foresman and Company, 1982. This book provides an introduction to identifying, measuring and developing performance in organizations. It is concerned with the completion of rating forms and with the process of performance appraisal and review systems in applied settings.

Cummings, L. L., and Schwab, Donald P. *Performance In Organizations: Determinants and Appraisal.* Glenview, IL: Scott, Foresman and Company, 1973. An integrated approach toward performance appraisal that focuses on organizational objectives and proceeds in developing a model that links the major components of the appraisal system.

DeVries, David L.; Morrison, Ann M.; Shullman, Sandra L.; and Grelach, Michael L. *Performance Appraisal on the Line.* New York: John Wiley & Sons, 1981. The authors explain how a performance appraisal system is put into place and run—cautioning that this is as important as which system is used. They offer guidelines on how to select and develop a performance appraisal system and how to conduct an appraisal suited to a given work environment. Different types of appraisal systems are compared in terms of cost-benefit analysis. The authors also suggest ways to gain organizational support for a performance appraisal system and discuss the legal implications of various systems.

Dornbusch, Sanford M., and Scott, W. Richard. *Evaluation and the Exercise of Authority: A Theory of Control Applied to Diverse Organizations.* San Francisco: Jossey-Bass Publishers, 1975. An interweaving of theoretical developments and empirical studies that recognizes evaluation as a complex and critical process. The authors identify four components of evaluation: (a) assigning a goal to a participant, (b) determining criteria to be employed in evaluating task performance, (c) selecting the samples of performance or outcomes that will be inspected, and (d) assessing the sampled performances with established criteria. They also contend that evaluation is frequently not a rational process.

Drucker, Peter F. *The Practice of Management.* New York: Harper and Row, 1954. In this classic, Drucker discusses the use of MBO and calls for the "substitution of management by self-control for management by domination." Drucker further states that managers must be able to measure their own performance on a continuing basis using clear, simple, rational, and relevant measures of performance in all key areas.

Fear, Richard A. *The Evaluation Interview, Rev. ed.* New York: McGraw-Hill, 1978. A classic in the field, this book presents what has become known as The Fear Method of Interviewing. It provides valuable guidance to personnel interviewers and other individuals involved in interviewing.

Fournies, Ferdinand F. *Coaching for Improved Work Performance.* New York: Van Nostrand, Reinhold Co., 1978. Theories of motivation are integrated into specific techniques useful in achieving optimum work performance. The author discusses five steps of coaching, which coaching technique is appropriate for a specific situation, how to use rewards and punishment, and how to recognize problem attitudes.

Goodale, James G. *The Fine Art of Interviewing.* Englewood Cliffs, NJ: Prentice-Hall, Inc., 1982. The author-consultant shows how to design and conduct interviews that allow the interviewer to be firmly in control. He emphasizes the need to prepare for the interview and to listen aggressively. As a foundation for his interview strategies, Goodale draws on psychological and business management research.

Henderson, Richard I. *Performance Appraisal: Theory to Practice.* Reston, VA: Reston Publishing Co., 1980. This book provides a detailed look at designing and implementing appraisal systems relevant to a broad range of job levels and responsibilities within modern corporations. It highlights efficient approaches to interviewing, counseling, training, and compensation planning that help management and employees alike as they work toward common performance goals.

How to Increase Sales and Profit Through Salesman Performance Evaluation. Chicago, IL: Dartnell Corp. Help your salesforce in meeting its sales and goals by analyzing seven basic measurement tools that assist in evaluating and pinpointing new and existing markets. There are also examples of reports useful in tracking the progress of sales personnel and ways to evaluate sales call activities.

How to Review and Evaluate Employee Performance. Chicago, IL: Dartnell Corp. This book describes a method for setting up a program to determine how well employees are performing. It provides guidelines to determine the need for performance analysis and review, and points out how to analyze and rate employee performance.

Hughes, Charles L. *Goal Setting.* New York: AMACOM, 1965. A practical guide that shows how to recognize employee needs for self-fulfillment and job satisfaction. Identifies tested methods for stimulating goal-seeking behavior in workers at all levels in the organization.

Humble, John W. *How to Manage By Objectives.* New York: AMACOM, 1978. A discussion of how MBO can be used as a tool for overcoming tactical errors commonly made by managers. Provides insights into when to use MBO and how to use it effectively.

Johnson, Robert G. *The Appraisal Interview Guide.* New York: AMACOM, 1979. Provides information on how to constructively criticize an employee. Shows how to make good use of a wide variety of appraisal forms and questionnaires.

Keil, E. C. *Performance Appraisal and the Manager.* New York: Lebhar-Friedman Books, 1977. Focusing on the performance appraisal interview, the author analyzes the opportunities available to managers for improving productivity and, at the same time, assisting employees grow and become more satisfied workers.

Kelley, Colleen. *Assertion Training: A Facilitator's Guide.* San Diego, CA: University Associates, 1979. A comprehensive guide for assertion trainers that provides special guidelines for facilitating assertion training. It provides ideas for working with anger and relating to protective and conversation skills.

Kellogg, Marion S. *What to Do About Performance Appraisal,* Rev. ed. New York: AMACOM, 1975. An outline on how to appraise performance and potential for such management uses as coaching, salary administration, employee growth, and career counseling. The book provides goal charts, summaries, and step-by-step plans to assist those involved in developing a performance appraisal system.

Kirkpatrick, Donald L. *How to Improve Performance Through Appraisal and Counseling.* New York: AMACOM, 1982. A review of the techniques of performance appraisal and coaching. The author covers such subjects as job analysis, standards of performance, appraisal, interviews, and coaching.

Lambert, Clark. *Field Sales Performance Appraisal.* New York: John Wiley & Sons, 1979. A guide to the measurement of performance of the field sales staff. The author describes how to develop a performance appraisal system that is customized to fit the particular needs of the sales force and the organization. Critical to the success of a sales force appraisal program is the formulation and implementation of a plan that links all parts of the process.

Latham, Gary P., and Wexley, Kenneth N. *Increasing Productivity Through Performance Appraisal.* Reading, MA: Addison-Wesley, 1981. Describes an effective approach to measuring an individual's performance. Provides a solid basis for promotion and compensation decisions. Emphasizes practical applications of the theoretical principles of goal setting, reinforcement, role clarity, and team building.

Lazer, Robert I., and Wikstrom, Walter S. *Appraising Managerial Performance: Current Practices and Future Directions, Report # 727.* New York: The Conference Board, Inc., 1977. A report on an extensive mid-1970s study of almost 300 businesses that found that approximately 75 percent of all respondents had formal appraisal programs. Although more than half of the businesses stated their programs were less than three years old, many problems were identified relative to their design and use.

Lefton, Robert E.; Buzzotta, V. R.; Sherberg, Manuel; and Karraker, Dean L. *Effective Motivation Through Performance Appraisal: Dimensional Appraisal Strategies.* New York: John Wiley & Sons, 1977. Through the use of two models, the authors show how to conduct performance appraisal with increased pay-offs. The two models, the Dimensional Model of Superior Appraisal Behavior and the Dimensional Model of Subordinate Appraisal Behavior, provide a basis for explaining how an effective performance appraisal system operates.

Lewis, James, Jr. *Appraising Teacher Performance*. West Nyack, NY: Parker Publishing Co., 1973. Provides the educator with a guide for implementing School Management By Objectives (SMBO), an approach to evaluating and improving the performance of teachers and administrators at every level.

Lopez, Felix M. *Evaluating Employee Performance*. Chicago, IL: Public Personnel Association, 1968. An analysis of techniques available for appraising performance and how they are useful with regard to the intended purpose of the appraisal. There is a particular focus on appraisal in the public sector.

_____. *Personnel Interviewing: Theory and Practice*, 2nd ed. New York: McGraw-Hill, 1975. This book provides background information and specific techniques that are valuable in improving interviewing skills. Interviewing activities in job analysis, performance appraisal, and employee career counseling are covered. Interview forms and a comprehensive bibliography are included.

Machiavelli, Nicolo. *The Prince*. New York: E. P. Dutton, 1952. This book, written in the sixteenth century, describes how authority is established by a leader. Honesty, integrity, deceit, cunning, manipulation, and many other human qualities are discussed from the perspective of the leader and followers. The concepts described by Machiavelli are as viable today as they were almost 500 years ago. The issues presented relate closely to the human barriers that block success in performance appraisal.

Mager, Robert F., and Pipe, Peter. *Analyzing Performance Problems or "You Really Ought a Wanna."* Belmont, CA: Fearon, 1970. Is there a performance discrepancy? If there is, the authors develop a flow diagram that assists in identifying performance problems and what to do with them. A quick-reference checklist provides a guide for determining what to do when an unacceptable performance situation arises.

Maier, N. R. F. *The Appraisal Interview: Objectives, Methods, and Skills*. New York: John Wiley, 1958. This classic categorizes appraisal methods into: (a) tell and sell, (b) tell and listen, and (c) problem solving. The author discusses each method and identifies where each is useful in improving superior–subordinate relations.

Maier, Norman R. F. *The Appraisal Interview: Three Basic Approaches*. San Diego, CA: University Associates, 1976. A discussion of the three dimensions of appraisal interviewing—objectives, methods, and skills—with a discussion of the principles of problem solving as related to the interview. The three approaches used in appraisal—sell, tell and listen, and problem solving—are explored and discussed in detail.

Mali, Paul. *Improving Total Productivity: MBO Strategies for Business, Government and Not-for-Profit Organizations*. New York: John Wiley & Sons, 1978. A step-by-step practical operating guideline on how the MBO strategy can be developed, installed, and managed. The book identifies 12 of the most critical areas of reduced performance and offers approaches to minimize efforts.

Management by Objectives. Cleveland, OH: Penton Publishing Co., 1970. A self-study guide that provides programmed learning on how to establish objectives, set standards for measuring performance, and conduct measurements to determine progress.

Margulies, Newton, and Wallace, John. *Organization Change: Techniques and Applications*. Glenview, IL: Scott, Foresman and Company, 1973. An excellent resource for those involved in designing and implementing a performance appraisal system. The authors present a systematic approach to bringing about organizational change. They provide knowledge and understanding to assist those willing to expend the effort to develop innovative approaches for improving human interaction within the organizational structure.

McConkey, Dale D. *How to Manage By Results,* 3rd ed. New York: AMACOM, 1977. Provides valuable instruction on how to make MBO work, focusing on procedures to increase productivity and improve communication and work flow, and stressing individual achievement and rewards for results achieved.

_____. *MBO for Nonprofit Organizations*. New York: AMACOM, 1975. Pragmatic and useful insights into MBO in nonprofit organizations, with case studies describing how particular organizations have implemented MBO programs.

McLean, Hugh A. *There Is A Better Way to Manage*. New York: AMACOM, 1982. The author integrates MBO with newer techniques to describe how managers can direct human potential toward the improvement of business results.

Migliore, R. Henry. *MBO: Blue Collar to Top Executive*. Rockville, MD: Bureau of National Affairs, 1977. The author recommends a review of the organizational environment before setting objectives. He further recommends the setting of objectives at every level. "How-to" advice is provided on setting and writing objectives at lower levels in the organization and in measuring MBO effectiveness.

Morrisey, George L. *Appraisal and Development Through Objectives and Results*. Reading, MA: Addison-Wesley, 1972. The philosophy and techniques of MBO are suitable and useful to employee appraisal and development. The author provides a variety of ways to apply goal setting to employee appraisal and development.

_____. *Management By Objectives and Results in the Public Sector*. Reading, MA: Addison-Wesley, 1970. This book focuses on the role of middle managers and supervisors in the operation of an MBO program. Barriers facing the effective implementation of MBO in the public sector are identified and brought to life.

Odiorne, George S. *MBO II: A System of Managerial Leadership for the 80's*. Belmont, CA: Fearon–Pitman Publishers, 1979. Odiorne states that the hardest part of MBO is making it work, but only two of the six chapters actually address this issue. MBO is seen as an overall way of managing an organization—public or private—a department, or an individual job. Many useful insights on implementing MBO are provided, such as 27 rules by managers who have made MBO work, the politics of implementing MBO, and a number of chapters on goal-setting techniques.

Olson, Richard Fischer. *Managing the Interview: A Self-Teaching Guide.* New York: John Wiley & Sons, 1980. An easy-to-follow, practical book that describes effective interviewing techniques and guideposts helpful to anyone who has responsibilities that involve the interviewing of employees. There are discussions on the skills necessary for conducting performance appraisal, employee counseling, and exit interviews.

_____. *Performance Appraisal: A Guide to Greater Productivity.* New York: John Wiley & Sons, 1981. A description of the inner process of assessing performance that includes how motivation, attitudes, and commitment of managers and subordinates determine what appraisal means. There is a discussion of a simple step-by-step process for conducting appraisals. The discussion includes a description of the 30 traps to avoid and the 50 techniques available for improving appraisals.

Patten, Thomas H., Jr. *A Manager's Guide to Performance Appraisal.* New York: The Free Press, 1982. The author states that an effective performance appraisal depends on a goal-oriented management philosophy that uses a management by objectives approach for identifying and rating levels of performance.

Porter, Lyman W.; Lawler, Edward E. III; and Hackman, J. Richard. *Behavior in Organizations.* New York: McGraw-Hill, 1975. The authors conclude that a good appraisal system must have the following characteristics: it must measure both behavior and results; it must be objective and tied to behavior; moderately difficult goals and standards must be set; subordinates must be able to influence the measures; time cycle of appraisal feedback must be appropriate to the task; subordinates must participate in setting goals and establishing measures; and appraisals must be effectively linked with the reward system.

Raia, Anthony P. *Managing by Objectives.* Glenview, IL: Scott, Foresman and Company, 1974. One of the pioneers of MBO provides excellent descriptions of the fundamental tools required to design and implement an effective MBO system.

Reddin, W. J., *Effective Management by Objectives: The 3-D Method of MBO.* New York: McGraw-Hill, 1971. A practical, explicit, and results-oriented approach to management by objectives. Through the use of examples, the author describes opportunities available to implement an MBO program.

Sashkin, Marshall. *Assessing Performance Appraisal.* San Diego, CA: University Associates, 1981. Using his ten principles, Sashkin provides a management-oriented approach for determining how well the performance appraisal program is working. Four self-administered assessment instruments are provided to diagnose how well his ten principles are being fulfilled.

Sloma, Richard S. *How to Measure Managerial Performance.* New York: Macmillan, 1980. A "how to" for implementing a workable MBO program. The author explains how to measure performance regardless of the manager's area of responsibility. Precise and well identified objectives, coupled with a good compensation program and adequate financial controls can lead to improved performance.

Smith, Manuel J. *When I Say No, I Feel Guilty.* New York: Bantam Books, 1975. Provides an assortment of verbal skills to combat manipulation by others. The author discusses his views that there are no absolutely right or wrong moral ways to behave, but ways to do what is best for oneself.

Smith, Howard P., and Brouner, Paul J. *Performance Appraisal and Human Development: A Practical Guide to Effective Managing.* Reading, MA: Addison-Wesley, 1977. Recognizing that the human resources of an organization are truly its most valuable assets, the authors provide an example-oriented approach for understanding how an appraisal system functions and the role management plays in developing an effective program.

Whisler, Thomas L., and Harper, Shirley F., eds. *Performance Appraisal, Research and Practice.* New York: Holt, Rinehart & Winston, 1962. A basic review of the elements that comprise the performance appraisal process. An excellent primer for anyone wishing to learn about performance appraisal.

Winstanley, Nathan B., ed. *Current Readings in Performance Appraisal.* Pittsburgh, PA: American Compensation Association, 1974. A broad and comprehensive review of what has been taking place during the past 15 years in the appraisal of employee performance. It focuses on emerging knowledge of the need for feedback in the appraisal process. In addition, it notes the trend away from rating scales, particularly when performance appraisal centers on personnel development.

Performance Appraisal

FILMS AND VIDEO CASSETTES [1]

A Recipe for Results: Making Management by Objectives Work, with Joe Batten. 32 minutes. Creative Media, Div. of Batten, Hudson, & Swab, Inc., 820 Keo Way, Des Moines, IA 50309.

Assessing Employee Potential. (5 tapes—63 minutes, 49 seconds). Resources for Education and Management, Inc., 544 Medlock Road, Decatur, GA 30030 (also provided in slide and filmstrip format).

Helping People Perform, with Peter Drucker. 23 minutes. BNA Communications, Bureau of National Affairs, 5615 Fishers Lane, Rockville, MD 20552.

How to Manage by Objectives Series, with George Odiorne. MBO, Inc., 157 Pontoosic Road, P. O. Box 10, Westfield, MA 01086.

1. *Escape from the Activity Trap,* 15 minutes.
2. *Management by Anticipation,* 15 minutes.
3. *Management by Commitment,* 15 minutes.
4. *Performance Review and Objectives Motivation,* 15 minutes.

How to Manage by Results Series, with Dale McConkey. American Media, 5907 Meredith Drive, Des Moines, IA 50324.

1. *MBO—What Does It Take?* 20 minutes.
2. *The Individual Manager and the MBO System,* 20 minutes.

Management by Objectives. (3 modules—27 minutes). Resources for Education and Management, Inc., 544 Medlock Road, Decatur, GA 30030 (also provided in slide and filmstrip format).

---

[1] Descriptive information on films, video cassettes, slides, filmstrips, and audio cassettes can be obtained from their respective producers.

Management by Objectives Series, with John Humble. BNA Communications, Bureau of National Affairs, 5615 Fishers Lane, Rockville, MD 20552.

1. *Focus the Future,* 27 minutes.
2. *Management by Objectives,* 30 minutes.
3. *Defining the Manager's Job,* 21 minutes.
4. *Peformance and Potential Review,* 21 minutes.
5. *Management Training,* 24 minutes.
6. *Colt: A Case History,* 25 minutes.

MBO and Performance Appraisal Series. Bosustow Productions, 1649 11th Street, Santa Monica, CA 90404.

1. *What Is MBO?* 13 minutes.
2. *Developing Objectives,* 14 minutes.
3. *Performance Appraisal,* 14 minutes.

Pay for Performance. BNA Communications, Bureau of National Affairs, 5615 Fishers Lane, Rockville, MD 20552.

Performance Appraisal. (3 modules—25 minutes, 30 seconds). Resources for Education and Management, Inc., 544 Medlock Road, Decatur, GA 30030 (also provided in slide and filmstrip format).

Performance Appraisal Program. ITC Entertainment, Inc., 115 E. 57th Street, New York, NY 10022.

Performance Appraisal: The Human Dynamics. CRM/McGraw-Hill Films, 110 Fifteenth Street, P. O. Box 641, Del Mar, CA 92104.

Performance Counseling and Appraisal Program. Management Decision Systems, Inc., P. O. Box 35, Darien, CT 06820.

The Nuts & Bolts of Performance Appraisal, with Joe Batten. 30 minutes. Creative Media, Div. of Batten, Batten, Hudson & Swab, Inc., 820 Keo Way, Des Moines, IA 50309.

Where Are You? Where Are You Going? 24 minutes. Roundtable Films, 113 North San Vicente Boulevard, Beverly Hills, CA 90211.

Who Wants to Play God? 20 minutes. American Media, Inc., 5907 Meredith Drive, Des Moines, IA 50324.

You're Coming Along Fine. 23 minutes. Roundtable Films, 113 North San Vicente Boulevard, Beverly Hills, CA 90211.

Interviewing

A Measure of Understanding. 29 minutes. Roundtable Films, 113 North San Vicente Boulevard, Beverly Hills, CA 90211.

Communication: The Non-Verbal Agenda. 30 minutes. CRM/McGraw-Hill Films, 110 Fifteenth Street, Del Mar, CA 92104.

Discipline—A Matter of Judgment. 12 minutes. National Educational Media, 1601 Devonshire Street, Chatsworth, CA 91311.

Face to Face: Coaching for Improved Work Performance, with Ferdinand F. Fournies. 27 minutes. Cally Curtis Co., 1111 N. Las Palmes Avenue, Hollywood, CA 90038.

How Am I Doing? 25 minutes. XICOM Video Arts, Sterling Forest, Tuxedo, NY 10987.

I'd Like a Word with You. 28 minutes. XICOM Video Arts, Sterling Forest, Tuxedo, NY 10987.

Interviewing Skills. (6 cassettes—64 minutes, 16 seconds). Resources for Education and Management, Inc., 544 Medlock Road, Decatur, GA 30030 (also provided in slide and filmstrip format).

Listening. 14 minutes. Roundtable/Rank, 113 North San Vicente Boulevard, Beverly Hills, CA 90211.

Listening for Results. 10 minutes. Roundtable Films, 113 North San Vicente Boulevard, Beverly Hills, CA 90211.

Listening: The Problem Solver. 20 minutes. Barr Films, P. O. Box 5667, Pasadena, CA 91107.

Listen to Communicate Program. CRM/McGraw-Hill Films, P. O. Box 641, 110 Fifteenth Street, Del Mar, CA 92104.

Pass It On. 15 minutes. Cally Curtis Co., 1111 North Las Palmes Avenue, Hollywood, CA 90038.

Tell Me About Yourself. 27 minutes. Roundtable Films, 113 North San Vicente Boulevard, Beverly Hills, CA 90211.

The Correct Way of Correcting. 24 minutes. Roundtable Films, 113 North San Vicente Boulevard, Beverly Hills, CA 90211.

The Discipline Interview. 16 minutes. Roundtable Films, 113 North San Vicente Boulevard, Beverly Hills, CA 90211.

The Face-to-Face Payoff: Dynamics of the Interview, with Joe Batten. 30 minutes. Creative Media, Div. of Batten, Batten, Hudson, & Swab, Inc., 820 Keo Way, Des Moines, IA 50309.

The Power of Listening. 30 minutes. CRM/McGraw-Hill Films, P. O. Box 641, 110 Fifteenth Street, Del Mar, CA 92104.

The Rewards of Rewarding. 24 minutes. Roundtable Films 113 North San Vicente Boulevard, Beverly Hills, CA 90211.

When I Say No, I Feel Guilty. 25 minutes. Cally Curtis Company, 1111 N. Las Palmes Avenue, Hollywood, CA 90038.

You're Not Listening. 20 minutes. Barr Films, P. O. Box 5667, Pasadena, CA 91107.

Assessing Employee Potential. Resources for Education and Management, Inc., 544 Medlock Road, Decatur, GA 30030.

SLIDES AND FILMSTRIPS

Interviewing Skills. Resources for Education and Management, Inc., 544 Medlock Road, Decatur, GA 30030.

Management by Objectives. Resources for Education and Management, Inc., 544 Medlock Road, Decatur, GA 30030.

Performance Appraisal. Resources for Education and Management, Inc., 544 Medlock Road, Decatur, GA 30030.

AUDIO CASSETTES The AMACOM division of American Management Associations, 135 West 50th Street, New York, NY 10020, produces a wide variety of audio cassettes. Following are some of the titles that are useful in performance appraisal training:

Appraisal & Career Counseling Interview, 1 tape

Assertiveness for Career and Personal Success, 6 tapes, (additional workbooks available)

How to Evaluate Performance and Assess Potential, 6 tapes

How to Interview Effectively, 6 tapes

Listen and Be Listened To, 6 tapes

Listen Your Way to Success, 3 tapes

Managing by Objectives, 6 tapes

Objective-Focused Management, George S. Odiorne

The Information Interview, 1 tape

The Positive No: Managers' Guide to Dealing with Superiors, Peers, & Subordinates, 3 tapes

The Problem-Employee Interview, 1 tape

Other Producers:

Appraising Performance: An Interview-Skills Course, Norman R. F. Maier. University Associates, Inc., 7596 Eads Avenue, LaJolla, CA 92037.

Executive Skills, with George S. Odiorne. 12 tapes. MBO, Inc., 157 Pontoosic Road, P. O. Box 10, Westfield, MA 01086.

Management Assessment Centers, Joseph L. Moses. Management Decision Systems, Inc., P. O. Box 35, Darien, CT 06820.

Performance Appraisal, Herbert H. Meyer. Management Decision Systems, Inc., P. O. Box 35, Darien, CT 06820.

Performance Dynamics, Felix M. Lopez. Universal Training Systems Co., 7101 N. Cicero, Lincolnwood, IL 60646.

Supervisory Skills. 12 tapes. MBO, Inc., 157 Pontoosic Road, P. O. Box 10, Westfield, MA 01086.

TRAINING PROGRAMS Many different kinds of organizations provide training programs on performance appraisal. The following list identifies some organizations that currently offer these services. In addition, universities and community colleges throughout the nation provide training programs that relate to many of the components of performance appraisal. It is quite likely that the nearest college or university would develop a tailor-made training program for any organization that identifies such a need and requests such a service.

American Compensation Association (ACA), P. O. Box 1176, Scottsdale, AZ 85250

American Management Associations (AMA), 135 West 50th Street, New York, NY 10020

American Society for Personnel Administration (ASPA), 19 Church Street, Berea, OH 44017

Applied Management Seminars International, 1700 Ygnacio Valley Road, #220, Walnut Creek, CA 94596

Center for Creative Leadership, 5000 Laurinda Drive, P. O. Box P-1, Greensboro, NC 27402

Development Dimensions, Inc., 250 Mt. Lebanon Boulevard, Pittsburgh, PA 15234

Industrial Relations Counselors, Inc., P. O. Box 1550, New York, NY 10019

PENTON—University Seminar, 420 Lexington Avenue, Suite 2846, New York, NY 10017

Index

NAMES

ORGANIZATIONS

TERMS